Mitch Hepburn

Neil McKenty

Mitch Hepburn

MCCLELLAND AND STEWART LIMITED / *Toronto* • *Montreal*

"Published on the occasion of the
Centennial of Canadian Confederation
and subsidized by the Centennial Commission."

"Ouvrage publié à l'occasion du Centenaire de la
Confédération Canadienne, grâce à une
subvention de la Commission du Centenaire".

Contents

List of Illustrations

With former heavyweight champion Gene Tunney
at Bannockburn

"I'll give Premier Duplessis and his policies
a blanket endorsement."

The Premier with his friends at his
forty-second birthday party.

"I hope I leave this world a little better place."

"We are in this thing because of the little people."

"A politician must have a sense of humour."
At Saints and Sinners Meeting, New York, 1941.

"King Must Go."

"I'm a precedent buster."

"My government's greatest contribution was
in the field of health."

"I hope I'll never forget the people
on the back concessions."

The Last Campaign, 1945.

"I have made mistakes."

Preface

This is not the Life and Times of Mitchell Hepburn, Premier of Ontario from 1934 to 1942. The materials for a work of that scope are unavailable if, indeed, some of them exist at all. Neither is it a portrait of Ontario's eleventh Premier. The social and economic frame for a full portrait is lacking. Rather, the book is intended to be a political profile of the man who has been considered one of the most colourful Premiers in the province's history.

The profile developed from research into Hepburn's victory in the Ontario election of 1934 carried out at the University of Toronto under the direction of Dr. John T. Saywell, now Dean of Arts and Science at York University. To expand that into a book seemed an interesting challenge and Centennial project because so little has been written concerning Ontario's Premiers.

Some of the problems raised in *Mitch Hepburn* require further research and development. The lack of certain material made this inevitable. Fortunately, the raw material for an interesting story was available. The main thing, it seemed to me, was to tell that story interestingly. Others will more fully analyze Mitchell Hepburn's motives, assess his record, and estimate his place in Canada's history. My primary aim was to sketch a profile of the man in action.

Professor Ramsay Cook of the University of Toronto read the entire manuscript, as did Richard M. Alway who has done extensive research on the Hepburn period. Professor H. Blair Neatby of Carleton University read portions of it. I am grateful for their suggestions. The staffs of the Provincial Archives of Ontario and the Public Archives of Canada were invariably helpful. I am also indebted to the Centennial Commission for a grant of $1,500.

That the book was completed is due most of all to the generosity of Canada's English-speaking Jesuits, particularly the Jesuit Provincial, the Reverend Angus J. Macdougall. The Jesuits provided financial support and freedom from other duties for research and writing. My thanks, also, to those many friends whose enthusiasm for the project exceeded my ability to do it justice.

I hope that students will find the book useful, and that the general reader, especially those Mitch Hepburn affectionately referred to as "the people on the back concessions," will find it enjoyable.

N. MCK.

chapter 1

Under the Shadow

There was no hint of discontent, no portent of future trouble in the applause that filled Aylmer's stifling town hall on that warm June afternoon in 1906. After a long meeting during which thirteen other nominees withdrew, the Reformers of East Elgin had finally chosen a candidate to contest the federal by-election scheduled for October 4. What was more, the slim young nominee standing on the platform acknowledging the cheers looked like a winner. There was a smile on his face and just the hint of a devilish twinkle in his eyes as Billy Hepburn* waved to the applauding delegates. Droplets of perspiration had formed on his trim black moustache. It had been an exhausting afternoon for Billy Hepburn. As he stood there, wearing his fashionable fawn vest, he still looked debonair and dapper, younger than his thirty-five years.

He waited for the cheering to subside. Then in a strong voice, which carried effortlessly through the jammed hall, Billy Hepburn began to speak. He would accept the nomination, but he would have backed any other winner. Yes, he knew about the rumours going around the riding; he had been in charge of Liberal patronage for the past two years but, despite what anyone said, he had managed it honestly. As for the stories about his personal life, well no man in his home district near Union would call him "a whisky barrel."

Let his accusers come to his farm in Yarmouth township and ask his neighbours about that. Those "dirty stories" had cost him the federal election in 1904 when he lost by a handful of votes. This time, Billy Hepburn concluded, to more cheering from the East Elgin Liberals, this

---

* At that time the family name was pronounced "Heeburn," but later on Billy Hepburn's son, Mitchell, who would become Ontario's eleventh Premier, was usually called "Hepburn."

time he would be a winner. The strongly Liberal St. Thomas *Evening Journal* agreed: "It was a triumphant day for Mr. Hepburn, and his election would appear to be an assured certainty."

On that afternoon in 1906, as the East Elgin Reformers streamed out into the warm June sunshine, there were solid reasons to believe that their nominee would win back the traditionally Tory riding. Billy Hepburn had already proved himself a canny politician and a substantial vote-getter. In his first try for elective office in 1901, he headed the polls for council in Yarmouth Township. Re-elected the two following years, he ran for Reeve in 1904 and won with a handsome majority. "Full of vigour, open-hearted, genial, a good speaker," Billy Hepburn contested Elgin East for the federal Liberals in the 1904 general election. Out of more than four thousand ballots cast, he lost by just twenty-one votes.[1]

That near victory in a Conservative riding was an astonishing feat for so young a man. Already affable, easy-going Billy Hepburn had built up a strong following, especially among the younger folk in his home Township of Yarmouth. A part of Elgin County (named in 1852 after Canada's great Governor-General, Lord Elgin), that belt of land stretching for sixty miles along the northern shore of Lake Erie, Yarmouth Township comprised the rich rectangular strip extending from the lake shore to beyond the county seat, St. Thomas, so called for Colonel Thomas Talbot (the "St." was "prefixed for euphony"), who pioneered the area in 1803. Later South Yarmouth (where the Hepburns settled near the hamlet of Union four miles south of St. Thomas) would be described as "a land of noble farms, good roads, fruitful orchards, and rich, hospitable homes." It was also a land whose sturdy pioneers, busy cutting a living out of the wilderness, had little patience with the established forms, religious or political. They flocked to St. Thomas to hear William Lyon Mackenzie denounce "the family compact." A force from Yarmouth and other nearby townships gathered to support Mackenzie in "the trouble" of 1837, and a Yarmouth man was hanged at London for treason.[2] Whether they were attacking a tree or the establishment, the pioneers of Yarmouth could make the splinters fly.

When Billy Hepburn first tried for a federal seat in 1904, there had been Hepburns in Yarmouth township for sixty years. Fifteen members of the Hepburn clan sailed from Dundee, Scotland, on July 18, 1843, to make their fortunes in the new world. Among them was a boy of ten, the first Mitchell Hepburn, born in Newburgh, "a town on the River Tay, in the kingdom of Fife, as the old Scottish folk used to call that country." After a hazardous three-month journey, these hardy border-clan people settled in Yarmouth Township along the old gravel road between St. Thomas and Port Stanley. Armed with the perseverance and thrift of their Fifeshire forbears, the Hepburns were determined to hew homes from the wilderness at a time, the first Mitchell Hepburn recalled many years later, when St. Thomas, soon to become a railroad centre, was not much more than a hamlet in the woods.

The Hepburns succeeded admirably, none more so than Mitchell Hepburn himself, the grandfather of the future Premier of Ontario. By 1863, Mitchell Hepburn had amassed 118 acres of land near Union. About the same time he also acquired a wife, Eliza Johnson, a Yarmouth girl, one of whose uncles had served with William Lyon Mackenzie in 1837. During the early years of their marriage, saddened by the deaths of all four of their children, they adopted* a baby son, William Frederick, a special blessing for Eliza who proudly watched Billy grow into a fine-looking boy.

In these years Mitchell Hepburn Sr. was increasing his land holdings, and by 1890, when young Billy was nineteen, his father had acquired nearly seven hundred acres. A cheese factory had been built, and a fine dairy herd developed. The herd was Billy's responsibility, requiring a good part of his spare time.[3] Billy Hepburn knew that his father meant business, and business meant a hard day's work. Part of a normal man's business was to acquire a wife, and there was no objection when, in 1892, still only twenty-one, Billy Hepburn decided it was time he did just that. By then Billy Hepburn had a mind of his own, and he had no doubts about the girl he wanted to marry.

A few miles away, in the neighbouring township of Southwold, lived the Fulton family. In 1836, five strapping Fulton brothers had come to Southwold from "Ballemoney," Antrim County, Ireland. One of the brothers, James, had married Annie McPherson, and from that fruitful union were born six sons and four daughters. Only one of the girls, Margaret, born on New Year's Day, 1871, had ever been crowned "the belle of Southwold." In 1892, Maggie Fulton, as everyone called her, was a lovely young woman of twenty-one, rather slim with dark upswept hair. She was "the pretty Miss Fulton," and Billy Hepburn's attraction was reciprocated.

The happy couple were soon making wedding plans which included a big new house, the gift of Mitchell Hepburn Sr., just a stone's throw from the homestead. Billy worked on their new home, a splendid three-story, white-brick structure set in a green meadow off the Fruit Ridge Road. Billy Hepburn and Maggie Fulton were married and moved into their new home. Life for the newlyweds began placidly and was blessed by the birth of a girl, Irene, on August 5, 1895. A year later, on August 12, 1896, in an upstairs bedroom overlooking the fields of Yarmouth,

---

* Because there was no adoption law at that time, children were usually indentured.

Maggie bore her second child, a son, Mitchell Frederick Jr., named after his grandfather, a son who cried lustily and was destined thirty-seven years later to become the Prime Minister of Ontario.

These were exciting weeks at the Hepburn house: a son was born, and a month earlier Wilfrid Laurier was sworn in as Reform Prime Minister. "Old Mitch," as he came to be known, was pleased with his new grandson and the new government. Long before he had brought his own staunch brand of liberalism from his native Fifeshire. Through the years he had actively supported Reform candidates in Elgin, though he had no personal interest in running for office himself. Not so with the more gregarious Billy. He liked people and he liked politics. Shortly after he headed the poll for Yarmouth Council in 1901, Billy decided to strike out on his own. Whether "Old Mitch's" spartan regime on the farm was too confining, or whether business life seemed to offer more opportunities, Billy Hepburn moved his young family into St. Thomas to go into the implement-selling business.[4]

There, on a September morning in 1902, his son, Mitchell, aged six, probably accompanied by Maggie, walked from their home on Queen Street to the three-storey, forbidding red-brick building, the Wellington Street School. The teacher Miss "Allie" Pye was reassuring as she began taking down the names of her fifty-one, well-scrubbed Grade I youngsters. "Mitchell Hepburn Jr." replied the lad with the slick dark hair and high voice, as he began his first day at school. Young Mitch remained only two years at Wellington Street. In the spring of 1904, with his parents and his sister Irene, he moved back to the farm near Union. Perhaps his father had not found selling farm machinery in Yarmouth and Southwold as lucrative as he had expected. In any event, his election as Reeve of Yarmouth in 1904, by "a handsome majority," had whetted his interest in politics. In March of that year, against ten other nominees, he won the East Elgin Reform nomination for the federal general election. "A bright, aggressive, capable young man," the Liberal *Evening Journal* described Billy, and added, "the seal of victory is upon Mr. Hepburn. . . . He is young. He is popular. He has no enemies." The Tories, who brought their leader Robert Borden into the riding, were taking no chances that the upstart from Yarmouth would cause an upset. He didn't. Billy Hepburn ran a strong campaign, losing by just twenty-one votes in over four thousand cast, the best Reform showing in the riding in years.

In November, 1904, when Billy Hepburn's father first ran for the federal House, young Mitch was just eight, old enough to hear his father speak from those Elgin platforms – Yarmouth Centre, New Sarum, Springfield – where he would stand addressing his audience's children twenty years later.* Most of young Mitch's time in the fall of 1904, however, was spent at Union School, just over a mile from his home. Union School was a one-room frame building heated by a big wood stove and at first young Mitch found it a bewildering change from Wellington Street and the ordered Miss "Allie" Pye. At Union, Mitch had a teacher who could not teach very well and who could not keep order at all. In the fall of 1904, if a pupil at Union School did not like the location of his desk, he picked up his books and moved without so much as a by-your-leave. Sooner or later something was bound to blow, and something did. One noon-hour, while the seventy or so students were crowding through the narrow door for afternoon classes, Mitch and two other lads placed a handful of giant firecrackers into the blazing old box stove. The ensuing blast blew the door off. Predictably, the teacher blew up too. The licking with a stiff wooden pointer, which Mitch and his two accomplices suffered in full view of the class, as one of them remembered later, "really took hold."

Fortunately for the good of education at Union, a new teacher soon took hold. Unlike his predecessor, David Weir was a splendid teacher. For about two years young Mitch Hepburn developed rapidly under Weir. The boy excelled in the oral recitation periods held once or twice a month on Friday afternoons. Anything connected with history or current events intrigued him, and Dave Weir encouraged this interest. According to one recollection, during a class period Weir caught Mitch examining pictures of Sir Wilfrid Laurier and Ontario's Premier, the Honourable George Ross. As punishment, Weir ordered the lad to deliver a speech on the two men the very next day. That night, with his father's help, Mitch wrote his first political speech, memorized it, and delivered it on schedule. But there was more than study and speech-making at Union School. Weir promoted sports – football, skating and hockey on the pond, tobogganing. Young Mitch Hepburn, not as robust as some of his fellows, enjoyed the sports, particularly tobogganing at which he was considered expert.[5]

These early years – working and playing at Union School; secure with his parents and his sister, Irene, in the house on Fruit Ridge Road; frequently walking through the back fields to visit "Old Mitch"; enjoying the companionship of his dogs and rabbits – these were happy years for Mitch Hepburn Jr. When school ended for the year, in June, 1906, he was not quite ten, a healthy contented boy. At that time no one could have foreseen that his father's growing involvement in politics would shatter some of the happiness so soon and forever.

On the sunny morning of September 17, 1906, the government patrol boat *Vigilant* steamed through the waters of Lake Erie into the harbour

---

*   Billy Hepburn ran in Elgin East, his son would later represent Elgin West in the federal House. The boundaries of the two ridings were frequently changed so that some areas appeared at various times in both.

of Port Burwell. On board was William F. Hepburn, Reform candidate in East Elgin for the federal by-election called for October 4 because the sitting Conservative member had resigned. Beside him stood the Honourable A. B. Aylesworth, federal Minister of Justice and the Honourable C. S. Hyman, acting Minister of Public Works. They were there to examine the harbour improvements and to help Billy Hepburn's campaign.

The loudest cheers of the election meeting at the Oddfellows' Hall were evoked by Hepburn's promise that no matter what was said about him he would make no derogatory references to his Conservative opponent, the wealthy David Marshall of Aylmer. The *Evening Journal* in St. Thomas was taking care of that in every edition. Marshall's major sins were that he had money; he owned a Russell car worth more than three thousand dollars (apparently in storage for the remainder of the campaign); he headed Canadian Canners Ltd., in Aylmer; he did not pay enough for farmers' corn; and he was the candidate of the trusts and big business.

The next night, in David Marshall's stronghold of Aylmer, Billy Hepburn, never at a loss for words, gave one of his best fighting speeches. Mopping perspiration from his face, he paid tribute to the ladies who had arranged the crowded meeting. Then he took dead aim at the charges that were being hurled against him through the riding: the old-guard Liberals opposed him; he misused his control of patronage for personal gain; he bet on the horses and was too friendly with the sporting fraternity; he drank too much.* Billy Hepburn did not know what else his opponents could say, but if they had other accusations he hoped they would make them at once. Even if worse things were said, he was in this fight to the finish. "I can beat them anyhow," Billy Hepburn promised as he invited the electors to "go to the polls and give 'the boy from Yarmouth' a chance."

Two days later, his campaign moving into high gear with the *Evening Journal* proclaiming that even prominent Conservatives were conceding his victory, Billy Hepburn's chance was gone, his promising political career was in ruins, and his family's happiness was threatened. Friday evening, September 21, he failed to appear at a scheduled meeting in Copenhagen, just north of Port Bruce, where the voters were well pleased with the harbour improvements he had obtained for them. Next morning, a cryptic paragraph appeared on page one of the *Evening Journal*: "Mr. W. F. Hepburn, Liberal candidate for Elgin East, has tendered his resignation." That afternoon the Reformers would meet in Aylmer to choose a new candidate.[6]

Rumours swept the riding. Had Justice Minister Aylesworth and other Liberal officials forced Hepburn out because they had decided he was a sure loser? Had the old-guard Reformers been too much for "the young colts" who had strongly supported him? It was an anxious group, a pale Billy Hepburn with them, who crowded into the Reform club rooms in Aylmer that Saturday afternoon, September 22, to choose a new candidate and to hear the first version of what was soon to be called "the Orwell Affair." Behind locked doors, in a room depressed by heat and bitterness, the Reform president recounted "the dastardly plot" that had forced their candidate's sudden resignation.

On the evening of August 1, after a long day's canvassing in the Belmont district, Billy Hepburn arrived about seven-thirty at the Albion House, a hostelry in the hamlet of Orwell half-way between St. Thomas and Aylmer. It was late, his horse was tired, so he decided to put up for the night. He ordered supper, finished some correspondence, retired shortly after eight, and slept soundly for nearly twelve hours. Next morning he breakfasted and left the Albion House to resume his canvass south of Orwell.

A few days later, David Butler, the proprietor of the Albion House, informed Hepburn that two women "of alleged ill repute" had visited his House on the night in question, one of them remaining until morning. Unless Hepburn paid him five hundred dollars, Butler threatened to connect him in an immoral way with the women and ruin his election chances. Butler intimated that the Conservatives, including candidate David Marshall, were behind the plot. Billy Hepburn flatly refused to pay any hush money. Accordingly, after a long delay, on August 25, the district Licence Inspector, William Andrews, laid a charge of keeping a disorderly house against Butler. No attempt was made to press this charge. Instead, the plan was to hold the case off until a few days before the election, then confront Hepburn with a subpoena to appear as a

* Some of these charges came to the attention of leading Liberals in Ottawa, including Sir Wilfrid Laurier himself. On June 26, two days before the official nomination, W. S. Caron, a prominent Aylmer Reformer, wrote the Prime Minister and enclosed a petition protesting Hepburn's impending nomination. A second letter reached Laurier on July 4 with the rumour that Hepburn was alleged to have shared in the profits of government-dredging operations in his riding. To the first correspondent, who concluded "that it is desirable and urgent that Mr. Hepburn should be induced not to enter into the contest," the Prime Minister merely observed "that I have it an invariable practice never to interfere with the choice of the candidates." With his second informant, Laurier was more explicit: "These insinuations against Hepburn do not seem to be well-founded. It is a matter, however, which will have to be cleared in the riding itself." To that end, the Liberal Chieftan passed on the protests to the Hon. C. S. Hyman, Acting Minister of Public Works and top Liberal strategist in Western Ontario, who promised to take the matter in hand and hoped "it may be possible to avoid trouble." (W. Laurier to W. S. Caron, June 26, 1906; H. H. Miller to W. Laurier, July 4, 1906; W. Laurier to H. H. Miller, July 7, 1906; W. Laurier to C. S. Hyman, June 26, 1906; C. S. Hyman to W. Laurier, July 3, 1906; PAC Laurier Papers).

witness in the action, thereby implicating him in disorderly and immoral conduct. His defeat by Marshall would be certain.

Despite the "dastardly plot" that had forced his resignation, many of the Liberals at the Aylmer meeting cheered Hepburn when he rose to speak and urged him to continue in the contest. Billy Hepburn, though promising to support Granville Haight, the surprised and somewhat lack-lustre candidate chosen to succeed him, stuck by his decision to retire. He explained to the press, "There was a tendency . . . to destroy my home life, and I refused to stand it any longer, and so I resigned." In a public statement, he confessed that he would "suffer injury that may prove irreparable from this base conspiracy." He promised again to fight for the new candidate's election and thanked the many friends in East Elgin who had stood loyally by him "under the shadow." Then Billy Hepburn left for home and Maggie and the children and the memory of what might have been.[7]

Those memories were made more poignant by the cheers which greeted him on every platform during the next few days. True to his word, Billy Hepburn campaigned hard for his successor with the theme that a Reform victory would vindicate his own good name. The affair at the Orwell Hotel became the central issue of the campaign. David Marshall denied he had anything to do with it and threatened to sue anyone who repeated that insinuation. It was repeated, especially on the afternoon of September 27, when Licence Inspector Andrews, a Tory appointee, served Hepburn with a subpoena to appear at the trial of one, David Butler, charged with keeping a disorderly house at Orwell. With what appeared unnecessary callousness, the summons was handed to Hepburn surrounded by his friends as he emerged from Granville Haight's official nomination meeting in Aylmer.

So just four days before the crucial election, on Monday morning, October 1, the Council Chamber at Aylmer was jammed when Magistrate Frank Hunt ascended the bench at 10:07 A.M. to hear the charge that David Butler kept a disorderly house. Among the spectators sat Billy Hepburn, still dapper, still debonair, but most of his lively sparkle gone. During the next two days the case against Butler unfolded. The astonishing thing about it was that Butler himself was the chief prosecution witness. He testified that Hepburn had not retired early on the night in question, that several times he had been ordered to bring liquor to Hepburn's bedroom quarters where he found the Reform candidate with a woman of low reputation. Sometime after midnight Hepburn had ordered his rig, driven off, and later returned and retired with a second woman. Several times since then he and Hepburn, at the latter's request, had discussed the matter with Mahlon Boughner, a Yarmouth farmer. The purpose of these visits was to induce Boughner, a friend of Provincial Conservative Member, Andrew Brower, to use his influence to have any charges dropped. Boughner testified that some weeks previously Butler had handed him a statement giving his version of the Orwell Affair, and he corroborated the testimony about Hepburn's request that the charges be dropped.

Chief witness for the defence in the anomalous position of defending Butler, his accuser, against disorderly conduct, was Billy Hepburn. There had been no women, he had slept soundly all night. Yes, he had talked with Boughner but at Butler's request. He had refused to play Butler's blackmail game. Under three hours of gruelling questioning by both the Crown and defence lawyers, Billy Hepburn lost some of his composure but stuck to his testimony. Each day after court, as he had promised, he was on the platform campaigning for Granville Haight and his own reputation.

Just two days before the election when Magistrate Hunt handed down his decision, Billy Hepburn was cheered at Springfield and Belmont, cheered despite the verdict. On the strength of Butler's testimony alone, the Magistrate found Butler guilty of keeping a disorderly house at Orwell. Almost certainly that decision influenced the election result. Granville Haight, Hepburn's replacement, lost to Marshall, the wealthy Aylmer businessman, by seventy-three votes. A few days later, Magistrate Hunt cancelled David Butler's hotel licence at Orwell, fined him fifty dollars and $16.50 costs with the option of one month's imprisonment at hard labour.[8]

That was the end of the first round in the Orwell affair. Strong legal talent from Toronto now appeared in Elgin to assist Butler, and the conviction was appealed. The appeal was heard almost immediately at the Court House in St. Thomas before the highly respected Judge C. Wesley Colter. The Judge was much interested in why Inspector Andrews had delayed prosecuting the case until just before the election. He was baffled by the Inspector's answers and many other aspects of the Orwell affair. "This is a very peculiar case. I have never heard anything like it, and I have never had anything at all approaching it in all my experience . . . I don't expect to arrive at the whole truth in this case, and I don't think that will ever be revealed until the Day of Judgment."

Nevertheless, Judge Colter did his best to arrive at the truth. He noted that Hepburn was, in fact, the real defendant in the case, yet a defendant unable to call witnesses on his own behalf. Butler's whole testimony was "absurd and untrue," including the allegation that Conservative officials had put him up to it. The Judge also found it remarkable that Boughner, who testified against Butler, now had signed the bond for appeal to reverse Butler's conviction. He further found that Butler himself had brought the two women to his hotel for immoral purposes but that Hepburn was in no way involved with them. On that score the conviction would stand. The whole affair, concluded Judge Colter, "was a foul and most wicked conspiracy . . . with a view to making a victim of an innocent man."

"Colter Judgment Vindicates Hepburn" ran the heading in the St. Thomas *Times* for November 8, 1906, but this was not the end of the Orwell Affair, and for Billy Hepburn the vindication was already too late. He assessed the damage – his political hopes blasted; his reputation attacked; his loved ones hurt – and he decided it would be easier to leave Elgin and start afresh.[9] When he left his home and his family to stay with relatives in the American Mid-West, Billy Hepburn felt himself still to be "under the shadow."

chapter 2

The Boy from Yarmouth

When his father left Elgin so suddenly, his political career in ruins, Mitchell Hepburn Jr. was ten years old, still at Union School, a lithe lad who played touch football and hiked across Yarmouth on picnics. The Orwell Affair was to change all that. Yarmouth, home of the Hepburns for more than sixty years, was no longer home for Maggie and her two children.

Now a young matron in her mid-thirties, Maggie left her wedding home on Fruit Ridge Road, all her dear friends and family in Yarmouth and Southwold, to be with her husband in St. Paul, Minnesota. His business ventures did not turn out as well as he had hoped. Not long after coming to St. Paul, he moved Maggie and his two children to Winnipeg. There, with the resiliency so typical of the young, Mitchell Hepburn Jr., whatever the pressures on his parents, had no trouble adjusting to his new life. Early in 1909, he was writing his uncle, Sam Fulton, back home in Southwold, about his academic record: "In our monthly report at school I stood first. I got Spell (80) Arith (80) Geog (83) Hist. (90) Gram 95." Even so the spelling sometimes slipped. "I may be home this sumer," Mitch wrote his uncle hopefully. He missed his tobogganing. "The weather is quite nice we have quite a bit of snow. There is no hills here to sleigh ride on so I built a little slide." Young Mitch asked anxiously about his colt "Brino," left behind when the family moved West and, like any twelve-year-old, mentioned his distaste for letter-writing. "I do not go skating much. I only write to you, Louie [Maggie's sister] and Grandpa and I would rather take a liking [*sic*] than write a letter but I like to get them."

A few days later, early in March of 1909, Maggie herself wrote to her brother, Sam Fulton; she had more to worry about now than the family's financial difficulties. The shadow of the Orwell Affair had now reached the West:

> Well, Sam, Will came home tonight nearly broken hearted he seen in the paper out here that Brower swore Will told him that the Orwell affair was true. Will says that it is a lie he never told Brower any such thing. He is worried to death to think it is in the paper out here. It is terrible to think they will swear to such lies when Will cannot be there to deni them.

Maggie added, almost despairing that the shadow of Orwell would never lift. "Poor Will he is worried terrible. They will kill him yet with that old thing stirring it up forever."[1]

Maggie had good reason for concern. Despite her brother Sam's charitable assurance that there was no publicity at home, the Orwell Affair had again burst into the headlines of newspapers all over Western Ontario. Ever since Judge Colter's vindication of her husband nearly three years before, ugly rumours had swirled through Elgin that the Tories had tried to ruin Billy Hepburn. Finally, the Conservative Government at Queen's Park appointed the Provincial License Inspector, Eudo Saunders, to determine whether political pressure had been exerted on his underling, Inspector William Andrews, to delay prosecuting the Orwell case in order to embarrass Billy Hepburn politically.

Inspector Saunders' investigation began at St. Thomas on March 9, 1909. Immediately it produced startling headlines in the local papers: "Hepburn To Be Tried For Perjury; Hepburn To Return To Testify." Billy Hepburn did not appear. He had been advised, explained lawyer Andrew Grant, an old family friend, not to do so unless all other witnesses were produced. This was impossible because David Butler, against whom the original charge of keeping a disorderly house had been laid, apparently could not be found. Further testimony provided the interesting information that Butler had neither paid his fine nor gone to prison, and that Mahlon Boughner, who testified against him at the original trial, had loaned Butler nearly six hundred dollars for legal expenses. Boughner also maintained that David Marshall, M.P. for East Elgin, had a moral obligation to repay this money, a suggestion that big businessman Marshall promptly denied.

If this testimony was intriguing, what was adduced against Billy Hepburn himself was more damaging. It was now stated under oath that both Hepburn and Butler had been involved in a disorderly celebration with questionable lady friends at the Orwell Hotel; that after Butler's conviction Magistrate Hunt was convinced gross perjury had been committed at the trial; that Billy Hepburn had requested Andrew Brower, the provincial Conservative member, to try to suppress the charges for the sake of Maggie and the children, but that Magistrate Hunt had intended to press them. Shortly afterwards Billy Hepburn left Elgin. In his report to the Ontario Government, Inspector Saunders found that there had been no Tory conspiracy, and that the Orwell Affair started when Hepburn and Butler quarrelled. He concluded there was "no reasonable doubt that Hepburn was the victim of his own indiscretion."[2] Only time would reveal what damage that conclusion about his father would do to the personality and career of Mitchell Hepburn Jr.

A few months later, Maggie, discouraged by her husband's financial difficulties, distressed by his growing estrangement from Mitchell Hepburn Sr., and lonesome for her friends and relatives at home, decided to return for a while to Elgin.[3] The children, Mitch and Irene, accompanied her, but her husband remained behind, still "under the shadow." Maggie did not return immediately to the home on Fruit Ridge Road which Billy Hepburn had built for their wedding. Instead, she rented a house in St. Thomas. From there, early in September, 1910, Mitch Hepburn Jr., now fourteen, began his high school career at the big red-brick St. Thomas Collegiate.

On his first morning in St. Thomas Collegiate, Mitch Hepburn Jr. sat in Form 1A with forty-two other students, a gangling lad, his dark hair slicked back from a prominent forehead above mischievous blue eyes, the easy smile and dimpled chin of later fame already in evidence. Mitch Hepburn began his high school career with a lively curious mind and an agile physique. He exercised the one on the flying rings in the gymnasium, the other as business manager of the football team.

Too restless and active to concentrate on homework for long, Mitch in his first year stood third in his class with an average just below seventy-five per cent. He recorded full marks in one of his Latin tests. It was in history that Mitch Hepburn excelled, and he was always proud of the hundred he once received in that subject in his second year. To his teacher, George Gray, a first-class pedagogue, Mitch Hepburn was "a wide-awake boy," capable and just possibly brilliant. "It was always a joy to see him in my history class. He was always asking intelligent questions that opened up the matter and led to lively discussions. Mitch Hepburn loved a good argument, and he handled himself well even then." He also handled himself well on the debating team where a fellow-debater, James Finlay (later a minister of the United Church), recalled that "he had a sharp incisive mind quickly detecting flaws in arguments or errors in fact. Even when his opponents were not mistaken in fact, Mitch had a way of persuading the judges that it was so."[4] This was a skill that the young debater (who had dreams of a career in law) would hone to a rare sharpness on the hustings.

All too soon for any vague plans about a legal career to materialize (plans his parsimonious grandfather almost certainly would have

opposed), Mitch Hepburn's formal schooling ended with dramatic sud-
denness in an incident that illustrated several of his abiding traits: stub-
bornness under pressure, loyalty to his friends, and a bristling hostility to
the establishment right or wrong. This time the establishment, in the
form of school authorities, would seem, at the very least, to have been
misinformed.

On October 7, 1912, with many of the Collegiate's students, Mitch
attended the Ontario Hydro's display of electrical farming appliances near
St. Thomas. The highlight of the afternoon came at four-thirty when Dora
and Dorothy, two placid cows, were subjected to an electrical milker. The
St. Thomas *Journal* remarked, somewhat incredulously, that the cows
seemed to enjoy the experience.

Mitch and a couple of his school chums climbed into a windmill to
see the proceedings a little better, and when the chief of Ontario Hydro,
Adam Beck, black bowler and all, mounted a democrat to address the
crowd of three thousand, the possibilities of that bowler became irresist-
ible. An apple thrown from the windmill was a perfect strike. Beyond
denting Beck's hat and his dignity, no harm was done. Or so Mitch Hepburn, who enjoyed the caper as much as his classmates, thought. When
he returned to school two days later, Mitch Hepburn was surprised to be
accused of throwing the apple and then outraged when, in face of his
vigorous denial, he was ordered to leave school until he revealed the
culprit or apologized to Adam Beck himself. In an impulsive, on-the-spot
decision, the boy walked to his classroom where his history teacher,
George Gray, unaware of trouble, saw him scoop all his books from his
desk, snatch his cap from its peg in the vestibule, and stride out the door
without a word to anyone. It was typical and it was final. Mitch Hepburn
did not waste much time looking back. He marched into the Merchants
Bank and was hired as a ledger keeper. After a few weeks, he transferred
to the Bank of Commerce on November 22, 1912.*[5]

For the next three years, Mitch Hepburn remained with the bank, a
period almost equally divided among branches in St. Thomas, Winnipeg,
and Port Stanley. The young junior, trim and smart in his grey business
suit, with his ready smile and nimble wit, liked banking, and the bank's
customers liked him. So vigorously, in fact, did he drum up business
among the farmers of Yarmouth and Southwold that his well pleased
manager, William Whiteside, cautioned him more than once to be careful,
a trait that Mitch Hepburn neither then nor later ever developed.

A transfer to a Winnipeg branch of the bank late in 1913 reunited
Mitch with his family. Shortly after her boy had joined the bank, Maggie
with Irene travelled west again to be with Billy Hepburn hoping that this
time the loneliness would not be so unbearable and that her husband's
prospects would improve.

Much as Mitch enjoyed being with his family, he passed the liveliest period in his early years at the bank in Port Stanley where he was stationed for most of 1915. "The Port," about nine miles south of St. Thomas on Lake Erie, was a thriving fishing village and, despite the war, enjoyed a booming summer tourist business. At the Port Stanley sub-branch, Mitch and his sociable, live-wire teller, William Carnwith, constituted the entire staff. They lived in rooms over the bank, but in the fine summer weather their rooms were usually empty. "The Port" offered too many attractions. There was the "Bachelors' Club," a group of gay blades who kept things humming on the social front. Bill Carnwith and Mitch had no trouble fitting into this once their bank shades were drawn for the day. They swam, canoed, hunted squirrels, promenaded the girls in the cool lake breezes to the end of the board walk on Sundays (beyond that it was strictly out of bounds for the ladies), and saved their money for Bert Niosi, Guy Lombardo, and the other name bands at Hopkins' Casino.

There was dancing, too, and card parties and social evenings at Conrad School near Fingal in Southwold, a few miles from "The Port." The district's best square dancers performed there, and John Burton, a progressive farmer from Fingal, easily rated that category. In all probability it was at a social evening at Conrad School (everyone called it "Coon's School"), some time in the spring of 1915, that Mitch Hepburn first noticed John Burton's daughter, Eva, a slim, dark-haired girl of fifteen. John Burton's small modernized farm outside Fingal was about seven miles from the big Hepburn place on Fruit Ridge Road. Eva's father had once been a school teacher, and his views on farming and politics, pronounced and articulate, were considered well-advanced, almost socialistic. In the provincial election of 1905, John Burton had run on the Socialist ticket. Among those who had campaigned against him was Billy Hepburn. John Burton lost that election decisively, but he never lost his lively interest in politics, his progressive thinking on subjects like agriculture, erosion, and education, or his proclivity for wide reading.

Perhaps the fact her father had been a teacher influenced the rather quiet Eva Maxine Burton to think of that vocation. When she graduated from the Fingal Continuation School, in 1917, however, she was still almost a year away from her eighteenth birthday, a prerequisite for entering Normal School. She decided to spend a year at home, where her household duties were not so onerous that there was not time to see more of Mitch Hepburn. She had seen him frequently already, at the dances

---

* It was also typical of Mitch Hepburn that he remained a life-long friend of the chap who did the apple-throwing, and years later, when he had become Premier, held no grudge against the teacher, by then an official in the education department, who was alleged to have been responsible for the misunderstanding.

at Coon's School, and at barn raisings in Southwold, where the young banker spent his time climbing beams "like a weasel."

In the summer of 1917, there were more opportunities for Mitch to see Eva. He had left the bank and was now helping his hard-pressed grandfather on the farm. The situation had not worked out with Billy Hepburn in Winnipeg so that Maggie and Irene were home again. Sometime in the summer of 1917, "Old Mitch" (still living in the family homestead but remarried some years after the death of Eliza, his first wife) gave his grandson two hundred acres of land on the Fruit Ridge Road. Early that fall, young Mitch Hepburn decided to make a business deal. He sold a field of beans and with the proceeds bought a Ford car. That made it easier running down to Fingal to pick up Eva for a dancing date at Hopkins' Casino. Braving Elgin's winter drifts with a horse and cutter was a more formidable proposition. No matter how treacherous the roads or how warm the invitation, Mitch would never spend a night with the Burtons. His grandfather expected him up at the crack of dawn to help with the chores. He was.[6]

In the spring of 1918, "Old Mitch" was in his eighty-fifth year, his tall frame stooped a little now, his beard snowy, his eyes still piercing. He wanted Mitch to stay on the land. But Mitch was young and there was a war on. Shortly after it began, his attempt to go overseas while he was with the bank in Winnipeg was thwarted by his parents' protests that he was underage. Early in 1916, he had trained for a brief period at London with an Elgin Regiment. Now Maggie, like "Old Mitch," needed her boy's help to keep the farm going. But the military situation changed that. On May 23, 1918, Mitch Hepburn enlisted in the first Depot Battalion Western Ontario Regiment at London. Two weeks later he was released for reenlistment with the Royal Air Force and left to begin his training at Long Branch, Toronto.

Almost every weekend Mitch managed to drive his Ford back to Yarmouth. He helped out on the farm and was able to see Eva regularly. On one of these weekend trips, an accident occurred that terminated Mitch Hepburn's brief military career and could easily have ended his life. Three of his service buddies were in the Ford with Mitch who was driving. When one of them asked to take a turn at the wheel, he readily agreed. The chap's nerve far exceeded his driving experience. The Ford hit a patch of loose gravel, spun out of control across a ditch, and crashed through a fence before overturning in a field, its wheels spinning crazily.[7]

Happily neither Mitch nor his companions were seriously injured, but the severe shaking up, followed by a bout of pneumonia at Long Branch, put him into a military hospital for a time and hastened his military discharge. It also hastened his romance. When she heard about Mitch's accident, Eva Burton already had her room reserved at the London Normal School for the fall term. The accident and Mitch's imminent discharge from the RAF changed that. Mitch convinced the young lady from Southwold (who had replaced other young ladies in his affections) that, for the wife of a young progressive farmer, becoming a teacher was just a waste of time. Maggie, a Southwold girl herself, readily agreed. So on September 11, 1918, in Knox Presbyterian Church in St. Thomas, at a quiet ceremony, Eva Maxine Burton became Mrs. Mitchell F. Hepburn Jr. The groom had only three days' leave. Mitch and Eva spent a brief honeymoon in Toronto, trying to see the sights between check-ins at the Long Branch barracks. It was an exciting if somewhat hectic way to begin a married life.[8]

When Mitch was discharged the couple settled down with Maggie in the house on Fruit Ridge Road to begin farming in earnest. Thanks to his grandfather, who kept a stern paternal eye on things from the old homestead nearby, Mitch's holdings had now increased to three hundred acres. The young husband, just turned twenty-two, attacked farming with that whirlwind of activity so typical of all his endeavours. He organized a co-operative dairy, slung the heavy milk cans himself for shipment to a Windsor dairy, built a cheese factory, and experimented with tobacco crops. Long hours and slim profits marked his early years of married life. They were made harder when both a girl and a boy born to the couple died in infancy. Eva found this heavy sadness easier to bear because of the warm relationship that had developed between her and Mitch's mother. The Hepburn home was again saddened on October 15, 1922, when "Old Mitch" died "leaving an honoured name," commented the *Times-Journal*, "that will always be associated with the county pioneers." He also left an estate (mostly in property and mortgages) which exceeded $150,000. His grandson was one of the chief beneficiaries.[9]

Settling his grandfather's estate and managing his own growing holdings demanded most of Mitch Hepburn's energies in the early 1920's. But not all. There was time to talk, and talk for Mitch Hepburn meant politics. Time to talk to Eva's father, John Burton, with his advanced views on conservation and education; time to talk to Albert Roberts in St. Thomas with his sparkling wit and dim views of the combines, for all his alleged socialism, a sensible thinker and, like John Burton, a wide reader, open to fresh ideas and experiments that would not basically disturb the *status quo*; time to talk to Judge Colter, who had believed in his father's innocence and was a solid low-tariff man; time, between hoisting milk cans, to talk to the farmers along Elgin's back concessions, to imbibe their "populism," their bias against the big-wigs and entrenched power, and to develop those fundamental rural characteristics of business acumen and thrift which had made most of them reasonably prosperous.

Considering his background and his position as a hard-working young farmer, it was not surprising that Mitch Hepburn gravitated toward the

United Farmers of Ontario, that successful lobby for the squirearchy in Ontario, which under Premier E. C. Drury formed the Government at Queen's Park from 1919 to 1923. Though he was one of the five charter members of the United Farmers of Ontario in East Elgin, and served for several years as secretary, Mitch Hepburn seems to have been more interested in the UFO's economic co-operative programs than in its political activities. He took little part in the East Elgin provincial election campaign of 1923 when the UFO candidate was soundly defeated by a Conservative. Two years later, in the fall of 1925, Mitch Hepburn was back in the Liberal camp where his grandfather and Billy Hepburn had always been.

The West Elgin Liberals were delighted to have the enthusiastic young man whom the *Times-Journal* called the "leading Progressive of the district" on their side for the federal election in 1925. Slim and boyish, a ready smile never far from his dimpled chin, the farmer from Yarmouth aroused more cheers – and jeers – than any other speaker the Liberals put up. At Temperance Hall in the Tory stronghold of Talbotville on Elgin's northern boundary, "Mr. Hepburn," reported the *Times-Journal*, "not only held his own in the verbal engagement but his temper as well." He ticked off the shortcomings of Conservative leader Arthur Meighen's backers. When a heckler loudly referred to one prominent Liberal jailed for his financial speculations, Mitch Hepburn smiled slightly, smoothly agreed that Liberals wanted justice for all, then to the crowd's delight remarked: "You Tories send your grafters over to England to get knighted and then they have the audacity to try to get back into power."

Even in 1925, Mitch Hepburn knew his Elgin audiences. He had arranged their loans at the bank, sold their milk in his co-op, danced and played cards with them at Coon's School. He knew what they wanted, and he wanted it too. "What the agriculturalist needs today are the abolition of the Senate . . . cheaper freight rates, and the breaking up of the Atlantic shipping combine."[10] The earnest speaker, the smile and the cheers, the snapping retorts were all reminiscent of another campaign. They reminded the older listeners of Billy Hepburn. The effect was not enough to elect a Liberal in West Elgin, but it made Mitch Hepburn's reputation as the best stump speaker in the county.

Officials of the West Elgin Liberal Association remembered Mitch Hepburn's efforts when the defeat of Arthur Meighen's short-lived Conservative administration in the Commons forced the country into another general election in 1926. This time they wanted a winner, and to men like J. A. McPherson, Alex Darrach, Judge Wesley Colter, and other leading Grits, Mitch Hepburn looked like a possible winner. There was one obstacle. Now living comfortably in St. Thomas, Maggie had not forgotten the shadow of Orwell, nor her husband's enduring exile. She remembered what he had said many times: "A good way to get in trouble is to get into politics. It is like putting your head in a pail and asking someone to hit it." Maggie wanted no more of that. Mitch would be better out of it. Accordingly, despite the cheers that greeted his appearance at the Liberal nomination on July 28, Mitch Hepburn withdrew his name, and the disorganized meeting finally named William Tolmie, "the bean king of Aldborough," and twice-defeated federal candidate, to contest the riding.

The following week deputations of prominent Liberals descended on Bannockburn, the Hepburn farm, and in her St. Thomas home they impressed upon Maggie the opportunity for Mitch if he accepted the nomination, the hopelessness of the Liberal cause if he did not. Probably it was the arguments of the distinguished Judge Colter, who had cleared her husband twenty years before, that caused Maggie to consent, despite her misgivings that what had happened to her husband might one day happen to her son. Her son, who had been rearing to go all along, was overjoyed to obtain his mother's approval.[11] To Mitch Hepburn, not yet thirty – a popular and somewhat restless young man who had worked in the exciting world outside Elgin, and savoured the cheers of the crowds – life on the farm was a bit too confining, the importunities of prominent men too heady to be rejected. Then there was always that old score of his father's to settle with the Tories.

The happy Liberals had no trouble inducing William Tolmie, busy hoeing his beans, to withdraw. Another convention was arranged, and on the sultry night of August 12, his thirtieth birthday, wearing a double-breasted, blue pin-striped suit, looking not much older than when he had spun on the flying rings at the Collegiate, Mitch Hepburn walked out onto the stifling stage of St. Thomas's Masonic Temple to accept the Liberal nomination for the riding of West Elgin. As the cheers mounted around him, the smile on Mitch Hepburn's face widened. He raised his right arm slowly, almost self-consciously, to acknowledge the loud hurrahs of his neighbours from Yarmouth. It was an enthusiastic crowd, but Mitch Hepburn knew that he would have an uphill fight. The county had not gone Liberal since the year he was born. To regain it, he must cut heavily into the normal Conservative majority, retain his base of progressive rural support (to ensure that he would run as an Independent Liberal), and win a sizeable chunk of the railroad vote in St. Thomas.

Declaring that if elected he would be his own man, subservient to no party whip, and employing the slogan once used by his father, "Give the boy from Yarmouth a chance," Mitch Hepburn began a whirlwind campaign, which left normally staid Elgin county standing on its ear and laughing in its milk cans. Backed by a corps of seasoned professionals, J. B. Davidson, Alex Darrach, Percy Dennis, J. A. McPherson, and enthusiastic squads of young people never seen before on the hustings, Mitch Hepburn stood on many of the platforms from which his father had spoken twenty years before. If he were not deluging his audiences with facts and figures on the tariff and freight rates (both should be lowered), he was convulsing them with laughter. When his opponent, the three-hundred-pound, good-natured Hugh McKillop, a two-time Tory winner, wisely declined Hepburn's brash challenge to a series of joint debates, Mitch would tell every audience that McKillop might weigh three-hundred pounds but he had never pulled his weight in Ottawa. All the time he was there, Hughie had only made one speech – to ask a page boy to close a door because he was in a draft. After the audience had stopped laughing, Mitch told them that, although he was only half his opponent's size, he would double McKillop's legislative efforts.

"Cyclonic, sharp, and witty," was the way one newsman described Mitch Hepburn's speeches. It was a good description of his whole campaign, a light, jabbing, laughter-filled wing-ding which McKillop, with more money, more advertising, more speakers, and a safe riding (even Mackenzie King and Liberal officials in Toronto had not counted on Elgin) never took seriously. Not, that is, until they started to count the votes on election night and the presses of the Tory *Times-Journal* began to roll out the black headline: "Elgin West Liberal First Time in Thirty Years." The delirious Liberals swarmed down Talbot Street; the brasses of Elgin's regimental band blared, and a thousand brooms, set afire, blazed merrily in the night. The cheers reached the open window of the *Times-Journal* building, where the winning returns from Yarmouth had just come in, and where a smiling young man with Eva beside him was praising the women and thanking the labour voters and saying, above the cheering, "I am going to try to make you who voted for me, and you who didn't vote for me, proud of me."[12]

The old shadow had gone and Elgin, which had denied Billy Hepburn almost twenty years before, had now given "the boy from Yarmouth" his chance.

chapter 3

Member for Elgin West

Victory for "the boy from Yarmouth" was an exhilarating experience. Mitch Hepburn had turned over Elgin West for the first time in thirty years, transforming a Tory majority of nearly two thousand in 1925 into a squeaky Liberal win by 178 votes. Publicly, Mitch Hepburn attributed his up-set victory to the ladies, the labour vote, and a young enthusiastic organization. Still, he could hardly be faulted for believing (what many were saying) that his own smiling personality and stump-splintering speaking ability had provided the margin of victory. He had won without much help from the Liberal Party organization. Now he intended to carry that independence to Ottawa. There he would be his own man.

The back benches of the House of Commons are far duller than the huzzahs and excitement of a victorious campaign. When he arrived in Ottawa early in December of 1926, for the opening of the session, Mitch Hepburn discovered that a hero in Elgin was just a name on a desk on Parliament Hill. To a friend back home, who urged him to make the "rafters of the House of Commons ring with the voice of the boy from Elgin," Mitch Hepburn wrote: "We private members have been given to understand by the leaders of the Government that this early session is going to be handled as quickly as possible, and any member who tries to display his eloquence at this early stage is liable to be ejected by the hook route." To remain under wraps for the time being ("rest assured . . . when the opportunity does present itself, I will try to do my stuff for the satisfaction of the boys back home") was a situation the youthful, some-what cocky representative from West Elgin was prepared to abide. But he would not suffer lightly any slight or snub, no matter where it originated. What seemed to be a deliberate humiliation came from an unexpected quarter.

When Mitch Hepburn first took his seat, he discovered with rising resentment that if his assigned desk were any further removed from the Government's front bench, he would have been out in the lobby. Still flushed with his own victory and eager to show the Cabinet what he could do, Mitch Hepburn was outraged. He could scarcely hear the debates; many of the Speaker's rulings escaped him. Mitch Hepburn did not propose to accept this cavalier treatment lying down. He blamed it on the newly appointed Minister of Public Works, the Honourable J. C. Elliott of London. As Mackenzie King's senior Minister from Western Ontario, Elliott had a special responsibility for the constituencies in that area. Mitch Hepburn's anger increased when he heard that Elliott had gone over his head to deal directly with the patronage in West Elgin. That was too much for the sensitive farmer from Yarmouth. Although he would continue to support the government, he threatened to leave the Liberal section and move to the cross-benches. A reported threat by Elliott to "read him out of the party" only hardened Hepburn's resolve.

All this brashness from a new member was a bit surprising and would certainly come to the attention of that gentleman who, above all else, prized party loyalty. Busy with the Imperial Conference in London in the fall of 1926, Mackenzie King scarcely had time to shake hands with the new members before Christmas. On his return, he was informed of the contretemps with Hepburn over seating arrangements and heard protests from some of Mitch's constituents, notably the land conveyor Alex Darrach who had supported Billy Hepburn in the ill-fated election of 1906. Darrach knew King personally, and he assured the Prime Minister that he had no more ardent and spirited supporter than Hepburn, but he "will not be the puppet of the Minister of Public works." He urged King to give the West Elgin member "some personal attention. It will repay you both. He is young and aggressive, and, as such persons often are, sensitive. . . ."

No point of friction was too minor for Mackenzie King's soothing oil. Patiently he explained to Darrach that seats were assigned by seniority. Therefore, "the new members, no matter how brilliant they may be, had to be given seats less advantageous than some others who may be inferior in debating strength and ability." Hepburn's threat to move out of the Liberal section, in King's opinion, was ill-advised. "I hope," he urged Darrach, "you will do all in your power to dissuade Mr. Hepburn from taking, on any account, a seat on the cross-benches. . . . No matter how loyal his support to the Government might be, he would prejudice his own interests in the eyes of all the members of the Party." Nevertheless, King was optimistic that his young supporter's grievances could be settled amicably: "I shall hope that before Parliament reassembles Mr. Hepburn will not allow either his feelings or his judgment to be affected by anything that may have transpired up to the present. As to the future, I think we can work that out together."

Mackenzie King lost no time, once Parliament reassembled early in February of 1927, trying to clear up his rambunctious follower's problems. He called Mitch Hepburn in for a chat which apparently smoothed things out. The Member for Elgin West, impressed by the Prime Minister ("He is certainly a man of outstanding ability") settled down to the routine work of Parliament. For several years he was to serve on two important committees (Banking and Commerce and Soldiers' Pensions) which fulfilled his growing interest in financial matters and his humanitarian instincts. He was especially pleased to help returned soldiers. "I have been very successful of late in handling pension cases," he wrote to one constituent. "I take a very keen personal interest in matters of this kind, and you may rest assured I consider it a privilege to do anything in my power."[1]

The Member for Elgin West faithfully attended to his constituents' requests, no matter how insignificant or inane they might be: he obtained information for a student's essay on agricultural problems; promised to support tighter laws against chicken thievery, should such legislation be introduced; protested that a flashing light in the Dexter Cafe at St. Thomas was interfering with radio reception; hoped that the boys at Port Stanley would be pleased with the new fog-horn system in the village; and asked those questions in the House that a Member interested in farming affairs and the railroad road vote back home was expected to ask. His major parliamentary speeches on the budget debates were, for the most part, sober, fact-filled efforts devoted exclusively to the problems of the South-Western Ontario farmer. They stressed the major theme of Hepburn's Ottawa years, the lowering of the tariff, and he frequently complained in private about the Government's lackadaisical response to this Liberal policy plank. Gradually the Member for Elgin West became a leading spokesman for the low-tariff wing of the Liberal Party, whom C. G. "Chubby" Power of Quebec South recommended to Mackenzie King as one of the members best equipped for hit-and-run debating.[2]

These energies were vigorously displayed in Mitch Hepburn's attack on the Sun Life Assurance Company. A private bill to increase Sun Life's capitalized stock had failed to pass because many members, including Mitch Hepburn, claimed that the whole thing was merely a scheme to benefit the shareholders at the expense of the policy holders. By the time the bill was introduced a second time in the 1928 session, several prominent Liberals (like Senator Raoul Dandurand, Government Senate leader) had been added to the company's board of directors, and Mackenzie King himself was not unsympathetic to the bill's passage.

Nevertheless Mitch Hepburn continued his opposition. His father had fought and lost to the manager of a Canning combine in 1906, and for him the Sun Life bill represented the attempt of the large interests to exploit the little man. "This company," he charged, "is attempting a stock

manipulating scheme which is not in the best interests of the policy-
holders. . . . Stock manipulations and stock watering are all too common
in this country." This was the authentic voice of Yarmouth Township
speaking, the small independent rural farmer expressing his resentment
against the established interests. Quite apart from the merits of the case,
it was a politically popular position, and the bill was killed a second time.
Only after Sun Life dropped its increased capitalization request did its
reorganization bill finally pass in the 1929 session with the Member for
Elgin West joining his Party to support it.[3]

On the whole, Mitch Hepburn found his early years as a Liberal
back-bencher at Ottawa, representing a relatively unimportant rural
riding, rather dull. At times his frustration in the Commons, combined
with the responsibility of his farm at home, seemed too much. "Sometimes," he wrote a friend in the spring of 1928, "I get terribly 'fed up'
with the whole game and wonder, after all, whether it's worth the price."
Once again he protested to the Minister of Public Works, J. C. Elliott,
about his interference in the patronage for West Elgin: "I think when a
Member is giving loyal support to the Govt., he is at least deserving of
what I would properly term fair consideration." Nursing this sensitivity,
which over the years was to grow, Mitch Hepburn found more and more
time for conviviality and partying with the boys from "Dynamite Alley,"
as it was called in the House, men who made friends easily and enjoyed
a good time, members like E. G. "Eddie" Odette (Essex East), Dr. James
Rutherford (Kent), Eccles Gott (Essex South), Malcolm "Mac" Lang,
Mitch Hepburn's office mate (Temiskaming South), Ross Gray (Lambton
West), and the popular Member from Quebec South, C. G. "Chubby"
Power. There was the occasional enjoyable excursion from the capital:
"Odette and about forty of us Members are leaving tonight on a trip
to Detroit & Border Cities. . . . It is somewhat of a coincidence in the
itinerary that in inspecting the industries of Windsor they end up in the
afternoon at the Salt Works and go from there to Hiram Walkers'
Distilleries."[4]

Mitch Hepburn was usually happy to get away from the confining
party discipline of Ottawa and back to the hustings where his reputation
had first been made. In September, 1927, he delivered several speeches to
help the Liberals in a by-election in North Huron only to see the UFO
candidate siphon off enough rural votes to enable the Conservatives to
win. Later that fall, when an official of the West Elgin UFO berated him
for attacking the UFO in North Huron, Mitch Hepburn welcomed the
opportunity to deliver a broadside against that wing of the farmer Party
dominated by J. J. Morrison, long-time UFO secretary, and Miss Agnes
Macphail (UFO federal Member for Grey North). They believed that
farmers as a group should be represented in Parliament by farmer members. At a meeting at Dutton in Central Elgin, Hepburn ridiculed the

"group government" theory. Then dramatically waving a sheet of paper in front of his farm audience, Mitch Hepburn, using a tactic he would make famous in later campaigns, tore into the "cool, calculating, and cunning" Morrison for accepting an exhorbitant salary and padding the UFO payroll with his own relatives.[5] This damaging charge not only increased the tension in the UFO between the Morrison faction and the former Premier, E. C. Drury, who opposed the "group government" theory; it also increased Mitch Hepburn's reputation as a rough-and-tumble political in-fighter, fearlessly prepared to take on "the big interests" wherever he found them.

This reputation was put to the test again when Mitch Hepburn's friend, Eccles Gott, the Tory high-protection representative from Essex South, challenged the Member for Elgin West to a joint debate on Liberal low-tarriff policies. The Hepburn-Gott debate, in St. Thomas on the afternoon of April 27, 1929, was a high point in Mitch Hepburn's forensic career. In Parliament and out, Gott had argued that Western Ontario tobacco growers would benefit if the duty on imported tobacco were increased. Leaving nothing to chance, Mitch Hepburn wrote to every major tobacco company in Canada asking a series of carefully worked out questions about the effect such an increase would have on domestic tobacco prices. Armed with their replies, Mitch Hepburn, flanked by a contingent of Ottawa Liberals come to Elgin to see the fun, walked into the Masonic Temple at St. Thomas on Saturday afternoon, April 27. There was standing room only in the hall, jammed with upwards of a thousand spectators, mostly farmers, with another five hundred standing outside unable to get in, all attracted by the promise of a sizzling verbal afternoon. Mitch and Ecc, as the two speakers referred to each other, did not disappoint them.

To protect the Western Ontario market for tobacco, fruit, and vegetables, Gott maintained, the tariff against similar American commodities should be raised.. This would both stimulate domestic production and increase the farmers' profits. Gott delivered a rambling speech attacking the Liberal budget, Mackenzie King, and the way the chairman handled the meeting, his remarks frequently interrupted by hecklers demanding he stick to the tariff. When Mitch Hepburn rose to reply, the applause left no doubt that St. Thomas was his home ground. He took note of the many points raised by his friend. In trying to answer, he felt like King Solomon must have felt when he was leaving home and was about to bid his six hundred wives good-bye; he did not know where to start. After the roar of laughter subsided, Mitch allowed it was only natural that he and Ecc should differ. "After all, as the Indian said, it was a good thing that everybody didn't love his squaw the way he loved her."

Then, in colourful, home-spun language, Mitch Hepburn stated the thesis that he had been hammering at for three years in Ottawa: in any tariff war, especially with the United States, the Canadian farmer, though he might benefit briefly, in the long run would suffer. He quoted a barrage of figures and statistics from China, the United States, Australia, and Canada to demonstrate what a higher tariff, even on selected items, would do: it would eventually raise the over-all cost of imports and/or increase domestic production so as to glut the market. In the first instance, the farmer would pay more for necessities like fertilizer; in the second, prices would be depressed, and the farmer would be out of pocket. Either way the farmer suffered. The simple fact was, Mitch Hepburn concluded, Canada was a fertile land, blessed by God but beset by high-tariff advocates who wanted to change the natural flow of trade and block nature's abundance. "They don't want to enjoy the fruits of the land. Instead of us having it God's way, they want us to have it Gott's way."

As the laughing Elgin farmers spilled out into Talbot Street, it was evident that Mitch Hepburn had scored a debating victory and had given the Tory protection policy one of its worst drubbings ever on an Ontario public platform. Some of the Liberals who gathered at the Grand Central Hotel after the meeting were mightily impressed with the performance of the Member for Elgin West. R. J. Deachman of the Consumers' League immediately wrote to Senator Andrew Haydon, Mackenzie King's top political organizer, that Hepburn had "proved himself in the contest an exceedingly able man." Haydon replied that "it would be difficult to have Hepburn's performance very freely duplicated within the Liberal Party."

Encouraged by his growing reputation as "a good platform man," Mitch Hepburn intervened more frequently in the debates of the 1930 session. Now he took on the leader of the Opposition, the Honourable Richard Bedford Bennett himself. Referring to a speech Bennett had made in his own riding of Port Stanley, which advocated higher protection for the dairy industry, Hepburn described the opposition leader as seen by Elgin's farmers. "Words literally flowed from his lips. If any word hesitated, it was swept to destruction by the thousands that surged in its wake as the Honourable Gentleman was carried along on the flood tide of his verbosity. His verbal machine gun killed the lowly mosquito by the thousands." As for Mackenzie King's much-maligned statement that he would give no money to Tory Governments for relief purposes, Mitch Hepburn saw nothing wrong with that. "If I had been in his position I think I might have said a lot worse. I don't blame him."[6]

There was another matter, though, that brought Hepburn and Mackenzie King into conflict – probably the first difference over a specific policy between them. The dispute arose over granting clearances to vessels carrying liquor to the United States, then under prohibition and thirsty for imported spirits, a matter that affected some of the Lake Erie ports in Hepburn's riding. The Royal Commission on Customs and Excise, which had reported in 1927, had recommended against granting clearances. After hesitating for two years, partly because he did not want to seem subservient to American demands on the question, King had decided by the session of 1930 to introduce legislation to stop liquor clearances and was prepared to resign if Parliament did not support him.

Opposition quickly developed, especially from Ontario Liberal Members, many of whom saw no reason why Canada should help the American authorities enforce prohibition. At a meeting of the Ontario Liberal Management Committee in Toronto in January, attended by many federal Liberals including Hepburn, all but two members of the Committee voted to continue liquor clearances. As he explained in a letter, "I am absolutely opposed to such a motion, and said definitely that I am forced to vote against this matter. The question of the possibility of the bill being killed in the Senate was brought up, and I am surprised the P.M. declared he would call for immediate dissolution of the House, and make liquor clearances a federal issue." After lunching with King late in January, Mitch Hepburn had not changed his mind. "I still maintain," he wrote to an Ontario Liberal, "that the Prime Minister is making a serious mistake regarding his proposition to cancel Clearance Papers. In fact, I have yet to find anyone in this riding in sympathy with such a move." Alex Darrach wrote King to warn him "that if Mr. Hepburn supports your bill I am afraid it will defeat him. We cannot afford to have him defeated. . . . It is freely admitted that he is the only useful member the riding has ever had."

Undeterred, at the first caucus of the session Mackenzie King, in an astonishing philippic combining high moral fervour and party loyalty, swung the caucus behind the measure. When it came to a vote in the House, only eleven individuals opposed it. Mitch Hepburn was not among them, and King was pleased. He wrote Alex Darrach: "I have felt, from the beginning, that Hepburn was wrong in the view he took as to the political significance of the measure. . . . I must say, however, that he has played the game very well, and, I believe will be strengthened as a consequence, rather than weakened, in his constituency."[7]

When King called an election for July 28, 1930, Mitch Hepburn needed all the help he could get in his constituency. Several problems militated against his holding a riding that the provincial Conservatives had won in October, 1929. There was rising unemployment and the growing sentiment for higher tariffs. Whatever the political danger, Hepburn never wavered in his support of freer trade. At a meeting of farmers in the spring of 1930, he differed with every other speaker and warned his listeners that more protection would mean lower farm profits. To one newspaperman, unaccustomed to so rare a display of political courage, Mitch Hepburn explained: "They may crucify me, but I cannot betray them. These are the people I have grown up among. These are my friends. Am I to lead them up a blind alley? Never, I shall go back to the farm . . . far, far better to be a good farmer than a dishonest politician."

Mitch Hepburn did not intend to go back to the farm without a fight. To offset another problem, the lack of newspaper support (the St. Thomas *Times-Journal* and the powerful London *Free Press* were solidly Tory), the eager young Elgin Liberals developed a novel scheme. Periodically during the campaign they sent the friendly London *Advertiser* to lists of voters. Within forty-eight hours of the voting, seven thousand *Advertisers* blanketed the riding. These were no substitute for the candidate himself, who was in demand for meetings all through southern Ontario while many Conservatives headed by R. B. Bennett spoke in Elgin. "I am having a good stiff fight here in Elgin," Hepburn told a friend, "and can see now that the Tories are determined to regain the seat." He was even forced to refute the charge, made against his father nearly twenty-five years before, that he was a drunkard. As election day approached and a distinct Tory trend developed across the country, even Liberals were conceding West Elgin. Some of them predicted that Hepburn would lose his deposit.

When the votes were counted on election night, R. B. Bennett's Conservatives swept into power at Ottawa, the Liberals dropped six seats in Ontario, but Mitch Hepburn held Elgin West by a sharply increased majority (1,437 votes) over retired clothier, Jack Dowler, the Tory candidate.[8] Most surprising of all was Hepburn's strength in the city of St. Thomas, where he won the railway poll and almost pulled even with the Tory urban vote. This was an astonishing display of vote-getting power, a display that did not go unnoticed by Liberal Party brass. It was viewed with particular interest by several Ontario provincial Liberals who were again in the market for fresh leadership after twenty-five years out of power.

When Mitch Hepburn went to Ottawa in September of 1930 for the special session called by Prime Minister Bennett, several Ontario Liberals began to take a long look at the member for Elgin West. They saw a young man, just turned thirty-four, married to an attractive wife, who made friends quickly and seemed to possess inexhaustible energy. If his rhetoric at times was on the bombastic side, his political record was orthodox enough. A consistent low-tariff man, he had retained his rural support despite growing protectionist sentiment and his own attacks on the UFO organization. On the matter of social and economic reform, he was certainly no radical. He had supported old-age pensions and had mentioned once in passing the eight-hour day and a minimum wage for men.

There were no radical tendencies there to rock the boat. His attack on Sun Life and the big interests was a bit overdone, but it was politically popular and could be put down to inexperience and youthful exuberance (as could the reports of excessive roistering with some of the boys in Ottawa). There was some question of his party loyalty, but the record showed that when the chips were down and the whips on the Member for Elgin West had gone along. Mackenzie King's attitude was more difficult to ascertain. There were rumours that King was neither impressed with Hepburn's ability nor amused by some of his extra-parliamentary antics. These were just rumours. Much more tangible was that solid victory in an Ontario rural-urban riding.

As Mitch Hepburn moved to the Liberal front benches for the special September session of Parliament, relishing his role in Opposition, twitting the new Prime Minister R. B. Bennett more easily (referring to Bennett's promise to end unemployment or perish, Hepburn remarked, "It is significant . . . that he has provided for any physical contingency by having as his chief whip a gentleman who, I understand, has been an undertaker"), people were spoken to, letters were written, approaches were made. Nothing definite. Just straws in the wind. Still concrete enough that late in September one of Mitch Hepburn's close friends from Elgin, Colin Campbell, wrote that he was "pleased to hear what you had to say about the Ontario situation but dont [sic] be in too big a hurry until they assure you off [sic] all arrangements."[9]

The Member for Elgin West was in no hurry. But the Ontario situation would not wait.

chapter 4

The Heather Afire

The situation of the Liberal Party in Ontario in 1930 was a mess. Since last in power in 1905, the Party had lost eight general elections, discarded seven leaders, and in the election of 1929 won only fourteen of the 112 seats at Queen's Park. As one disillusioned Liberal put it, the Party had lost not only its structure but its soul.

This was all too true. Under its great leader Sir Oliver Mowat, who was Premier from 1872 to 1896, the provincial Liberals were a reform party with progressive policies – close to the people, solidly based in the cities, with strong appeal to the working man, sure of a high proportion of the Catholic vote, both Irish and French; sure, too of substantial rural support. Under subsequent leaders, this rural-urban-religious coalition, so carefully constructed by Mowat, gradually disintegrated, so that by 1930 the Liberal Party in Ontario was moribund. There were a number of reasons for its demise but one was of paramount importance. The Party, particularly in the period from 1911 to 1917, under the leadership of Newton Wesley Rowell, a high-minded, able, austere Methodist lawyer, had changed courses. Rowell obscured the Party's progressive program by channelling its reforming zeal into a moral crusade against the evils of booze.

This campaign for prohibition transformed the Liberals from a broadly based coalition of voting groups into a minor political sect. By emphasizing the salvific effects of prohibition, Rowell alienated large portions of the urban vote, labour support, the minority Catholic community, and the growing ethnic groups. The energetic Harley Dewart, leader from 1918 to 1923, tried to revive the Liberal reform program but, after some limited success in which the Party's urban vote increased appreciably, the prohibitionists proved too much for him and Dewart resigned. In the provincial election of 1929, the Ontario provincial Liberal

Party was not much more than a rural Protestant splinter group, narrowly based on a dozen predominantly dry ridings, its policies bankrupt, its leadership pathetically weak.

For all the moral fervour they expended on the liquor issue, and all the defeats they sustained because of it, the Liberals had been beating a dying horse for at least two general elections. By 1930, prohibition (introduced as a wartime measure by the Conservative Government of Sir William Hearst) had, as a legislative enactment, come and gone. With the return of the soldiers and the growth of the cities after the war, changing social and economic conditions were reflected in the diminishing majorities for prohibition in the three referendums on the matter taken between 1919 and 1924. By that time the gregarious, politically astute Howard Ferguson (who had led the Tories to an overwhelming victory over E. C. Drury's Farmer Government in 1923) had realized that votes could be bottled. Controlled "suds" was a better political bet than enforced sobriety. So Ferguson began to nudge his somewhat reluctant Party toward a moderate "wet" policy. In 1925, he introduced 4.4 beer, a cross between alcohol and soda water which was dubbed "Fergie's Foam." When the voters downed that without any political hangover, Ferguson decided on a bolder step. He fought the 1926 general election on the issue of liquor sale under government control.

The Liberals and William E. N. Sinclair, the steady, colourless, pedestrian Oshawa lawyer, their temporary leader since 1923, fought hard to keep the province safe from demon rum. That is, the Liberals who remained: the cities and large towns were gone, so were labour and the Irish Catholics. The province's French Canadians, still leery of Howard Ferguson's Orange-dominated Party, were screaming for mercy, but there was none. Plodding along, trying to face both ways on the liquor issue (first maintaining it was out of politics, then advocating that the people should vote on it in another referendum), pipe-smoking William Sinclair and his little band of prohibitionists finally fought the campaign on yet another version of Rowell's "ban-the-bar" policy. Ferguson could convince "dry" Tories to accept a measure of control easier than Sinclair could force "wet" liberals to swallow prohibition. It was the difference between a lump of sugar and a big stick with nothing at the end of it but a pure conscience and a long drink of water.

By the late 1920's the consciences of the majority of Ontario's voters were not that pure, and most Liberals had had their fill of cold water. Ferguson won the election of 1926 easily. The following year a measure of government control under the Liquor Control Act came into force, and the Liberal party fragmented into half a dozen dissident groups. There were the "dry" Sinclair Liberals, comprising most of the members at Queen's Park, still determined to hang onto their narrow base of rural Protestant "dry" votes. Their position was stronger than their numbers suggested because they had the support, on the liquor issue, of the Toronto *Globe* and Joseph E. Atkinson's Toronto *Star*. The remaining Liberal groups, among whom there was considerable overlapping, had one thing in common: they all thought it was time the Ontario Liberals looked for fresh leadership.

The Liberal Party's dissatisfied element included the reform Liberals hoping to steer the party again into the progressive tradition of Mowat and its earlier years. Atkinson of the *Star* was a reform Liberal, as was that Laurier Liberal and progressive, Arthur Wentworth Roebuck, with his appeal to the labouring class, won by frequent defences of working men in the courts. Reform Liberalism was especially strong among the young Liberals, like Paul Martin of Windsor and J. C. McRuer of Toronto, in the Twentieth-Century Liberal Clubs. Reform Liberals were usually, but not always, "wet" liberals, men like Percy Parker, the Toronto oil and mining magnate, Arthur Slaght, an able Toronto lawyer, and Harry Sifton, the power baron. Finally, there was "the federal gang" (as Sinclair's group called them) in the Reford building at the corner of Wellington and Bay streets, the powerful Ontario federal contingent like Senators William McGuire and James Spence; the former King Cabinet Ministers, Peter Heenan from Kenora, James Malcolm from Kinkardine, W. D. Euler from Kitchener, and London's J. C. Elliott. They functioned through the Ontario Liberal Association, an organization that Sinclair, like Rowell before him, had ignored by setting up his own provincial office.[1]

Whatever their differences, these Liberal groups wanted a change in the provincial leadership. Before the disastrous election of 1926, Joseph Atkinson had advised Mackenzie King that "the party's position in federal affairs would be much improved if it were possible to strengthen the leadership of the party in the legislature." Periodically there were demands for a party convention (one had not been held since 1923 when Sinclair had been chosen temporary leader at a Queen's Park caucus), and these increased after the debacle of 1929. Sinclair himself complained to Mackenzie King about the lack of party funds, the absence of organization ("The party is dead in the ridings") and said that opinion favoured a convention. After the federal election of 1930 (in which the party lost six Ontario seats), agitation for a provincial convention increased. Sinclair, who had unsuccessfully asked King for a senatorship ("It would solve some of the Ontario difficulties provincially and place the party where it could say which way it wanted to go"), again pressed upon the federal leader the urgency of a convention even if the wet-dry controversy broke wide open. King wrote to Sinclair on August 19, 1930, that he was inclined to favour a convention "but only on one condition, namely, that we know pretty well in advance what is likely to be its outcome."

That was the problem that Senator A. C. Hardy, President of the Ontario Liberal Association, underlined again for King when he informed him he was calling together the Ontario Liberal Management Committee to discuss a convention. "The question of leadership is a very harassing one and I don't know what the outcome will be." Despite this uncertainty, the Management Committee decided to call a convention in Toronto for the middle of December, 1930.[2] Two problems would face the delegates: choice of a leader and a policy on the liquor question. The leader would have a profound bearing on the temperance question and would likely determine the course of the Party for years to come. Were the Ontario provincial Liberals to remain a narrow rural splinter group or were they to return to their program of progressive reform and thereby regain power with a new urban-Catholic-labour coalition?

Through the autumn of 1930, as the convention approached, the names of potential Liberal leaders emerged: Peter Heenan, former federal Labour Minister; James Malcolm, once King's Minister of Trade and Commerce; Arthur Roebuck, the courtly, wing-collared Toronto lawyer; S. C. Tweed, provincial Member for Waterloo North, president of an insurance company with numerous big-business connections; some of the younger Liberals favoured Paul Martin of Windsor. Through September and October, another name was also being mentioned with increasing frequency. On October 21, the Toronto *Star* noted that "a quiet boom is going on in favour of M. F. Hepburn, M.P. for Elgin West." Hepburn's supporters, mostly younger people and by no means organized, stressed the fact that he was "young and vigorous, a good speaker, and likely to capture the imagination of the people."

Before the fall of 1930, the federal Member for Elgin West had not concerned himself much with provincial politics. By October, his interest had quickened. Late that month he spoke in the provincial by-election in Waterloo South, a seat the Liberals surprisingly won back from the Conservatives. On October 30, Mitch Hepburn came to Toronto to make one of the most significant speeches of his career. Gathered to hear him in the rooms over Hunt's Store at the corner of Yonge and Bloor was the Toronto Men's Liberal Club. Present to size up "the boy from Yarmouth," some of the seventy-five meeting him for the first time, were the leaders of Ontario Liberalism – Percy Parker, Senators McGuire and Spence, Harry Johnson, Secretary of the Ontario Liberal Association. Mitch Hepburn lost no time displaying his platform wares. He rocked his audience with a comparison ("There are only two absolute monarchs in the world – Haile Selassie and Howard Ferguson") and delighted them with his forthright declaration on the liquor issue. Prohibition was no longer a public question, and he thanked God "because that means that next time we are going to be able to get out in the open and fight Ferguson on his record which I think is the most damnable ever."[3]

When Mitch Hepburn sat down at Hunt's that night, the enthusiastic politicians rushed up to shake his hand. They were looking for a winner, and many thought they had found one. Percy Parker described the impression made by Hepburn to Mackenzie King: "He created something akin to a sensation, and after the dinner was over expressions were heard that this was the man for Leader." Which was all very well, but there was strong opposition to Mitch Hepburn's becoming provincial leader, opposition lead by Mackenzie King himself. He disapproved of Hepburn's way of life, and some of his convivial friends and their drinking habits (an opinion shared by the powerful Atkinson of the *Star*). Moreover, King was opposed to opening the Elgin West seat which he felt the Tories would win in a by-election, a position he made clear to several prominent Ontario Liberals, including Mitch Hepburn himself, at a luncheon meeting at Laurier House early in November. King's opposition was more than verbal. After abandoning his earlier suggestion that Sinclair should hang onto the leadership for a time, King brought pressure to bear on his friend Percy Parker to run himself, and failing that he thought it preferable to place the affairs of the provincial Party under a provisional committee until after the next general election.

Although the federal leader claimed throughout that he did not want to interfere in the internal affairs of the provincial Party, nor would he block Hepburn's preferment, he actively lined up support for Parker during a visit to Toronto and wrote to Hepburn's friends in Elgin urging them to persuade their member not to run. Hepburn's long-time Elgin supporter, Alex Darrach, needed no persuasion. "Mitch has the abilities of a kind which will make him useful to you," he wrote King, "but they are not of the cool, calculating kind" required by a provincial leader.[4]

Despite King's efforts, the pressure on Hepburn to stand was mounting. Telegrams, letters, and phone calls poured into Lakeland, Florida, where he had been holidaying with his family since early November. On November 26, Hepburn wrote to Arthur Roebuck (who was considering running for the leadership himself), that King wanted him to remain in Ottawa: "I am very perplexed and quite at a loss to make a definite decision." Then he tentatively decided to run if he could do so without splitting the Party or alienating King. No doubt the importunities of his friends (Percy Parker had decided not to stand and wrote King that he considered Hepburn "would be the best man who is really available and have so told him") had their effect on Mitch Hepburn, who, despite his antipathy for the "big interests," was becoming increasingly susceptible to the blandishments of the powerful. One of Mitch Hepburn's old friends, Albert Roberts, wrote to King a week before the convention: "Flattery is a most subtle and deadly weapon. I am afraid that the agents of 'big interests' are preparing a political grave for one whom they wish to bury, and are employing a most effective implement for the digging."5

There were other considerations too. Mitch Hepburn had never cut the swath he had hoped as the Member for Elgin West. The young man whose ancestors had fought against the "Family Compact" in 1837, whose father had been crushed by the "big interests" in 1906, had gone to Ottawa in 1926 as a swash-bucking independent, only to discover another establishment. The hierarchy of that establishment, tightly controlled by Mackenzie King himself, never considered Elgin West very important politically and never took its exuberant member very seriously. Hints that Mitch Hepburn might one day receive a Cabinet post, perhaps agriculture, seemed more unrealizable than ever. At the same time, influential friends like Percy Parker were telling him that instead of sitting on the back bench at Ottawa he had the ability to manage the team and lead it to victory at Queen's Park. It was a powerful inducement to an impressionable young man who, if he could not define power, had realized for some time that he wanted more of it.

Despite this drive for power and the assurances of his friends that he could attain it, Mitch Hepburn had to reckon not only with King's opposition but with the reluctance of most West Elgin Liberals to see him leave the federal field. They judged he had a better political future in Ottawa and were concerned that his health was too precarious for provincial leadership. On December 11, tanned and rested from his Florida holiday, he attended a meeting of prominent Liberals in Toronto, including several key members of "the federal gang," among them Senators Spence and McGuire, James Malcolm, Harry Johnson, and Percy Parker. At this meeting a new strategy was worked out to broaden the Party's narrow dry rural base. It involved Sinclair's retiring from the leadership in favour of the provincial Member for Waterloo North, Sidney Tweed, a man the Party managers felt they could live with. Apparently all those present, including Mitchell Hepburn, concurred in this decision, and an emissary was dispatched to obtain Sinclair's consent. Mackenzie King was delighted and wrote a friend in Elgin that Hepburn's decision not to run "is a wise one."6

The only trouble with this "back-room" strategy was that it underestimated Sinclair. On Monday, December 15, the eve of the convention, it became apparent that he was in the fight to stay. A statement was given to the press that the Queen's Park Liberals, including S. C. Tweed, had unanimously endorsed Sinclair's leadership. Now, it seemed that all bets were off. A good part of Monday a smiling Mitch Hepburn greeted delegates at the King Edward Hotel. Other leadership possibilities were mentioned – Peter Heenan, Harry Sifton, Arthur Roebuck, Elmore Philpott (who had just resigned as an editor of the *Globe* to run) – but most delegates now believed that the fight would lie between Sinclair and Hepburn, a confrontation that would confirm the rural, small-town direction of the Party over the past twenty years or reverse it, a struggle that no matter who won would result in a serious split.

Senator Hardy opened the convention at eleven o'clock on Tuesday morning, December 16. After a stormy session, the delegates decided to modify the prohibition plank. This was a victory for the urban-wet wing, but it would be nullified if a dry leader were chosen. The same day the Toronto *Star* reported that Mitchell Hepburn had definitely decided not to run. In his hotel rooms, pressure was being exerted on Sinclair to withdraw in favour of Tweed, and the Party leaders, including Hepburn, thought the Oshawa lawyer would eventually buckle. To the large federal contingent of senators and members attending the convention, this still seemed the best solution. It would meet King's wishes about Hepburn and at the same time rid the party of its dry leadership. The whole trouble was that on the eve of the ballotting a stubborn Sinclair showed no signs of buckling. All day Tuesday he had met delegates in his hotel rooms. That night he was too busy to attend a Twentieth-Century Liberal Club banquet in the Crystal Ballroom of the King Edward Hotel, a banquet addressed by Mitch Hepburn who delivered a short punchy attack on Ferguson and Bennett ("Lord Gopher of Calgary") which left the delegates in high good humour.

As the diners streamed out of the Crystal balloom to return to their rooms or gather in little groups all over the hotel, a few wandered into the Yellow Room on the second floor where a bar had been set up. They were excited and a little bewildered about the leadership question. The room began to fill up. Younger members drifted in, Paul Martin and W. P. Mulock among them. The managers of the federal gang were there – Senators Spence and McGuire and Percy Parker, and reformers like Roebuck and Patrick Donnelly, and some of the boys from Elgin, Wilson Mills and Colin Campbell. It was approaching midnight, and the Yellow Room, lively with conviviality, was crowded. There was a good deal of talk about Mitch Hepburn's speech earlier in the evening. Then someone mentioned that spell-binder he had delivered a few weeks before at Hunt's and quickly a current of enthusiasm crackled through the room, smoky and jammed now with 150 delegates from all parts of the province. One name kept emerging from the chatter. There was only one man who could do it, only one who could rebuild the Party, only one who could win. A messenger was sent to Room 325 at the Prince George a short distance away.

When Mitch Hepburn appeared in the doorway to the Yellow Room, through the haze he saw that it was filled with friends from Ottawa, from Elgin, from the North, from Toronto. They told him that all efforts to force Sinclair out had failed. Mitch Hepburn should take it; otherwise the convention would be a disaster; otherwise the Party would collapse. Wilson Mills, President of West Elgin's Liberals, demurred. He explained why they wanted their Member to remain at Ottawa. There were cries of protest. Without Mitch there was no hope of victory. Delegate after delegate urged him to stand. Finally, Peter Heenan concluded a fiery exhortation by promising he would tour the province with Mitch and together they would "set the heather on fire."

Reporters listening in the corridor outside heard a thundering roll of cheers, then silence. Inside, someone had shoved a chair close to Mitch Hepburn. He stood up, his face was grey with fatigue, but the smile was there. He was a good Liberal, and he would go now where it was plain he had to go; he would accept the leadership if they wanted him. He turned to his supporters from West Elgin, some with tears in their eyes. He was sorry to give up Elgin, but he was prepared to do what his friends from all over the province wanted him to do. With the balloting to begin in less than twelve hours, a tired but triumphant Mitch Hepburn returned to his rooms at the Prince George.

Still, when nominations were called for a Liberal leader, on the wintry afternoon of December 17, 1930, the outcome, for all the enthusiasm in the Yellow Room, was by no means certain. Sinclair had given no sign. As he walked into the convention hall with Mrs. Sinclair by his side, he indicated to Atkinson of the *Star* that he was staying. He sat close to the press table with his wife, tired, a slightly worried look on his face, toying with the bowl of his pipe, fiddling with a ballot pad on his knee. He sat there as the nominations droned on and three of the nominees (including Heenan and Roebuck) quickly withdrew. He looked up as a roar of cheering greeted Mitchell F. Hepburn; waited again to hear his own name put in nomination, then tapping out his pipe, his square jaws clenched, Sinclair walked to the platform, looking neither to right or left, borne up by a wave of applause at least equal to Mitch Hepburn's. He adjusted the microphone, looked out at the six hundred delegates, out at his friends from Ontario South and all the little crossroads of the province expecting a fighting speech from their old chief.

He began quietly; he could see a good majority for him in the convention, but that would leave all the old problems. Sinclair had made his decision, made it only moments before, perhaps when he heard that roar of applause for the Member from Elgin and knew that the majority and confirmation he craved were gone. He had done his best for seven years, Sinclair said, but apparently his best had not been good enough. "No, no!" came a cry. The speaker brushed the interruption aside and went on with a slight glance at the candidates behind him. "So I stand aside today in the hope and with the conviction that a new start will make things better in Ontario. I hope it will be better. At least, if it is not, I shall know that I have not stood in the way." Then accompanied by his wife and the singing of "For He's a Jolly Good Fellow," the leader of rural Ontario Liberalism walked out of the hall, not even waiting to cast his ballot.

The vote was an anti-climax. Only Elmore Philpott, never considered a serious candidate, and Mitchell Hepburn remained. A hush fell over the six hundred delegates when the chairman approached the microphone to read the results: "Mr. Hepburn has been elected leader of the Liberal Party in Ontario." Delegates rose to their feet cheering and waving programs wildly as three husky friends from Elgin carried the leader-elect to the platform. They watched and cheered again as he stood there, looking not much more than a boy in his blue suit and bright red tie, his black hair brushed back from a high forehead, his slate-blue eyes darting around the hall, the Hepburn smile flashing as he noticed the Elgin delegation.

The cheers died. The clear, high-pitched voice began. The words sounded like his father's twenty-five years before. He was young, but he hoped they wouldn't hold that against him; he was willing to learn. The words came more quickly now, without notes, sounding a growing confidence. "I go forward as Ontario leader filled with optimism. I know I am going to succeed . . . I'll supply the pep and ginger and you people hold the brakes. And we will never stop till we get to Queen's Park." It was heady stuff for Liberals who had not had a winner for a quarter century. A serious, unsmiling Mitch Hepburn concluded, "I will do my best and I hope, that, when my span of life is done, I will leave the world a little better place than I found it."[7]

To the excited delegates leaving the King Edward and heading for home – to the Toronto Liberals and the labour men, the French Canadians and the Irish Catholics, the delegations from the North – to all these who had supported the smiling young man in the red tie, to them the heather was already afire.

chapter 5

Rum, Romanism, and Power

The cheers of the Liberal convention behind him, Mitch Hepburn returned to Florida to spend Christmas with Eva and his mother Maggie and gather strength for the battle ahead. Already there were indications what an uphill fight it would be. Reaction to the choice of "the boy from Yarmouth" as Liberal leader was, to say the least, mixed. Conservative papers like the Toronto *Telegram,* which viewed his previous record pretty much as a joke, were downright hostile. More serious was the response of the Liberal Toronto *Star* and its publisher Joseph Atkinson. After several days of silence on the convention's nominee, the *Star* suggested that the Liberals might have better chosen a leader acceptable to the prohibitionists. Rumours spread that disgruntled Liberals would break away to form a dry farmers' party. Some of Hepburn's old St. Thomas supporters were incensed at the choice. "I think," Alex Darrach wrote to Mackenzie King, "he is a very foolish young man." Darrach did not like his former protégée's wet views and added, "He is entirely unfitted by nature and by training for the difficult task he has undertaken . . . I regard the selection as a supreme act of folly." Darrach warned King that Hepburn was "riding for a fall."

Whatever his personal opinion, Mackenzie King, always the good Party man, acted to strengthen his new Ontario lieutenant's position. He told Hepburn that he was "pleased that you reversed your previous decision and allowed your name to go before the convention." (He was even more pleased that Hepburn had decided to retain his federal Elgin seat.) He promised him complete co-operation and support ("I know enough of the difficulties and problems of a political leader to be able to enter very sympathetically into your feelings"), and urged Hepburn to "immediately secure from those around you the guarantee of co-operation in a financial way . . . for purposes of organization."

Among a number of Ontario Liberals to whom King wrote urging support for Hepburn was the deposed leader, William Sinclair. "You will find Hepburn a very pleasant and delightful young fellow to work with," he wrote, exhorting Sinclair to "go out of your way to demonstrate the cordiality of your co-operation with him." Sinclair's reply was a warning of future trouble. After explaining to King that he had lost the leadership because of the "federal gang" led by Peter Heenan, he added: "You suggest that I aid Hepburn. I do not see how I can be of much assistance. His friends are not my friends. Whatever faults I may have, I know he is of a much inferior type of mind to my own. . . . His chief qualifications consist in making rabid speeches, one sentence of which at any time may be his undoing." Sinclair, too, hinted at the possibility of a dissident provincial Liberal Party.[1]

So the newly elected Liberal leader began the year 1931 without a seat at Queen's Park, House leader Sinclair hostile, with only a dozen members in a Legislature of 112, party funds depleted, facing a well-heeled Conservative majority. Despite all his talk of "pep and ginger," Hepburn's chances of leading the Liberals to Queen's Park after so many years in the wilderness looked bleak at the beginning of 1931. What the Liberals needed was an issue or a miracle, perhaps both.

During the next three years not one but three issues emerged, all of them related to and complicated by the depression. Liquor, religion, and electricity were the stuff of politics in Ontario during the early 1930's. In the previous decade the province's expanding industrial-urban complex required more electrical power. This demand could not be met within the province because jurisdiction over Ontario's boundary waters, the Ottawa, St. Lawrence, and Niagara rivers, had not yet been settled by the governments involved. Faced with this difficulty, the Conservative Government of Howard Ferguson, though still committed in principle to the traditional public ownership policy of Ontario hydro, turned to private sources to fill the increased power demands. Between 1926 and 1930, the Government signed contracts with four private Quebec Power Companies: Beauharnois, Light, Heat, and Power; Maclaren-Quebec; Gatineau; and Ottawa Valley. Within the province, the Government purchased the Dominion Power and Transmission Company, serving the Hamilton area; the Madawaska Company, supplying the Renfrew-Pembroke district; and guaranteed to buy power annually from the Ontario Power Service Corporation in Northern Ontario, a subsidiary of the Abitibi Company. Based on the projected increase in demand, these transactions (which provided some 891,000 horsepower for immediate and future delivery) seemed eminently sensible and caused little comment at the time.[2] It was only when the depression struck, the generators slowed down, and the question of unused power became entangled with charges of graft and corruption in the signing of the contracts that hydro became an issue that almost jolted the Government out of power.

The depression also complicated the religious issue. Over the years the province's Roman Catholics had periodically agitated for more public support for their separate schools. Specifically, they wanted a share of corporation and public utility taxes. The astute Howard Ferguson stayed clear of this potentially dangerous issue by making minor concessions without granting the principle. He increased separate school grants in individual instances and he mollified one group of Catholics by modifying the hated Regulation Seventeen, which had restricted French teaching in the schools. The success of Ferguson's "under the table policy" was evident in the elections of 1926 and 1929 when the traditionally Liberal Catholic vote went heavily Conservative. The worsening economic situation, however, made it more difficult than ever for the Catholics (a low income group) to finance their elementary school system. Accordingly, in 1932, the Catholic Taxpayers' Association was established. With the blessing of the bishops but under direct control of laymen, the CTA soon became a province-wide, parish-based organization designed to convince the government that, in equity, Catholics had a right to more public tax support for their schools. Under the dynamic direction of the acerbic, persistent Martin J. Quinn, it also became a pressure group that any politician could ignore only at his peril.[3]

The liquor question, also affected by the depression, was another political problem in the early thirties. There was little enough relaxation in hard times for the lower economic classes. Why could not a working man in a city go into a pub and enjoy a drink of beer? As it was, spirits could only be purchased at government stores. Moreover, in a period of shrinking revenues and growing government deficits, the wet wing of the Tory party thirstily eyed the freer distribution of beer and wine as an untapped keg of revenue.

Dominating all these issues and related to them was the depression, the leit-motif of "the hungry thirties," easy enough to translate into statistics, virtually unmeasurable in terms of psychological and political impact. Every politician had to face up to the implications of nearly half a million people on relief; of the married labourer in Sudbury who considered himself lucky if he could make twenty-two dollars a week; of the thousands hopelessly tramping the dusty streets who could not earn a nickel; of the unemployed family of four in Toronto where the mother had to eke out a weekly subsistence on four dollars and twenty cents relief money.[4]

More than any other, the politician who had to face up to the problem of the depression was George Stewart Henry, the fifty-nine-year-old Member for York East, and the man who, on December 15, 1930, two days before Mitchell Hepburn's selection, had succeeded Howard Ferguson (newly appointed Canadian High Commissioner in London) as Ontario's fourth Conservative Prime Minister. "A plain, blunt honest man" were the adjectives usually used to describe George Henry. After politics (he had represented East York since 1913), George Henry's interests lay in farming at his home near Oriole outside Toronto, the milk business (President of Farmers Dairy), and mortgages (National Trust), all of which had proved quite profitable. A stable, reliable man was George Henry ("There's as much romance about the Premier of Ontario as about a first mortgage or a bottle of milk"), a man who taught Sunday school at Oriole and could be counted on to "plough a straight furrow." The effervescent Howard Ferguson, during his eight years in the Premier's chair, had made Toryism in Ontario an enthusiastic religious revival of which he was high priest; George Henry would tend to make it a limited company of which he was managing director.[5]

Nothing much happened during George Henry's first session as Premier in 1931 to suggest that the man who had kept Farmers Dairy solidly in the black could not keep the Tory Government out of the red. For that matter, nothing much happened during most of his first year as leader to encourage Mitch Hepburn. To the disgust of more militant Liberals, the House leader, William Sinclair, was not even on speaking terms with Hepburn. Although Conservative majorities were cut, the Liberals lost three by-elections.

After fighting two by-elections, attending to his parliamentary duties in Ottawa, managing his growing Bannockburn farms, and trying to pep up the organization in the Ontario constituencies, a tired Mitch Hepburn entered hospital in St. Thomas in June, 1931, for major surgery. The operation, removal of a kidney, was successful but was the occasion of rumours that Hepburn's health was not up to the task of leadership. Mackenzie King, who had asked a St. Thomas friend to have flowers sent to the hospital ("I should think a few roses or any spring flowers would be quite appropriate") wrote to his former Ontario Cabinet Minister, James Malcolm, "that Mitch is doing as well as can be expected. The little fellow has been very plucky about the whole affair." In the same letter, King speculated "whether he will ever be sufficiently strong to continue in the position of leadership . . . I imagine he has wished many times that he had accepted the counsel of his older friends and not allowed himself to be too quickly precipitated into the task which he assumed, the duties of which, we must all agree, he has met with considerable ability, courage and fortitude."

By the fall of 1931, Mitch Hepburn, feeling better, was fighting the South Wellington by-election. This time he had an issue custom-made for his barn-storming platform abilities. Hepburn pressed a question that he had raised in a speech at Milton in the spring. There, after underlining his own belief in continued public ownership of Hydro, the Liberal chief, rattling off figures, claimed that Hydro had sold out to private interests in Quebec, had vastly overbought, and that the Ontario taxpayer was paying for this folly in higher charges. In the fall of 1931, Mitch Hepburn could embellish his indictment of Hydro waste and extravagance with charges of graft and corruption. During the summer, evidence given at a parliamentary investigation in Ottawa into the Beauharnois Company's relations with the previous King administration, besides revealing that the company had contributed heavily to federal Liberal campaign funds, also suggested that Ontario Tories had profited handsomely when the Beauharnois contract was signed.

The President of Beauharnois, R. O. Sweezey, the man building a multi-million-dollar power empire on the friendship of federal Liberals and an eighty-three-foot waterfall near Montreal, testified that he had given $125,000 to one John Aird Jr. This money had been paid the day before Howard Ferguson, in the fall of 1929, had arranged for Ontario to take 250,000 horsepower from Beauharnois. According to Sweezey, Aird had said he was a representative of the Ontario Conservative Party and a political contribution would be in order because Beauharnois "would probably be having a lot of dealings with the Ontario Government, and gratefulness was always considered an important factor in dealing with democratic governments."

On the stand, Aird was not very clear about what he did to earn the money (which he had deposited in eleven Toronto banks), but he denied that it was a political contribution or that one cent of it had gone to the Ontario Conservative Party. Aird (son of Sir John Aird of the Canadian Bank of Commerce), an engineer by profession, operated two companies, one in construction, the other in masonry, formerly with Imperial Oil, sometime president of a woolen mill that had gone broke, an associate builder of the Lord Nelson Hotel in Halifax, and withal a keen student of hydro affairs, volunteered another piece of information. When the Ontario Hydro Commission had purchased the Madawaska properties near Renfrew in 1929, he had received $50,000 for his "services."

Although the Ottawa Committee found that there was no evidence that any of the $125,000 payment to Aird had gone to any political party (the Ontario Liberal Party admitted receiving a routine $2,000 campaign contribution from Sweezey), Mitch Hepburn used the revelations with telling effect in the South Wellington by-election in November, 1931. The Conservatives confidently expected to win. Instead, the popular young Liberal candidate, Paul Munro, turned over nearly 1,800 votes to register a stunning upset. Writing to King about his victory, Munro stressed the "valiant work at great cost to his health" done in the riding by Hepburn.[6]

South Wellington was the most heartening provincial Liberal victory in years. It revealed the growing co-operation between the Party and

Harry Nixon's Progressives.* This co-operation, a significant development of Hepburn's first year as leader, was essential if the Liberals were
not to lose another general election through three-cornered contests.
Nixon and Hepburn were old personal and political friends from UFO
days, and the Progressive leader, writing later to Mackenzie King, gave
full credit to Hepburn for the closer ties between the Progressives and the
Liberals:

> I have felt for many years that it was utter folly for the Liberals and
> Progressives to fight one another . . . but previously met a very cold
> reception to any overtures I made, but, I am very happy to say, that
> in the new Liberal leader, Mr. Hepburn, I find an entirely different
> attitude and expect that the result in Ontario in the next Provincial
> election will amaze even the most optimistic.

Nixon for all practical purposes replaced Sinclair as Hepburn's lieutenant in the Ontario House. This was evident early in 1932, when the
demands for a full probe into Hydro affairs grew. Even most of the Conservative press thought that the payments to the mysterious and affluent
John Aird Jr. should be investigated. There were charges too that the
contracts signed with the Quebec power companies were outrageously
prodigal, that the 100,000 horsepower contracted for from the Ontario
Power Service Corporation should be examined, and that the twenty-one
million dollars the Government paid for the Dominion Power and Transmission Company was too high. After he had all the contracts scrutinized
by government auditors, George Henry wrote Howard Ferguson that he
was prepared to have a short inquiry into some aspects of Hydro but did
not expect any trouble.

The inquiry, begun in February, 1932, was one of the longest and
most ill-starred in Ontario's history. The first royal commissioner finally
resigned because of ill health, his successor died, and it was only in
November, 1932, that Justices W. R. Riddell and G. H. Sedgewick
brought in their report. It gave Hydro and the Government a complete
bill of health. The Commissioners found that the $50,000 paid to John
Aird Jr. on the Madawaska purchase was for "services" rendered, though
these were never spelled out. Mitch Hepburn was "shocked" at the
findings.

He and his Ontario lieutenants, particularly the able, arrogant Toronto
lawyer, Arthur Slaght, kept digging into the Hydro contracts. Early in
1933, they hit pay dirt. Rumours had been circulating for some time that
all was not well with the Ontario Power Service Corporation, the subsidiary of the Abitibi Company set up to produce power in the Abitibi
Canyon north of Sudbury. Ontario Hydro, with an eye on the develop-

ing power needs of the North, had contracted to buy 100,000 horsepower annually from the OPSC. When the depression struck, the parent Abitibi Company, in June, 1932, defaulted on its bond payments. Anxious to save the power project, the Henry Government quite legitimately began negotiations to take over the faultering power subsidiary. These negotiations were near completion in March, 1933, when questions began to appear on the order paper at Queen's Park asking whether any of the OPSC bonds (which had substantially recovered their original market value when news of the take-over became known) were held by George Henry or Arthur Meighen (Conservative Senate leader appointed to the Ontario Hydro Commission by Henry in June, 1931) or by any of the companies with which the two gentlemen were associated.

These questions (supplemented by several attacks on Meighen's integrity by Mitchell Hepburn) ticked ominously on the order paper for some weeks before setting off an explosion that nearly blew George Stewart Henry out of the Premier's chair. On April 5, 1933, amid speculation that he would resign within hours, George Henry looking pale and shaken, rose to tell a hushed legislature that in the summer of 1930 (shortly after he had made a fortune from the sale of a milk company), he had invested $25,000 in OPSC bonds, and companies of which Hydro Commissioner Meighen was a director held several hundred thousand dollars worth as well.

Although his personal loss on the bonds was substantially cut by his Government's take-over, the Premier denied any impropriety. "I do not propose to enter into any excuses on the matter," he told the House and added, "In all sincerity I want to say that when this problem first came to me I never thought about my personal interest." Henry's honesty was less in question in the transaction than his political judgment. To admit that he had all but forgotten that he had $25,000 tucked away in a concern his Government saved from bankruptcy was a political blunder of monumental proportions. The Premier later admitted to Howard Ferguson, "I will never forgive myself."[7] Whether the ordinary voters, to whom $25,000 was an unbelievable fortune, would forgive him, was another question. For the moment, George Henry survived.

The hydro disclosures obscured for a time the pressure being exerted on the Henry Government from another quarter. Since 1932, the Catholic Taxpayers' Association had developed a grass-roots organization in more than eighty per cent of the Catholic parishes across the province.

---

*   Harry Nixon, a forty-year-old farmer from St. George, was born and brought up a Conservative. He later joined the UFO and became a Minister in Premier E. C. Drury's Farmer Government in 1919. After its defeat in 1923, Nixon, who retained his Brant seat, joined the Progressives, that loose political grouping of farmers whose main goal was freer trade.

A vigorous and sustained campaign was mounted to gain Catholics a share of corporation and utility taxes for their elementary schools. Pamphlets, circulars, and letters blanketed the province, parish meetings were held, sermons preached on the rights of Catholics. Deputations descended on Queen's Park insisting that Henry meet the Catholics' legitimate requests. The man who demanded an answer with growing impatience, often with less finesse than firmness, in the end with a gun pressed to George Henry's temple – loaded, so it was claimed, with a quarter of a million Catholic votes – was Martin J. Quinn, the astute, undiplomatic, and indefatigable chairman of the Catholic Taxpayers' Association.

At the same time, Orange lodges from one end of Ontario to the other made it clear what would happen to George Henry if he gave the Catholics a cent. Martin Quinn maintained that reasonable Protestants would support the Catholic claims, and as for the Orangemen, he would simply outvote them. "If the Government does not grant our request," he warned Henry publicly, "we will go quietly to the polls and cast 250,000 votes, and try to elect a Government which will give us justice." That kind of statement, besides enraging the Orangemen, suggested that Quinn and the CTA had elicited some kind of secret pledge from Hepburn to help the Catholic schools. Reinforcing this theory was the fact that Quinn himself and many members of the CTA's executive were Liberals. Early in 1933, Martin Quinn, somewhat disillusioned with Henry's evasions on the question, wrote to Hepburn. He informed the Liberal chief that his friend and Ontario's Catholic Senator, William McGuire, had assured him that Hepburn was "entirely in sympathy with the position we take, and may be counted upon to support any legislation that the Government may initiate." Hepburn merely replied that the Liberal position would be announced when the Government adopted a definite policy on the school question.

Hepburn realized that he was on extremely delicate ground. Presumably most of the Orangemen would vote Tory anyway, but he could not afford to antagonize moderate Protestant opinion by seeming to favour the Catholics, especially when it was already being charged that too many of his close friends and backers were Catholic, men like Peter Heenan and Frank O'Connor, the President of Laura Secord. If he were to form a Government, he must regain a sizeable share of the traditionally Liberal Catholic vote, lost in the two previous elections on the prohibition issue and the reported anti-Catholicism of former Liberal leaders like Newton Wesley Rowell.

Hepburn moved carefully on the religious issue. In March, 1933, he conferred with Quinn and Senator McGuire. As Quinn recalled this meeting later, Hepburn would seem to have made a definite commitment to support the Catholic request. In a letter to Hepburn, he referred to "the arrangement made between you and me at a conference in March,

1933, arranged by our mutual friend, Senator McGuire." Just a few days after the conference, however, Hepburn was disappointed to discover that apparently Quinn was not all that pleased with whatever "arrangement" had been made. He noted to a friend: "I am returning the Quinn letter. I was rather disappointed at the personal reference, as I thought we had a pretty clear understanding with regard to this very subject. In any event, he seemed to be entirely satisfied after an interview I had with him and Senator McGuire." In view of subsequent events, it is only natural to assume that Hepburn promised to consider the Catholics' request sympathetically, perhaps even pledged privately some tax relief. In public he kept absolutely quiet, reasoning no doubt that the real pressure was on Henry and that the Liberals had less to lose by silence than the Premier had already lost by procrastination.

Former Premier Ferguson (who had toured Ontario's fall fairs in 1933 taking, as he put it, the political pulse of the people for Henry) warned the Premier after his trip that in "the school question you have your most delicate and difficult problem." Ferguson urged the Premier to move swiftly and set up a commission that hopefully would recommend the whole problem be settled by the courts. Henry did not move swiftly, much to Ferguson's disgust, Catholic annoyance, and Orange fears. Finally, on the last day of the 1934 pre-election session, Henry announced to the legislature that stated questions to clarify the tax position of Catholics would be submitted to the courts. This belated compromise satisfied none of the opposing factions, but it did put the matter on ice until the militantly Protestant Toronto *Telegram* defrosted it again in the final days of the election campaign.[8]

If Henry's ineptness in Hydro matters and his dilatoriness on the school question weakened the government, that old bugbear, prohibition, almost destroyed the Liberals and their new leader. From the time Hepburn became leader, there were rumours that the Conservative wet-wing, led by Attorney General William Price, was pressing Henry to adopt a "loosening" policy on sale of spirits by making wine and beer available in hotels and restaurants. Whatever his personal feelings, the Premier had much to gain by a "loosening" policy which, at one stroke, would bolster sagging Government revenues, deflect the voters' attention from any weaknesses in the administration's record, and almost certainly split the opposition down the middle. From London, Howard Ferguson was urging this move.

Mitch Hepburn's problem was to peel the dry label from his party without alienating the prohibitionist Liberals or jeopardizing his alliance with Harry Nixon's dry Progressives. He had already stated publicly at Sudbury (much to Nixon's annoyance), "We as a Liberal Party are no longer supporting the cause of prohibition, and never will so long as I am leader of the Party." He was careful not to go beyond this negative statement. As he explained to his supporter, M. W. Rossie of the London *Advertiser*: "If we oppose the Henry beer policy we will go down to defeat in the same manner as we did in the campaigns of 1923-6-9." He thought his best hope of holding the Party together was to wait Henry out: "I have no thought of proposing a definite policy and will certainly wait until Henry puts his cards on the table."

It was a long wait that unnerved the edgy Liberals. The Premier did not put his cards on the table until nearly the end of the 1934 pre-election session. Then to thunderous desk-thumping from the massed Tories, Attorney General Price introduced the liquor legislation, which permitted sale of wine and beer in hotels on a local option basis and contained a rider guaranteed to split the opposition wide open: the legislation would not come into force until after the election. As the delighted Tories listened, both Price and Henry assured them that this would be *the* issue.

At first the dry Liberals in the Legislature, prompted by frantic pressure from Hepburn (he sent telegrams and letters to the Liberal members and despatched Ontario Liberal President T. B. McQuesten to Queen's Park to maintain a solid front), decided to "acquiese" in the legislation. But when a recorded vote was taken a few days later, three Liberals (including Dr. George McQuibban who had replaced Sinclair as House leader) openly spoke against the measure; they were joined by six other Liberals and Progressives in opposing the "loosening" bill which easily passed with the unanimous support of the Tories. Despite all Hepburn's efforts to hold them in line, the Liberals had again disintegrated on the liquor question. In Sudbury, a disillusioned Mitch Hepburn announced that he was returning to Toronto immediately "to find out what circumstances made these men change their minds and do a right-about-face."[9] The Conservatives, hydro scandals and religious strife forgotten, were jubilant as they left Queen's Park for home. On the eve of the campaign, their liquor policy, bottled and tested in two elections, had again been carried out of the Tory wine cellar, a peculiar vintage guaranteed to give Grits a hangover and to make Tories flush with victory. A lot of people had underestimated good old George Henry: he could sell milk, teach a satisfactory Sunday school class, and whether they liked it or not in April, 1934, a good many Liberals had to admit that he could mix a damned good drink.

Shortly after the Liberal debacle on the liquor vote, the respected Windsor *Star* advised the disorganized Party to hold a convention to straighten out its affairs. One of his Western Ontario supporters wrote to a discouraged Mitch Hepburn: "Right now you couldn't elect the Prince of Wales as a Liberal in any Essex seat." It all seemed a sorry ending to almost three years of effort on the part of Hepburn criss-crossing the constituencies and speaking from innumerable platforms to reorganize the Party.*

Before the vote on the liquor issue, there was evidence that the attempt of Mitch Hepburn and his friends to rebuild the Party by constructing the old urban-labour alliance, win back the farmers, the English and French Catholics, and capture the growing ethnic vote was succeeding. Largely as a result of Hepburn's personal negotiations, Harry Nixon's Progressives were now openly allied with the Liberals, and a significant remnant of the old UFO Party, headed by former Premier E. C. Drury himself, was supporting Hepburn. So was the only UFO candidate running in the election, Farquhar Oliver; and Duncan Marshall, a former agricultural Minister in Alberta, had been promised a Liberal Cabinet post.

With the farmers responding to a farmer leader, Hepburn wooed the labour vote. There were indications that depressed conditions and Hepburn's somewhat radical rhetoric were having their effect. Strong labour men like Arthur W. Roebuck, David Croll, then Mayor of Windsor, and Morrison MacBride, former Labour Member at Queen's Park from Brantford, were all running as Liberals. In the West York by-election in May, 1932, Hepburn openly urged an amalgamation of Liberal, Progressive, and labour forces to fight the reactionary Tories. He assured his labour audience, "I swing well to the left where even some Liberals will not follow me." The Conservatives retained the riding, but only because the labour candidate drew enough votes from the Liberals to permit the Government man to win.

When the Henry Government used tanks and machine guns to break up a strike of furniture workers in Stratford in the fall of 1933, Hepburn came down on the side of the workers. "My sympathy," he told an audience in East Kent, "lies with those people who are the victims of circumstances beyond their control, and not with the manufacturers who are increasing prices and cutting wages at the same time." Also designed to appeal to the workers in a time of depression were some of Hepburn's plans for better times. These included good doses of inflation and rigid government economy (if he were elected he promised that the exodus of supernumeraries from Queen's Park would dwarf the annual Orange parade).† With the newly formed Ontario Co-operative Commonwealth Federation (with which Hepburn had been unable to effect a working alliance) hopelessly split on the issue of "Red" support, and the Government tarnished with an anti-labour image, Hepburn made the most

---

* Although Hepburn led the way, some of the others who aided were Senator A. C. Hardy, Harry Johnson, Percy Parker, Frank O'Connor, Arthur G. Slaght, Peter Heenan, Arthur Roebuck, and J. C. M. German.

† Much to the chagrin of Prime Minister Bennett, some federal Liberals, and some of his own advisors, fearful of undermining confidence in business institutions, Hepburn also renewed his attack on the financial policies of the Sun Life Company. (CAR, 1932, p. 73.)

of his opportunity to win the working vote back to Liberalism. The Catholics too seemed to be coming into line. Hepburn, an avowed "wet," had been careful not to shut the door on increased help for Catholic schools. Strong French Catholic candidates like Paul Leduc in Ottawa and the popular Theodore "Theo" Legault in Nipissing were trying to regain the vote that Ferguson had captured.

Despite the note of radicalism in some of his speeches, Mackenzie King himself was impressed with Hepburn's efforts to rebuild the provincial Party in Ontario. In the spring of 1932, King wrote to Hepburn's old friend and advisor, Albert Roberts, in St. Thomas: "Hepburn has made steady progress ever since his election as leader of the Party." There were weak spots but they would be overcome: "Mitch may be and is extreme in many things he says and this brings on his head much in the way of criticism. . . . It is out of pummelling of this kind that profounder judgments are evolved and I have not the least doubt that as time goes on Mitch will moderate considerably."[10]

Not all were as pleased as King about Hepburn's effort to reconstruct the Ontario Party. The dry rural splinter group in the Legislature led by Sinclair was not pleased at all. Sinclair himself expected to regain the leadership. He thought it was only a matter of time until the Party, disgusted by Hepburn's high-pressure tactics and personal excesses, would reject the new leader. At the annual provincial Liberal meeting held in London in October, 1931, the Sinclair forces, led by William Moore, federal Member for Ontario (Sinclair's provincial riding), tried to break Hepburn's hold on the Party machinery. "I was considerably worried for a while," Hepburn wrote a friend after the meeting, "but more than pleased at the finish of the meeting to witness the complete rout of the Moore forces."

This internal Party dissension, complicated by recurring spells of ill health, and more frequently punctuated by bouts of drinking, induced in Hepburn considerable depression and discouragement. The effort to attend his parliamentary duties at Ottawa, run the party by remote control in Ontario, and manage Bannockburn farms seemed to be too much. "May I state quite frankly," he sharply replied to one request for a political speech in the fall of 1932, "that it would be impossible for me to lose any more time . . . running around the province like a greyhound. I have given unselfishly of my time, and now I feel that I have to look after my own interests."

On October 14, 1932, Hepburn told his friend and backer, Percy Parker, it was possible "that I shall retire from the leadership before the annual meeting on November 18." Despite the fact that Senator Arthur Hardy sent him financial help fairly regularly, Hepburn was discouraged about the lack of Party funds (he thought that the Toronto office would have to be closed) and complained that the Party had let him down in a financial way. "As you are fully aware," he explained to Colonel William P. Mulock on October 21, 1932, "the Party has not lived up to any of its obligations. So far as I am concerned, I have done everything possible to carry out my responsibilities. There is a limit to everything and I have just about reached mine." Mitch Hepburn, however, was resilient. By the time of the annual provincial Liberal meeting in Ottawa in November, 1932, he had recovered his zest, the delegates gave him a rousing vote of confidence, and the leader took off with Peter Heenan for an organizational tour of the North.

Internal Party squabbling continued and would continue, Hepburn was convinced, as long as Sinclair was House leader at Queen's Park. A dangerous situation arose early in 1933, when well-founded rumours from Toronto indicated that Sinclair and one or two other Liberals wanted to join a coalition government with Henry. "I just put in four hectic days in Toronto," Hepburn wrote a friend, "straightening out the situation in the Legislature. Sinclair has proved himself to be an absolute traitor to the cause." This could not go on. In the fall of 1933, Hepburn quietly prepared the way to oust the embittered Sinclair. These efforts culminated in an eighth-floor suite of the King Edward Hotel on January 6, 1934, when the Legislative members present voted overwhelmingly to replace Sinclair as House leader with Dr. George McQuibban, the bachelor country doctor from Alma who had delivered upwards of three thousand babies and promised to deliver a slam-bang Opposition attack at Queen's Park. "This," he said, "will be no political petting party."[11]

McQuibban, a dry Liberal like his predecessor and never close to Hepburn personally, was not much of an improvement on the lacklustre Sinclair. Nor was the outside Liberal "board of strategy" trying to run things from Harry Johnson's Liberal office in Toronto much help. The pre-election 1934 session of the Legislature was more or less a disaster for the Liberals. Attempts by Hepburn and his "board of strategy" to develop scandal issues (an Orillia magistrate, it was alleged, had trafficked in offices; an Elgin county employee of the Highway Department had padded the payrolls) fizzled out like damp firecrackers. By turning down Henry's offer of an acclamation in East Kent (partly because King was still opposed to his resigning his federal Elgin seat), Hepburn left himself open to Henry's taunts to enter the Legislature and "quit shouting from behind the barn." The dismal performance of the Liberals in the 1934 pre-election session culminated in the Party's division on the liquor legislation. Early in April, Charles Dunning, King's former Minister, bet federal organizer Norman Lambert that Hepburn would not win Ontario. Most objective observers at the time would have agreed with him.

As the campaign began, Hepburn's leadership itself remained a question mark. Two of the leading Liberal papers in the province, the *Globe* and the Toronto *Star,* rarely mentioned the Liberal leader in their editorials. The Ottawa *Citizen* was more emphatic and stated that Hepburn had not been an impressive opposition leader. He indulged in too many wild unsubstantiated charges. Still, the *Citizen* added hopefully, he is young and he may grow. Hepburn was young indeed; at thirty-seven he was one of the youngest political leaders in the province's history. Yet, despite his youth and inexperience, there was already evident in Hepburn that elusive characteristic so prominent in most leaders of men, a trait that commanded total loyalty from his friends and engendered deep hostility in his enemies. This was an indefinable charisma that made Mitchell Hepburn not so much an enigma as a sign of contradiction, able to stir passions in himself and in others, a power which if controlled might take him to the heights but undisciplined would destroy him.

This ability to move people, this magnetic quality which often left his audiences mesmerized and his enemies cold with fury, was the key to Hepburn the politician. If the tenets of his political philosophy were blurred, the effect of his personality was almost instantaneous. "You either hate his guts or you love the guy," remarked one of Hepburn's Elgin friends, "there's no middle course."[12] To those who loved him, especially the farmers and families of Elgin County, Mitch Hepburn was "one of the boys," a big, uncomplicated generous man who made friends quickly and stuck with them loyally through thick and thin; those who hated his guts considered him a ruthless, vulgar, unprincipled back-concession politician on the make, a fast-talking upstart who combined the worst defects of Huey Long and Walter Winchell.

On the surface there was no such ambivalence about the Conservative leadership. George Henry had brought the Party through the pre-election session with colours flying. The biggest threat to more years of power was not Hepburn's bombast but the depression itself. While he pondered an election date, Henry was cheered by figures that showed the relief rolls were dropping and conditions, especially in the rural areas, were improving. The Government could do something to hasten the improvement. Relief allowances were raised; workers' wages in the North increased; several multi-million-dollar public works' projects were announced; and Henry requested federal Prime Minister R. B. Bennett to "sweeten the situation" by speeding up federal works' programs. Nothing much for the moment was being said about hydro or the school question. That left the track clear to run the election on the liquor issue. After desperate pulling and tugging, Hepburn had finally convinced his Party, if elected, to implement the Henry liquor measure unchanged. When House leader George McQuibban refused to accept that, it became questionable how long Hepburn's papered-over policy would hold together.

To win a mathematical majority in the Legislature (reduced from 112 to ninety seats since the last election), the Liberals needed to turn over twenty-eight seats. The redistribution bill was not calculated to help the

Party in the province as a whole or in Hepburn's riding of Elgin. Two townships had been taken from Elgin. "This is not supposed to have helped improve the chances of Mr. Hepburn," Henry drily wrote to Howard Ferguson and added, "we should feel our party not unduly handicapped because of the changes."[13] In April, on the eve of the campaign, it seemed that, despite the depression, the Conservatives could defend their years in power more easily than the Liberals could turn over twenty-eight seats. Or so George Henry probably thought as he pondered an optimum election date, pondered much too long for some of his followers, impatient to give the Grits another drubbing on the liquor issue.

There was one man who did not intend to sit around waiting for the Premier to make up his mind to call an election. Suddenly and ferociously, in a manner typical of his political tactics and belligerent campaign style, Mitchell Hepburn stepped up his attack on the Tory administration. At Perth in the first week of May, Hepburn charged that a "toll-gate" existed in the liquor industry. Before a foreign distillery could sell its wares to the Liquor Control Board, it had to appoint an agent, usually a Tory "ward-heeler" who collected a commission, a portion of which went into the Conservative Party war-chest. The Liberal leader, never at a loss for figures, reeled off a few for his overflowing Perth audience. The Liquor Board listed two or three hundred brands. On the assumption that it required $10,000 to have each one listed, the "toll-gate" amounted to three million dollars yearly. The Liberal chief promised to name names of Tory officials implicated in this swindle. (Before the campaign was over, he named several, including Harry Price, Conservative member for York West, and Mines Minister Charles McCrea.)

The outraged Conservatives denied the charges which the Kingston *Whig-Standard* said were serious but wholly unsubstantiated: "So far all that Mr. Hepburn has done is to establish doubts in the public mind." The attack of the Liberal chief had done more than that. At a time when the prohibition wing of his own Party was still balking on the liquor issue, he had managed to transfer the whole question to another and safer dimension, from the morality of drinking, which was at least debatable, to the immorality of graft, in high places, which was not. Whether the charges (and a dozen others made during the campaign) stood up or not was not the point. The scatter-gun attack commanded headlines and kept the Government on the defensive.

The strategy of the Liberal leader was clear. The election must be fought on the record of the Henry Government. In Hepburn's rhetoric that record was as simple and unsatisfactory as a relief voucher. At a time of hardship and economic distress, the Government had run up an appalling public debt at Queen's Park. What was worse, all those Tory financiers were bleeding the little man of his hard-earned cash through stupid mismanagement if not bare-faced corruption. This time the Conservatives would not bamboozle the people with beer; this time the issue was not to be the Tory liquor policy but the Tory mess at Queen's Park. Hepburn would clean up that mess and clean it up fast.

On taking office the Liberals would slash the administrative cost of government by fifty per cent; all those superfluous boards and commissions that drew fat salaries would be abolished; and those extravagant hydro contracts might just be cancelled. Hepburn had astonishing ability to take a complicated issue, translate it into easily grasped bread-and-butter language, dramatize it, and wrap it in emotional overtones. He had as well the priceless gift of establishing almost immediate rapport with "the little man" and the "have nots," a power unmatched by any other Ontario politician in the hungry thirties.

As the campaign developed, it was not the Liberal platform (which, except for pledges to better labour conditions, was largely negative) but the Hepburn personality that emerged as the chief issue.* He was becoming, according to the *Globe,* "the most forceful drawing-card Ontario politics has seen for years." Large enthusiastic crowds turned out everywhere to see and hear the man who with a flow of barbed-wire eloquence laced with humour could tear the Tories to shreds and bring the people cheering to their feet. That was the Liberal leader at his platform best, the man who could convulse a tired crowd with laughter when there was not much to laugh about.

One warm May night in Midland they came to see him: farmers from the back concessions near Georgian Bay; housewives hanging onto their children; clerks and stenographers from town; sailors off the Great Lakes boats, nearly five thousand of them jammed into the Midland arena and spilled out into the streets. It was the biggest meeting of the election campaign. Inside the sweltering building, the crowd waited patiently, almost apathetically, many of them looking worn and tired, some of them obviously on relief. They waited while the opening speeches droned on for the Liberal leader.

Finally he appeared, striding down the aisle preceded by a piper, flanked by his aides, a tall slim man just under six feet in height, wearing a double-breasted blue suit. His round face with its dimpled chin looked youthful and chubby; his eyes, below a high pale forehead, were slate-blue. Suddenly the atmosphere in the arena changed. An electric interest crackled through the crowd as people swerved round to see the thirty-seven-year-old farmer from Elgin who wanted to be Premier of Ontario. As he bounded onto the platform, there was a burst of clapping. Quickly, Mitch Hepburn turned to face the crowd, his right hand shot out and up to acknowledge the growing applause. Then his face broke into a flashing smile. Before he had said a word, Hepburn's magnetic personality triggered a charge of enthusiasm and friendliness that exploded through the arena in the roaring chant, "We want Mitch!"

Without using a note, Mitch Hepburn ripped into "the malodorous record of Tory administration." He described the Government's work program ("Where there are ditches on the highways, they're filling them in, and where there aren't ditches, they're digging them"), and ridiculed a Tory campaign paper, *The Straight Furrow,* which pictured big businessman George Henry as a working dirt farmer ("They tell me 'Honest George' hasn't worn overalls since he gave up wearing three-cornered pants – diapers – sixty-five years ago"). As the crowd rocked with laughter, Mitch Hepburn promised that Ontario would have a new deal under the Liberals. "There will be no more Lieutenant Governors in this province," he vowed, "until we get out of the present period of depression." Nor would there be any more Tory Cabinet ministers riding around in well-upholstered limousines at the public's expense. "If we are elected we are going to line up all the limousines at Queen's Park and sell them to the highest bidder." If this threat seemed phony (the Tories acidly inquired if Hepburn and his ministers intended riding to Queen's Park on bicycles), the cheers that it evoked were not. Hepburn knew his crowds. Many in those crowds were on relief, men and women to whom a basket of groceries was a luxury and a car a symbol of injustice, a sort of capitalistic sin. At one stroke, Hepburn dramatized his economy program and associated the callous Tories with affluence and waste.[14]

Stubbornly George Henry and the Tories tried to answer the shrill Liberal onslaught. By the time the Premier had replied to one charge, Hepburn and his chief platform lieutenants (Roebuck, Slaght, Duncan Marshall, and J. C. McRuer) were at other meetings waving affidavits purporting to prove more examples of Tory graft and malfeasance. The Tory Party had taken a "rake off" from companies supplying typewriters at Queen's Park; there had been graft in the construction of an addition to the building itself. Finally Henry and his aides (Highways Minister Leopold Macaulay, Attorney General William Price, and Mines Minister Charles McCrea), growing desperate, tried to link Hepburn with the radicals, the Reds, and the CCF. If he were elected, British institutions would topple and property would be confiscated. Newspaper advertisements headed "Do you want to be a Kulak?" showed a grim, tight-lipped Hepburn lashing cringing farmers with a bull-whip.

If this comical attempt to make Hepburn into a Communist bothered him any, the Liberal leader gave no signs of it. As the campaign moved into its final weeks, and his crowds grew in size and enthusiasm, he

---

*   When Henry finally announced that the election would be held on June 19, Hepburn resigned his federal seat in Elgin.

became more confident, while setting a fantastic pace, racing from village
to town to city in the big black car driven by his Elgin friend, George
Ponsford, speaking as often as four times a day in the critical ridings of
south-western Ontario. At Windsor shortly before voting day, Hepburn
was in his best form for a record crowd of ten thousand. He convulsed
the audience with his description of the Premier:

> Honest George they call him, and Charlie McCrea says he hasn't a
> dishonest hair in his head. That's fair enough because he's bald. . . .
> Why, honest George is the man who forgot he had 25,000 tucked
> away in Abitibi bonds. He forgot he was a director of a company that
> had 200,000 in it, and he forgot the Right Honourable Arthur
> Meighen's companies had 300,000 invested in it. . . . I feel sorry for
> Honest George. All he has is about a million or so that he made out
> of Acme Dairy. If any of you farmers water your milk you go to jail.
> But if you water your stock you get to be Premier of Ontario.

A few days before the voting, Hepburn was confronted again with
the dangerous Catholic school issue. The Toronto *Telegram* published a
letter from Martin Quinn virtually ordering Catholics to vote against the
Government because Henry had double-crossed them. The *Telegram* and
the Orange lodges demanded to know whether the Liberal leader had
sold out to the Catholics. Despite extreme pressure, Hepburn refused to
panic. At Aylmer, in heavily Protestant country, he said his last word on
the school question: "I'm a Protestant, a Mason, and Knight of Pythias,
but I do believe in fairness to our Catholic friends. They have asked me
for no concessions but they will get a fair hearing when they do." That
said, Mitch Hepburn led a roaring motorcade through Elgin to St.
Thomas and Bannockburn to wait the results on June 19. In the six weeks
of the campaign, he had travelled more than seven thousand miles, had
spoken more than a hundred times to crowds as far north as Kapuskasing
and as far east as Vankleek Hill on the Quebec border. According to the
veteran newsmen accompanying him, the effort had been maximum and
unprecedented, a flat-out run to topple the biggest Conservative majority
in Ontario's history.[15]

It was election night in Ontario. Mitch Hepburn, his wife, their close
Elgin friends and Party workers, were at the Masonic Temple in St.
Thomas packed into a dingy oblong kitchen containing a gas range,
steam boilers, and an old sink. The Liberal leader, his hair ruffled, sat
with a scratch pad on his knee, hunched behind a telegraph operator
who was transmitting the returns from a temporary wire to a battered
typewriter. Within minutes the advance poll for Elgin reported: a 190-
vote majority for "the boy from Yarmouth." Wiping his face with a

crumpled handkerchief Mitch Hepburn looked up exultantly at his wife on a table behind him. "Elgin is mine; now for the province."

In less than three hours the province was his – in the greatest Liberal victory in its history. The North went solidly Liberal. Not a single Conservative was elected west of Toronto. Only a handful of seats in Toronto and the hard core of solidly Orange ridings in Eastern Ontario stayed with George Henry who, while retaining his own seat, saw eight of his twelve ministers defeated. Final returns showed sixty-six Liberals elected to seventeen Conservatives.*

While the Liberal seats piled up, the roars and cheers increased from the crowds massed outside the Masonic Temple in Talbot street. Elgin was celebrating the election of its first Premier, the youngest in Ontario's history. From the railway yards, whistles shrieked and bells clanged; outside the Liberal headquarters rockets burst in the air; and from the marquee of the Capitol Theatre across the street, a searchlight played on the second-story window of the Masonic Temple. There, bathed in light, wearing a smile as wide as Elgin County, with his wife ("she has stood loyally beside me"), an excited Mitch Hepburn shouted above the din. "The spirit of Elgin went all over Ontario today and swept the Liberals into power. . . . It would be impossible for me to tell you in the fullness of my heart what you have done in rolling out the greatest majority ever accorded a candidate in Elgin county."

While Elgin feted its Premier-elect and the people of Ontario waited expectantly for Mitchell Hepburn to move into the Premier's chair at Queen's Park, George Stewart Henry, in his quiet manner, expressed the mood of the province that he had served so faithfully for so long. His last letter to Howard Ferguson on the election of 1934 was both a postscript on an era and a prophecy for the future. The people of Ontario, predicted George Henry, "are in for interesting times."[16]

---

* The three Progressives and one UFO member elected would bring the effective Liberal total to seventy.

chapter 6

Power Politics

At his Bannockburn farm, Mitchell Hepburn sat in the sun-room of his spacious white-brick farm home reminiscing with friends and reporters about the campaign. "The little guy does not get enough of the good things of life, and anyway it's good politics to give a hand to the majority." Whatever a cynic might make of that statement, and whatever his enemies said about the way he played politics (he played rough and he played to win), there was no doubt in Mitch Hepburn's heart about his purpose in the 1934 election: "Get this fact. We are in this thing because of the little fellow, the workman who isn't working any more, the farmer who is struggling against unbelievable odds. I've seen these people, talked to them, you can't credit their situation. We're in this thing because of them and for them. There is going to be a new deal in this province."

Confident, cocky, threatening to abolish the Lieutenant Governor and the speed limit ("I can't stand hypocrisy, it's the bunk"), from the moment the results of the voting were tallied, Mitch Hepburn took charge. More than any other factor, his dynamic leadership was responsible for the dimensions of the Liberal sweep, a fact acknowledged even by the Conservative press including Hepburn's hometown paper, the St. Thomas *Times-Journal*: "He electrified the province with his leadership, breathed life into a party that was moribund, radiated his own enthusiasm into the people and roused them into a frenzy which has resulted in one of the most smashing and overwhelming victories ever recorded in the history of Canadian politics."[1]

It was all very well to say, as many did, that the decisive factors in the Liberal victory were the depression, the unpopularity of R. B. Bennett's Conservative Government, and George Henry's ineptness. Undoubtedly these contributed to the results. But the voters' distress had to be nurtured and inflamed until all their anger turned against a Government which was allegedly squandering their money and was inured to their hardships. The man who focussed that uneasiness, who made the Tory Government not so much a victim of the depression as its cause, was Mitchell Hepburn. To identify the record of the Henry Government with the depression, to interchange and confuse the two in such a way that cause and effect became blurred, was sound political strategy: but strategy had to be implemented; the dry facts and figures charged with emotion; the issues isolated and dramatized and driven home with an impact that would carry through to the ballot boxes. That was primarily the leader's task, and the leadership provided by Hepburn in the election of 1934 was almost perfectly equated to the times. The times were depressed, the people tired and apathetic and discouraged; Mitchell Hepburn, with his boyish exuberance, his inexhaustible energy, his rousing oratory which often bordered on rank class appeal, provided a refreshing alternative to stale platforms and tired politicians. Still, reactionary Tory governments had recently been ousted in British Columbia and Nova Scotia, and perhaps anyone could have defeated George Henry in Ontario in 1934. If the Liberals had not changed leaders in 1930, would slow-moving, pipe-smoking William Sinclair have beaten him? Considering the division within the Liberal Party, probably not; certainly not by the record majority that Mitch Hepburn piled up.

Perhaps the result could be explained by George Henry's bumbling. As one aide of the Premier put it, if George Henry crossed a pasture containing one "cow flap," he would step on it. But the "cow flaps" were there for Mitch Hepburn to step into too. By a dazzling display of political footwork, he avoided them. It was claimed by the Toronto *Telegram* and many Conservative leaders that the Catholic vote elected Hepburn. Donald M. Hogarth, the mining magnate from Northern Ontario, formerly the provincial Member for Port Arthur and chief Tory strategist, explained to federal Conservative Robert Manion that the Catholics voted ninety-eight per cent Liberal and their vote cost Henry thirty seats. An examination of the way in which the religious issue developed and an analysis of the Catholic vote indicate that had there been no school question, the 1934 election results would have been substantially the same.[2] When all the factors in the 1934 political upheaval, including the dimensions of the sweep, are examined, one factor stands out: the leadership of Mitchell Hepburn. For the first time in thirty years the Liberals offered a genuine alternative to the ruling regime at Queen's Park. That alternative was not so much a program as a man. The man Hepburn in the early thirties (like T. D. Pattullo in British Columbia) was the antithesis of the traditional, rather stuffy, stand-pat middle-class leader of a political party. His friendliness and folksiness, his dynamism, his belligerency, and even his personal excesses differentiated him from previous leaders.

So did the speed with which he moved into the Premier's chair. After a short holiday at Roche's Point on Lake Simcoe, the summer estate of his friend Frank O'Connor, the Premier-elect, refreshed by sunning and swimming, returned to Toronto, his Cabinet already chosen. On the warm evening of July 10, 1934, about eight o'clock, Mitch Hepburn stepped out of the King Edward Hotel. His red campaign handkerchief protruded from the pocket of the dark business suit he was wearing; a bright crimson tie and a white carnation in the lapel added a dash of colour; in his hand the Premier-elect carried a light gray fedora. "Let's go," he grinned, as he jumped into a borrowed car for the short drive to Chorley Park with his Cabinet to be sworn in by Lieutenant Governor Herbert Bruce as Ontario's eleventh (and fifth Liberal) Premier. (Mrs. Bruce, who watched the ceremony, noted in her diary: "Hepburn does not look as bad as his photos make him out to be, and his Cabinet look quite a decent lot of men.")

The Cabinet contained no real surprises. Those men who had helped Hepburn most in the campaign were included: Harry Nixon as Provincial Secretary, Arthur Wentworth Roebuck as Attorney General and Minister of Labour, David Croll (sworn in on the Talmud) as Minister of Welfare. Peter Heenan had resigned his federal seat to become Minister of Lands and Forests and the Irish Catholic representative in the Cabinet which was reduced to ten as an economy measure. Duncan Marshall, Minister of Agriculture; Dr. Leonard J. Simpson, Education; Dr. Albert Faulkner, Health; Paul Leduc, Mines, and T. B. McQuesten, the solid business representative from Hamilton, Highways and Public Works, rounded out a ministry, in which Hepburn himself retained the Treasury portfolio. "The Hepburn Cabinet," remarked the Toronto *Star*, "has been chosen with care and should give a good account of itself." The *Star's* crusty publisher Joseph Atkinson had somewhat warmed up to the young Premier. "I think," he wrote to Mackenzie King, "Hepburn is strengthening the Liberal cause in Ontario. This is so at present whatever may be the result ultimately. My opinion of him has become more favourable since the elections." (Apparently winning an election compensated, in Atkinson's mind, for Hepburn's personal defects.) The federal chief too seemed pleased by Hepburn's progress. As was his custom, King took no public part in the provincial campaign, but during its progress he wrote Hepburn a warm letter of encouragement urging him to conserve his energies, decline social invitations, and obtain lots of rest (a recipe for well-being that Mitch Hepburn ignored then and later).

Immediately following the election, the Ontario leader travelled to Ottawa to consult the federal chieftan. At that time he insisted he would make his own decisions, "But I realize I am a young man and my leader at Ottawa can give me valuable advice." One piece of advice that King insisted on was that federal and provincial affairs should be kept separate: "As I said to you in our first conversation after the elections, I feel your colleagues would resent any attempt on my part to go over their heads, in matters which were likely to be of concern to them or to their departments; also that I was sure you yourself would feel embarrassed were I to be making suggestions, with which you might not agree."[3]

Now that Hepburn's Cabinet had been chosen and sworn in, King wrote to express his pleasure. "The Government, I think, is a good one and vastly superior to anything the province has had since Sir James Whitney's day." Its superiority aside, the Hepburn Government was certainly one of the fastest-moving in the province's history. After cutting its salary and implementing Henry's beer legislation, it moved swiftly to implement the campaign promise to slash the costs of government. In this respect Hepburn's priorities, despite his radical rhetoric, revealed his basic conservative approach: "The first job is to overhaul the machinery of government. That means two things as I see it. First, eliminate inefficiency – rip out deadwood, political appointees, hangers-on, those who draw big salaries for doing little. Second, cut out unnecessary functions of government – those that have outlived their usefulness or are too paternal."

With a stroke of the pen, all civil servants appointed since October, 1933, were fired. Work was temporarily halted on the new Hydro office building on University Avenue. The Hydro Commission and engineers like F. A. Gaby were replaced. Commissions and boards at Queen's Park were amalgamated or abolished entirely. Every game warden in the province was dismissed and 183 bee-keepers (a keeper for every bee in the province, quipped the Premier) lost their jobs. Ontario House in London, England, was closed, and the Government cancelled the province's display at the Canadian National Exhibition.

Premier Hepburn himself lost no opportunity to implement his politically popular economy program. He referred to a Hydro employee being paid $3,000 a year "and doing absolutely nothing. The man is still doing the same thing but he is not getting paid for it." Even George Henry was forced to pay a bill of $3,004.45 for services and repairs to his personal car when he was Premier. By the end of July it was estimated that the Government's retrenchment program had saved the province more than a million dollars, at what cost to the civil service no one could then estimate.*

The economy program reached a kind of orgiastic climax at Varsity Stadium in Toronto on August 27, 1934, when eight thousand cheering taxpayers watched the Tory "grand fleet" of forty-seven cars auctioned off

---

* Later the Toronto magazine *Saturday Night* judged the worst defect of the Hepburn administration to be its treatment of the civil service. Undoubtedly some incompetent Tory holdovers should have been dismissed. But the personal distress and injury to morale caused by the wholesale firings of many faithful government employees could scarcely be justified even on economy grounds.

for approximately $34,000. George S. Henry's gray Packard limousine, hoisted in the air on a special elevated runaway, brought $1,500. When Senator Hardy protested to Hepburn that this car auction was undignified, the new Premier heatedly replied: "Regardless of whether you consider it burlesque or not, I am telling you this action of ours is going to meet with the whole-hearted approval of the rank and file of the taxpayers. You can have too much dignity in government."

Some, like the Toronto *Mail and Empire,* disagreed. After comparing Hepburn to Louisiana's Huey Long, the paper remarked that the "slaughter" of civil-service firings "reminds us of the beheadings which took place during the reign of terror during the French Revolution." Mitch Hepburn's assessment of the taxpayers was probably more accurate. Suffering from the depression, they approved the economy program. They approved, too, the score of investigations and royal commissions busy all over the province examining everything in the Tory record from the books of the Temiskaming and Nothern Ontario Railway to the files of George Drew, Ontario Securities Commissioner. Summarily fired, Drew accused Attorney General Roebuck of rifling his office and was described by Roebuck in turn as having "the manners of a boor, the venom of a traducer." Most publicized of the investigations – one that King advised Hepburn to hold – was the Smith-Latchford Commission into the affairs of Hydro, especially the dealings of George Henry and Arthur Meighen with the Ontario Power Service Corporation. Meighen was incensed by this witch hunt into his affairs. "This is the most diabolical political inquisition ever held outside of Turkey," he complained to a friend. "The conduct of it would put to shame Pontius Pilate." Meighen and Henry were more incensed when the Smith-Latchford Commission found that both gentlemen had acted improperly in the matter of the Ontario Power Service Corporation bonds.*[4]

What with firing Tories, trying to find jobs for importunate friends, and attending Liberal victory parties, the summer of 1934 was a busy one for the Premier. A month after the election, St. Thomas threw the biggest party in its history in honour of Mitch Hepburn and his Cabinet. By mid-afternoon of July 19, despite intermittent showers and threatening skies, the city had literally closed up shop to toast the first Government of Ontario headed by a son of Elgin. All day, from Brantford to the Windsor border, trains, buses, and cars flowed into the city, and a crowd estimated at fifty thousand people gathered in Pinafore Park. The affair ended with a spectacular display of fireworks climaxed by a forty-foot-high portrait of Mitch Hepburn outlined in white fire against the dark sky.[5]

Fun and games had their place in the summer of 1934, but so did politics. Prime Minister R. B. Bennett, after four years in power, had called a "little general election" in five Ontario constituencies (including Hepburn's old West Elgin seat) for September. Mackenzie King, anxious to win all five seats in order to force a general election, wanted Hepburn's organization to handle all the Ontario ridings and asked Hepburn himself to devote special attention to Elgin. Mitch Hepburn campaigned hard for the federal Liberals and returned home several times to help his friend, Wilson Mills, a fruit-grower from Sparta, retain Elgin. At a large meeting at the Granite Rink in St. Thomas, he shared the platform with King, praising him as the greatest Canadian statesman since Laurier. The federal leader responded by saying, "I have followed Mr. Hepburn and I want to say that we want him not for three months or three years, but we want to see him in the public life of Canada for the next fifty years." Undoubtedly Mitch Hepburn's efforts and those of his organization helped the federal Liberals retain Elgin and pick up two seats from the Tories in the September by-elections. His strenuous campaigning forced him take to his bed exhausted.[6]

Lacking administrative experience, with just two years of high school and some junior work in the bank, Hepburn found the move from running a farm to managing the affairs of Ontario a difficult one. His Government, its ministers exercising considerable autonomy, seemed to settle down quickly and to move with despatch. But there had been difficulties and disappointments right from election day. Despite the apparent good relations between Hepburn and King, friction continued between the provincial Liberal organization and some of the federal people. When Ontario federal Liberals wanted to have their own men taken care of at Queen's Park, they frequently met a cool reception. From the outset Hepburn tightened his grip on the Ontario organization. On one occasion, when discussing the September by-elections with Norman Lambert, he threated "to call on K. in Ottawa and tell him to pull off his brigands," and he himself would win all the by-elections for the federal Liberals. King and Hepburn resolved the difficulties in a personal interview, but friction with the federal Liberals did not end.

In his own sphere Hepburn had not been able to recruit some of the men he wanted for his Cabinet. The former federal Minister from Kitchener, W. D. Euler, with King's approval, had turned down the chairmanship of Ontario Hydro. Another young Liberal, George Fulford, newly elected Member for Leeds, rejected a Cabinet post. Cabinet-making, civil-service reorganization, and federal campaigning took their toll. Late in August, Paul Martin, an early and enthusiastic Hepburn supporter from Windsor, told Norman Lambert: "Hepburn had told him he hadn't slept for a week; and had admitted being all at sea respecting his current problems." Martin was of the opinion, moveover "that the H.

---

* Another Commission found that Conservative organizer Harry Price and the former Mines Minister, Charles McCrea, had been involved in a liquor "toll-gate" system, as Hepburn had charged in the 1934 campaign. (*Globe,* July 11, 1935)

Government is unsoundly based and could not stand up: that Mitch hadn't got the men he wanted: that he had yielded to silly promises re app't of cabinet ministers." Martin added the interesting comment that the provincial Liberals' all-out effort in the September by-elections indicated "that Hepburn and a number of the Ontario group had their eyes on Ottawa."

Whatever his long-range plans, Mitch Hepburn's eyes in the fall of 1934 were not on Ottawa. On October 24, he told Norman Lambert over lunch at Queen's Park that "he was fed up and was going to West Indies."[7] Early in December, Mitch Hepburn, his nerves frayed, and physically tuckered out, purchased some light clothes and left with his friends Arthur Slaght and Frank O'Connor for a trip to Bermuda, Nassau, and Cuba. There would be little enough time to enjoy the seductive sunny diversions of the south before Mitch Hepburn's first legislative session began early in 1935.

By one o'clock on the wintry afternoon of February 20, 1935, the crowds were already gathered at Queen's Park. Inside, the long corridors were jammed with men in their ascots, their ladies in fur wraps. By two-fifteen, the Legislative galleries were packed. Outside, four guns barked a fifteen-gun salute as Lieutenant Governor Herbert Bruce arrived with a company of Royal Canadian Dragoons to open the first session of Ontario's Nineteenth Parliament. At two-forty-seven, an unprecedented cheer rose from the galleries. Through the oak doors of the chamber, still tanned from his southern trip, looking younger than his thirty-eight years, in morning coat and striped pants, walked Mitchell Hepburn, entering the Legislature for the first time as Premier. By his side, wearing a graceful gown of blue crêpe, with train and a shoulder bouquet of orchids and violets, stood Mrs. Hepburn. The Premier smiled slightly as he heard the applause from the galleries, punctured by one voice shouting, "Atta boy, Mitch!"

People expected excitement at Queen's Park, and they were not disappointed. Even before the session began there had been fireworks. The Premier aroused a storm of protest when he and his Cabinet had declined to attend the traditional state dinner given by the Lieutenant Governor on the eve of the session, whereupon Dr. Bruce cancelled the function. To cut unnecessary expenses and frills further, the Speaker's tea on opening day was also cancelled. There would be "no teacup juggling," said the Premier, and even if there was criticism in Toronto and elsewhere ("Canada's Huey Long," snorted the *Cobourg World,* "has gone further in stupidity than even his most violent detractors could have hoped"), Hepburn maintained, "the man in the back concession is applauding what I am doing."[8]

Before what came to be called "the thunder, lightning, and waterpower" session was concluded, Mitch Hepburn aroused more applause and provoked more criticism than probably any other Premier in the province's history. Quickly his earthy wit dominated the house. During debates, many of which were a warmed-over version of the 1934 campaign, he completely outclassed Opposition leader George Henry. When Henry protested that he would leave public life with a clear conscience, the Premier snapped with a smile, "Your conscience is like your appendix, an inactive organ." When the Opposition leader demanded that answers to questions be read, not tabled, the Premier, always impatient of procedure and protocol, listened to his Attorney General read aloud for twenty-five minutes, then, angry and red-faced, cut him off: "This fiasco and waste of time is not going on. It may have been an established procedure to read these questions, but it will be suspended for the present at least." When the Opposition threatened to obstruct a Government bill, Hepburn warned: "This bill is going through in its present form without us dotting one 'i' or crossing one 't.' " There were cries of "dictator" and "iron heel" when Hepburn, angered at what he considered useless queries, threatened to "wipe the order paper clear at one stroke." Once in a particularly bitter exchange with the Opposition leader, the Premier used the word "brazen," an epithet that Liberal Speaker Norman Hipel ruled out of order. "I cannot accept your ruling, Mr. Speaker. I regret that I can't, but I will have to appeal to a vote of the House." The House sustained Hepburn against his own Speaker in an unprecedented vote.[9]

These exchanges were mild compared to the major debate of the 1935 session dealing with the Quebec Hydro contracts. For three years Hepburn had attacked these contracts signed by the Ferguson Government in the late 1920's as wasteful. The Liberal leader had promised action; the time for action had come. A week after the Legislature opened, Attorney General Roebuck (also a Hydro Commissioner) began a sustained attack on the contracts that the previous Commission had signed with Beauharnois, Gatineau, Maclaren's, and the Ottawa Valley Co. In a marathon nine-hour speech, spread over three days, Roebuck contended the province was paying millions annually for power not being used. What was the solution? The contracts had been in force for some years. The province's hard-pressed taxpayers wanted to know the answer to that question, so did the Opposition, the hydro bondholders, and the financial community growing uneasy as they read the Attorney General's assault on the "big interests." In the final speech of his nine-hour trilogy, Roebuck spelled out what his solution would be. Excepting the contract with Gatineau, he announced to the House, "All three of these contracts are not only outrageous and inequitable, but illegal and unenforceable." This contention was based on Roebuck's view that, because the agreements involved interprovincial works and power lines, they were under federal jurisdiction and beyond the legal capacities of Ontario and Quebec to negotiate.

For the first time the ugly word "repudiation" was heard. The hydro bonds dropped in value. Hepburn took no part in the debate, but when rumours of a Cabinet split spread, he insisted "that the Cabinet, to a man, is right behind Mr. Roebuck." Some Cabinet members were a long way behind him. There was a division in the Cabinet, not about whether the contracts should be renegotiated (even George Henry's Government had favoured that) but on the much more contentious question of their legality. Hepburn himself seems to have hesitated about outright repudiation. Certainly some of his ministers did. Harry Nixon, Duncan Marshall, and David Croll thought the contracts were legal.[10] Day after day, packed galleries watched the hottest session since 1923, waiting for the Premier to announce the Government's decision on the contracts.

On April Fool's Day, Premier Hepburn left no doubt about the Government's policy. He rose to introduce the Power Bill, declaring all existing agreements with the three Quebec companies to be "illegal, void, and unenforceable." To make the Government's case air-tight, a clause in the bill barred any recourse to the courts by the companies concerned or any other parties. Purchase of power would be continued from Gatineau, but the contracts with Beauharnois, Maclaren's, and Ottawa Valley would be cancelled. The Premier estimated that the annual savings to the province would exceed two hundred million dollars. He regretted any loss to the bondholders but, as he told the house, there was no alternative:

> This is the most difficult task I have attempted in my nine years of public life. But . . . Ontario today is in an impossible position. . . . The Province is bound for a period of 40 years to purchase huge quantities of unwanted power from Quebec – an amount which is beyond the capacity of industry to absorb. . . . Undoubtedly there will be criticism, undoubtedly the bond market will go down. This is to be regretted but we feel there is no other course.

Criticism there was. Liberal desk-thumping at the "repudiation" policy would not drown out the howls of protest both within and without the Legislature. The *Financial Times* of London expressed its disapproval; questions were asked in the British House of Commons; the Investment Dealers' Association of Canada ran four-column advertisements in the daily papers headed, "Is a Contract Approved by the Government of Ontario Nothing But a Scrap of Paper?"; the *Mail and Empire* compared the Government's action to Germany's repudiation of the rights of Belgium in 1914; small investors and the province's credit would both be injured. In Ottawa, W. D. Euler, Hepburn's original choice to run Ontario Hydro, was "very angry" and told Norman Lambert "he intended to denounce the whole action." As opposition mounted, Mitch Hepburn reacted as he always did to opposition, he angrily dug in. "We're not going to budge one iota," he told the press. "If the tactics of the financial interests are to stampede us, they are sadly mistaken, for we will not budge from our situation."

Mitch Hepburn did not budge. On Monday, April 8, 1935, debate began on the Power Bill, "the most iniquitous measure," said George Henry, "ever presented to an Ontario Legislature." The Opposition leader urged the Government to negotiate a fair settlement with the bond-holders and threatened to oppose "repudiation" to the end. The Premier was just as adamant. "If we have to sit here until noon tomorrow," he snapped, "this bill is going to get a second reading." On and on the debate went as the galleries emptied and refilled, members spelled each other off, slept fitfully, alarm clocks burring intermittently in the caucus rooms to warn an exhausted speaker it was his turn – on and on non-stop for twenty-six hours and thirty minutes, a record for Ontario. Once when George Henry returned from a short snooze he found a vase of fresh flowers on his desk with the card, "Say it with flowers," signed by the Premier. Finally, at five-thirty in the afternoon of Tuesday, April 9, the groggy House passed second reading by forty-two to fifteen.

There was still no let-up. Along with other bills, the Government intended to drive for final passage of the Hydro legislation. "We said the bill was going through," said a grim Hepburn. "It is going through." Through Tuesday night the debate raged. There were lighter moments. As midnight approached, the Premier summoned a tired page boy. A moment later the boy was excitedly running through the press gallery whispering, "The Premier just asked me a moment ago if we'd like more boys up here or a jump in pay. Gee, I told him all right. I said, 'Give us the extra jack.' " Finally on Thursday, April 11, at 8:40 P.M., after almost four solid days of sitting, to thunderous applause from the galleries and desk-thumping from the Liberals, the Power Bill (which would not go into effect until formally proclaimed at a later unspecified date) passed by fifty-seven votes to seventeen.* Led by Dr. A. Des Rosiers (Russell), the Liberals broke into "Allouette" and a pleased Roebuck promised the Bill's supporters that they would "in the years to come, look back with pride on their actions."

A week later, after another series of late-night sessions to clear the order paper (a frazzled George Henry complained, "There's no reason why we should be driven like dogs until we're ready to drop"), the

---

* Former Conservative Minister of Mines, Charles McCrea, and the expert on constitutional law, Professor W. P. M. Kennedy of the University of Toronto, advised Lieutenant Governor Bruce to sign the "repudiation Bill." However, if the stability of the province was adversely affected in the American and London markets, they thought that would give Bruce the "chance to call upon Hepburn to resign, & then call upon the Liberal W. E. N. Sinclair to form a new Gov. or ask for a General election." (Journal of Mrs. H. Bruce, April 10, 1935)

"thunder, lightning, and water-power" session ended. It had been an exciting period in which Mitch Hepburn rode herd on the members. Even the Conservative *Mail and Empire,* vigorous in its opposition to the Power Bill, admitted that Hepburn "directed the business of the house with expedition and left no doubt among his many supporters that he is in command."[11]

Not long after the Power Bill controversy ended, Mitch Hepburn was again fighting the financial interests. Determined to obtain money for the province as cheaply as possible, he travelled to New York with his friend, J. P. Bickell, a rough-and-ready "Bay street cowboy" and millionaire mining magnate, to survey the possibilities of the American money market. Hepburn stated, on his return, that he would "smash" the high interest rates charged by the banks on provincial loans. On June 5, the Government advertised for bids, to close a week later, on fifteen million dollars of low-yield debentures, the first such transaction since the hydro fight. Expecting no difficulty with this offering, the Premier left for a short fishing trip in the Algoma area. With him were some of the leaders from the business and mining world with whom he now felt at home, men like Ed Flynn, Democratic boss from New York, and Sell 'Em Ben Smith,* New York financier, Jesse Jones, head of the Reconstruction Finance Corporation, and Jack Bickell. "We had a fine trip," beamed the Premier on his return, June 12. "I caught a twelve-and-a-half pound fish. . . ." Next day Mitch Hepburn was struggling with bigger fish. "No surrender to Money Barons is Pledge of Hepburn," read the *Globe's* headline, occasioned by the incredible fact that the Ontario Government had not received a single bid for its bond offering.

This lack of confidence by the business community left Mitch Hepburn hurt and angry. He accused the financial interests of ganging up against the Government because of its Power Bill: "The plain issue is whether the country is to be governed by elected representatives or by dictators in control of the machinery of money." The financial community denied any conspiracy. The respected London *Financial News* was biting. In view of the repudiation of the contracts, "It is small wonder that the reputation of the present Ontario Government stinks in the nostrils of the financial world. It is unnecessary for Mr. Hepburn to look further than this for an explanation of the failure of his Bond issue."

Mitch Hepburn, whose father's political career had been blighted by the "big interests," did not take that lying down. The Government would by-pass the regular financial channels and "a province-to-people" loan would be organized. As for the banks that had boycotted the loan, Hepburn warned, "It will be my pleasant duty to impose a tax on those who make the most money out of the least effort." It was a typical Hepburn reaction and an excellent political issue: "We'll give the fellows on the back concessions a chance to laugh while the other fellow squirms."

The original fifteen-million-dollar issue was replaced by a twenty-million-dollar, "province-to-people" loan (so-called because it was hoped most of the amount would be subscribed by small investors), which an elated Premier announced on June 19 had been over-subscribed.[12] Despite all the talk of a "people's loan," however, most of the offering was taken by the big institutions, the insurance companies, and the banks, for the simple reason that its terms were better than those of the first offering. Probably in the short run, Mitch Hepburn's 1935 victory over the power barons (which would almost certainly be tested in the courts), and his tussle with the money interests, had helped him politically. But it was questionable whether, even on the back concessions, such displays of personal pique and raw political power would be helpful over the long haul.

The rate of interest on provincial bonds was a dull business, and Mitch Hepburn seemed relieved to return to the hustings in the summer of 1935 for the federal election campaign. Early in the year he had told an Elgin political meeting: "When the election is announced, I am going to take the field and fight just as hard for the Right Honourable W. L. Mackenzie King as I fought for this Province. I am going from one end of Canada to the other in support of Mr. King." Mitch Hepburn was as good as his word. In April, when King sent an emissary to ask if he would help finance the Ontario campaign, Hepburn agreed on condition that some of the federal field organizers did not interfere. On May 10, King's top political strategist, the tactful, astute organizer, Norman Lambert, Secretary of the National Liberal Federation, asked the federal leader to speak to Hepburn's friend and millionaire backer, Frank O'Connor of Laura Secord, about financial help for the election. At the time King, still smarting from the trouble with Beauharnois over campaign funds, declined: "He said he did not want to put himself under any obligation to O'C.; that he had had a lesson from the Beauharnois affair . . . and never again wd. he put himself in the power of any man. He did not trust an Irish Catholic drinking man any too far anyhow."

King's trust for "an Irish Catholic drinking man" seemed to deepen in almost direct proportion to the need for campaign money. He later contacted O'Connor and other Ontario Liberals and assured Lambert "that everything would be ready" for him. While Lambert tried to line up Hepburn's friends for financial help, the Premier himself was impatient to hit the campaign trail. King left no doubt how heavily he was counting on

---

*   Bernard E. ("Sell 'Em Ben") Smith, an American millionaire, reportedly obtained his nickname at the time of the 1929 stockmarket crash. Smith was away on a plane trip and several of his holdings were wiped out before he could reach a telephone and frantically shout to his brokers, "Sell 'Em, Sell 'Em." (*Evening Telegram,* July 28, 1938)

Hepburn's help. "I should like to say," he wrote on August 6, 1935, "how much I hope you and your colleagues will take as active a part in the present campaign as you may find possible." King invited Hepburn to share the platform with him at the official opening of the Ontario campaign in Woodstock on August 13. The Ontario Premier accepted and told the large Woodstock audience: "I want to take this opportunity of pledging to Mr. King my loyal and undivided support in this campaign." Pointing to Hepburn on the platform, Mackenzie King was no less laudatory: "There you have the promise of one who will be second to none in furthering the policies of Liberalism throughout the country."[13]

At the end of August, Mitch Hepburn, looking tanned and cool in a white linen summer suit, left Union Station in Toronto to begin furthering the policies of Liberalism in the West. Before formally opening his western tour at Winnipeg, Mitch Hepburn, never noted for his long letters, wrote twice at some length to King. In his opinion, he explained, the two major issues in the campaign were trade reciprocity and monetary reform. After informing King that his health was none too good (just prior to leaving Toronto he received the result of a heart examination which "rather alarms me"), he made the kind of request that usually did nothing to ensure a healthy relationship with Mackenzie King. For some time Premier Hepburn had advocated a lower federal tax on gold mines. Within a few days, he noted, one of the mining magnates, J. P. Bickell, "a very intimate friend of mine and a good supporter of the Party," would be in to see the federal leader. Would it not be a good idea, Hepburn wondered, if he and King made a joint policy announcement concerning the mining tax? "Do not exert yourself unduly in the campaign," King replied. He was less definite about helping Bickell and the mining men: "I will keep in mind the other matter referred to . . . and if need be will communicate with you further in reference thereto."

If Mitch Hepburn found that reaction rather cool, he did not permit it to abate the zest of his political campaigning from coast to coast. Aided by the dulcet tones of Wishart Campbell, "the golden baritone," he toured the West ridiculing the "funny-money" Social Credit theories of Alberta's Premier, William Aberhart ("Governments have only the money they take out of the pockets of the people. Only over in Alberta Mr. Aberhart has a different idea. And if it works no one else will have to"), toured the Maritimes, made a brief foray into Quebec, and two swings through Ontario stressing before generally good audiences his two major themes: reciprocity and monetary reform, including easier money, and a nationally owned central bank. At the same time he urged his Ontario organization to go all out for King: "I do hope," he wrote Attorney General Roebuck, "that all the Ministers will go the limit in Ontario. We need at least fifty seats to assure a Liberal Government at Ottawa." How much Hepburn's presence (and that of his hard-working ministers) meant in Ontario is indicated by a letter Tory mastermind Donald M. Hogarth wrote to Dr. Robert Manion (Fort William) on the eve of the voting: "If it were not for the mechanics and power of the provincial Government which has been exercised to the limit, King would not be in the picture in this province at all." Hogarth still predicted that the Tories would win a minimum of forty Ontario seats.

In fact, Mackenzie King, aided by the depression and R. B. Bennett's unpopularity, swept the country. In Ontario, the Tories held only twenty-five seats, while the Liberals more than doubled their representation to fifty-six. Mitch Hepburn, fighting off a heavy cold which had curtailed his final campaign appearances, was especially pleased that Wilson Mills easily held Elgin and that his friends Colin Campbell (Frontenac-Addington) and Arthur Slaght (Parry Sound) had won Ontario seats. To a cheering crowd in St. Thomas on election night, Hepburn praised Mackenzie King as a great economist and conciliator. Now that King was again Prime Minister, it would be easier to pass progressive legislation at Queen's Park. "With the co-operation that I know I will receive from Ottawa, I am hopeful that your Government in Toronto can accomplish much on your behalf."[14]

The hope was soon dashed. Within a week Mitch Hepburn, exhausted from campaigning and high living and worried by his medical prognosis, informed King that he would soon resign the Ontario premiership. For his part, Mackenzie King made it unmistakeably clear that his idea of federal co-operation with Queen's Park differed considerably from Hepburn's. This difference between the older and younger man reflected a fundamental dissimilarity in their viewpoints and values, a dissimiliarity that had existed almost from the beginning of their association.

Late in the fall of 1932, at the time of the annual Ontario Liberal meeting in Ottawa, Mackenzie King held a dinner party at Laurier House. It was a small dinner for Mr. and Mrs. Hepburn, and the day before, King had asked Hepburn for a list of those he would like to have invited. As King subsequently explained to one of the guests, "I fear I did not make clear to him at the time that my table would seat only a certain number, and the result was that as I did not hear from him until late on Saturday afternoon, I could not arrange at that time to accommodate more than could comfortably be seated at the table." The methodical, orderly King could not cope when, at the last-minute, a thoughtless Mitch Hepburn (accustomed to his wife's preparing for unexpected guests at Bannockburn on a moment's notice) showed up with more people than anticipated. King rationalized the situation by saying, "It arose apparently through Mr. Hepburn and myself each acting on our own without full knowledge of what the other was doing."

Over the years it was not so much a lack of knowledge of what the other was doing (though that obtained too) as a fundamental difference in personalities which plagued the relationship between King and Hepburn, until eventually embarrassment at a dinner party escalated into recrimination and distrust concerning policies. From the beginning Mitch Hepburn, an undisciplined young man with a quick intelligence complicated by emotions bordering on the juvenile, could never hope to understand the cautious, calculating King, the enigma of Kingsmere, with his qualifications on everything from friendships to policies. For his part, Mackenzie King, ever readier to boast of friendship than to experience it, never comprehended or fully trusted the bumptious member from Elgin who came to Ottawa and immediately started raising hell about the seat assigned him in the Commons. In King's stylized lexicon of propriety, there was a way to do things, and making scenes with one's betters was not acceptable. Over the years, Mackenzie King saw no reason to change his first impression of Hepburn as somewhat unreliable and a possible trouble-maker.

King was a past-master at hiding his real feelings (sometimes even from himself) so that in the early years there was no public hint of his attitude toward Hepburn. The younger man, unsure of himself and sensitive, seems often to have questioned King's friendship. He was upset when King (who had a good reason) declined to attend a Hepburn meeting in Peterborough in 1932. At the time Paul Martin tried to reassure the Ontario leader. King, he wrote, "spoke most enthusiastically of you and I would be inclined to look upon him as a friend." This friendship, such as it was, endured for some years, but King's real feeling never changed. After Hepburn won the premiership in 1934 and travelled to Ottawa to discuss his plans with King, the federal leader confided his impressions to Norman Lambert. "He described Hepburn as unreliable and a bit crooked in his dealings with people."

Hepburn had not been in office six months when King spoke to Lambert "about attempt in Ont. to create a Liberal machine," King's fear of a Hepburn machine in Ontario was partly based on growing conflict between the provincial and federal Liberal organizations over control of finances and the choosing of federal candidates. In a number of ridings like Fort William, Port Arthur, Hamilton West, Ottawa West, and Sault Ste. Marie, there is no doubt that the Hepburn organization tried to control federal nominations. Disputes over finances also increased. At a meeting in Toronto in the spring of 1935 to raise federal campaign funds, the treasurer of the Ontario Liberal Association, Frank O'Connor, told Norman Lambert that the Ontario Government had settled a number of long-standing accounts with a large contractor for two and a half million dollars "and 200 th[ousand] had been left; but Hepburn had said it cd. not be used for Fed'l purposes." Lambert informed King of this bonanza and of Hepburn's attitude.

Nevertheless, during the 1935 federal election, King was happy to have Hepburn's help, and the Premier literally wore himself out campaigning from coast to coast. In addition to his personal contributions, totalling $25,000 to the federal campaign, Hepburn's chief financial backer, Frank O'Connor, appears to have worked assiduously among the mining men to solicit federal campaign funds.* (O'Connor, however, rejected a suggestion by Senator Donat Raymond, the chief federal fund collector in Quebec, that O'Connor contribute $100,000 to the campaign in return for Vincent Massey's "influence for Senatorship.")†[15]

Both O'Connor and Hepburn felt that they had contributed heavily to the 1935 federal victory, particularly in Ontario. They considered their efforts entitled them to some consideration. The day after the election, O'Connor called Norman Lambert: "& wanted K. to remember this is a time of young men, 'a young man cabinet'," and also requested that he be appointed to the CNR's Board of Trustees. Stories appeared in the press that Liberals who were friends of Mitchell Hepburn, men like Colin Campbell and Arthur Slaght, perhaps even Hepburn himself, would be members of the new King Cabinet.‡ Beyond denying that he would go to Ottawa Mitch Hepburn said nothing publicly. On October 21, however, he wrote a brief letter to Mackenzie King. After renewing his congratulations to the victorious federal chief, he outlined the qualifications of one of his closest political associates, Arthur G. Slaght, Toronto lawyer and Member-elect for Parry Sound. He did not mention that most Ontario

---

* Funds officially subscribed in Ontario toward the federal campaign of 1935 totalled $558,478.10, of which nearly half was expended within the province. From an examination of the list of subscribers (Labatt's at $19,000 and the Canadian General Electric Company at $25,000 were among the largest contributors), there is no way of determining just how much of the total was collected through Hepburn's Ontario organization. Some of Hepburn's close friends and their concerns, in addition to Frank O'Connor ($25,000), contributed. These included J. P. Bickell ($8,000), Algoma Steel ($10,000), Larry McGuinness ($1,000), and "Sell 'Em Ben" Smith ($5,000). Presumably, too, there were other contributions that did not pass through the National Liberal Federation. (Lambert Papers, statement of 1935 federal campaign subscription in Ontario, March 31, 1936).

† Vincent Massey was then President of the National Liberal Federation.

‡ In his memoirs, Charles A. Bowman, editor of the Ottawa *Citizen* from 1914 to 1945, recounts that toward the end of the 1935 federal campaign, he mentioned Premier Hepburn to Mackenzie King as a possible federal Minister of Finance. According to Bowman's recollection, King replied by recalling Sir Wilfrid Laurier's advice to him many years earlier: "Never in your cabinet include a man – no matter how able – who is addicted to over-indulgence in liquor." (Charles A. Bowman, *Ottawa Editor* [Sydney, British Columbia: Gray's Publishing Company, 1966], p. 201)

newspapers were predicting Slaght was a certainty for the Cabinet, probably as Justice Minister.

The new Prime Minister replied by return mail on October 22. "I cannot say," he began, "how much pleasure your letter of yesterday, received this morning, has given to me. Having so recently gone through the experience of forming a ministry yourself, I can see that you more than appreciate the exacting nature of the duties imposed on one who is in the midst of that task." To prove his pleasure at receiving Hepburn's letter, King wrote the Ontario leader a lecture, five pages long, on the need to maintain strict separation of federal and provincial jurisdictions. This was especially true now when a Dominion-provincial conference would soon be held, and King wanted to be able to assure all the premiers that no one of them had been consulted in the formation of the federal Government. That was "why I thought it well not to communicate with yourself . . . and why I did not, as you might naturally have expected, seek your counsel and advice at an early moment." King reminded Hepburn of their discussion when the Ontario Cabinet was being formed in 1934: "You will also recall that I made no suggestion of any kind as to the personnel of your ministry. You asked me my advice on one or two matters which had to do with cabinet formation, and I gave you what, out of my experience and what I had heard and learned from Sir Wilfrid Laurier, I felt might be helpful in that connection."

Hepburn did not miss the point. King's letter was formally correct and constitutionally air-tight. Hepburn had no right to expect that any man he might suggest would receive preferment from King. The Ontario leader could take responsibility for holding Elgin (at King's request); he could go all out in Ontario and across the country to help return King to power; his close associates in Ontario could raise federal campaign funds (again at King's request); but to suggest to King that one of Hepburn's friends might make a good Cabinet minister deserved what it got – a patronizing lecture on constitutional properties. It is true, as J. W. Pickersgill notes in the *Mackenzie King Record* that Hepburn felt "his support was a large factor in achieving the Liberal sweep in Ontario." A good portion of the Ontario press and the province's politicians felt so too. It may also be true, as Pickersgill writes, that Hepburn "expected to be consulted about the composition of Mackenzie King's Cabinet; indeed he tendered unsolicited advice which was not followed. He and his friends were known to be very resentful of the appointment to the Cabinet in 1935 of C. D. Howe and Norman Rogers whom they regarded as non-professional outsiders."*[16] Still, it seems that King might have been a little less insensitive to Hepburn's temperament and a little more appreciative of his campaign contribution. Not one Hepburn man received an appointment to any position in the King administration of 1935.

The day that Hepburn received King's letter – a letter that he never forgot or forgave – his personal aide, "Eddie" Wooliver, announced that the Premier would accept no more calls after ten o'clock in the evening at his King Edward Suite. Plagued by newsmen, office-seekers, and hangers-on, exhausted from the federal campaign, disappointed and hurt by King's attitude, enervated by bronchitis and insomnia, Mitch Hepburn was again experiencing a bout of physical debility and emotional depression. He decided it was time to call it quits.

On November 5, 1935, the *Mail and Empire*'s headline announced, "Hepburn to Quit Politics after 1936 Session." To his stunned Ontario supporters, Mitch Hepburn explained: "I simply can't carry on. I can't do justice to the Party, the people, or myself in my present condition." When he heard the news, Mackenzie King phoned his regrets, and the Toronto *Globe* commented: "There is nobody in sight among Ontario's public men big enough to begin to fill the place that Mitchell Hepburn has made for himself in the life of this province."

A change of clime altered Mitch Hepburn's attitude. There was a quick and pleasant November trip to Miami, accompanied by Jack Bickell and Frank O'Connor. There was warm sunshine, good companionship, a stop in New York, and a tour of the nightclubs with Broadway columnist Ed Sullivan, who described the Premier as "one of the most interesting men this reporter has ever met." In the first week of December, Hepburn returned to Queen's Park, much refreshed, "determined to carry on as long as my health permits." He did not waste any time going into action. Negotiations with the Quebec hydro companies had dragged on for months. Hepburn announced, "We're through," and the Power Act, cancelling the contracts, was proclaimed.

On December 8, 1935, the Premier and his aides left for the Dominion-Provincial Conference at Ottawa. It was Hepburn's first meeting with the federal authorities since his rebuff after the campaign. It was not a happy experience. The relief grant to Ontario was almost doubled, but Hepburn's suggestion to save some millions of dollars annually by refunding the provincial debts received a cool reception from Finance Minister Charles Dunning and most of the other participants. Perhaps that and the fact that he was still choked up with bronchitis prompted Hepburn to leave the conference shortly before it ended, thus missing a dinner with Mackenzie King and the other premiers. Still feeling far from well, Mitch Hepburn left almost immediately to spend the Christmas of 1935 with his family in Miami, amid rumours that his days of power at Queen's Park were numbered.[17]

---

* It is interesting that King told Norman Lambert that Howe's appointment was a favour to Vincent Massey and the National Liberal Federation. (Lambert Diary, October 23, 1935)

chapter 7

Tools of Rome

After he returned from Florida for the 1936 session, looking a bit more rested, talk of retirement muted for the moment, Mitch Hepburn dominated provincial politics by the sheer force of his personality. His colourful unpredictability generated a kind of excitement that kept the Legislature, the public galleries, and the whole province on edge. At any moment, he was capable of pulling switches and blowing fuses. He did that by introducing the first motion of censure in the Chamber in thirty-four years. The motion condemned former Attorney General William Price for using "contemptible, vulgar language." Price was alleged to have accused a Liberal member of being not only willing but anxious "to kiss a certain part of another member's anatomy to curry political favour." After one of the bitterest debates in years, the motion of censure on Price passed. The former Attorney General had the last word. "Imagine Mitch Hepburn," Price said, "being shocked at vulgarity."[1]

The controversy concerning the censure motion was sedate compared to the main debate of the session, the question of giving Catholics more help for their elementary schools. Since Hepburn had come to power in 1934, there had been rumours that he would do something for the Catholics. The problem was that the statutes guaranteeing the existence of separate schools in Ontario (primarily the Scott Act of 1863 and the British North America Act itself) did not take into account the subsequent industrial development of the province; they made no obligatory provision for the Catholics to share in corporation and public-utility taxes. The Catholics thought they were entitled to a portion of tax support from these sources, just as Protestant school supporters in Quebec shared them. The Catholic Taxpayers' Association and its president, Martin J. Quinn (who felt that the Catholic vote had contributed heavily to Hepburn's victory in 1934) were disappointed when no school legislation was introduced in the 1935 session. On several occasions Hepburn indicated that he thought the Catholics had a case. To a deputation of the CTA headed by Quinn, which he received at Queen's Park in January, 1935, Hepburn, while refusing any commitment, made an oblique reference to the fact that Catholics received little or no corporation tax revenue: "There's no doubt in my mind that when the original school act was drafted they did not anticipate, at that time, that we were going into an industrial age such as we are in at the present time."

To a large Protestant and Orange delegation, which called on him in February, 1935, to protest any concessions to Catholic schools, the Premier was outspoken: "We won't be cowed by any propaganda that is carried on. . . . We know that, politically, you have leaned pretty much in one direction in the past. You are only dangerous to those who fear you. We are going to judge this thing on its merits." When Quinn, however, disturbed by rumours that there would be no legislation in 1935, referred to Hepburn's "pledges," and warned him of "the grave political potentialities of failure to deal with the matter at the present session," Mitch Hepburn, who never succumbed to that kind of language, merely had his secretary acknowledge receipt of the letter (a procedure that brought more threats from the irascible Quinn.) After the end of the 1935 session, the Premier appointed a committee to look into the whole financial structure of provincial education, and the matter rested there.*[2]

Nothing much was heard publicly of the separate school question until February of 1936, when rumours appeared in the press that new school legislation was being prepared. The rumours stirred up a storm of activity among the Orange lodges and the CTA. Protestant protests poured into Hepburn's office. Martin Quinn kept up his unrelenting campaign. In a letter to one of Hepburn's Elgin constituents (passed on to the Premier), Quinn fell back on his major threat. He wrote, "The desire of our people will be registered at the ballot boxes in the way of protest or of gratitude, and, as a Liberal, I do hope that it will be in the latter direction." Then Quinn overplayed his hand. In a speech at Oshawa on February 9, 1936, he was reported by the Toronto *Star* (which had been a supporter of the Catholic cause) to have threatened that if the Hepburn Government did not give separate schools a just share of school taxes, the CTA would defeat it at the next election. Immediately on reading this report of his speech, Quinn telegraphed the Premier to deny categorically that he had threatened the Government. Unfortunately for Quinn, Hepburn received a verbatim account of Quinn's remarks which indicated that

---

* One of the advisors appointed to the committee was the chief inspector of public and separate schools, V. K. Greer, who had been partly responsible nearly twenty-five years before for Mitch Hepburn's leaving the St. Thomas Collegiate over the Sir Adam Beck apple-throwing incident.

these had been "toned down" by a Catholic priest in Oshawa before they were sent to the Toronto newspaper. One of the "censored" remarks referred to Hepburn: "If that bird doesn't come across now we'll kick him out."

Angered by this intemperate outburst, the Premier coldly informed Quinn that the separate school question would be settled "on its merits regardless of any threats or political repercussions." The Toronto *Star* characterized Quinn's Oshawa speech as "indireet" and "defiant," and warned that threats of Catholic political domination would structure "a united Protestantism at the polls." Joseph Atkinson forwarded a letter from a reader to the Premier which he felt expressed a popular view:

> I have been travelling a lot in the past few months and I want to say this, that there is ten times more feeling below the surface than one would surmise among the Protestants. I and my family are all Liberals and the hard-working kind too, but we are all Protestant and good old Presbyterians, what the Liberal Party used to be, and while we want to be Liberals we won't see the party turned into any Bobtail or fifth wheel for the Roman Catholics. If the R.C.'s dominate it we have to get out. We do not believe in any Separate Schools any more than George Brown.

While Protestant protests mounted, the Cabinet and the Liberal caucus wrestled with the problem through February and March of 1936. Though in public the Premier minimized intra-party conflict, he was not so sanguine in private. Writing to a political friend in Nova Scotia in March, Hepburn admitted: "We are having great difficulty in getting our members in agreement in regard to the proposed Separate School Bill. While I agree with regard to the justice of the matter, we are very much concerned as to the possible political repercussions."

Over the last weekend of March, rumours spread that the Premier would resign if his followers did not support the separate school bill. Reports circulated too that at least three Cabinet ministers and seventeen members would quit if their leader did. Whatever truth there was to these speculations, Hepburn decided to stay, and his followers decided to stay with him on the school question. He told the press: "As far as my own personal well-being is concerned, I should step out of office. My doctors insist I should. But I can't let my colleagues and my supporters down now especially at a time like this. There is such a thing as loyalty to one's friends, you know. So I intend going through with this job until after the next election if it kills me."[3]

The savage debate on the school bill seemed a greater threat to the health of the short-handed Opposition than to that of the Premier. On April 3, 1936, as Orangemen and Catholic priests jostled each other in the packed galleries, Mitchell Hepburn rose to introduce the contentious bill. The measure contained two major provisions: corporations (which hitherto had an option in the matter) were now obliged to divide their taxes for school support in proportion to the creed of their shareholders; if the corporations were so complex or widespread that the beliefs of their shareholders could not be determined, the taxes would be apportioned in each municipality according to the ratio of Protestants and Catholics in the community (not, as the Catholics had requested, on the basis of school population). No provision was made for another Catholic request, a share of public-utility taxes.

The Premier was alternatingly jocular and serious as he spoke for twenty minutes, introducing the first legislation to help Catholic school supporters in seventy years. "The present Government," he said, "has decided to deal with this question now out in the open." He realized that some would be offended and none would be satisfied: "Let me say . . . that I realize full well that this Government has not gone as far in this matter as the separate school supporters would like us to go. And I realize that we have gone much further than some holding the opposite opinion want us to go. I can only say . . . that I hope this bill does not provoke what we in Ontario want least of all – a religious controversy."

As the Premier sat down to the applause of the Liberals, pages scurried from the galleries with congratulatory notes. One of Hepburn's friends, Percy Parker (who had serious doubts about the legislation), said simply, "You spoke like a great statesman." Undoubtedly his short speech introducing the school bill – clear, concise, temperate – was one of the best Mitch Hepburn had ever made. But he was under no illusions about what lay ahead, even though he could write lightly to his friend "Chubby" Power, "Yesterday I introduced the contentious school issue. I have definitely now aligned myself in the camp of those who eat fish on Friday." What Hepburn had wished least of all to provoke, a religious controversy, was soon raging as Protestant Ontario gave every evidence of resisting the measure. "An Infamous Betrayal of Public Schools" was the Toronto *Telegram's* terse summary of the new legislation. In many Protestant pulpits on Sunday, April 5, the separate school act was denounced. The Premier himself stated that if the legislation were defeated he would resign.

For ten straight hours, beginning on Monday, April 6, the House debated the bill. Attorney General Arthur Roebuck made a strong speech in its favour. He was backed by Education Minister Dr. L. J. Simpson in the face of solid Tory opposition. George Henry reiterated the position he took in 1934: the question should go to the courts for a decision. Vainly, Roebuck tried to force Henry to concede that he would repeal the act if returned to power. "Is the honourable gentleman hot or cold," Roebuck sarcastically asked, "is he white or black?" "Let me tell you," retorted a white-faced Henry, "that I am red-blooded." That was Mitch Hepburn's cue to crack: "Not red blood but tomato-juice." When the House rose at two-twenty-five on Tuesday morning, April 7, the Tories were still battling, and the bill seemed no nearer passage.

If the protests streaming into Queen's Park were any indication, the bill would never pass. Even C. G. Power, a Catholic himself, while praising the Premier's political courage, warned Hepburn that "knowing my own breed, I doubt whether you will get very much thanks from them for it." When the debate resumed on Wednesday, April 8, before packed galleries, Tory front-bencher Leopold Macaulay dared the Premier to call off the whips, and a worried Percy Parker sent Hepburn a memorandum warning that a large number of Liberal members would vote against the bill "were it not for a profound sense of loyalty to yourself."

It was nearly four o'clock on Thursday morning, April 9, when the Premier rose to announce dramatically that his life had been threatened. Despite threats and protests, he would press on with the bill. "I am not lacking in courage. I have the conviction that I am doing the right thing." Past governments had increased grants periodically to separate schools here and there, but some more rational plan was needed than this hit-and-miss method. "What is more obvious, "the Premier asked, "than to use the taxation from these people to equip and maintain the schools. These children are wards of the state. They have just as much right to an education in this province as other children." Then as the dawn and the vote approached, Mitch Hepburn wound up for the Liberals by taunting the Opposition: "This Government is not a Government of the horse-and-buggy days . . . Go on and make your appeal to religious and racial prejudice. . . . The Tory party has done it before. . . . We are not going to make an appeal to prejudice but to reason."

Both prejudice and reason played their part in the decisive vote on the bill about five o'clock in the morning of April 9, when the legislation passed sixty-five to twenty. Three Liberals, including former house leader Dr. George McQuibban, bolted the party to join seventeen Conservatives in voting against the measure. Three other Liberals, among them William Sinclair, were absent. The next afternoon the house prorogued. Mitch Hepburn, weary but smiling, seemed unperturbed by threats from the Orangemen and a Tory promise to repeal the legislation "at the earliest opportunity." Martin Quinn and the Catholics emerged from the session of 1936 with the first significant legislative aid for their schools since 1863.[4]

Through the hot summer of 1936, the separate school controversy raged, both in the press and on public platforms. The Premier received hundreds of letters, most of them opposed to his stand, some of them downright abusive. "You are a twister and a prevaricator and a traitor to Protestants and the insolent way you twitted the Opposition stamps you as an impudent cur," wrote one disgruntled Protestant. The conflict was heightened by the Conservative leadership convention held in May, 1936, to name a successor to George Henry. One of the most vociferous candidates, George Drew, maintained that the school bill harmed Protestants (because it unjustly increased their tax load) and did not really help Catholics ("It is utterly unworkable and can only lead to endless litigation"). Drew was defeated in a surprisingly close leadership race by W. Earl Rowe, forty-two-year-old farmer, sulky driver, and federal Member (Dufferin-Simcoe) from Newton Robinson.

The Conservatives resolved to repeal the legislation when returned to power. "Ladies and gentlemen," Earl Rowe told the Party faithful at the convention in the Royal York, "it's going to be repealed as sure as you sit here." The Tories now thought they had an issue with which to nail Hepburn's hide to the wall. The lines seemed clearly drawn for what would be, according to the Toronto *Telegram,* "the major issue in the next provincial elections." If the religious question was to dominate, Mitch Hepburn intended to do the best he could with it. Through the blistering summer of 1936, he ranged through the province on an extended speaking tour in which he defended the school legislation. "I do not care if all the Tories in Toronto howl from now until the next election," he told a Niagara Falls meeting, "they cannot take away the rights of the separate school supporters." Angrily he vowed Earl Rowe would regret his slur at Orillia that the Liberals were "tools of Rome." To an overflow audience of his own constituents at St. Thomas, the Premier was unequivocal: "May I say that this act will never be repealed, Earl Rowe notwithstanding. . . . It is sound, right and fair. . . . I don't want to fight an election on a religious issue, but if the Tories force me I may have to."[5]

Mitch Hepburn fought an election on the religious issue sooner than he expected. On October 15, 1936, the Conservative Member for East Hastings, James Hill, died. A by-election was called for December 9 in the riding about 150 miles east of Toronto. East Hastings was a long narrow constituency stretching from the Bay of Quinte in the south almost to Algonquin Park in the north. Except for the county seat, Belleville, the riding was predominantly rural, with a heavy Orange population. There was only one separate school, and the Catholics numbered little more than twenty per cent. Though the riding was traditionally Conservative, Hill had held it by only 418 votes in the Liberal sweep of 1934, and Mitch Hepburn thought he could regain the seat. To do so he planned personally to captain an all-out effort in which his Government's record would be the issue and his own prestige as Premier would be squarely on the line.

The two capable young candidates, both doctors, Harold E. Welsh, the Conservative from Roslin, and Harold A. Boyce, his Liberal opponent from Deseronto, were soon drowned out by the strident oratory emanating from the squads of outsiders pouring into every corner of the riding. The central issue quickly emerged. "They will come to East Hastings with a lot of chloride of lime," warned one Tory worthy, speaking of the separate school bill. "They will try to bury their dead cat, but they can't get near it. It smells too bad." Earl Rowe, facing the first test of his leadership in East Hastings, used much less inflammatory language, but he stressed the school matter in all his speeches and promised at Maynooth and elsewhere to repeal the "clumsiest legislation ever put on Ontario's statutes."

The man who spear-headed the attack on the school legislation in East Hastings was the gentleman Earl Rowe had appointed his Ontario campaign manager, George A. Drew. All over the 3,600-mile-square riding, big broad-shouldered handsome George Drew tore into the school act and lashed at Hepburn's friendship with the Catholic candy millionaire Frank O'Connor: "If the Roman Catholics of this province say to me, a Protestant, 'We are going to bring our faith into politics,' " Drew told a meeting at Bancroft, "then I say to them right now, 'The war is on.' " "Who is this Mussolini," Drew taunted Hepburn, "this puppet of Frank O'Connor?" A Liberal vote, Drew warned a crowd at Deseronto, was a vote to continue the O'Connor dictatorship in Ontario. No statement of George Drew's during the East Hastings campaign, or during his entire subsequent political career (despite his contention he had been misquoted), received more notoriety than his remarks about the French made at the hamlet of Plainfield. "It is not unfair to remind the French," Drew reportedly said, "that they are a defeated race, and that their rights are rights only because of the tolerance by the English element who, with all respect to the minority, must be regarded as the dominant race."

This appeal to religious and racial prejudices was supplemented by an effective, if quite unauthorized, whispering campaign in the riding's back concessions. The Premier's wife was a secret Catholic. "I wouldn't care if she was a Catholic," retorted Hepburn, "she's a darn fine looking girl." Crowns on the King's Highways would be replaced by romish crosses; a papal residence was being prepared at Casa Loma. In this sort of campaign, everybody seemed to be losing except the pickpockets from the city who were cleaning up at the packed meetings.

Against this massive attack on their school bill, the Liberals retaliated with everything they could muster. It was reported that William "Billy" Fraser, federal Liberal Member from neighbouring Northumberland riding and chief political "fixer" for Central Ontario, had moved his entire campaign machinery into East Hastings. So did Colin Campbell, the Premier's friend and federal Member for Frontenac-Addington. In the latter part of November, almost every train arriving in Belleville from Toronto carried Cabinet ministers, Legislative members, and men like Arthur Slaght to strengthen the Liberal team. Even Wishart Campbell, "the golden-voiced baritone," tried his repertoire on the stolid farmers.

After gulping down a hot meal at the Hotel Quinte, the Grit phalanx fanned out over the riding to explain the Government's record and plead for a fair hearing on the school bill.

Personally leading the Government's fight was Mitch Hepburn. In the campaign's latter stages, he literally lived in the riding, travelling its frozen roads in a small car, speeding from Point Anne in the south to Fort Stewart in the north to fight for his record. People waited in the dark wintry nights, waited at Maynooth in the heart of the Orange country and Eldorado and Bannockburn, waited to see and hear for the first time in their lives the King's First Minister in Ontario. Bundled in a fur coat against the icy blasts, Mitch Hepburn, cramped and tired from the twisting ride, would step from his car and walk briskly into a small hall (often an Orange hall) its frosted windows warmly lit by the flames of a woodstove inside. His fur coat off, his suit crumpled, his blue tie askew, the Prime Minister of Ontario stood there, the platform creaking, his face flushed. He began to speak in a voce raspy from days and nights of campaigning in the dead of winter. In simple phrases, his big hands and shoulders gesticulating, he appealed to the hearts of those in the back concessions. From a dim corner at the rear, a heavy-set swarthy woodsman, who had tramped his way four or five miles through the cold darkness to the meeting, muttered: "So that's Hepburn. Well, I'll be jiggered."

That was Hepburn in East Hastings in the winter of 1936, fighting, right or wrong, for what he believed, fighting for his friends, trying through the zero nights and the snow drifts to convince these tough honest Protestants that his school bill was fair and, despite the odds, sounding confident that he would win. It was hard not to like Mitch Hepburn, and the farmers of East Hastings liked him. They liked him when he said to them: "They can hammer me all over the lot as long as you people on the back concessions stick with me." Would they stick with him in East Hastings? It was not a religious issue but an economic one, he explained to the crowds. "The Government merely provided for a fair and equitable distribution of corporation taxes as between the public and the separate schools – in other words they settled not a religious question but an economic one." The farmers of East Hastings and of the province would benefit, he noted, because now the city corporations would share more of the tax load. No, said the Premier, there had never been any secret agreement between him and Frank O'Connor, but Frank O'Connor was a friend of his, and he did not intend to give up that friendship no matter what George Drew, Earl Rowe, and Toronto's Catholic-baiting Baptist minister, the Reverend T. T. Shields, had to say about it.

As election day, December 9, approached, the inflammatory speeches on both sides became more heated. Even Edward VIII and Mrs. Simpson, playing out the abdication crisis in far-away London, did not unduly distract the attention of the province from the fight in East Hastings. The

Globe and Mail warned that "the bitterness of the campaign was arousing hatreds reminiscent of the Middle Ages. And it is not farfetched to speak of bloodshed as a possible result." The rabid oratory reached its climax at a public debate between Rowe and Hepburn on December 2 at Madoc, its hotels bulging with visitors. There was more bitterness in the jammed, noisy Armouries where the debate was held than between the two leaders. In fact, there was so much noise, fist-fighting, and heckling that the debators could seldom be heard. "I have never known him to be anything but a gentleman," Rowe said of the Premier, who was literally howled down when his turn for a short rebuttal came. Mitch Hepburn, still smiling, picked up his notes amid the pandemonium and turned back to his seat beside his wife who was close to tears. Earlier in the campaign he had told a more friendly Madoc audience that "if defeat is the penalty for doing what is fair and just, then send us down to defeat." "I am confident," Earl Rowe predicted, "the voters will say to the Government . . . 'Hands off the public schools.' "

Snow was so heavy in parts of East Hastings that some of the eighty-five per cent turn-out of the voters skied to the polls. As Edward VIII prepared to give up his throne for the woman he loved, the new King's loyal subjects in East Hastings sent Hepburn's Liberal candidate, Dr. Harold Boyce, down to a crushing defeat. Conservative Dr. Harold Welsh raised the previous Tory majority of 418 to 1,136. Considering the massive effort of the Liberals, led by the Premier himself, it was a stunning set-back. A tired, dispirited Mitch Hepburn (who had told Lieutenant Governor Bruce two weeks before the voting "that he had to win or he would quit") explained to a friend that the "by-election was fought purely on religious bigotry." The result in East Hastings, commented the *Globe and Mail* (which supported the Government record but disagreed with the school bill), "has condemned the School Assessment Act and this alone. In a riding traditionally Conservative and Orange, this is not surprising." The whole province was now aroused on the religious question, and it was questionable whether Mitch Hepburn could carry a general election on the issue. Many of his closest supporters doubted it. Frank O'Connor, whose name had been besmirched from one end of East Hastings to the other as the Catholic millionaire puppeteer pulling the Party's strings, was fed up. He told Hepburn he was through collecting funds both provincially and federally. "E. Hastings he said," according to Lambert's diary, "cost 33,000. He wd. not continue either federal or prov.'l financial activities."[6] Despite this enormous expenditure for those days in a single riding and his own campaigning, Mitch Hepburn's appeal to the back concessions in East Hastings had been rejected. It was his first defeat in a ten-year political career. If Mitch Hepburn were to remain in office, he needed a broader power base and another issue.

A broader base was also necessary because, through 1936, despite efforts on both sides to improve the situation, friction between Queen's Park and the federal Liberals continued. One of Hepburn's friends had now received recognition from Mackenzie King: Frank O'Connor, "the hard drinking Irish Catholic," was named a Senator. This did not placate Hepburn, still stung by King's attitude after the 1935 campaign. The Ontario Premier instructed Harry Johnson, secretary of the provincial organization, not to invite any federal Cabinet minister or member to share a platform with Queen's Park Liberals.

Later, Hepburn wrote "Chubby" Power that he wanted to discuss "the strained relationship which now exists between the two governments." When, however, the federal Government cut its relief grants to the provinces without notifying him in advance, Hepburn angrily decided to tighten the financial squeeze on the federal Liberals. Norman Lambert, in Toronto to collect party funds, noted in his diary on April 18, 1936:

> Saw O'Connor . . . who told me that Mitch very sore at Ottawa over relief adjustments & alleged failure of Ottawa to notify him or Peter H[eenan] – M[itch] had asked Frank O'C not to send any money from Ontario to Ottawa – O'C. said he would talk to Mitch later about it. He wanted K[ing] to make overtures toward reconciliation etc. & He (F.) intended to approach King about it.
>
> Saw Harry Nixon who thought that 80% of trouble was due to their own ministers.

One of the main areas of friction was in the Department of Highways. The Minister, T. B. McQuesten, resented what he considered Ottawa's lack of co-operation on highway construction. At the same time, some Ontario federal Liberal officials were annoyed at the way McQuesten was distributing contracts.[7] From time to time tension between the two Governments eased, but these changes seemed to depend on shifting moods rather than on anything more basic. The underlying causes of the trouble persisted. These involved both policies and personalities. To Mitch Hepburn and some of his ministers, largely dependent on federal action before they could formulate their own programs to combat the depression, King's policies often seemed to lack any over-all plan or long-range objectives. If Ottawa was floundering in the area of economic policy (as often during these years it was), Queen's Park was bound to be affected.

To King and most of his Cabinet, Mitch Hepburn's demands often seemed exorbitant and unpolitic, his excitable temperament impossible. The drift at Ottawa, coupled with the personality of Mitch Hepburn, made a genuine rapprochement impossible. Hepburn was determined to show Ottawa that he held the whip hand in his own province. He continued to interfere with financial contributions to the federal Party. This caused increasing concern to Norman Lambert. Near the end of April, Frank O'Connor told Lambert in Ottawa "that Mitch had forbidden him to send any money here." Furthermore, O'Connor expressed surprise that Hepburn had discovered the federal account number. On May 29, Lambert asked O'Connor "whether or not Hepburn had Ontario still under the ban." The answer from one of Hepburn's closest friends indicates that fear was complicating Hepburn's relationship even with his intimate associates: "He said he had done nothing towards collecting his amounts because he didn't want Hepburn to hear that he was doing anything. He referred particularly to Jack Bickell who he assumed had said to Hepburn that O'C. had solicited 10m. from him for federal purposes." Lambert "explained that this situation cdnt. go on." This information was passed on to Mackenzie King. A short time later O'Connor seemed less fearful of flouting Hepburn's ban on collecting federal funds in Ontario. He phoned Lambert and "said he wd. send 2m. tomorrow night. He said he wasn't going to pay any attention to Mitch's suggestion about collecting."

Toward the end of 1936, the break between Hepburn and the federal Liberal organization was formalized. On November 5, Norman Lambert wrote Hepburn a conciliatory letter inviting him, "as a personal favour," to attend the annual meeting of the National Liberal Federation in Ottawa in December. Hepburn's reply to this invitation was chilling:

> During the past few months I have given a great deal of thought to the question of the relationship which should exist between the Ontario Association and your Federation, and after many conferences with my colleagues it has been decided that we will not be represented at your annual meeting. I am also asking Mr. Johnson to keep his organization separate and distinct from yours.

Hepburn continued, "In future it will be our intention, and may I make this very clear, to keep our organization separate and apart from yours." This would seriously complicate federal organization and financing in Ontario. Mackenzie King with his monumental ability to ignore a problem where there was one, seemed unperturbed. Lambert showed him Hepburn's reply. "His attitude to Mitch's letter was that it didn't affect him: that any feeling of antagonism must be towards somebody else."

But to someone like Norman Lambert, responsible for the Ontario federal Liberal organization, the problem was serious. Hepburn issued fresh orders to Ontario lieutenants like Frank O'Connor to give no more financial aid to Ottawa. He forbade them to attend the annual meeting of the National Liberal Federation in December. (O'Connor explained rather lamely to Lambert that by not going they "would help pave the way later to better understanding between Ottawa and Toronto.") Lambert suspected, with some reason, that Hepburn was behind a plan that emerged suddenly at the meeting to oust the whole Ontario executive and replace them with his own people. Lambert moved quickly, the attempt failed, and he informed King why he felt it was "part of a plan originated in Ont. to get control of National organization."[8] At the close of 1936, paving the way "to better understanding between Ottawa and Toronto" would require considerable cement.

Toward the end of 1936, besides his prickly relations with Ottawa and the disastrous East Hastings by-election, Mitch Hepburn was preoccupied again with the problem of Hydro contracts. During the year, both in the Legislature and the courts, the Government's action in cancelling the contracts had been criticized. In November, the Ontario Appeal Court declared the Power Act *ultra vires* in so far as it had required the Attorney General's permission to bring action against the province. This cleared the way for a series of suits by the Ottawa Valley and Beauharnois Companies. (Revised contracts with Gatineau and Maclaren's had been announced in February, 1936). Publicly, Mitch Hepburn seemed unperturbed by the court's decision against one aspect of his legislation. "This is a temporary hollow victory for Earl Rowe, the Tory Party, and the power barons of St. James Street." He added, "This Government in the public interest will fight to a finish and, I repeat, will never pay."[9] Yet as he said those words, influences were coming to bear that induced Mitch Hepburn to change his position not only on the Hydro contracts but on a number of other policies as well.

As the "boy from Yarmouth," Mitch Hepburn had always been proud of his rural background and his special appeal to "the back concessions." He was proud too of his brief sojourn in the business world with the Bank of Commerce. Later in his career, Mitch Hepburn never permitted his tilts against big business in the abstract to interfere with his widening friendships for big businessmen in the flesh. Before he became Premier, Hepburn had associations with some of Toronto's wealthy entrepreneurs. Percy Parker, the oil and mining magnate, was one of Hepburn's closest backers and friends.

When he was campaigning for the premiership, Mitch Hepburn met a number of prominent members of the business and financial community in the Centurion Club, a group of Toronto businessmen dedicated to electing a Government expressing liberals ideals at Queen's Park. The Centurion Club included among its members men like J. H. Gundy, Bethune Smith, and Latham Burns. Other friends of Mitch Hepburn's during this period were the wealthy J. P. Bickell and, of course, Frank O'Connor who controlled both Laura Secord and its American subsidiary Fanny Farmer. After he became Premier, it was not surprising that Mitch Hepburn's associations with the "Bay Street crowd" became warmer and wider. Sitting in the Premier's chair and living in a King Edward Hotel suite was a far cry from the days near the Elgin village of Union when Mitch Hepburn sold a field of beans to make a payment on a car. Most men would have changed somewhat in the transition; Mitch Hepburn was no exception. The lad who got along well with the manager of the Bank of Commerce in St. Thomas now had no trouble with the New York financier, Sell 'Em Ben Smith.

Among the members of the Centurion Club and a business protégé of Percy Parker was a fast-rising young Toronto stock-broker named George Clement McCullagh. Born in London, Ontario, in 1905, nine years after Mitch Hepburn's birth, a few miles away, George McCullagh, son of hard-working, lower-class parents, sold newspapers to help his family make ends meet. The newsboy soon became a young man in a hurry. In just over twenty years, he moved from selling papers to the *Globe's* circulation department (where he led the way in sales) to the paper's financial page, and thence to a Toronto brokerage office, where he made a tidy personal fortune in the thirties on the spectacular rise of gold stocks. McCullagh's brokerage connections and his astuteness enabled him to gain the confidence of mining millionaire William Wright. In the fall of 1936, Wright's millions helped McCullagh buy both the Liberal *Globe* and the Tory *Mail and Empire* and found the *Globe and Mail*.

As a Liberal and a friend of Percy Parker, McCullagh helped in the Hepburn election of 1934. About two years later, in September, 1936, Hepburn appointed McCullagh the youngest Governor in the history of the University of Toronto. On that occasion, Hepburn said: "Mr. Mc-Cullagh is an outstanding young businessman . . . a man with great executive ability and a very keen financial mind. In addition, he is possessed of a most charming personality." Relations between the handsome, hard-driving McCullagh and the Premier determined to give Ontario "a new deal" were close enough when McCullagh established the newspaper in November that he felt it necessary to publish a front-page statement denying that prominent Liberals, specifically Mitch Hepburn and Frank O'Connor, "had any part in buying or acquiring control of the *Globe and Mail* or in the negotiations leading up to the purchase." One of those who had heard the rumours was Norman Lambert. Shortly after the newspaper merger, Harry Johnson told Lambert "that Hepburn had had to do a job for both papers before things were lined up for Geo. McC. & that it was definitely true that Mitch was the principal factor in getting McC. in the newspaper situation; that he had been considered the brightest of the young men in that group." Whatever assistance Hepburn gave McCullagh in forming the *Globe and Mail*, the young publisher wrote to tell King that he had great admiration for Hepburn but thought he should jettison some of his Cabinet ministers.[10]

Less than a month after its first issue, the *Globe and Mail* ran an editorial entitled "Price of Repudiation." The editorial strongly denounced the Government's cancelling of the hydro contracts. In effect, said the editorial, the Government had declared "that if one does not like the debts contracted it need not pay. . . . For the sake of the good name of the province and the welfare of innocent investors, the *Globe and Mail* believes new contracts should be made with each company separately." This attack on Government policy was interesting in view of the close friendship that existed between McCullagh and Hepburn. Even more interesting was the reaction of the Toronto *Telegram* which suggested that the editorial was a "sham attack" whose main purpose was to enable Hepburn to get off the hook on the hydro contracts. Mitch Hepburn's violent reaction to the editorial indicated that the battle was genuine. After all-day Cabinet conferences on December 17, 1936 (in which Attorney General Roebuck figured prominently), the Government issued a statement charging the *Globe and Mail* with pleading "the interests of the financial ring whose yoke the Government has struck from the neck of power users." It would take more than the purchase of a newspaper "to frighten the Government into submission." Hepburn conceded, nevertheless, that he was willing to negotiate a settlement.

McCullagh's reply to Hepburn's extreme language was mild. The *Globe and Mail* stated in hurt tones that to suggest its motives were dishonest was irrelevant and "in bad taste." Still, the Premier's open-minded attitude toward further negotiations with the hydro companies was very "fair and reasonable." Next day, when Hepburn continued his attack by challenging William Wright, principal *Globe and Mail* shareholder, to buy 50,000 horsepower for $750,000, "and thereby assist the Government" to dispose of surplus power, the *Globe and Mail* merely noted that "this reference to Mr. Wright is uncalled for and childish," and once again congratulated the Premier on his readiness to negotiate. Perhaps that also was the point stressed at the dinner McCullagh enjoyed with Hepburn at his Bannockburn farms just before his paper's first assault on the hydro contracts.[11]

So the year 1936 ended with several things up in the air: the Premier's relations with Ottawa; the hydro legislation; and the separate school question. Most up in the air of all – or so it seemed – was Mitch Hepburn's relationship with the successful young publisher George Clement McCullagh.

chapter 8

Riding with General Motors

At the Crystal Ball Room of the King Edward Hotel, as corks popped and the orchestra blared, a child contortionist labelled "1937" stepped into.the limelight at the stroke of midnight. The New Year had come in with a bang. For Ontario's politicians, the year 1937 was to be a long series of bangs, one crisis succeeding another like a string of exploding firecrackers.

Even when he was not on the scene, Mitch Hepburn was almost invariably at the centre of the political revelry. In the first week of 1937, he made a quick trip to Oshawa to buy a new car from his friend Samuel McLaughlin, President of General Motors. "My dear Sam," he wrote on January 4, "it must be some satisfaction for you to know that Messrs. Bickell, O'Connor, and Hepburn are now speeding around in the new 1937 McLaughlin-Buick. . . . It is one of the best Buicks I have ever driven, and I have been driving them for the past fifteen years."[1] In a few weeks the Premier would be in communication with Sam McLaughlin again; this time the matter would be more serious than a smooth-riding Buick.

The new year had just begun when the Premier announced that the Legislature would meet early, on January 19, in order to pass special legislation to protect the province against any judicial decisions that might affect Hydro adversely. The need for such a session became evident when the courts awarded damages against the Government to two of the Quebec power companies (Beauharnois and Ottawa Valley), and despite the repudiation act of 1936 found that their contracts with Ontario Hydro were valid, which meant that Hydro must take all the power contracted for from the companies by the agreements signed by the Conservatives. Hepburn said the companies "haven't a chance of collecting anything." To charges by Earl Rowe that the province was facing a power shortage, the Premier replied, "I am fully confident that the power needs of this province are looked after for many years to come." To be on the safe side, Hepburn ordered his hydro officials to make a survey of Ontario's power requirements.

The Premier had other afflictions more pressing than the hydro situation. His chronic bronchitis had flared up again, complicating his old kidney trouble. In mid-January, his doctor ordered him to take an extended rest in a dry climate. "I don't know when I'll be back," the Premier told newsmen. "I know I feel terrible – that's all," he added as he prepared to leave for Arizona with his family for a holiday. While the Premier was in Arizona (quite disenchanted at first with the unseasonably cold weather), Acting-Premier Harry Nixon was left to mind the store for the special session at Queen's Park dealing with hydro legislation. The purpose of the new bills was to place Hydro on the same plane as Crown property beyond the jurisdiction of any court decision. Again it was Attorney General Roebuck who led off for the Government. Again it was a marathon performance. In a three-hour address on January 20, Roebuck scored "this stock bunkum" of a power shortage. When the Tory Opposition charged that the legislation was un-British and disrespectful to the courts, the Attorney General accused them of "serving their masters, the Quebec power interests faithfully and well."

Not only the Opposition but a growing number of Liberal members were becoming apprehensive about the new power bills. The attitude of the *Globe and Mail* was having its effect. "The Legislature of the Province of Ontario," wrote the paper, "cannot with impunity defame the character of Hydro or of the Courts by passing the wretched bill offered it." George McCullagh was so angered by Roebuck's speech that he phoned the Premier in Arizona to protest. Hepburn's vacation was also interrupted by warnings from his own members. Liberal whip Harold Kirby (Eglinton) wrote that "a number of our strongest members are becoming disturbed." Hydro's chief engineer, Thomas Hogg, prepared a memorandum for Acting Premier Harry Nixon and wrote Hepburn that unless a new contract were negotiated with the Ottawa Valley Company (which with Ontario controlled the Chats Falls power development at Niagara), hydro reserves "will not be sufficient to meet the demand during the winter season 1938-9."

Nixon, sceptical of the hydro legislation from the beginning, informed the Premier that, Roebuck's position to the contrary, Ottawa Valley was willing to settle. He added that he was impressed with Hogg's opinion "that the situation is really alarming, that the demand for power is increasing rapidly, and that we going [sic] to be embarrassed by next fall" unless some accommodation could be made. Nixon added: "The Province is tremendously inflamed over the legislation now before the House, and the Members are disturbed to such an extent that I doubt very much if they can be held in line – the whole trouble being that they have no confidence in the A. G. [Attorney General]."

To make certain that the Premier understood the situation, Nixon gave Hogg's memorandum on a possible power shortage to David Croll and asked the Labour Minister (who had replaced Roebuck in that portfolio) to fly to Tucson on the weekend of January 23 to place the case for negotiations with Ottawa Valley before the Premier at his holiday retreat. Despite these behind-the-scenes manoeuvres, the misgivings of some members of the Liberal majority and the spirited opposition of the Tories (George Henry called the absent Premier a "juvenile Hitler" for saying that the province would not honour the contracts no matter what the courts decided), the new power legislation passed on January 29 and the House adjourned. The bills explicitly stated that Hydro could not be sued without the consent of the Attorney General.

The *Globe and Mail's* opinion of the legislation was caustic. "It is a good bet that Mr. Roebuck's 1937 measure is not worth a lead dime in any court of competent jurisdiction."[2] A letter written on January 29 by the paper's publisher to Hepburn was not at all caustic, but it revealed much about the relationship between the publisher and the Premier. George McCullagh reiterated his misgivings about the power legislation. He was very dubious about the wisdom of the bills; only time would prove whether or not the Attorney General's course was justified. Much later Roebuck claimed that, shortly after the East Hastings by-election in December, McCullagh had asked Hepburn to dismiss him from the Government. The publisher denied this, although a few days after he established the *Globe and Mail* on November 23, 1936, and prior to the East Hastings by-election, McCullagh informed Lieutenant Governor Bruce that he was "out to move Roebuck, Croll & Heenan from the Cabinet."

There is no reason why the ambitious publisher of an influential metropolitan newspaper should not advise the Premier of Ontario about the personnel of his Government. There is even less reason to speculate about this in view of McCullagh's complete letter to the Premier on January 29, 1937. After noting his displeasure with the hydro bills, McCullagh switched from power politics at Queen's Park to the tickertape on Bay Street. The market had been generally quiet in the post-Christmas season. Mitch Hepburn had not really missed anything of moment by being on vacation in Arizona. But George McCullagh himself had been on the job, and part of that job was to keep an eye on Mitch Hepburn's investment portfolio. In fact, since the Premier had been away, the publisher and one-time broker had come across an interesting speculative stock called Hyslop Gold Mines. In addition to purchasing shares for himself, George McCullagh had also bought a block for Mitch Hepburn. (Of course, the Premier's name did not appear anywhere in the transaction.) Because the purchase price (eleven cents a share) had doubled in a period of two weeks, it looked as though the publisher and the Premier were onto a good thing.

It was to be expected that George McCullagh, who had made a good deal of money on the rise of gold stocks, would know a good thing when he saw it. Some time previously, for example, he had invested in Kerr Addison stock. After a successful drilling campaign, Kerr Addison had risen from the purchase price of fifteen cents a share to between $3.50 and $4.00. The same engineer who had worked Kerr Addison so successfully was now at the Hyslop property. With any luck at all, the publisher could run the Premier's investment in Hyslop gold into some real money. It was, to be sure, a gambling stock, but then both George McCullagh and Mitch Hepburn were, in their own way, gamblers.

Mitch Hepburn had utilized his big-business and political friendships (including that of George McCullagh) to win the premiership of Ontario. Each man had helped the other on the road to the top. In a sense, they were partners in power. The one friend buying a block of stock for the other was just one facet of that partnership. So it was quite natural that the publisher should keep Mitch Hepburn informed of the state of his portfolio. Once he had assured the Premier that his investment portfolio was in good shape, George McCullagh turned to Hepburn's health. He urged him to remain on holiday until he was completely recovered.[3]

Mitch Hepburn paid more attention to George McCullagh's market tips than he did to his medical advice. By the time the publisher's letter arrived in Tucson, the Premier had decided to cut his holiday short and return home. Although he was feeling much better and had lost sixteen pounds, the Arizona vacation had been somewhat of a disappointment. Unseasonably cold weather had contributed to this. But the real reason for the Premier's early return was the hydro situation. When Croll had made his flying visit to Tucson on January 24, Hepburn had given him permission for the Government to press negotiations with the Ottawa Valley Company. Acting Premier Nixon, ignoring Hydro Chairman Stewart Lyon and Commissioner Roebuck (who knew nothing of Hogg's memorandum to Hepburn warning of a possible power shortage), immediately ordered hydro officials to work out a settlement with Ottawa Valley. So smoothly did these negotiations proceed that Nixon reported to Hepburn on February 5 that he expected a satisfactory agreement within a matter of hours.

Snags developed, however, and Hepburn hurried back to Queen's Park on February 9. "We are all tangled up in our Hydro negotiations," he explained to Frank O'Connor, "and apparently are not making much headway." He told O'Connor that he was particularly worried about two points: "The first which enabled the company to withdraw power for resale in Quebec, which in effect, meant we had no contract and second, Ontario agreed to absorb any taxation which might be levied over the thirty-year period of the contract by either the Federal or Provincial Government." When these points were settled to Ontario's satisfaction, the Government, on February 12, 1937, signed a new contract with Ottawa Valley at a lower price ($12.50 a horsepower against $15.00), and somewhat better terms than the original one signed by the Tories. Hepburn, who had repeated so many times that he would never settle with any of the Quebec companies, announced, "A settlement of some kind has been inevitable, and the present one is as advantageous as under the circumstances could be expected." George McCullagh and the *Globe and Mail* were pleased, while the *Telegram* still thought the whole business had been a political sham battle:

> The net result of the Hydro uproar is that Mr. Hepburn is covered with fictitious glory as Mitch the Giant-Killer, and Hydro is buying power at terms on which the power company has been willing to sell. The same result might have been attained without the stage-play, but it would not have been so politically useful to Mr. Hepburn and his Government.

The *Telegram* aside, by his settlement with Ottawa Valley, Mitch Hepburn had made a somewhat better deal than the original one. He also had pleased George McCullagh and retained his reputation on the back concessions. Seen in those terms, it was not a bad settlement, not bad at all.[4]

Four days after the agreement with Ottawa Valley, the House resumed its sittings on February 16, 1937. Now that new contracts hed been negotiated with all the Quebec power companies except Beauharnois, presumably there would be something on the agenda other than hydro. With a refurbished Mitch Hepburn again leading the Government, there was. One of the Premier's vacation companions in Arizona (and a near-casualty in a wild car ride he had there with Sell 'Em Ben Smith) was Sir James Dunn, the eccentric, flamboyant, arrogant, and convivial New Brunswick-born financial magnate. Among other techniques used by Sir James to construct his corporate empire was that of buying up large blocks of depressed stocks and bonds. He had done this with the twice-bankrupt Algoma Steel Company. After Hepburn came to power in 1934, Dunn, who by then had acquired control of Algoma Steel, asked the Government to incorporate the reorganized company. This was done but the company's mines were still inactive because the ore could not be withdrawn economically enough.

To remedy this, presumably on the theory that what was good for Algoma was good for Ontario, Dunn approached Hepburn about Government help to make his company viable. Mitch Hepburn wrote his friend, Jim Curran, the editor of the Sault Ste. Marie *Daily Star,* that Sir James was "very anxious to discuss with the Government the possibility of reviving the scheme of subsidizing his company for the purpose of developing the iron ore bounty situated north of the Soo." The premier asked the knowledgeable Curran for his views. "I am frank to confess that I am quite ignorant about the iron-ore industry and will have to be guided by the views of those who have given this matter a great deal of thought and study." Curran replied that the subsidy scheme would be of immense benefit for Northern Ontario development.

So a day before the House opened, Sir James, at a banquet in Sudbury, was able to announce that the Hepburn Government would revive the bounty on iron-ore production to approximately a dollar for each ton of iron-ore recovered. This subsidy would begin on January 1, 1939, and continue for a ten-year period. In return for this aid, his company planned to spend approximately $1.5 million developing the Helen iron-ore deposits in the Michipicoten area. This announcement triggered one of the most acrimonious incidents of the session, an incident that did not concern the subsidy itself which even the Opposition generally supported (though the *Telegram* noted acidy that had a Tory Government introduced it, "There might have been talk about the Iron Barons"). The trouble rose because the sitting Liberal Member for the Sault, Dr. A. D. Roberts, thought that he, not Sir James Dunn, should have announced the subsidy. Dr. Roberts' resentment at what he considered unjust and cavalier treatment smouldered for several weeks, then burst like an angry flare on the startled Legislature. Premier Hepburn was at a conference in his office when the Member for the Sault, one of the House's better speakers, read a telegram he had sent the Premier hours after Dunn's announcement of the bounty. The house grew silent as Roberts said he "was astounded to hear private financier announce Government policy while the people's elected representative, who for two years loyally supported a supposedly democratic Government," was ignored. Liberal members stiffened as Dr. Roberts concluded. "I am discouraged but not defeated by such discourtesy and cheap autocracy."

Never since he had come to power had one of his own supporters so openly defied the Premier. Corridors and lobbies buzzed with speculation about how he would deal with this public criticism. Mitch Hepburn's response was swift and ruthless. Next afternoon, March 5, a quiet Chamber and packed galleries watched him rise shortly after the House opened. He began in a low voice: "It sometimes falls to the duty of a Leader to perform an unpleasant but necessary task. I feel obligated to reprimand the Honorable Member for Sault Ste. Marie for an unwarranted and ungentlemanly attack on Sir James Dunn and myself. It is an unpleasant task and I am sure the sympathy of the House goes out to a leader in a case like this." So far as the announcement of the bounty was concerned, the Premier explained, Sir James Dunn had a perfect right to reveal the plans of his own company.

Then, as he invariably did when crossed personally, Mitch Hepburn plunged in the knife. What had nettled Dr. Roberts, he explained, was that Algoma officials had refused the doctor's request for a medical contract with the company: "Dr. Roberts was unable to blackmail the company into giving him a job on the company payroll in consideration for his then support of the iron-ore bill." The Premier then revealed how he dealt with a member who stepped out of line: "I have a certain responsibility toward my party and I intend to purge my associates of the influence of a member guilty of this conduct. Mr. Speaker, on Monday of next week I am going to ask you to move him to the Opposition benches." Hepburn sat down in silence. Swiftly and irrevocably he had read a fellow member out of the Party under circumstances that had neither precedent nor parallel in the Legislative history of the province. In a cold voice, Dr. Roberts denied the Premier's allegation about impropriety in patronage and requested that the case be referred to the House Committee on Privileges and Elections.*[5]

Any resentment the Liberal caucus may have felt toward the Premier for his harsh treatment of a fellow member was quickly dispelled in the thunderous applause that greeted Hepburn's 1937 budget speech. After many dark years of deficits, Ontario at last had a "sunshine budget." In a rosy ninety-minute speech, the Premier (who was also Provincial Treasurer) announced a substantial reduction in the gross provincial debt, a new subsidy for municipalities, lowering of several taxes including complete abolition of the amusement tax, and (on net ordinary revenues of eighty millions) a surplus of more than seven million dollars, twelve times that forecast. As the Liberals pounded their desks, the faces of George Henry (who had remained Tory House leader) and the Opposition lengthened at the sunny financial picture sketched by Hepburn. He looked at the stony Tory faces with a grin: "I couldn't collect much amusement tax over there right now." In a glowing tribute to Hepburn for his sound financial policies, the *Globe and Mail* hailed the budget as "an amazing record, unprecedented and unexpected for times like these."[6]

If his "sunshine" budget was the administrative highlight of Mitch Hepburn's third session as Premier, the persistent separate school problem provided the most drama. Since the Liberals' defeat in the East Hastings by-election, hydro matters had supplanted the religious issue. The Conservatives were still committed to the school bill's repeal, and Catholic leaders were increasingly disappointed about the practical effects of the Act. It was impossible to determine for purposes of assessment who were Catholic school supporters in large complex corporations. In Hamilton and Toronto, this difficulty was so great and there was so much litigation that the financial position of the Catholic schools was actually worse than before the contentious legislation had been passed.

One of those most disillusioned with the Act was Martin J. Quinn who had worked so hard for its passage and who blamed two of Hepburn's Catholic advisers, Lands and Forests Minister Peter Heenan and Senator William McGuire, for much of the problem. In a letter that seemed to lack some of his old fire, Quinn, on February 22, 1937, complained to the Premier about the defective legislation and added with his usual acerbity: "If the Government are not prepared to pass legislation that will give effect, under existing conditions, to the rights that undoubtedly were intended to be given to separate school supporters under the original legislation, then we ask that the amendments of last session be repealed, so that we may occupy a position at least as favourable as that enjoyed prior to their passage."

Hepburn was long past answering Quinn's letters personally, but he did not conceal his anger from Frank O'Connor at this communication "which I believe will cause considerable trouble if given publicity." Nor did he conceal his opinion of Quinn: "As you know, I have absolutely no use for him. I believe he is so hot-headed and irresponsible that he makes little headway in any undertaking. It seems rather an anomaly that while we are still being severely criticized by the opposition for the measure which gave benefit to the Separate School supporters, such a letter should be received from Quinn."

In a brief, acrimonious reference to the Act in the middle of the 1937 session, Hepburn again angrily denied a charge by Tory W. E. Baird (High Park) that he had made a "bargain" with Frank O'Connor and the Catholics. At that time the Liberal majority easily defeated a Conservative amendment regretting that the school bill would not be repealed. Less than three weeks later, on March 23, 1937, House leader George Henry moved second reading of a bill that would have repealed the school legislation. Presumably the Government would again vote it down. Instead, in a surprising manoeuvre, which may well have caught most of his own followers off guard, Hepburn moved the adjournment of the debate.

Next morning the *Globe and Mail* ran a front-page editorial entitled: "Mr. Hepburn's Duty Is Clear." If the school question were the major issue in any provincial campaign, "the Province will be rent in a way likely to make recovery impossible for decades." The *Globe and Mail* "believes it to be in the best interest of Catholics and Protestants alike that [the legislation] be stricken from the statute books." More ominously, the editorial warned that George McCullagh's paper could not commend the Hepburn Government to the electorate unless the separate school bill was repealed.

---

*   Subsequently, at Dr. Roberts' request, the investigation was dropped. He admitted privately to the Premier that his actions had been "indiscreet," but he was not asked to stand in the provincial election of 1937. (PAO Hepburn Papers, Dr. A. D. Roberts to M. F. Hepburn, May 27, 1937.)

That same night in the Legislature, after a day of tense conferences with his colleagues, Mitch Hepburn rose to speak on the Tory motion to repeal the separate school bill which he had fought so hard and so long to make law. His face was set and serious: "It seems to be my unfortunate lot on many occasions to be in a position not envied by anyone." Until the bitter by-election in East Hastings, he had hoped that the province would acquiesce in the legislation. He could not accept the statements of men like Baptist minister T. T. Shields that Catholics were disloyal citizens, nor could he countenance the "absolute intimidation" resorted to by George Drew in East Hastings.

Still, the bill, which he had hoped "would bring a greater degree of equity to a religious minority," was not working out. To desk-thumping from the Tories, the Premier then said he was going to accept reluctantly George Henry's motion to repeal the legislation. "It is with a certain amount of trepidation tempered with regret that I do so." He referred to the words of his boyhood idol, Sir Wilfrid Laurier. "I do not want to open the door of power with a bloody key," and he commended those words to Earl Rowe, George Drew, and their allies. "It is my responsibility to forestall the possibility of a religious war in this province. I am man enough to stand up and take it on the chin for what is for me a bitter pill."

The Opposition gloating across from him would not have the opportunity to make the pill any more bitter. "I am going to move," concluded the Premier, "seconded by Mr. Nixon of Brant, that the question be now put." For a moment this parliamentary tactic, which amounted to closure on further debate, stunned the Tories. But only for a moment. Then it detonated what the *Globe and Mail* called the "worst explosion in legislative history." That tough little Tory gamecock, Leopold Macaulay, who had understood he was to be allowed to speak on the bill, jumped up screaming at the Premier: "I'm going to have my say. You change the rules in the middle of the game. It is a rotten dirty trick. You may be a dictator but you can't do this to us – in the name of democracy." With the legislature in an uproar, Speaker Norman Hipel vainly shouting for order, and Mitch Hepburn, sitting white-faced and silent, Macaulay, his eyes flashing angrily behind his glasses, moved out into the aisle in front of his seat, shook his fist up at the press gallery, and shouted: "Take this down, you fellows. It is the dirtiest, rottenest trick ever."

As Macaulay continued to shout above the din of Liberals crying, "Sit down!" the Sergeant-at-Arms, Captain Charles Rutherford, V.C., was seen advancing toward him. Although he tried to shake him off, Captain Rutherford firmly grasped Macaulay by the arm, wheeled quickly, and smartly marched the protesting Member for York South out of the Chamber where bedlam had broken out. A Union Jack quickly appeared, and George Challies (Grenville-Dundas) draped Macaulay's empty chair with it. When Speaker Hipel restored order, the vote on the separate school legislation was finally taken. The bill was repealed eighty votes to nothing.[7]

So ended the only attempt in nearly three-quarters of a century to legislate financial support for Catholic elementary schools. "Premier Hepburn," exulted George McCullagh in the *Globe and Mail,* "has exhibited the courage of high statesmanship." Most of the electors, Catholic and Protestant alike, seemed to agree. The parish priest of St. Patrick's Church in Galt, Father E. A. Doyle, told the Premier that his action was "another display of that manly sincerity and rugged honesty which have marked your public career. More power to you." Old-time Liberals, who thought it would be political suicide to go to the country on the separate school issue, were surprised and delighted. Hepburn's friend, Senator Hardy, wrote: "Well, by God, if that did not give the other side a body blow, then they never will get one." The Toronto *Telegram* was pleased to see "its campaign against Premier Hepburn's concessions to Separate Schools crowned with success," but it could not resist a final dig at both the Premier and the *Globe and Mail*: "With an oily rectitude . . . it calls upon the public to applaud the courage of a burglar who drops the stove which he finds too hot to carry off."

Some Catholics, though reassured by the Premier's words when he repealed Bill 138 ("I want to give the definite assurance to the Catholic minority of Ontario that the Liberal Party will give justice and equity to all people regardless of race or religion"), were disappointed to see so many years of effort end in failure. None more so than Martin J. Quinn. When the legislation was originally passed, Quinn estimated that it "will give us a good deal more than the best the Bishops ever asked or hoped for." Now that it had been repealed, Quinn was outraged. He blamed George McCullagh for the Government's reversal. Under the circumstances, the bill would almost certainly have been repealed or at least drastically modified whether McCullagh had intervened or not. Ontario's Protestant majority was not prepared to accept at that time what they considered unwarranted financial "concessions" to the Catholics. Catholic leadership on the question was hopelessly at odds, and after East Hastings, the political danger in the legislation (despite its continued support by Ministers like Leduc and Croll) made repeal inevitable.

If many Catholics were disappointed, they still credited Mitch Hepburn with trying to do justice for their schools. That the attempt failed did not detract from his sincerity and courage when politicians preceding him had equivocated. Archbishop James Charles McGuigan of Toronto expressed this feeling. He regretted the repeal but stated that the legislation "recognized a principle and manifested an honest effort to give some measure of justice to the Catholic minority."

After the repeal of the school bill, the Government quickly cleared the order paper, and on March 25, 1937, what the *Globe and Mail* called "the most hectic session in the history of the Ontario Legislature" prorogued. Happy to escape Queen's Park, Mitch Hepburn met his friends and famous trans-Atlantic flyers, Dick Merrill and Jack Lambie, and with his secretary, Roy Elmhirst, flew to Miami for a well-deserved holiday.[8] Events were in train, however, that would force the Premier to cut short his Florida vacation and would precipitate the biggest labour crisis in the province's history.

During his campaign for the premiership, Mitch Hepburn made no statement that received more publicity than his remark, "I swing far to the left where even some Liberals will not follow me." Those words, spoken during the West York by-election in May, 1932, constituted an open bid for the substantial labour vote in that riding. In the minds of men like George Henry, the words labelled Hepburn a radical if not a Red. One prescient observer noted at the time that Mitch Hepburn never staked out his claim in the vast untracked country of radical reform. He did not stake it out then or ever. In the earliest years of his political career in Elgin, Mitch Hepburn belonged to the United Farmers of Ontario, an organization that could be considered radical to the extent that it advocated political gimmicks like the direct referendum, recall of judges, and in some instances class government. If the UFO was politically radical in this narrow sense, most of the farmers who belonged to it were socially conservative. Mitch Hepburn himself was more interested in the co-operative marketing features of the UFO program than in its political planks.

While federal Member for Elgin in the House of Commons, Hepburn showed himself to be a traditional *laissez-faire* liberal coated with an emotional antagonism to the business barons. When he entered provincial politics, Hepburn's remedy for the faultering economy was not to introduce innovations in the economic and social order, such as the CCF advocated. His rhetoric was radical; his policies were not. What Hepburn emphasized in the campaign of 1934 was not radical reform but the elimination of corruption at Queen's Park, drastic economies in the administration of government, no increase in the provincial debt, and the crowning benefit of all this, a balanced budget. This program was basically conservative in so far as it was an attempt to restore conditions that were associated with prosperity before the depression. That the Hepburn program of 1934 was fundamentally conservative was noted by an editorial in *The Canadian Forum* shortly after the election. "It is at least evident that the electors did not declare themselves in favour of an alernative and positive policy of reform in their general "Swing to the left.'" Consequently, continued the *Forum*, the result of the 1934 Hepburn sweep was "negative."

This analysis was correct. What gave the 1934 campaign its air of excitement and challenge was not commitment to reform (except on the part of men like Roebuck and Croll) but Hepburn's radical rhetoric, his evangelical fervour, his promise not of reform but revival. He was on the side of the little man (where most of the voters were) against the tycoons, and it was essentially in this role that Mitch Hepburn considered himself a "reformer." At a meeting in Elgin shortly after the election of 1934, Hepburn himself put this succinctly. "I'm an out-an-out reformer and I'll fight against the protected interests to the end." So a reputation for reform was built on rhetoric, on fighting the Sun Life, on cutting the power barons down to size, on selling Tory cars at Varsity Stadium (an action that was colourful and flamboyant, certainly, but whose purpose was basically conservative, to help balance the budget). A few months after the Liberal sweep of 1934, there was no incongruity in *The Canadian Forum's* entitling an article "That Tory Hepburn."[9]

That is not to say that Mitch Hepburn did not combine a liberal humanitarian instinct with his traditional rural conservatism. His untiring work for war veterans and his support of old-age pensions during his years as a federal Member illustrate this. But his humanitarianism was a matter of the heart rather than the head, a feeling for the underdog rather than a positive commitment to ameliorate the social order. The less Government interference with the social and economic fabric the better was a principle Hepburn had expressed in the House of Commons long before he came to Queen's Park and started flying around the country with Sir James Dunn, Jack Bickell, and Sell 'Em Ben Smith. His Government's intervention to aid Dunn and Algoma Steel (for which Sir James was so grateful he promised the Premier he would campaign among his workers for him in the next election) seems to run counter to Hepburn's aim of minimal government interference. He rationalized it quite easily as merely the Government's attempt to put one of the primary, free-enterprise industries back into profitable production, an aim supported by most conservatives.

Nowhere does the tension between Mitch Hepburn's liberal humanitarian instincts and his social conservative traditions emerge more clearly than in his attitude toward labour. Hepburn's practical experience with labour was limited to Bannockburn farms. There, at times, he employed upward of thirty men (some of whom he had gone to great trouble to bring out from Europe). Often he went out of his way to display kindness to these men and their families. He was much closer to his able farm manager, William Tapsell, and his hired help than he was to the corporate tycoons who tried to reduce the price paid for his tobacco. But a workman should know his place, Bannockburn was being run to show a profit, and a man who did not do an honest day's work received short shrift from Mitch Hepburn. He was a fair, honest employer; there was no labour trouble, but at Bannockburn Mitch Hepburn was on the side of management.

That was about the extent of Hepburn's practical experience with labour before 1934. As Premier, his first contacts with labour were friendly. When the Conservative Mayor of Toronto, William Stewart, announced in July, 1934, that he would not receive the large group of "hunger marchers" converging on the city, the Premier and Attorney General Roebuck (then also Minister of Labour) arranged to meet them at Queen's Park. "These marchers are entitled to every courtesy," Hepburn said. "If they are down and out, they are to be regarded as unfortunate and it is the purpose of this government to help them on their way back to recovery."

Of more help than kindly words to the "down and out" was the labour legislation introduced by the Hepburn Government during its first session in 1935. The Industrial Standards Act, piloted through the House by Arthur Roebuck, was one of the most advanced pieces of labour legislation ever placed on the statute books. The Act provided that where workers and employers representing a preponderant group in any industry agreed upon minimum standards of wages and hours in the presence of a government representative, these rates and hours were to be imposed on the rest of the industry in the province or in a designated area. The purpose of the Act was to equalize wage rates and raise them to a level where a decent standard of living would be maintained for factory employees. It was aimed at cleaning up the sweat-shop conditions which had prevailed in the province.

Many, including labour leaders, hailed the Industrial Standards Act as enlightened legislation, and Mitchell Hepburn, as head of the Government which introduced it, must be given full credit. At the same time, it is interesting that the man primarily responsible for the Industrial Standards Act, Arthur Roebuck, was not at all comfortable in the Government during most of its first session. So unhappy was the Attorney General and Labour Minister that the federal seat of Trinity was being held open for him should he decide to resign and run for the House of Commons, a plan approved by Mackenzie King. Some of this tension between several members and Roebuck rose because of the hydro contracts. Some, however, was caused by the Attorney General's advocating legislation that represented more Government intervention in industry. Before the legislation passed, the Premier publicly stated that the best way to help labour was not to regiment industry but to cut Government expenses. After the Industrial Standards Act had been in operation for about a year, one of Hepburn's small "c" conservative advisers,* the federal Liberal Member for Northumberland, William Fraser, wrote from Trenton to protest against the deleterious effects the Act was having on the clothing industry.

"Knowing you as I do," Fraser wrote the Premier, "I do not believe that the Act is consistent with your own ideas." Hepburn replied: "I am frank to confess that I never was enamoured with the Industrial Standards Act and have tried to keep the brakes on as much as possible."[10]

From the time he had come to power, Premier Hepburn's attitude toward labour unrest and disturbances reflected the conservative-humanitarian sides of his make-up. In April, 1935, when hunger marchers complained to Queen's Park that their families were starving, the Premier gave up part of his Easter holiday, toured their homes in Toronto's suburbs, spoke to their wives ("Good morning, Madam, my name is Hepburn. I just came to see how you and your family are getting along. Are you getting enough food?), and returned to Queen's Park where he ordered that two thousand mattresses be distributed to the poor and that the Government's relief allowance be increased. That same month a disturbance at Crowland, near Welland, where relief recipients refused to continue public works until their allowances were further increased, revealed Hepburn's stern rural conservatism. He ordered extra provincial police into the area, visited the strikers himself to warn them against "outside agitators," and threatened their leaders with jail if there was any further disturbance. If they did not accept the Government's terms "then it's war to the finish." When the strikers capitulated, the *Globe* congratulated the Premier for breaking the back of the Crowland strike.[11]

This attitude of Mitch Hepburn's toward labour agitation in the thirties was consistent with his rural conservative background and his interpretation of business-like government. As an economy-minded Premier, his aim was to balance the budget. Labour agitation for higher wages and relief allowances must be put down because the first would threaten the primary industries like the mines on which the province's economy depended and the second would be an unwarranted drain on the treasury. Furthermore, Mitch Hepburn never evinced much concern with or understanding of the aspirations of organized labour. These aspirations, such as a contract between employer and employees and the process of collective bargaining itself, were not recognized by the general citizen in the thirties to the extent that they later became acceptable. In those years, the word "union" was often a dirty epithet. Mitch Hepburn was much less concerned with labour's aims than with its apparent threat to law and order and the province's economy.

That threat seemed more ominous in the early months of 1937. With the peak of the depression passed, and industry beginning to make gains,

---

* Many of Mitch Hepburn's friends, the men who encouraged his leadership and supported his campaign for Queen's Park – men like Arthur Slaght, Percy Parker, Bethune Smith, and Senators A. C. Hardy, James Spence, and Frank O'Connor – were, in many respects, small "c" conservatives. So, for that matter, was Harry Nixon.

labour also wanted a bigger slice of the economic pie. If Ontario's citizens and leaders had any doubts about this, they had only to look at the neighbouring state of Michigan. There the Congress of Industrial Organizations, formed and led by John L. Lewis in opposition to the American Federation of Labour and the craft unions, had split the labour movement. Violence and sit-down strikes at the automotive plants in Flint, Michigan, by the United Auto Workers, a CIO affiliate seemed to many in Ontario an example of the bloody price that must be paid once the working man got out of hand. The CIO, it was alleged, was riddled with Reds (a wild exaggeration that contained, like most exaggerations, an element of truth), and the burly John L. Lewis was considered by the public only a cut above the bandits in the Kremlin itself.

Early in 1937, the CIO spilled over into Ontario where an attempt was made to organize the workers of the Holmes Foundry at Port Edward near Sarnia. At the beginning of March, some seventy union members, provoked by management's persistent refusal to negotiate with the workers, staged a sit-down strike on the plant's premises. Violence (instigated by the non-strikers) ensued, and arrests were made. Mitch Hepburn's reaction was prompt and predictable in view of what he had been saying for several years concerning labour agitation. He told the Legislature: "Those who participate in sit-down strikes are trespassers and trespassing is illegal in this province. . . . There will be no sit-down strikes in Ontario! This Government is going to maintain law and order at all costs."

On the same day that he made that statement (which had the support of the Opposition and the vast majority of the province's citizens), Mitch Hepburn's minister of Labour, David Croll, announced Ontario's first minimum wage for men (an action that scarcely supports the thesis that by the spring of 1937 Hepburn was simply anti-labour). Business profits were increasing, Croll explained to the House, but not wages: "Labour feels quite rightly that it should have a stake in the returning prosperity. We fully agree." Croll then warned: "It takes no prophet to predict that without Government action 1937 will be a year of industrial disturbance." Presumably Mitch Hepburn, who had promised (but not emphasized) a minimum wage bill in the 1934 campaign, agreed with his Minister of Labor. But Government action could cut two ways, and Mitch Hepburn had always been more committed to economic advance and the maintenance of law and order than to social justice.

In the spring of 1937, the Premier had, or thought he had, evidence that law and order in the province was being threatened by the CIO's attempt to invade Ontario's labour scene. There had been trouble at Sarnia and elsewhere. Hepburn knew too that a "wildcat" strike had occurred at the General Motors plant in Oshawa where negotiations toward a new contract were proceeding, and where a slim, dark-haired young UAW official from Detroit, Hugh Thompson, was attempting, with considerable success, to organize the workers. "Keep the Agitators Out," warned the *Globe and Mail,* referring to Thompson. In the Legislature, the Premier's language echoed that of George McCullagh. Ontario would have no truck or trade with outside labour agitators: "We are not going to tolerate them, and I point that out to those people now in this country – professional agitators from the United States – to agitate and foment unrest in our industrial areas." If municipalities could not maintain law and order, the Premier promised to use "the full strength of the Provincial Police and other resources at the Government's disposal." He was "right behind any reform as long as it is brought about by orderly and constructive methods. But I will not tolerate the sit-down strike in this Province of ours. In the first place, it is nothing but illegal trespass. In the second place, it is against law and order."[12]

Hepburn had already suffered a set-back in his attempt to "keep the agitators out." As early as February 24, the Premier had contacted his friend, the Minister of National Defence, Ian Mackenzie, to inquire whether CIO agents could be prevented from entering Canada. When conferences among Mackenzie, Labour Minister Norman Rogers, and the Mines and Resources Minister T. A. Crerar produced no immediate results, Hepburn telephoned Crerar on March 3 requesting him to bar certain American labour representatives from Canada including Hugh Thompson. Immediately Crerar ordered an immigration official to investigate Thompson's record. There was a file on Thompson at Queen's Park in the Department of Labour. Crerar's man examined that "but was unable to find anything that looked dangerous." An interview with Thompson in Oshawa was no more helpful. Thirty-four years old, Hugh Thompson had been born in Ireland, lived in Canada for ten years, married an American, had been legally admitted into the United States. He returned to Canada and was not advocating sit-down strikes "nor anything beyond the usual course that strikes ordinarily take in this country."

Crerar immediately forwarded this information to Hepburn with his opinion that, so far as Thompson and other accredited representatives of international unions were concerned, he could not "see how we can legally exercise discrimination against them, unless they encourage in Canada any illegal activities." This policy, perfectly justified by the evidence at Crerar's disposal, was one that Mitch Hepburn apparently never understood or accepted. Later, when trouble broke out at Oshawa, he wrote to Senator Hardy: "The thing that annoys me so is that the Dominion seemed powerless to act . . . when I gave them full information regarding the activities of John L. Lewis's paid agitators in Canada. Had they been thrown out of Canada at that time, we would have had industrial peace, which means so much to the period of recovery."[13]

That was the labour situation at General Motors in the last week of March when the Legislature prorogued. The Premier's reversal on the separate school legislation, not the possibility of trouble at Oshawa, commanded the headlines. When Mitch Hepburn left for his Florida holiday, he gave no indication that he expected trouble at Oshawa. Negotiations there between management and the company union headed by Charles Millard (who had resigned his job at General Motors) were continuing. Millard presented the employees' revised demands, which included higher wages and better working conditions, to G.M. on March 31. These demands, on which both sides were in substantiated agreement, did not seem to pose a strike threat. This arose from another issue gradually coming more sharply into focus. Who really represented the workers? G.M. maintained it was the company union headed by Charles Millard (whom they considered an employee on leave of absence). Most of the workers claimed it was Local 222 of the United Auto Workers (a CIO affiliate) which Hugh Thompson had been organizing and of which Millard and the executive of the company union were, in fact, members.

G.M.'s Plant Manager, James B. Highfield, had refused to negotiate with the workers' committee if it contained CIO representatives, specifically Hugh Thompson. G.M.'s Vice-President and General Manager, Harry Carmichael, said the only snag to a settlement was the question of CIO affiliation. This problem was not resolved in a meeting in Labour Minister Croll's office on April 2 between management and the workers' committee headed by Millard who insisted he was there not by virtue of his former job at G.M. but as an international representative of the UAW. The meeting was amicable although Plant Manager Highfield took exception to Croll's remarks about G.M.'s labour relations: "I have often said," Croll told Highfield, "that you and Harry Carmichael and your organization of General Motors take a lot of trouble to build good cars. If you took as much trouble to build good will amongst your men, you wouldn't have a mess of this kind." Croll was of the opinion that "the mess" could be cleaned up with the help of the personnel of his department (especially his chief labour conciliator Louis Fine), and he left the city for a holiday in the Southern United States. At a further meeting, G.M. again refused to sign a contract with the UAW-CIO, and the *Globe and Mail* noted that the threat of a strike was more serious as the recognition of the CIO affiliate had now become "the central issue."

At this point, Mitch Hepburn unexpectedly ended his holiday and returned to Toronto. He had planned a driving trip into Florida's lovely Lake Wales district, but as he explained to George Fulford (Leeds), "I had to make a hurried trip back by plane in order to reach here at the time of a very acute labour crisis, brought about by the activities of John L. Lewis's paid propagandists in Canada. . . . Ontario is just seething with labour troubles." About seven o'clock on the morning of April 8, the phone rang in the Premier's suite at the King Edward. The threatened strike at General Motors had begun when the workers, without incident, left the plant just after the morning shift started. In Oshawa, Hugh Thompson, the chief "of John L. Lewis's paid propagandists in Canada," announced, "It will be peaceful picketing and violence will not be tolerated." Millard was quick to add, "A sit-down strike was never contemplated for Oshawa."[14]

The Premier was not taking any chances. He knew that the CIO had been associated with sit-down strikes and violence in Michigan; he knew that George McCullagh had warned the *Globe and Mail's* readers: "Along with the motor industry, steel plants, pulp and paper mills, and the mines are in the contemplated line of march. . . ." He knew, too, that in 1936 the total production from Ontario's gold mines was valued at $83,000,000 of which $29,000,000 was distributed in dividends. He knew (if by chance he did not, George McCullagh would tell him) what would happen to those mining profits if the CIO moved into the Northern Ontario mining fields.

Quickly Mitch Hepburn dressed, grabbed a bite to eat, listened to the latest reports on the labour situation, then picked up the phone. He called federal Justice Minister Ernest Lapointe, and followed up his call by a telegram urgently requesting "that assistance of Dominion police be made available to maintain law and order in strike areas. . . . Report just submitted to me," Hepburn's telegram concluded, "indicates situation becoming very acute and violence anticipated any minute." That morning's report from the Provincial Police in Oshawa detailed to report to Queen's Park said that the strike had begun peacefully. The Premier, however, was receiving information almost hourly from other sources. One of these was a lawyer (on the scene in Oshawa) connected with General Motors.

The federal Government responded immediately to Hepburn's request for aid. The Premier had communicated with the Justice Minister before noon on Thursday. "Your telegram received," Lapointe replied at 2:14 P.M. the same day. "Seventy men unmounted will leave at four o'clock for Toronto. Stop. Thirty three men all ranks mounted will leave at six o'clock for Toronto. Stop. All to be placed at your disposal with understanding that all expenses as usual will be paid by Province." That night the Royal Canadian Mounted Police rolled into Toronto. One *Globe and Mail* man described the scene as they detrained: "They strolled from the Union station in groups of two, ten, and so on, carrying suitcases, like any ordinary civilian. . . . Some wore blue slacks, others riding breeches; some had the far-famed Stetson hats, others had forage caps." He noted somewhat disappointedly, "There were no signs of horses or armaments."[15]

While this striking force was unpacking its suitcases and bedding down for the night at University Armouries, the Premier, who had taken charge of the Government's negotiating team (both Roebuck and Croll were still on Easter holidays), had completed a round of meetings at

Queen's Park. At their conclusion, he issued a statement that was almost a carbon copy (or possibly the original) of George McCullagh's lead editorial next morning. "This is the first open attempt on the part of Lewis and his CIO to assume the position of dominating and dictating to Canadian industry. . . . We believe the time for a showdown is at the start." Any knuckling under to the CIO at Oshawa would lead eventually to an assault on the mining and timber industries. "I counsel and request those Canadian employees who are ill-advised by outside propagandists that they should stop, look, and listen before any serious trouble develops." If the strike continued indefinitely, the Premier warned, relief would be cut off to the strikers (a step that David Croll, before the strike began, had assured the workers would not be taken).

On Friday morning, April 9, after a conference with Charles Millard and the workers' committee at Queen's Park, the Premier seemed more optimistic about a quick settlement. He was "very much impressed" with the reasonableness of the strike delegation. He had no immediate intention of sending police to Oshawa: "The police are standing by only in case trouble develops and gets beyond the control of the municipality and I – as it is my duty – must send extra help." The Premier decided to remain at his desk over the weekend. On Saturday, April 10, the negotiations took a turn for the worse. The only major stumbling block to a settlement was the recognition of the UAW-CIO as the bargaining unit for the employees. On Saturday morning, Hepburn's conference with the strikers collapsed because he refused to see Hugh Thompson. As the young CIO representative sat outside the Premier's office twiddling his thumbs, Hepburn told the press: "Thompson is the issue in the strike right now. . . . I will have nothing to do with any paid agitator from a foreign country. . . . I still adhere to that attitude and from it I positively will not budge."

To compound the Premier's problems, another "paid agitator from a foreign country" arrived in Oshawa from Detroit on Saturday, no less a person than the president of the United Auto Workers, the bespectacled Homer Martin, thirty-three, graduate of Yale and a former Baptist minister, a remarkable young man whose mild collegiate manner belied the fact that he did not beat around the bush. On Saturday night, before a mass meeting of 2,500 G.M. workers in Oshawa, Martin warned: "General Motors of Canada, whether the Premier likes it or not, will meet the international union." It was a fiery speech from the American union president: "Herr Hepburn will discover that democracy in Canada is a good deal older than he is . . . I don't care whether I meet the Premier or not. I'm not really interested in meeting him. I could go to almost any museum in the country and find mummies. I'm interested in meeting General Motors and I'm going to meet General Motors."

Language of that kind was sure to stiffen the Premier's antipathy toward foreign agitators and (despite assurances from Mayor Alex Hall that all was peaceful in Oshawa) escalate in his own mind the threat of violence. Accordingly, on Tuesday, Hepburn wired Lapointe for reinforcements: "Situation at Oshawa becoming more intense and would request that at least another hundred Dominion police be sent to Toronto where services will be available in case of disorder. Please wire reply quickly as possible." At the same time he telegraphed to Prime Minister King angrily protesting Labour Minister Norman Rogers' reported offer to mediate the strike. (Rogers' intervention had been requested by Oshawa's Mayor Hall, a request supported by the G.M. workers.) "I deeply resent," Hepburn told King, "the unwarranted interference on the part of the Honorable Norman McL. Rogers who projected himself into the strike issue and definitely played into the hands of the Tory Mayor of Oshawa. . . . While I have not consulted with General Motors' executives I am satisfied they will not be a party to such treachery or make my present unhappy lot more embarrassing."

The Premier concluded his telegram to King with a sentence that sounded like a communication between independent states on the verge of war: "This action is quite in common with the treatment that this Government has received from most of your ministers, and in my opinion constitutes an overt act." George McCullagh, fearful that Ottawa's intervention might cause G.M. to cave in on the crucial issue of CIO recognition, agreed. In a front-page editorial, entitled "Canada's Man of the Hour," the *Globe and Mail* hailed Hepburn as the man who "has taken up the battle without Ottawa's aid, in spite of Ottawa's refusal to help him when he requested assistance six weeks ago, and he is the man to see it through."

Mackenzie King immediately tried to set Hepburn's mind at rest on the matter of federal intervention. Rogers' offer to mediate, he told the Premier, "had been misunderstood or misconstrued." The federal Government had no intention of intervening unless both parties requested it and not even then if Queen's Park was still active in the matter. So much for the "overt act." Relations between Hepburn and the federal authorities were strained further when Lapointe wired on Wednesday that "having regard to our responsibilities in all parts of the Dominion" it would not be possible to send extra police to Toronto. This refusal of co-operation from the federal authorities was the final straw. "In view of vacillating attitude taken by your Government," Hepburn informed Lapointe, Ontario would look after its own law enforcement. He requested the Justice Minister to remove the special RCMP detachments in Toronto forthwith, and Lapointe immediately complied.[16]

Mitch Hepburn was as good as his word. He had already begun to organize a task force "to maintain law and order in this province." These special constables would reinforce the regular Provincial Police, seventy-five of whom were on constant alert at Queen's Park where, according to one observer, they spent their time playing cards and exercising with dumbbells while waiting bulletins from Oshawa. The special constables, soon dubbed "Hepburn's Hussars," eventually numbered about four hundred. Many of them were recruited among university students and veterans' organizations. The plan was to provide uniforms, training, and twenty-five dollars weekly pay while on call. Equipment was scarce. The Premier, however, had been in communication with a firm in New Haven, Connecticut, suppliers of "everything in police equipment except uniforms" which assured him that special gases, automatic riot guns, handcuffs, revolvers, high-powered lights, and holsters could be shipped immediately. Presumably on the supposition that cavalry might be needed, the Eglinton Hunt Club offered the Government sixty horses. The officers and non-commissioned officers of the 133rd Battalion, Canadian Expeditionary Force, wired Hepburn that they were prepared to take up arms again to keep "foreign malcontents" out of Canada.

As the clatter of marching men, under the command of that veteran of the imperial wars, Colonel Ian Hunter (Liberal, St. Patrick), sounded on Toronto's drill squares, officials in Oshawa became increasingly annoyed. Mayor Alex Hall (who had been dismissed by the Hepburn Government as Crown Attorney in 1934) wired the Premier inviting him to visit Oshawa unannounced "to see first-hand the behaviour of the men and remarkable condition of law and order existing." The city of Oshawa did seem to be a peaceful spot. The strikers were in a jolly almost festive mood. Before walking off the job, they had participated in the biggest pay day in G.M.'s history. Although beverage rooms were closed as a precautionary measure, movie theaters were filled, and downtown streets were jammed with strollers. Committees organized sports and entertainments for the men not on the picket lines.

Meanwhile, in addition to difficulties with federal and municipal authorities, the Premier faced trouble in his own Cabinet. For several days there had been rumours that Labour Minister Croll and Attorney General Roebuck (two men McCullagh had promised to eliminate) were on their way out. Both men were back in their offices at Queen's Park, but the Premier (who had not held a formal Cabinet meeting since the strike began) had seen Roebuck only once and Croll not at all. On Tuesday, Hepburn told the press, "In the course of time I will want to know, of course, if every member of the Government is solidly behind me in our fight against the forces of John L. Lewis and of Communism, which are now marching hand in hand."

Time did not take long to run its course. Next morning, Wednesday April 14, the Premier marched into his office, summoned the press and his secretary, Roy Elmhirst, and said peremptorily, "Take a letter." The letter, sent immediately to Roebuck (who for several days had fruitlessly tried to contact the Premier both by phone and personally) and Croll, demanded their resignations "since it is quite clear to me that you are not in accord with the policy of the Government in fighting against the inroads of the Lewis organization and Communism in general." The Premier admitted "the decision I have arrived at is one that is causing me both grief and unhappiness," but he assured his two powerful Ministers that there was "nothing personal in this matter and I hope that in future I shall always enjoy your friendship as I have in the past."

Within hours Hepburn had received the resignations of Arthur Roebuck, whom George McCullagh had time and again told him was a menace to public life, and of David Croll who said in his letter of resignation that he preferred walking with the workers to riding with General Motors. Neither man resigned as a matter of principle. Both men still thought that the record of the Hepburn Government was, in the main, a good record. Despite differences of opinion about the labour issue at Oshawa (which neither Minister expressed publicly prior to his resignation), both had been prepared to remain in the Government. Croll and Roebuck were dismissed because Mitch Hepburn was too committed emotionally now to brook even opposition by silence. "Time," predicted the Toronto *Star*, "will vindicate Mr. Roebuck and Mr. Croll."[17]

As the Hepburn reform forces packed their bags, the Hepburn police forces increased. Two hundred more special constables were sworn in. Special instructions were sent to all Crown attornies to issue warrants for the arrest of any of Lewis's agents who attempted to create any form of lawlessness in the province. The Premier was again optimistic about an early settlement. On Thursday, April 15, he wrote T. E. Wilson of the Oshawa *Times* (strongly anti-CIO), "To my way of thinking the company has met practically every reasonable request and I am sure is prepared to consumate an agreement with its workers at the earliest possible moment." In Oshawa, the strikers who expected (and thought they had been promised) substantial financial help from the international union in Detroit, were digging in for a long siege.

The possibility of a drawn-out strike increased on Saturday when negotiations at Queen's Park between Hepburn and some of the workers' committee broke off on a note of tragi-comedy. Hugh Thompson was there again, twiddling his thumbs outside the Premier's door. So was Charles Millard, still claiming to be a representative of the UAW, and J. L. Cohen, the Toronto lawyer representing the CIO. That morning Hepburn had received a secret memorandum from his secretary, Roy Elmhirst (prepared by another Toronto lawyer), claiming that "Cohen is an old-time Communist and must be watched very carefully in any negotiations."

As the meeting progressed, an aide informed the Premier that Thompson, Millard, and Cohen were using a room outside his office known as the Premier's "vault" to make phone calls to UAW officials (including Homer Martin) asking for instructions. His face flushed with anger, the

Prime Minister jumped up from the meeting, marched out of his office, and told the union men: "That ends it. Good afternoon. I'll have no more of this remote control." Turning on his heel, he strode away. A somewhat bewildered Hugh Thompson, who had seen newsmen lounging in the Premier's vault, protested that he thought it was a coffee shop. Cohen quietly observed that Hepburn was an admirable host but seemed to lack the prime qualities of a conciliator, "calm, objective judgment, and self-control."

Now ten days old (during which period not a single strike arrest had been made in Oshawa), the strike showed no signs of settlement. The Premier had already warned of possible wide-spread violence when he announced that he had "definite knowledge" (which came from the general manager of Hollinger Mines and other company agents) that the CIO was trying to organize strikes in the Northern Ontario mining areas. "Let me tell Lewis and his gang here and now that they'll never get their greedy paws on the mines of Northern Ontario." The mine owners backed him. Jack P. Bickell, the Premier's long-time friend and the President of McIntyre – Porcupine Mines, and J. R. Timmins, head of Hollinger Consolidated Mines (which in 1936 had declared a profit of fifty per cent on total production), said that rather than submit to CIO domination they would shut down their mines.

If the owners could shut down their mines, the strikers at Oshawa could continue to shut G.M. On Monday evening, April 19, they brought tears to the eyes of Mayor Hall when they howled down his offer of further concessions from management and held out for full recognition of Local 222 of the UAW. Something had already occurred in Detroit, however, that had weakened the strikers' position. Officials of the UAW had decided that the dispute in Oshawa must be settled between the local UAW union and G.M. This meant, in effect, that the powerful financial resources of the international union would not be at the disposal of the strikers, support they had counted on all along. Their morale was still high, but cracks were appearing in the solid front to continue the strike. On Tuesday morning, April 20, a secret delegation of eleven strikers visited Hepburn at Queen's Park and reportedly told him that fifteen hundred men wanted to return to work.[18]

Perhaps it was this meeting, and the information that the international union had refused financial support, that prompted Premier Hepburn to resort to an extraordinary action. The President of General Motors, Colonel R. S. McLaughlin, was at sea on the *Queen of Bermuda* which was expected to dock in New York on Thursday. On Tuesday, the Premier sent a wireless to G.M.'s President: "Would urgently request that you advise Carmichael to suspend any negotiations with strikers until your return Thursday morning. Would also ask you to give no statements regarding situation until I have had chance to confer with you. Confidential reports indicate total collapse of strike imminent."

Next day, Wednesday, a settlement seemed imminent, when strike officials appeared to have backed down on the matter of CIO recognition. After several hours of conferences with G.M. Vice-President, Harry Carmichael, and the CIO barrister, J. L. Cohen, a statement was issued from Queen's Park: "Mr. Cohen stated that neither he nor Mr. Millard were instructed by or represented the Committee known as the CIO." Early on Wednesday evening, the Premier received a hurriedly scribbled memorandum addressed to the *Globe and Mail's* Douglas E. Oliver, further indicating that the CIO representatives were wavering:

> Thompson leaving by fast car for Toronto to catch six P.M. train for Washington. Since Martin failed to get here today, Thompson is hightailing to him. Thompson will confer Washington tomorrow morning with Martin and John Lewis. Says now he'll fly back here tomorrow afternoon with Martin. Obvious he needs help and is running out to get hand strengthened.

The CIO had not abandoned the field entirely, however. On Thursday afternoon, *Globe and Mail* man Oliver received another secret communication that was marked for the urgent attention of the Premier. It contained the information that one Claude R. Kramer, a CIO agent from Massilon, Ohio, was now registered at the Genosha hotel in Oshawa. So far as the strikers were concerned, the CIO issue was still crucial. The memorandum continued:

> The feeling in Union headquarters as voiced . . . by many men at 3:20 is that CIO is still dominant in picture. They say even if negotiating committee agree to local settlement barring CIO that at mass meeting will take matters out of hands of negotiating committee and hold out for recognition of International Union. Kramer's being here certainly holds potential dynamite.

The dynamite holed up in the Genosha hotel never exploded. Like the crucial CIO issue and the strike itself, it fizzled out in an ambiguous sputtering of semantics. After nearly five hours of meetings at Queen's Park on Thursday, led by Harry Carmichael for the company and Charles Millard for the strikers, a smiling Mitch Hepburn announced that "a complete agreement" had been reached. Next day, Friday, April 23, on the sixteenth day of the strike, the G.M. employees assembled in the Oshawa Armouries (the use of which had been readily granted to Hepburn by the federal government) and voted overwhelmingly to accept the settlement.

Chief of Police Owen Friend congratulated the men of their good behaviour (no one had been arrested in connection with the strike); the tents that had sheltered the pickets at night were struck; boxing bouts were laid on for the afternoon; a dance was planned for that night; and Mayor Hall, to resounding cheers, said he would see immediately about opening the beverage rooms. The Oshawa strike was over.[19]

Who had won? The men had gained concessions from General Motors in the matter of wages, working conditions, and seniority rights. What of the central issue, the recognition of Local 222 of the UAW, a CIO affiliate? Whom did G.M. actually sign a contract with? According to Ross Harkness in his biography of Joseph E. Atkinson, the *Star* publisher had suggested to the union that the contract should be between the company and "its employees who are members of the UAW" without any reference to the CIO. Whether or not as a result of Atkinson's suggestion, this was the formula that was used, with the significant omission of any mention of the UAW. The crucial clause in the agreement, signed by Millard and the others representing the workers, read: "This agreement covering the Oshawa Factory of the company is signed by the union employees hereunder who signed on behalf of themselves and their successors in office representing the employees of the company who are members of the local union."

What did that mean? There was no doubt what it meant to Hugh Thompson and Homer Martin (whom Hepburn once more tried, unsuccessfully, to have federal Minister Crerar bar from Canada because "it is known they are members of organization in United States whose acts have been wholly illegal"). The two CIO agitators returned to Oshawa in triumph to address a victory celebration. They scoffed at the contention of the company, the *Globe and Mail,* and Mitch Hepburn that the CIO had not been recognized. They maintained that the agreement had been signed by men who were members of the UAW, that the Oshawa local was in fact a UAW local and, therefore, a CIO affiliate. "The settlement is a complete victory for the CIO," said Martin. An elated Hugh Thompson was no longer twiddling his thumbs: "The strike was not settled at Queen's Park," he boasted. "It was settled at Grand Boulevard and Woodward Avenue, Detroit, between a foreign corporation and 'foreign agitators.' " The local's President, Charles Millard, was just as vehement: "The agreement is with the local union. I know and they know and the world knows that the union has been recognized. All of this business of trying to avoid saying so in so many words is just child's play."

Still, the Premier, George McCullagh, and G.M. contended that the agreement (which was to run concurrently with the contract signed between G.M. in the United States and the UAW) was an agreement between G.M. of Canada and its employees at Oshawa. The fact that neither the UAW nor the CIO was mentioned explicitly meant that there had been no recognition of the international union. "The agreement reached is a victory for those opposed to Lewisism," said the *Globe and Mail*. "The CIO is not mentioned in the settlement pact. . . . No matter what false and flimsy claims may be put forth by Lewis agents and their comrades, the Reds, the CIO is repudiated." After the enormous effort that George Mc-Cullagh had made on his editorial and news pages and in conferences with Hepburn to keep the foreign agitators out, it was a rather disappointed editorial. Later McCullagh admitted that the victory over Lewisism had not been so complete. He blamed weak-kneed American industrialists for permitting the CIO to gain a foothold in Oshawa. Writing to the President of the Steel Company of Canada, R. H. McMaster, McCullagh conceded that had it not been for prominent industrial leaders in the United States, he would have more decisively defeated the CIO, and kept them out of Canada. In any event, the argument concerning semantics soon became academic. As a result of the strike, the UAW-CIO had gained *de facto* if not *de jure* recognition in Oshawa.

There was an air of unreality in this final dispute over terminology, as there had been over the whole strike. The central issue, the right of employees to sign a contract with the union of their choice (a principle by no means firmly established in Ontario labour relations at that time), was obscured by other issues. The case for that right was put succinctly by David Croll when in resigning he reminded Hepburn

> that the working people have a right to form their own associations for the purpose of collective bargaining; that they have the privilege of joining the lawful union of their choice; that if they, in their wisdom and in their knowledge of the conditions under which they work, consider that they should make the final resort to a strike, then that too is their right; and having struck they shall not be molested if they picket peacefully and within the law.[20]

That was well and good, but in Mitch Hepburn's view it did not give sufficient weight to two considerations: the CIO, tainted with Reds and involved in violence and sit-down strikes, posed a threat to law and order and to Ontario's economic welfare.

There is no question that in 1937 the majority of Ontario's citizens supported the case against the CIO put to them by Premier Hepburn. The right to sign freely a labour contract with the union of one's choice became hopelessly entangled in an emotional crusade against Communism and foreign economic domination. Mitch Hepburn did not create the climate in which these views prevailed: he was a product of that climate and articulated it. So did almost every newspaper in the province, Conservative or Liberal, led by George McCullagh's *Globe and Mail*. As the respected Windsor *Star,* writing from a heavy labour area, noted: "Public opinion is back of Mr. Hepburn. Canadians have seen and read enough of the results of CIO campaigning in Michigan to know that they want none of this stuff on our side of the line." American newspapers like the *New York Times* and the *Herald Tribune* (and letters from dozens of States) praised Hepburn's firmness in the face of CIO lawlessness.

The strike made strange bedfellows. Catholic priests and the Reverend T. T. Shields, whose tirades against Catholics (and Hepburn) in his Toronto Jarvis Street Baptist Church were distributed to the faithful almost weekly, supported the Premier. Speaking at all the Masses at St. Vincent de Paul Church in Toronto on Sunday, April 18, at the height of the strike, Father Melville Bolan thanked God that "the head of our established Government here has seen the Communist trend and has the courage to face it." The fat folders of congratulations on the Premier's CIO policy from clergymen were swelled by many letters from municipal officials and private citizens.

Naturally the business community was behind the Premier. In a note to Hepburn, the President of the Toronto Board of Trade voiced appreciation "of the prompt, energetic, patriotic, and statesman-like action you have taken to meet the challenge of foreign agitators." From the President of Libby, McNeill, and Libby, T. J. Taylor of Chatham, came praise for "the way you have handled the Oshawa strike situation – you deserve the admiration of every law-abiding citizen. I have yet to talk with anyone, regardless of Party, who has not similarly expressed himself."

Labour officials like A. R. Mosher, President of the All Canadian Congress of Labour, and J. O. Nix, Secretary-Treasurer of the Winnipeg Council of the Canadian Federation of Labour, praised Hepburn's efforts to maintain Canadian unions free from foreign domination. Mosher wrote the Premier: "Communists are determined to control the A. F. of L. unions in Canada as well as the CIO unions and a great mistake will be made if A. F. of L. unions in Canada are excluded from any efforts designed to curb domination by foreign agitators and Communists."

Backing for Hepburn's policy in the Oshawa strike was province-wide, broadly based and cut across party lines. Among the hundreds of letters and telegrams of commendation was one from Leamington containing the names of more than two hundred people who supported the Premier. "The enclosed names," said the writer, "will speak for themselves. There is no question how many names I could get to sign. It would only be how much time a man could give to same. Sixty to seventy-five per cent of the names on the enclosed are of Con. party. Every businessman in Leamington signed except those out of town. I did not go to the Jews."[21]

The chief opposition to Hepburn's CIO policy came not from the members of the official Opposition, which scarcely uttered a word (Leader Earl Rowe made one fence-straddling statement deprecating playing politics with labour strife and advocating law and order), but from Atkinson's

Liberal Toronto *Star*. Despite his early misgivings, Atkinson had supported Hepburn's Government fairly consistently since it had come to power. Shortly after the Oshawa strike began, Atkinson made a rare visit to Queen's Park. His purpose was to convince the Premier that he should permit the workers at Oshawa to choose their own union, even if that meant the CIO. When he refused (so Hepburn recalled later), Atkinson angrily threatened to break his political career. Atkinson denied this, and Harry Nixon who was present (and fully supported Hepburn's policy) recalled: "As was his way, Mitch over-dramatized what happened. The men disagreed, but I don't recall Mr. Atkinson making any threats."

Whatever happened (and Ross Harkness records that sometime in 1937 Atkinson came to the conclusion that Hepburn was a demagogue and a fascist), the *Star* mounted a sustained campaign against the Premier's policy. The Premier was denying labour a fundamental right. If capital had international connections, labour was entitled to them also. The recruiting of a standing police army was "the height of folly." Still, the *Star* professed not so much anger as disappointment at the Premier's actions and placed the major blame for his policy on the fact that "he has allowed himself to be captured by bad advisors. . . . It seems to us that it is too bad that Premier Hepburn should end in this way. He wins the applause of those would destroy him, and who gladly will." Just before the strike ended the *Star* observed: "The Oshawa employees were made pawns for the protection of the mine-owners from expected demands by their workers. That was the program and Mr. Hepburn and his advisers have carried it out." When the strike was over, the *Star* was more explicit:

> The Star has been a supporter of Premier Hepburn and we hated to go back on him in the case of the Oshawa strike. But we, as a Liberal newspaper, hated to see him suddenly become a more Tory premier than this province has ever seen in office. That is what he became.
>
> He acted upon his large fund of inexperience in connection with trade unionism which was greatly augmented by his intimacy with the new publisher of the *Globe and Mail,* who knows nothing of trade unionism, but who is deeply concerned with gold mining. These two young men seem to have decided to run away with the province and establish control of it.

Undoubtedly the *Globe and Mail's* publisher exercised considerable influence on Mitch Hepburn's anti-CIO policy. George McCullagh rated his importance more highly. Some years later he wrote to several corporation executives, including General Motors' President, Colonel R. S. McLaughlin. He then maintained that he and the *Globe and Mail* had provided the major opposition to the CIO threat in 1937. Whatever the

Premier had done to withstand CIO pressure was due, in large measure, to information he had received from McCullagh and at the latter's urging. In fact, McCullagh considered himself something of an expert on labour matters and union activities; it was this expertise he placed at the Premier's disposal at the time of the Oshawa strike. Primarily as a result of McCullagh's vigorous intervention and that of his paper Mitch Hepburn took a positive stand against foreign agitators and the CIO. In any event, that was how McCullagh remembered it.

Hepburn himself admitted McCullagh's influence, but it is difficult to believe that the publisher was the dominant force in Hepburn's anti-CIO policy. The Premier – with his rural conservative background; his interest in the advance of the primary industries like mining; his distrust of organized labour – needed no encouragement from McCullagh. As the British writer, Sir Anthony Jenkinson, who had seen both men in 1936, noted: "They seemed to be the best of friends, and indeed there was no fundamental reason why this should not be so since both had the same economic interests and social philosophy." If the influence of McCullagh and his paper did anything, it hardened Hepburn's resolve and inflated the possibility of violence, another of the unreal aspects of the strike. This gave the Premier the excuse, if he needed one, to deploy men and equipment to ward off a danger that always seemed remote and that the strike leaders had assured the authorities from the beginning would not develop.

Whatever is said of Mitch Hepburn's anti-CIO stand in retrospect, his policy was consistent with his rural conservative background and his previous statements on labour-management relations. The influence of George McCullagh and the other mining men merely reinforced his own instincts. He had fought the power barons; fighting John L. Lewis and the international labour barons was, in Mitch Hepburn's view, the same kind of fight. With his penchant for seeing complex problems in simplistic black-and-white terms, the Premier had no difficulty rationalizing his actions. As he explained to L. H. Dingman of the St. Thomas *Times-Journal,* it was "simply a case of a Government assuming its responsibilities and resisting an influx of Yankee racketeers with one intent in mind, that of creating disorder and chaos in Ontario."[22] Put that way, the issue in the Oshawa strike was indeed simple.

More to the point politically, that was the way most of Ontario's citizens, including Conservatives, saw it. If Mitch Hepburn had not quite stopped the foreign agitators at the border, he had stopped the Opposition dead in its tracks. The separate school issue and the hydro contracts had been forgotten. He had only to say the word and Mitch Hepburn could go to the country as the white knight who had blunted the lance of the Red invasion at the Detroit River. It looked like a dandy election issue.

Mitchell Hepburn's parents, William and Margaret,
and a future Ontario Premier, aged ten.

"A plain, blunt, honest" man,
Premier George S.Henry

"I go forward as Ontario
leader filled with
optimism." (December, ▮

The First Hepburn Cabinet, 1934. *Left to right:*
Paul Leduc
T.B.McQuesten
A.W.Roebuck
Peter Heenan
Premier Hepburn
H.C.Nixon
Duncan Marshall
Dr.L.Simpson
Dr.A.Faulkner
David Croll

"There's going to be a new deal
in this province." (1934 Campaign)

Wide World

Wide World

"There will be no sit-down strikes in this province."

Riding With General Motors
Left to right:
Harry J. Carmichael,
Vice-President of G.M.;
J.B. Highfield,
G.M. Plant Manager;
Premier Hepburn;
J.L. Cohen, union lawyer;
Charles Millard,
union official.

"Mr. McCullagh is
a most charming
personality."

Below: "George Drew
is a friend of mine."

The Globe and Mail

Toronto Star Syndicate

"M.F.Hepburn Bannockburn Farms."

Lieutenant Governor Herbert Bruce.

Right: Earl Rowe and "Sparkplug."

Far right: Mrs. Hepburn with Patricia, Peter, and Helen.

Skating on Lake Laurier.

Above right:
The Royal Visit, 1939.

Right:
With Jack Bickell.

Facing page:
The Premier and his Friends:
The Right Honourable
W.L.M.King and
Senator Frank O'Connor.

With Sir James Dunn of Algoma Steel.

London Free Press

Left: With former heavyweight
champion Gene Tunney
at Bannockburn.

Below: "I'll give Premier Duplessis
and his policies
a blanket endorsement."

The Globe and Mail

The Premier with his friends at his forty-second birthday party.

In front of the Premier:
An airplane pilot;
Judge Duncan Ross
   of St. Thomas;
L.J."Larry"McGuinness,
   Toronto distillery
   president;
Premier Maurice Duplessis;
an airplane pilot;

To the left of the Premier:
Unidentified man;
his Mother, Maggie;
his wife, Eva;
his son, Peter.

To the right of the Premier:
His daughter, Patricia;
Harry McLean, President
   of Dominion
   Construction;
William Tapsell, Manager
   of Bannockburn Farms.

Back row, behind
   the Premier:
Unidentified man;
Harry Johnson, Secretary,
   Ontario Liberal Ass'n.;
Sell 'Em Ben Smith,
   New York Financier;
Colin Campbell, Minister
   of Public Works;
L.J.Dingman, Publisher,
   St. Thomas *Times-
   Journal*;
L.B."Pete"Birdsall,
   reporter, St. Thomas
   Times-Journal.

"I hope I leave this world
a little better place."

Above: "We are in this thing because of the little people."

Left: "A politician must have a sense of humour."
At Saints and Sinners Meeting, New York, 1941.

Above right: "King Must Go."

Right: "I'm a precedent buster."

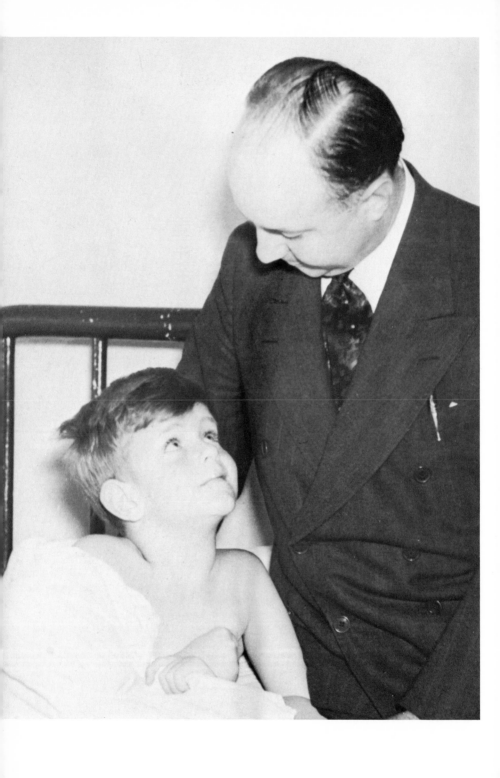

The Globe and Mail

Left: "My government's greatest
contribution was
in the field of health."

Above: "I hope I'll never forget
the people on the back
concessions."

Right: The Last Campaign, 1945.

London Free Press

"I have made mistakes."

chapter 9

Back to Power

With almost the entire province hailing his handling of the Oshawa strike, Mitch Hepburn's political position at the end of April, 1937, seemed unassailable. A large majority in the Legislature and the lack of any coherent labour policy on the part of Earl Rowe, the Tory's absentee provincial leader, gave Mitch Hepburn complete freedom for political manoeuvre. He could reorganize his Cabinet, replace David Croll and Arthur Roebuck, the two Ministers he had dismissed, and go through another session, or he could call a snap election. On a number of occasions, both publicly and privately, the Premier had indicated that he intended to hold another session before going to the country in 1938. No one, however, not even Mitch Hepburn, had made sufficient allowance for his own unpredictability.

On May 1, 1937, the banner headline across the Toronto *Star* read: "Hear Hepburn Seeks Union Government." The *Star's* news story elaborated on a rumour that the Premier had asked Earl Rowe to meet him a few days previously and had suggested to the astonished Conservative leader that a union government composed of Liberals and Conservatives should be formed. On May 4, the *Star's* speculations were more sensational: Hepburn had offered Rowe (whose followers held only seventeen seats in a House of ninety) the premiership and the right to name half the Cabinet. When pressed by newsmen, both leaders admitted they had met. It was quite normal, said the Premier. He had information of a confidential nature that he thought should be made available to the Opposition leader. There had been no proposal for a coalition.

Despite these demurs, the coalition scheme, incredible though it seemed, had been taken seriously in some quarters. It had been taken seriously enough by Mitch Hepburn himself that on Friday, April 23, the day the Oshawa strike ended, he told Lieutenant Governor Herbert Bruce "how

serious the trouble was getting in the Province and that he might be calling for a dissolution at any time and asking for a Union Government."
Home for the weekened, he had a chat with L. B. "Pete" Birdsall, a reporter on the Conservative St. Thomas *Times-Journal.* Hepburn asked
Birdsall, who was his political hound-dog in Elgin, to sniff out the attitude
toward coalition in his own riding. Birdsall consulted his Managing
Editor, Tom Keith, then later, on Sunday, April 25, sent Hepburn their
views which were generally favourable to the proposal. They advised Hepburn to move warily for a few days, feel out the other side, obtain a
definite understanding regarding future policies, and send out "kites" to
test the public's reaction. "As Tom puts it," explained Birdsall, "it might
save you a heap of embarrassment, even political suicide, if you get everything on a straight and most definite basis of understanding." Birdsall
doubted there would be any significant opposition in Elgin. "Personally,
I favour your idea."

In Toronto on Monday, April 26, the Premier moved more positively
to sound out the other side about union government. He accepted the
Lieutenant Governor's offer to help in any way he could, and informed
Bruce that he would be willing to take Wilfrid Heighington (St. David),
Drew, Rowe, and Robert Manion (Federal Conservative member for Fort
William) into his Cabinet (after dropping Peter Heenan, the third and
last member whom George McCullagh wanted ousted). He asked the
Lieutenant Governer to consult Rowe and Drew (the latter Mrs. Bruce
had noted in March, was "not working out well as a Party organizer")
separately. Later the Premier discussed the matter with Earl Rowe at a
secret meeting in a downtown Toronto hotel. Although they were not fully
elaborated at the time, two points emerged from this meeting to suggest
the genesis of Mitch Hepburn's extraordinary proposal: his bitterness
toward Mackenzie King and the influence of George McCullagh. "I will
never be satisfied until King's political heels go through the wringer," was
the way the Premier put it.

What better way to oust King eventually than to form strong union
governments in Ontario and Quebec. This was George Drew's strategy
("Drew is strongly for a National Government. Ontario and Quebec
National and Canada is well controlled," Mrs. Bruce noted at the time in
her journal) and Mitch Hepburn, increasingly blinded by his hatred of
King, shared it. Apparently too he agreed with the reasons advanced for
coalition by George McCullagh and several other mining men who had
been prominent in the anti-cio policy. A union government would not
only present a united front against the cio's Communistic threat to Ontario's economic well-being but would also deal more efficiently with other
problems, like hydro and civil-service reform. Rowe was told that if he
wished he could have the premiership himself (Hepburn offered to take
the agricultural portfolio or drop out altogether) and name half the Cabi-

net. Hepburn informed him that plentiful funds would be available to fight an election. Absolute secrecy was to be maintained (the *Star*'s story breached that), and it was agreed that Rowe would give his answer at ten-thirty on Friday morning, April 30.

An astonished Earl Rowe, taken aback by a plan that would virtually end the two-party system in Ontario, immediately brought the proposal to the attention of Conservative Party leaders in Ottawa. There the Liberals' chief organizer, Norman Lambert, who invariably noted a hair falling from a politician's head, recorded in his diary on Thursday, April 29: "Saw Col. Hogarth on the street with Hon. Dr. Manion. Understand Earl Rowe & Meighen also here." Lambert's sensitive political curiosity was aroused. It was soon satisfied. The next evening, Lambert had a visit from his friend, R. K. Finlayson, the personal secretary to R. B. Bennett. Finlayson, who sometimes informed Lambert of Bennett's policies before they were even formulated, had some information on Earl Rowe's flying visit to the capital:

> He told me that "Mitch" had seen Rowe re union govt. in Ont. He would offer Rowe half cabinet, & P. mshp. if he wanted it.
>
> Hogarth, & Meighen & Rowe had been here conferring with R. B. & while R. B. was inclined to union, Hogarth & Meighen were so much opposed to it Rowe went back with his mind made up to refuse.

Rowe would delay giving Hepburn his answer beyond the Friday morning deadline. There were two reasons for this: Bennett, leaving for the coronation of George VI, wanted to be off the scene before the story appeared, and the Conservative leaders feared that George McCullagh might try to pull some anti-labour chicanery on May 1 to force the coalition scheme.

Rowe did not delay long. Early in the first week of May, he rejected the proposal. By then, the *Star* had published the rumours, and Ontario Liberal officials acted swiftly to reassure members of their own Party, as much in the dark as the general public, about the plan. Late on Monday, May 3, Ontario Liberal Secretary Harry Johnson suggested to Hepburn: "Perhaps the best way of setting our people at rest on coalition is to ridicule it and show by the attitude of the Tory Party in nearly all the things you have done the impossibility of your having such minds in your council." That was exactly what Hepburn did the next night in Toronto at the annual banquet of the Ontario Women's Liberal Association. "The only idea of a coalition I know of," he laughed, "exists in the office of the President of the Toronto *Star*."[1]

If the President of the Toronto *Star,* Joseph Atkinson, publicized the rumours of coalition, there is no doubt that one of the moving forces behind the proposal was the publisher of the *Globe and Mail,* the thirty-two-year-old George C. McCullagh. McCullagh once told one of his employees that he made and unmade governments. Sometime during the Oshawa strike and the alleged threat of the CIO to the province's economy, especially the mines, McCullagh apparently decided to make one. Periodically, McCullagh articulated for his readers his views about the functions of governments, views that he would elaborate in the future. The key to good government was efficiency. Canada was so vastly over-governed it was almost nine countries instead of one. This cumbersome system was expensive, inefficient, and deleterious to economic development. Much of the debate in the Legislature was useless window-dressing, an artificial luxury that the province could not afford. Labour agitation, the hydro question, the matter of efficiency in the civil service could not be ignored indefinitely while parties jousted and jockeyed for political advantage. Why not form a strong union government combining the resources and brains of both Parties to face up to Ontario's problems?

Granted there were some specious advantages to the union-government proposal, it is still somewhat difficult to understand why Mitch Hepburn, with his large legislative majority, reacted as positively as he did to the plan. Later he claimed that he had serious reservations: "Personally I was not convinced of the need of such a coalition, but I listened to men who were pressing for such action." Pressing the hardest was McCullagh, and the Premier shared his impatience with what he considered archaic forms of democratic procedure, forms that seemed to hamper rather than expedite the province's business. To change the rules of procedure would be a tedious process, with little appeal for men of the impatient stamp of McCullagh and Hepburn. Union government seemed a simple, black-and-white short-cut to maximum efficiency. A businessman would think of it in those terms, but one would have expected a politician to take a longer look. George McCullagh notwithstanding, union government at that time in Ontario was a hair-brained scheme.

For all his personal charm and driving determination, McCullagh was as naïve about politics as he was successful in business. "He had no particular ideas regarding Dominion politics," wrote one observer in 1937, "except that radicalism should be fought on as wide a front as possible." In the business world, McCullagh, who had vowed to become a millionaire before he was thirty, was a hard-headed realist; in politics, he was an idealist with illusions. One of these illusions was that traditional constitutional processes could and should be tailored to the demands of economic efficiency, that the government of the province of Ontario could be run along the lines of the Wright-Hargreaves mining complex with an unelected Chairman of the Board calling the shots from the *Globe and Mail* offices.

The Premier should have realized that short-circuiting democratic processes and blowing up the two old Parties was too high a price to pay for efficiency in Government. Queen's Park could not be run simply like a successful corporate structure. That he thought so in the spring of 1937 illustrated several things about Mitch Hepburn: his disdain for traditional democratic processes, coupled with his growing fascination for untrammelled power; his weakness for neatly packaged solutions, especially when these were wrapped in the flattery of a powerful friend; and his increasing tendency (eventually to prove disastrous) of permitting his personal vendetta with Mackenzie King to dictate political decisions and policies.

Throughout the province, reaction to the coalition "kite" was puzzled. In Toronto, the *Evening Telegram,* pretty much in the dark about the affair, thought it was a good idea to combat "class warfare." The *Globe and Mail* was disappointed that the plan had been rejected. Only the *Star* came out decisively against union government, terming it "one of the most dangerous proposals in the history of Ontario politics." Hepburn's flirting with the plan was "a blunder so fatal that only prompt recognition of the natural result can save him. . . . It is easy to imagine from what politically amateurish source such a suggestion emanated. It is not so easy to imagine how an experienced politician came to accept it . . . a coalition against labour would be naked fascism."[2]

The published reports that Mitch Hepburn had supported the plan seemed calculated to damage the Liberals politically. The leader's political luck held, however, and ironically it was the Conservatives who were hurt by the proposal. On May 5, only a short time after he had definitely rejected the proffered union, Earl Rowe spoke at Arthur and tried to set the coalition rumours at rest so far as his own Party was concerned: "If any suggestion of coalition were even considered, who would we be uniting against? Coalition would either stifle constructive opposition in the Legislature of the Province, and give endorsation to the establishment of a dictatorship, or it would be a definite refusal by those charged with responsibility to institute progressive legislation." In carefully chosen words, the Tory leader then enunciated his Party's policy concerning labour unions: "The Liberal-Conservative party stands for the right of employees to bargain collectively through their own representatives, chosen by the workers through the medium of secret ballot free from improper influence, coercion, or intimidation."

The next day, the resignation of the chief Conservative organizer and Rowe's lieutenant in Ontario, George Drew, was announced. Drew had resigned, so he said, because he disagreed with his leader's labour policy and supported Hepburn's stand on unions: "I am in complete agreement with him that the CIO should be prevented from exploiting Canadian labour." The only trouble with that explanation (as the general public was to learn more than a year later, in December, 1938, when Drew replaced Rowe as Conservative leader) was that it was not fully accurate. Drew had actually resigned as organizer on April 30, five days before the Arthur speech. The immediate reason for his resignation was not a difference concerning labour policy (Rowe later claimed that the "policy was fully discussed with Col. Drew and received his endorsement before he considered resigning as organizer"). It was Rowe's refusal to accept the coalition plan that occasioned Drew's resignation.

Although Drew had been Hepburn's bitterest opponent in the East Hastings by-election, the *Star* reported that a rapprochement had been effected, and Drew would enter a union government, probably as Attorney General. (As early as April 25, in fact, Drew informed the Lieutenant Governor that he had been offered the Attorney Generalship in a union government. Dr. Bruce at that time "advised him to do nothing without taking Rowe with him, which he had not planned on doing." Three days later, Drew phoned Dr. Bruce to say "that he had more or less decided to join the Govt. even if Rowe did not and was preparing a statement.") Several times Drew urged Rowe to accept the union-government proposals. On the night of April 29, 1937, Rowe later recalled, when he was in Ottawa to confer with R. B. Bennett, Drew phoned him at the Chateau Laurier and begged him not to close the door on coalition until he could see him again. Next morning, at the Albany Club in Toronto, Drew made his final effort to persuade Rowe to accept. He failed. "I refused," Rowe recalled later, "and pointed out it would be a gross betrayal of their confidence for me as a leader to end the Conservative Party that way." Drew then told Rowe that he had had several interviews with powerful interests that were urging a coalition of the Parties and reiterated his reasons for union government, chief of which was that it could more effectively combat Communism and "effect reforms which every thinking person believes should be carried out, but which, in the very nature of party politics, are extremely difficult for any party to do."

It was a grand and glorious vision, a government gleaming with efficiency from the Eastern Counties to the Manitoba border. While the voice was the voice of George Drew, the Conservative leader may well have suspected that the hands behind the scheme were the hands of George McCullagh. In any event, as Rowe recalled the Albany Club meeting: "Col. Drew stated to me that the time had come to end the two-party system in Ontario, and he strongly favoured coalition and that unless I agreed to coalition he would resign. Col. Drew resigned that afternoon." George McCullagh was disgusted. "Is it any wonder Colonel Drew rebelled?" complained the *Globe and Mail*. "It is amazing that Honourable Earl Rowe finds anyone, except the Reds and the Pinks and others who thrive on discontent and agitation, to stay with him."

What was more amazing was that Mitch Hepburn had emerged from a sticky wicket not only unscathed but stronger than ever. By entertaining the coalition proposal, he retained the support of the *Globe and Mail*,

George McCullagh, and the mining men, threw the provincial Conservative Party into a tizzy that resulted in Earl Rowe's losing his chief lieutenant and retained his base on the back concessions. That was the report the Premier received from organizers in the field. On June 1, 1937, when coalition talk had almost ceased, he wrote confidentially to R. S. Colter, the Liberal Member for Haldimand-Norfolk: "From information I have received from our own organizers, it would appear that the rural people are solidly behind the Government, insofar as its labor policies are concerned. One of our men reported having interviewed fifty ardent Conservatives, thirty-seven of whom are heartily behind the administration."

Those figures, if accurate, would indicate a high defection of Conservative voters. Some Tory strategists were hopeful that the Party was returning to normal after the labour controversy and George Drew's damaging resignation. On May 17, Donald Hogarth expressed this hope to Dr. Robert Manion:

> Things are settling down a bit in the matter of the CIO controversy and I think some of the nabobs who in the past have at least given lip service to the Conservative party, are beginning to see that they have permitted themselves to be influenced by the ballyhoo and ridiculous propaganda inspired by the *Globe and Mail*. Out of it I think Earl has immeasurably increased his prestige, has established himself as a strong man who is not to be stampeded or forced to take an unsound position.[3]

If things were "settling down a bit" for the Conservatives, they soon blew sky-high again for the Liberals. The evening of June 3 was a pleasant one in Toronto, the temperature about sixty-five degrees. At Loew's Theatre on Yonge Street, the patrons for thirty-two cents could laugh at Wallace Beery in "The Good Old Soak." A couple of blocks away, at the Royal York Hotel, the officers of the Canadian Life Insurance Association were holding their annual banquet. The ballroom was crowded as the guest speaker, Premier Mitchell F. Hepburn, rose to address the company's executives and their wives.

Mitch Hepburn was in good form. Frequent applause punctuated his remarks as he ticked off the record of his Government. He reviewed the labour issue and promised again that he would never tolerate CIO lawlessness in the Province of Ontario. At this statement the clapping from the men and their well-gowned ladies was prolonged. Mitch Hepburn waited for it to cease before continuing: "I can speak only for Ontario. I cannot speak for Canada, because we have a vacillating Government at Ottawa. And now I am going to make a serious statement, one that will probably make a headline." The audience was quiet as Mitch Hepburn said: "I am a Reformer. But I am not a Mackenzie King Liberal any longer. I will tell the world that, and I hope he hears me."

The break, long in the making, was finally out in the open. The Premier elaborated his reasons for this extraordinary statement in a letter to his friend, the Liberal Premier of British Columbia, T. D. "Duff" Pattullo. He had "been deeply disappointed" at the federal Party's failure to carry out their 1935 campaign promises, particularly a lowering of the tariff and a genuine national bank. According to Hepburn, the federal leader had promised him, at the opening of the 1935 campaign, that both these policies would be adopted. "Neither promise has been fulfilled and the present setup of the so-called National Bank is a farce, a glaring example of the insincerity of King and his associates."

King's policy on relief payments and public works also rankled Hepburn. "Following his election, we endeavoured to settle with him regarding road construction, carried on largely to benefit the Federal party prior to and during the election, but we received much worse treatment than Bennett ever conceived of." Relief grants to Ontario, according to Hepburn, had been arbitrarily cut: "Rogers asked me to send officials to Ottawa to confer with regard to the general relief situation. On arrival there, our officials were told that everything had been settled by Order-in-Council and there was nothing more to discuss." Hepburn's complaint was that Ottawa's actions were conceived arbitrarily and executed unilaterally. "The attitude of King and his associates has been to treat the Ontario Government or anyone known to be friendly with our administration as so many burglars. Their whole policy has been one of studied insults, one heaped upon another."

The Ontario Premier did not intend to carry what he considered King's political unpopularity: "The King party, due to its callousness toward its own supporters, is in so much disfavour that I arrived at the point where I decided to break with them. I am quite prepared to answer for the sins of my own Government but not to carry King's as well." He referred to "the way they let me down during the CIO invasion of Ontario" and revealed that his treatment at the hands of King after the 1935 election still festered: "It is needless for me to point out that it was the friends of our Government who financed the federal candidates from Quebec to British Columbia. These men have been treated even more shamefully than the members of the Government." He then gave Pattullo an example of what he considered supreme federal ingratitude: "I indicated to King and Elliott last spring that we were seriously considering an appeal to the electors this fall, with the result that the Federal contribution to our mines and roads program has been practically cut in two. This was a further demonstration of appreciation on the part of those whom we supported so loyally during the Federal campaign." So far as he was concerned, Hepburn told Pattullo, "I am sick and disgusted with King and his whole outfit and want nothing more to do with them, politically or otherwise."

In his letter to Premier Pattullo outlining the genesis of his break with King, Mitch Hepburn did not refer to another source of friction causing the federal Liberals increasing concern: the Ontario Premier's continuing attempt not only to control all campaign finances in the province but also to name federal candidates. This effort accelerated after Hepburn, in November of 1936 formally notified federal organizer Norman Lambert that the provincial Liberals were breaking away from the federal organization. It came to a head in the federal by-election in West Hamilton in March, 1937. For several weeks prior to the by-election, there had been a struggle to control the naming of the Liberal candidate, between the provincial Liberals headed by Hepburn and his Minister of Highways and Public Works from Hamilton, T. B. McQuesten, and the federal Liberals whose strategy was directed by Norman Lambert and Hamilton organizer Bart Sullivan.

Lambert made several trips to Hamilton to try to arrange for the nomination of a suitable candidate. Among other things at stake was the control of patronage. Later Lambert summarized the struggle:

> Hamilton was dominated by a strong provincial Liberal organization under the control of Premier Mitchell Hepburn. . . . After an effort of several weeks in Hamilton to arrange for a suitable Liberal candidate, a nominating convention was held and resulted in the selection of the wrong man – one who represented the anti-federal machine of Mr. Hepburn and Mr. McQuesten, his Minister of Public Works. Mr. Kennedy O'Connor, the convention's choice, was defeated in the by-election, and West Hamilton was not redeemed until 1940, when it was won by Honourable Colin Gibson.

Because there was so much over-lapping between the Ottawa and Ontario organizations this friction at the constituency level and Hepburn's public breach with King complicated things enormously, especially for provincial Liberals. Not consulted about the split with the federal leader – uninformed, for the most part, about its real causes – the rank-and-file Liberal in the province was confused, his loyalties strained. One of Hepburn's friends, the Member for Leeds, George Fulford, told the Premier that there was much disappointment and resentment among the older Liberals in Leeds County over the break with King: "I find myself in a predicament because there is scarcely a thing you have done that I have not admired; and yet, on the other hand, I simply cannot and will not be disloyal to Mr. King."[4]

Most provincial Liberals experienced this predicament. One radical way to resolve it would have been to organize a new "left-wing" provincial Liberal party to oppose Hepburn under the leadership of a man like Arthur Roebuck. While some Liberals were vaguely considering this scheme, the Premier himself, with his usual despatch, was making plans to call an election. In May and June, he had assured his own followers privately that there would be no campaign in 1937 "unless," he wrote W. G. Nixon (Temiskaming), "some great crisis should develop, which I hope will not be the case." What had developed was not a great crisis but a great opportunity for the provincial Liberals to skewer the Conservatives on the CIO issue, an opportunity that a politician of Mitch Hepburn's stripe could not be expected to pass up. He told Pattullo confidentially on July 27, "I propose to dissolve the House within another six weeks. From reports we have from organizers and canvassers the situation looks very promising."

Once he had made up his mind, Mitch Hepburn moved swiftly to ensure that the situation would be more promising. He did a little fence-mending in his own riding of Elgin. Tenders were let for a new quarter-million-dollar swing-bridge at Port Stanley, a bridge that the southwestern voters of the riding had been promised by every politician in living memory. A mile from his farm home, Bannockburn, and four miles south of St. Thomas, construction began on a four-million-dollar mental hospital, the biggest Government project in the county's history. From Elgin, the Premier turned his attention to the province. His strategy was not so much to defend the record of his own administration (which David Croll, running as a straight Liberal "without labour pains," said was "a splendid one") but to define the issues so that Earl Rowe and the Tories would be on the defensive from the beginning. Before he announced an election date, Mitch Hepburn launched his campaign on August 12, 1937, surrounded by his ministers on a flower-strewn platform in lovely Pinafore Park in St. Thomas. It was his forty-first birthday and the eleventh anniversary of his first nomination.

Mitch Hepburn gave a fighting speech as he carved out the three issues on which the election would be fought. First was his anti-CIO policy. "The people will have to decide whether they want Lewis and lawlessness in this fair province of ours or whether they want it to remain a decent, law-abiding place in which to live." There was the need to protect Hydro users against the power barons and higher rates under the Tories. Finally the province required tighter succession-duty legislation to collect some fifty million dollars of estate taxes left untouched by the Conservatives when they were in power. (The succession-duty legislation passed by the Hepburn administration had been challenged in the courts; now the Premier promised to remedy any loopholes if returned to power.) If Hepburn could dominate the campaign with these issues, Rowe and the Tories would be placed in a hopeless position. With Mitch Hepburn on the attack, where he liked to be – and also on the side of law and order, lower hydro rates, and a "soak-the-rich" campaign – Earl Rowe might soon find himself defending foreign labour agitators, power barons, and deceased millionaires.

Mitch Hepburn lost no time putting Rowe and the Tories precisely in that position. In his third speech in as many days, the Premier told an enthusiastic crowd of nearly four thousand at an Oakville political picnic what would happen if the Tories won: lawless CIO agitators would be given free entry into the province to foment trouble (at Perth he elaborated on this to warn that American firms would be wary of establishing branches in the province should the Tories triumph); hydro rates (which were reduced a week before the election set for October 6) would go up and hydro would be dominated by the Quebec power barons; wealthy estates would again defraud the public treasury by avoiding succession duties. It was the 1934 campaign all over again – except that Mitch Hepburn really did not have to extend himself. The fact that George Henry and eight of his former ministers were running helped Hepburn immeasurably. Liberal advertising ridiculed "The Old Gang," picturing them bailing out the sinking Tory "Rowe Boat." "Scrape off the paint," Hepburn told a crowd at Beaverton, "and you have George Henry of Abitibi fame. . . . Mr. Rowe, for whom I have the highest regard personally, is just the front man. . . . His hands are tied, and George Henry will be treasurer again, if he gets the chance, and back you people will go to the era of debts and deficits."[5]

There was not much the Conservatives could do with that kind of attack; they could only try to counter Hepburn on the three issues he was stressing. The fact that they had to do this was a tribute to the Premier's choice of fighting ground. The most dangerous issue for Rowe was the CIO problem. Before the campaign began, some Tory strategists expected that the Premier would make the CIO his chief campaign plank and would misrepresent it in a manner difficult to refute. The trouble with Lewisism and the CIO issue was that in the campaign of 1937, as in the Oshawa strike itself, there was something unreal about it. To nail the CIO issue down, entangled as it was with Communism, was, to use a favourite phrase of Hepburn's, "like trying to nail jelly to the wall."

One Conservative who tried to do that was the man who succeeded George Drew as provincial campaign organizer, the respected Lindsay lawyer, Cecil Frost (brother of Leslie Frost, who would win Victoria for the Tories in 1937 and go on to become an Ontario Premier). In a letter to the *Globe and Mail*, Cecil Frost tried to nail Lewisism and the CIO issue to the wall:

If by "Lewisism" you mean sit-down strikes, sabotage or other criminal or illegal practices, the Liberal-Conservative Party would apply the same vigorous enforcement of law as it would against any other lawbreaker. If by vituperation against what you call "Lewisism" you mean the denial of the right of wage-earners to freedom of association, then may I point out there is not in existence and never has been any law, Provincial or Federal, to prevent such association. Neither Mr. Hepburn nor your paper have yet suggested the enactment of such a law.

Precisely. But emotional slogans are usually more effective on the hustings than dialectical distinctions.

That veteran Tory strategist, Donald Hogarth saw this early in the campaign. Referring to Rowe's sensible labour statement at Arthur, in which the Tory leader, like Cecil Frost, distinguished between illegal labour agitation and peaceful union organization, Hogarth prophetically warned Rowe of the political implications of his CIO policy:

I have felt for some time that our fortunes have been prejudiced by reason of misrepresentation and calculated propaganda in respect to your attitude on the CIO. . . . While your declaration of policy at Arthur would seemingly satisfy people who would reach their conclusion through facts, it is obvious to me that such is not the case as through press misrepresentation and propaganda, Hepburn is earmarked as the "Defender of the Faith," whilst you, as the leader of the Conservative party, are looked upon as a sympathizer of the CIO.

It was Hogarth's opinion (shared by Dr. Robert Manion) that before the CIO issue developed Hepburn had no chance of re-election. "I say without hesitation that he will sweep the Province if this is to be the issue on which the Election will be fought." Then Hogarth cut to the heart of the CIO as a political issue in 1937: "Please keep in mind that wherever I use the phrase 'CIO' I mean Communism. The general public have got it in their minds that the two things are associated and the fact that there is no substance to this impression cannot be got over to the public."

Indeed it could not, though horse-racer Earl Rowe, about as comfortable in front of a microphone as a skittish pacer at its first fall fair, gave it his best run. Again and again he told his audiences that his Party would not tolerate lawlessness in the province. When hecklers at Port Hope asked the Tory chief if he would keep foreign agitators out, he replied heatedly: "Mr. Hepburn admitted the other night he had no power to keep them out. It was just Huey Long political bluff. I tell you," he said smiling, "if Mr. Lewis or Mr. Hepburn breaks the law here after October 6, I'll put them both in the same jail."

Rowe's language at Sudbury was stronger. He charged that Hepburn's meddling had prolonged the Oshawa strike by a week, that his arbitrary action against the workers contained "the seeds of fascism." If Hepburn could by fiat outlaw a union, "why cannot some wilder Prime Minister say you cannot join some church, or some club or some other form of organization?" At St. Thomas, on the Premier's home ground, Rowe claimed that "Hepburn's Hussars" were merely organized to distribute Liberal patronage, then added caustically, "He threatened to throw John L. Lewis in jail if he came into Ontario and caused bloodshed. Who wouldn't?" In Oshawa, Rowe laid his position on the line: "The issue here was not law and order, but the right of free association."

It was simply no use. As the campaign moved into its final stretch, Hepburn increasingly stressed the issue to which his large crowds responded most enthusiastically. The CIO was mixed up with Communism; he had kept the CIO out; Earl Rowe and the Tories were against that policy. Therefore. . . . There were holes in that reasoning big enough to drive a pacer through. What Ontario was experiencing in the fall of 1937, however, was not a horse race but a barn-storming Hepburn political campaign. There was plenty of room in that for a little imagination. Mitch Hepburn had an excellent imagination. To the packed Granite Rink in St. Thomas, Federal Minister Ian Mackenzie beside him (with the assurance that the federal Liberals were behind him one hundred per cent), Hepburn explained why he had felt it necessary to recruit special forces at the time of the Oshawa strike: "The organization of that special force was well-advised, for our police had confidential reports that 15,000 Communists were ready to take part in any uprising whether it took place in Toronto or elsewhere. That special police force was not organized simply for the Oshawa strike."* As General Hogarth had warned Rowe, the CIO was firmly associated in the voters' minds with Communism and violence. Hepburn's entire campaign reinforced that association. Probably there was nothing Earl Rowe (or any other Conservative leader in 1937) could have done to make the voter realize that the connection was vastly exaggerated and, in any event, obscured the real question.

Rowe did not have much better luck with the other issues. He attempted to mount a serious campaign against the Hepburn Government's hydro policies. He contended that Hepburn's reckless cancelling of the contracts had left the province facing a power shortage. "Already the lives and the safety of the people of this province are endangered by the power shortage," Rowe told a meeting at Kemptville in Howard Ferguson's old riding. Mitch Hepburn replied that far from facing a shortage, the province held 120,000 horsepower in reserve and told a laughing audience at Beaverton that if sulky racer Earl Rowe did not know any more about horses than he did about horsepower he should get off the track: "Sometimes I think that Earl Rowe doesn't fully appreciate the

---

* Confidential reports reaching Hepburn during the Oshawa strike make no mention of this possible uprising. They do not indicate, in fact, evidence of violence anywhere. (PAO Hepburn Papers, 1937)

extent of 120,000 horsepower. I suggest that if he wants to find out some day he back that horse of his, Sparkplug, into the transmission lines, and I'll guarantee that Sparkplug will go a mile faster than he ever went before, and he'll drag Earl Rowe and all the remnants of the Tory Party along with him."

On hydro, as on labour, Mitch Hepburn had backed Rowe into a corner. The Premier explained the issue very simply: by cancelling the hydro contracts, he had given the province cheaper power; the Tories had fought the cancellation; therefore the election of the Tories would result in dearer power. Robert Manion warned Rowe of the danger: "The farmer vote may be opposed to you because of the decrease in power rates which Hepburn gave them through his repudiation." He urged Rowe to promise that the power rates would not go up. Rowe did this, pledging at the same time not to renew the contracts, but never to "hoist that black flag of repudiation again." These assurances availed little, as Hepburn played on the fears of higher hydro rates under the Tories. At Cobourg, in rural Northumberland, he made a statement that was by now vintage Hepburn. "If I have the choice between the power barons of Quebec and the farmers of the province of ours, I'm for the farmer every time."

It was the same with the succession-duty issue. When in office, according to Hepburn, the Tories had permitted millions in uncollected succession duties to slip through their hands. Most of these people were their wealthy friends, and they would not dare to investigate those estates now. There were at least forty-eight estates with uncollected duties running to seventy million dollars. "If you want all this money recovered, as it should be," the Premier said at Paris, "you need only vote for the present Government." In vain Rowe dared the Government to prosecute in the courts for uncollected duties. In vain (in one of the few memorable phrases of the campaign), the Tory chief accused Hepburn of "searching graveyards with a lantern." It was hopeless. Rowe was defending the big interests; Mitch Hepburn was on the side of the little man.[6]

Besides these frontal issues in the campaign of 1937, both leaders had to contend with threats from their rear. For the Premier the danger came from Martin Quinn and the separate school question; for the Conservative leader it was George Drew running as an independent Conservative, anti-CIO candidate in Wellington South. Quinn represented the more serious complication. By the time of the 1937 election, the intransigent Chairman of the Catholic Taxpayers' Association was convinced that the Premier, aided and abetted by the *Globe and Mail* (and the Catholic Cabinet Minister, Peter Heenan), had sold out the Catholics on the school issue. Though the *Globe and Mail* said the issue was dead, the Chairman was all for forcing Hepburn to make a public statement of his intentions before polling day.

On September 7, a month before the election, Quinn wrote a letter to Albert Murphy, a member of the CTA executive in London: "I have no confidence in Mr. Hepburn's willingness to go through with our legislation merely because he is convinced that such action is justified, and I am equally certain that in the absence of a pronouncement he will be prevented by his own followers and the *Globe and Mail* from doing so." If Hepburn did not make a statement by the following Friday, September 10, then, Quinn said, "I propose to ask him publicly for one." Murphy immediately phoned Quinn who reluctantly agreed to postpone his demand for a few days. It was to Hepburn's advantage to keep the school question out of the elections, and to accomplish this he worked through his French Catholic Mines Minister, Paul Leduc. Leduc was in close touch with Murphy who had replaced Quinn as the liaison between the CTA and the Government. On September 4, Murphy wrote Leduc: "I discussed the whole situation with Bishop Kidd [of London], and he agreed with me that silence on our part is essential at the present time." On September 10, Archbishop McGuigan of Toronto informed Quinn that the Ontario bishops, at a meeting in Ottawa on September 2, had decided that "Catholic papers and organizations should not discuss the school question during the election period, as no good can come of it, and our enemies might gladly seize upon anything said to make this an election issue."

The Conservative leader raised the issue on several occasions (as did George Henry and others), but he did not press it.* Rowe's main purpose was to smoke Hepburn out. "He owes the people a definite policy on this all-important issue," Rowe told a political meeting at Madoc. "What does he plan now?" He charged at Sault Ste. Marie that the Premier had deliberately bungled the school act and betrayed the Catholics. Although Rowe emphasized his complete support of the public school system, neither the Orange lodges nor the Toronto *Telegram* considered his position strong enough, and both these bastions of Toryism refused him a complete endorsement. Meanwhile, on September 27, Albert Murphy assured Hepburn that the Catholics would not raise the issue during the

---

* One prominent Conservative who felt that his Party had pussy-footed on the separate school issue in the campaign was Robert Manion, a Catholic, federal Member for Fort William, and soon to become national Tory leader. After the 1937 provincial election, he wrote to his son, complaining that he had been restricted to Northern Ontario for the provincial campaign: "It was only at the last moment that I came to believe it was a stupid Protestant campaign in which it was considered by the board of strategy that I should be kept somewhat in the background. . . . I have been telling a few straight truths to the Conservative group since the election, particularly that when a Party takes the silly attitude that it can ignore forty-two per cent of our people and still hope to win it shows rotten lack of brains. Our group has been catering to the extreme and bigotted [sic] Protestant group too damn long." (PAC Manion Papers, Robert Manion to his son, November 14, 1937)

campaign. This policy was "dictated by the continued trust in yourself and your Government inspired by your efforts in 1936," as well as the Premier's promise of a square deal for the Catholic elementary schools at the time that he had repealed the school bill. So the Catholics kept quiet while the more extreme Protestants were unhappy with Rowe's lack of militancy on the school issue.[7]

Hepburn succeeded admirably in excluding the contentious religious question from the 1937 campaign; Earl Rowe was less successful keeping his former chief organizer under wraps, with George Drew running as an Independent Conservative in Wellington South. That riding, glowed the *Globe and Mail,* should be gratified to have the opportunity "for representation by one of the keenest-minded, most outstanding men in public life." In his much-publicized campaign (also strongly supported by the *Telegram*), George Drew sounded not so much like a candidate running in a rural Ontario riding as a potential provincial leader. He made speeches outside the constituency, speeches that often sounded like the editorial pages of the *Globe and Mail.* Drew stressed the Communist threat to Canada; CIO organizers were "ruthless racketeers" and "worthless parasites." If he were elected, Drew would introduce legislation to control Communism. The *Globe and Mail* had previously advocated an Ontario version of Bill 98, the federal legislation dealing with subversives, which had been repealed.

In the interests of efficiency and good government, said Drew, the Legislature should be streamlined. The party system was too confining; often members were "nothing but pawns in the game of rigid party politics." "It is time to end the burlesque in the Legislature," Drew told an audience in his hometown of Guelph. Too often strong central Government was hamstrung by Party politics. The *Globe and Mail* had reached much the same conclusions expressed in a succinct sentence just before voting day: "There is no good reason for maintaining parties in a provincial campaign." Wisely Earl Rowe and his Party (which did not run a candidate in South Wellington) all but ignored Drew's philippics. When a heckler at Hamilton asked the Conservative leader where Drew was, Rowe snapped, "He may be with you but he is not with me . . . I have one hundred per cent loyal supporters in every riding except one, and I have never mentioned his name on any platform and I am not discussing it now."

As though the independent candidacy of his former lieutenant were not enough complication for the Conservative chief, the publisher of the *Globe and Mail* decided to take to the hustings against him. A few days before the voting, newspaper advertisements invited Ontario citizens to hear George McCullagh "Unmask the Politician." What they heard on a province-wide network the Saturday night before the election was a condemnation of the partisan political game as it was played in Canada; an indictment of Rowe for his CIO policy; unqualified support for George Drew; praise of Mitchell Hepburn's administrative record; and a bugle-blowing call to greatness with an emotional rendering of "Invictus" which the young publisher's wife had handed her husband before he left for the studio.

Earl Rowe (who told a Massey Hall crowd that his wife never gave him poetry to read) had nothing to match this. As for Mitch Hepburn, he did not need McCullagh's help. In the campaign's final days, everything was coming up roses. Despite his feud with Ottawa, at least half a dozen federal ministers were on the stump. Mackenzie King allowed that he had never experienced any serious difficulties with the Ontario Premier and he intended to vote for a Hepburn candidate. The Premier chose the scene of all the trouble for one of his final campaign appearances. His voice was a tired whisper, as he defended his CIO policy before a rambunctious meeting in the Oshawa Armouries. Fistfights broke out, and so large was the crowd that serious injuries were narrowly averted when several tiers of over-loaded seats crashed at the back of the Armouries. The Premier rode out the booing and near pandemonium to predict that his candidate in Oshawa, Gordon Conant, would be elected and his labour policy vindicated.

Earlier he told a meeting at Picton he had no doubt about the return of his Government or his own election in Elgin:

I'm just a human being like yourselves. If I have made mistakes, they have been mistakes of the heart. I have faith in the intelligence of people and all through this campaign I have appealed only to reason. They tell you of this terrible individual Hepburn, but the only thing I am going to say in my defence is that down in Elgin where I've always been a farmer and where I'll remain a farmer, they have given me increasing majorities, and this time they tell me they are going to give me the greatest ever of my long political career.[8]

They did indeed. Election day, October 6, 1937, was 1934 all over again. After voting with his wife at Union, and showing off his prize Percherons at his Bannockburn farm, Mitch Hepburn slipped into St. Thomas for a quick visit with his mother, Maggie, then went directly to the Masonic Temple on Talbot Street to hear the returns. It was the same dingy kitchen, with its uncovered pipes and the sink in the corner. The Premier was hunched over in a big chair with his wife, Eva, behind him, surrounded by Elgin Liberals, listening to the figures tapped out on the battered typewriter. Again the list of Liberal wins piled up headed by Elgin. Again an excited Mitch Hepburn jumped up: "It's a sweep, fellows, a sweep."

And it was, like 1934, a sweep. Because of the way in which the campaign had developed, especially on the CIO issue, no one had really expected the Conservatives to win. In contrast to the Hepburn forces (who were endorsed even by the Toronto *Star*), the Conservatives had little newspaper or financial support. As Donald Hogarth later explained to Robert Manion, the Liberals had so much campaign money "that they could not expend all that was handed to their organization." As for the Tories, "if it had not been for a couple of Conservative Dervishes, the campaign would have fallen flat from the lack of financial support."

Still, no one had anticipated a Liberal victory that would duplicate their 1934 sweep. Final figures showed that, while slightly increasing their share of the popular vote to just over fifty per cent (the Conservatives remained static at forty per cent), the Liberals dropped only three seats from their 1934 total. The Government won sixty-three seats to twenty-three for the Conservatives (a gain of six). Four other winners (two Progressives, one Independent Liberal, one UFO) gave the Government an effective total of sixty-seven. In Elgin, Mitch Hepburn won every municipality to pile up a record majority of nearly five thousand. The Premier won the heavily labour railroad poll by almost two to one.

Mitch Hepburn's win in Elgin was not surprising. Elgin still loved "the boy from Yarmouth." They would have loved him without the county's new roads, the swing-bridge at Port Stanley, and the mental hospital near St. Thomas. What was more surprising and more difficult to explain were some of the results in the rest of the province. In Centre-Simcoe, Hepburn's Minister of Education, Dr. Leonard Simpson, easily defeated Conservative leader Earl Rowe who, surrounded by his friends and neighbours at Newton Robinson, his farm home, congratulated "Premier Hepburn on his decisive victory," adding that he could take his first political defeat "as I have taken defeat in sports in days gone by." The defeated leader was not so magnanimous about what he considered "indifference of forces within our own ranks and those who thought they saw a short-cut to the seats of the mighty," an obvious reference to the defection of the business community and George Drew's advocacy of union government. Both Arthur Roebuck and David Croll, running as straight Liberals differing with Hepburn on his CIO policy, easily won re-election. In Oshawa, where the trouble began (and where former Liberal leader William Sinclair declined to stand), Gordon Conant held the seat for the Liberals. The Liberal vote in the city of Oshawa itself dropped sharply, most of it picked up by the CCF candidate.* The electors of Wellington South, however, lost a glorious opportunity to strike a blow against CIO lawlessness by decisively defeating Colonel George A. Drew.

Again the coalition of voting blocks that the Liberals had put together in 1934 held steady. The Catholics, the North, the farmers, even the workers for the most part, stayed with Hepburn. He had constructed an alliance between two groups of primary producers: the mining capitalists with the money, and the farmers on the back concessions with the votes. He had retained all his old platform magic and barbed-wire humour. At Tweed, he accused former Premier and Education Minister George Henry of putting an "amusement tax" on high school examination papers because, according to Henry, some pupils just tried for fun. This time round, thanks to the labour issue, he had the backing of the establishment, the financial interests, and the press.

Hepburn also retained in the 1937 campaign his sense of political strategy and his sensitivity to the breezes blowing at the grass roots. In 1934, he had out-generalled George Henry on the explosive liquor issue by transforming the question from one of the morality of drinking to the immorality of graft in Government circles; in 1937, on the politically dangerous labour question, he outmanoeuvred Earl Rowe by transposing the issue of labour's right to free bargaining into domination of Ontario's economy by foreign, Communistic agitators. It was a neat trick if one could get away with it. Mitch Hepburn got away with it.

There were times during the campaign when Mitch Hepburn referred proudly to his Government's record. As even Arthur Roebuck, David Croll, and the Toronto *Star* admitted, it was a generally good record. The Hepburn Government had cut taxes, paid a subsidy to municipalities, assumed the entire cost of the municipal share of Old Age Pensions and Mothers' allowances, just before the election passed an Order-in-Council for pensions to the blind (the first province in Canada to do so), slashed hydro rates, added some two thousand miles of county roads to the provincial system of highways, and announced the first budget surplus in years. It was not this record, however, but the Tories' weaknesses that were exploited in the campaign of 1937. Mitch Hepburn always felt more at home slamming his opponent against the ropes than standing at the centre of the ring reading a program of events.

The Premier now had the opportunity for a Cabinet reorganization. Replacements were needed for Croll and Roebuck; two Cabinet Ministers had been defeated, Agriculture Minister Duncan Marshall (Peel), and Health Minister Dr. Albert Faulkner (West Hastings). The Premier did not lack for advice on Cabinet appointments, particularly from the *Globe and Mail* which (excepting Drew's defeat) had been delighted with the election results. Hepburn had made glaring mistakes in the selection of his first Cabinet; now he had the opportunity to rectify these. In addition to other reforms – abolishing patronage, establishing a sound civil service based on ability – the newspaper hoped that Hepburn "perhaps could be so bold as to venture the assertion that the Provincial Legislatures are unwieldly and cumbersome and leeches on the taxpayers' money." Still,

---

* Over the province, the total CCF vote declined almost one-third from 1934, and the Party was not a significant factor in the election.

if a provincial Legislature were to remain in Ontario, the newspaper, in language that verged on the apocalyptic, described the man who should lead it: "On the horizon, endowed with a brilliant mind, supported by loyal fellow citizens, stands the figure of Mitchell F. Hepburn. To him has been thrown the torch, and by his acts he shall be judged. No man ever had a greater opportunity for genuine public service." It was an interesting editorial coming from the man who on August 28 had ventured to one of the Premier's friends his opinion of Hepburn and Rowe. According to McCullagh, neither the Premier nor the leader of the Opposition was fit to run a pub.

When he finished writing that editorial, George McCullagh dropped the Premier a note reiterating most of its leading ideas. He urged Mitch Hepburn to exhibit courage and foresight in choosing his new Cabinet. If only he did that, Hepburn's second administration would be immeasurably strengthened. McCullagh did not disguise his admiration for Hepburn's own ability and leadership capacity. Nevertheless, he pointed out that his government, during its first term, had been less effective than it might have been, because two or three of its ministers had not measured up. Now was the opportunity to coldly appraise the Cabinet, cut out the dead wood, and introduce new men into Hepburn's team. Moreover, McCullagh urged, if the Premier would only play down political partisanship, abolish patronage entirely, and slash government costs, he would make his mark on history and leave a legacy of statesmanship second to none. In his letter to the Premier on cabinet-making, McCullagh also provided one of the keys to the sometimes stormy relationship between the two men. He admitted that both of them had impetuous dispositions. Sometimes that made communication difficult. For that reason, among others, the publisher intimated that it might be wiser and more prudent if he stuck to his office and the job of running his newspaper and permitted Mitch Hepburn to run his government as best he could. A lot of politicians, both at Queen's Park and in Ottawa, would have agreed about the wisdom of that.[9]

With George McCullagh running his newspaper for the moment, Mitch Hepburn had the opportunity to "coldly appraise" his Cabinet. The appraisal did not take long. On Thanksgiving day, October 11, 1937, the Premier motored from St. Thomas to Toronto, met his old ministers, and next night in the green-carpeted offices of the Lieutenant Governor, the new Cabinet was sworn in, probably the fastest job of Cabinet-building in the province's history.

The key Cabinet appointment was that of the solid straight-laced Gordon Conant of Oshawa to the post of Attorney General. Other new ministers who would join the holdovers – Harry Nixon, Peter Heenan, Tim McQuesten, Paul Leduc, Dr. L. J. Simpson – included: Health, Harold Kirby (Eglinton); Welfare and Municipal Affairs, Eric W. Cross

(Haldimand-Norfolk); Agriculture, P. M. Dewan (Oxford); Labour, M. M. MacBride (Brantford); Public Works, Colin Campbell (Hepburn's long-time friend, again defeated in Addington, for whom a seat would be found). William L. Houck (Niagara Falls) was made Hydro Vice-Chairman and Minister without Portfolio. A. St. Clair Gordon (Kent West), also a Minister without Portfolio, increased the Cabinet to four-teen. It was a young Cabinet, the average age just forty-seven. The *Globe and Mail* was pleased with the new administration: "Mr. Hepburn's Cabinet is a marked improvement on his first one." Gordon Conant's appointment was "admirable in every way," though McCullagh was dis-appointed to find that Lands and Forests Minister Peter Heenan had not been dropped. The Toronto *Telegram* was much less enthusiastic about Hepburn's choices: "It is . . . a disappointment to find him surrounded in his new Cabinet by such a bunch of mediocrities as the Hon. Gentle-men who were sworn in yesterday."[10] This was too harsh. The new Minis-ters, if lacking the progressive zeal of a Croll or Roebuck, were, in the main, solid acquisitions. The thirty-two-year-old lawyer from Norfolk, Eric Cross, was a very able young man. Conant's appointment to the sensitive post of Attorney General would give the administration a more conservative hue, but there would be more harmony. Mitch Hepburn (and quite a few Liberal members for that matter) had never felt very comfortable with Arthur Roebuck.

One piece of unfinished business that required the Premier's immediate attention was what to do about Lieutenant Governor Herbert Bruce and his official residence, Chorley Park, that impressive structure of French, chateau-type architecture standing in fifteen acres of parkland overlook-ing the Rosedale ravine. Ever since the 1934 campaign, Hepburn had pledged that Chorley Park (which he would call "a haven for broken-down English aristocrats who should be paying for their rooms at the hotels") would be closed. When the 1937 election was called, Dr. Bruce had requested Hepburn not to raise the issue during the campaign, and the Premier complied.* Now that Bruce's term was to expire in a few weeks, the problem of Chorley Park and of his successor had to be faced immediately. Because this was a federal appointment, it could cause more friction between Queen's Park and Ottawa. Mackenzie King hoped not.

---

* On that occasion the Premier explained to the Bruces that it was Joseph Atkin-son of the *Star* who had forced him to attack Chorley Park in the 1934 cam-paign. He also referred to Atkinson's attitude in the Oshawa strike. "When Hep-burn refused to follow Atkinson's dictates over the CIO Atkinson in his office shrieked with rage, and when something was brought up with regard to the cor-rect report being put in the *Star*, he said, 'The Star will print what I tell it to.' " To this, the Lieutenant Governor's lady commented tartly, "The *Star* and Atkin-son are a menace to Society." (Journal of Mrs. Herbert Bruce, August 25, 1937)

King was optimistic that Hepburn's overwhelming victory with federal help had smoothed the situation over. Two days after the election, King expressed this hope to a prominent federal Liberal supporter, Toronto lawyer E. G. Long: "May I extend to you my warm congratulations on Tuesday's results. After all the Federal Ministers have done in the recent campaign, and Federal Members as well, I hope we have heard the last of any lack of co-operation between the Government at Ottawa and Toronto."

Fond hope. On October 8, King wrote the Ontario Premier noting that Dr. Bruce's term as Lieutenant Governor would expire on November 1. "My colleagues and I," King continued, "are prepared to recommend to His Excellency the extension of Dr. Bruce's term for at least another year, should His Honour be agreeable to continue in office for that length of time, and should this extension meet with your approval." King said that he had intimated this to Dr. Bruce but had explained to him that he wanted to confer with the Premier after the election, "and if the extension of his term for that period did not meet with your approval, I would wish to consider the matter further."

On the whole, Hepburn and the Lieutenant Governor had got on well since 1934. Often the Premier would visit Bruce at Chorley Park, though he would never take a meal there. Hepburn's refusal to attend the annual state banquet at the time of the Legislature's opening had ended that glittering affair. The Lieutenant Governor had been quite disappointed when the Premier had decided not to attend George VI's Coronation in May, 1937. He recorded his reaction in his autobiography, *Varied Operations*:

> I felt sure that this experience would be beneficial to him and alter his attitude toward society generally. He so far committed himself to say that he and Mrs. Hepburn would go if they could accompany us and that he would rely upon my advising him with regard to social functions and said that Mrs. Hepburn would be taking up with my wife the matter of clothes she would need. A few days later he informed me that he had changed his mind and decided not to go.

Except for the annoying problem of the closing of Government House, Dr. Bruce recalled that his relationship with his first minister "could not have been more pleasant." Hepburn himself brought up the matter of Bruce's term and Chorley Park on the night of October 12, when the cabinet was sworn in. To Bruce's utter "amazement he said that he was going to ask Mr. King to reappoint me for another term if I were willing to accept." Mrs. Bruce recorded the Premier's surprising *volte-face* in her journal:

He had changed his mind over the whole situation, realizing now what an important part a Lieut. Gov. played in the running of a Province, in these days of Communism we needed it and the House. Said that Herbert had shown him all this and was going to ask Mr. King to reappoint him. At the same time saying that he was all right at executive work but hated entertaining, and agreed that the Govt. should give an entertainment allowance as the Lieut. Gov. was the logical person to do it.

So the problem of the Lieutenant Governor's term and the closing of Chorley Park seemed to have been amicably settled on terms satisfactory both to the federal and provincial Liberal leaders.

In fact, something occurred that again caused Mitch Hepburn to reverse himself completely. Possibly it was resentment that a plan to have his defeated Agricultural Minister, Duncan Marshall, appointed a Senator had not been well received at Ottawa. He curtly wrote King that the federal leader's suggestion to extend Bruce's term was unacceptable to the Ontario Government.* Moreover, if King were interested in Hepburn's choice for Lieutenant Governor, he had just the man, none other than his defeated Minister of Agriculture:

> If you are seeking a nominee of this Government, I would suggest the name of the Honourable Duncan Marshall, who for many years past has rendered a great deal of service, both for the Provincial and Federal Liberal organizations. After consulting with my colleagues, I find they are all in agreement and insofar as the social obligations are concerned, we could place at Mr. Marshall's disposal both the offices of the Lieutenant Governor and the Speaker's Chamber which should suffice.

Mitch Hepburn continued: "In any appointment that you may make, please bear in mind that it is our intention to close Chorley Park on October 31." If all the ghosts of the King-Hepburn feud were to be resurrected, Halloween night seemed as appropriate a time as any.

On October 19, the Premier told the astonished Dr. Bruce of his decision to close Government House and of his intention to obtain "someone to take the position [of Lieutenant-Governor] who would entertain in the speaker's chambers." King was no more prepared to accept Hepburn's

---

* According to Dr. Bruce, the Premier told him on the night of October 12 that he favoured extending the Lieutenant Governor's term. Hepburn's letter to King categorically rejecting this plan is also dated October 12. Possibly there is an error in dates because it seems inconceivable that even Mitch Hepburn was capable of so swift a reversal.

suggestions concerning a federal appointment in 1937 than he had been in 1935. This time he decided to approach the provincial Premier directly. On the occasion of a trip to Toronto on October 22, King visited Hepburn at Queen's Park to see if some compromise could be reached. After the meeting, he told Dr. Bruce "he had spent a stormy hour and a half with Hepburn in the morning, who would not give way at all." Governor General Tweedsmuir, also in Toronto, gave Dr. Bruce his understanding of the difficulty. "Hepburn had asked King for a senatorship for Duncan Marshall . . . King had refused and as a retaliation Hepburn said he would close G. H. & asked for Marshall's appointment as Lieut. Gov." That evening at dinner at Chorley Park, Mackenzie King sat beside Mrs. Bruce: "He spent most of the time running down Hepburn and his behaviour. He attributes it all to drink. Said he did not win the first Prov. Election, a black dog could have won against George Henry. Was most emphatic about our staying on, and told me to tell Herbert that whatever happens we must stick it out." The Prime Minister again urged Dr. Bruce to accept another term: "He was most anxious to have Government House kept open and felt that by my good relations with Mr. Hepburn a deal could be made with the latter. . . . Mr. King expressed his willingness to appoint Mr. Marshall to the Senate, hoping that it would ensure Government House being kept open."[11]

Dr. Bruce seriously considered this proposal, encouraged by the almost unanimous approval in the press for an extension of his term. By now rumours of the possible appointment of Duncan Marshall were circulating freely. Marshall had begun his political career with the United Farmers of Alberta, where he had been a Cabinet Minister, later had come to Ontario where he had been a Liberal political organizer off and on for twenty years. As Mitch Hepburn's Agricultural Minister, Marshall was primarily known as the man who spent $18,000 for a Scottish bull, Millhill's Ransom, which later died prematurely at the Guelph Agricultural College. (At the time of the animal's sudden death, Premier Hepburn explained to the Legislature that Millhill's Ransom died of "acute gastritis" shortly after being inspected by the members of the Legislature's Agricultural Committee.) A good platform speaker, Marshall was a rough, haughty man, somewhat contemptuous of his constituents (who reciprocated by replacing him with Conservative Thomas L. Kennedy in the 1937 election), none too popular with either his Cabinet colleagues or the Liberal caucus.

Public opposition to the appointment of an anti-establishment man like Marshall increased all across the province. The Toronto *Telegram* warned: "The office of Lieutenant-Governor should be preserved from becoming the $10,000 haven for a discarded Member of the Cabinet." The *Globe and Mail* termed Marshall's rumoured appointment "ridiculous" and advised King not to make it "to please the whims of Mr. Hepburn." George McCullagh personally tried to salvage the situation. He had a long session with the Premier, in company with William Rundle, a strong Mackenzie King Liberal who told the Bruces what had occurred. The Premier, wrote Mrs. Bruce, "had let off very badly on King's treatment of him, and said he was through with him."

> He had never done a thing to help him, and he would never ask him to do anything again. It boiled down to McCullagh getting a promise out of him that if McCullagh could get an intermediary to ask King for a senatorship and it would be granted, would he keep G.H. open. He agreed but only on condition that Herbert was reappointed as Lieut. Gov. because he liked him.

Meanwhile, the fierce opposition in the press to Marshall's appointment was reflected by the Liberals themselves. It is extremely doubtful, despite Hepburn's assurance to King, that the Cabinet unanimously favoured Marshall. There was general support from rank-and-file Liberals for the closing of Chorley Park, but Marshall was another matter. A letter to the Premier from George Fulford, former provincial member for Leeds, was typical. "I do not intend to be presumptuous, but for God's sake don't make D. M. Lieutenant Governor." A prominent Torontonian who had backed Hepburn since 1934, Dr. Joseph Sullivan, said he was withdrawing his support unless the Premier changed his mind "which has become perverted on this issue." So vociferous had the controversy become that Dr. Bruce felt his own position was now intolerable. "The situation which had arisen," he noted in *Varied Operations,* "by this time had been taken up by the press which was loud in its denunciation of Mr. Hepburn's proposals. This put me in an embarrassing position, and on November 16 I sent my resignation to Ottawa and informed Mr. King that I would not accept another term." Mrs. Bruce recorded the last straw in her diary for November 15: "The climax came when this morning the Department refused to have the chimneys cleaned or give new electric light bulbs through a servant."

Moreover, the compromise that George McCullagh tried to arrange between King and Hepburn also failed because of the massive dislike and distrust of both leaders. Hepburn informed McCullagh that King could still help him by giving Marshall a Senatorship. But King, according to McCullagh, would not do this without a written request from Hepburn and a written promise that he would keep Chorley Park open. King himself was still seeking some kind of solution. He withheld the announcement of Dr. Bruce's resignation, sent another emissary to see Hepburn and by Tuesday, November 23, a compromise of sorts had been worked out and Ontario had a new Lieutenant Governor. He was Albert Matthews, sixty-four, member of a prominent Toronto brokerage firm, and a long-time King Liberal who had helped Hepburn in his election campaigns.

Matthews' appointment left Duncan Marshall an unemployed politician sitting on his farm near Oakville. He was grateful for the fight Mitch Hepburn had put up and there was always the Senate. He wrote Hepburn on November 25:

> I want you to know how much I appreciate the support you gave me re the office just filled. I know you stayed until the breaking point and nothing further was possible.
>   I also know that you are supporting me for the Senatorship which I will appreciate very much. In such a position I may be able to be of some assistance to you and if so will be at your command. I think we understand each other.[12]

A few weeks later Mackenzie King appointed Duncan Marshall to the Senate. Chorley Park was closed, never to be reopened as a residence for the Lieutenant Governor.

The controversy over Chorley Park and Duncan Marshall's appointment revealed much about Mitchell Hepburn: his contempt for tradition and the representatives of the establishment, even of the monarchy (partly a heritage of his dissenting Elgin background, partly an inherent hostility toward authority of any kind) complicated by a gauche uneasiness with social forms and graces; his tenacious loyalty to his friends (or those he thought were his friends); a willingness to use almost anything, even a high public office, to advance his fight with Mackenzie King; a growing inclination to ride rough-shod over the advice of his Liberal colleagues; the old habit of digging into a position, even an untenable one, when crossed or thwarted. The conflict also revealed something about the tactics and the shape of things to come in the King-Hepburn feud. The federal leader, patient, prepared to bide his time, calculating, preferring to work out a solution behind the scenes, opting for compromise rather than confrontation, refusing, above all, to come out into the open and fight; and Mitch Hepburn, fiery and unpredictable, increasingly losing the self-control so necessary in a public figure, trying to lure the older man onto a front-page brawl where Hepburn's invective could be brought to bear with maximum effect. Mackenzie King's superhuman ability to sit tight in the eye of the hurricane while the winds of criticism blew all about him was equalled only by Mitch Hepburn's frustration that his fulminations provoked nothing but silence.

These traits, particularly the strategy of Mackenzie King, were revealed in the controversy over hydro power, which erupted again in the latter part of 1937. During the election campaign Earl Rowe had tried to make a major issue of hydro by charging that because Hepburn cancelled the power contracts the province would soon be facing a critical power shortage. The Premier denied this, claiming that Ontario had ample power reserves. His Government's policy, he told a meeting at Thorold, was "to make our Province more and more dependent on our own power resources, and we propose to proceed very slowly as far as any further contracts with the Province of Quebec are concerned." All was not as rosy with Hydro, however, as Hepburn had led the electors to believe.

On June 8, 1937, before the Premier announced the election, he conferred at his farm home with the chief Municipal Hydro Engineer, R. T. Jeffery, who had requested the meeting. Jeffery told Hepburn that hydro affairs were fast drifting into chaos, that communications between Hydro Chairman T. Stewart Lyon and his staff engineers had broken down, and that the system was facing disaster unless some settlement could be reached with the Beauharnois Company, which had a suit before the courts for damages on the cancelled contract and back costs for the hydro contracted for. Hepburn listened courteously and advised Jeffery to take the matter up with his Ministers, Harry Nixon and Paul Leduc. Two weeks later, the Ontario Appeal Court confirmed the legality of the Beauharnois contract, and ordered Ontario to pay back costs and $600,000 in damages. Immediately the government decided to appeal the case to the Privy Council, an appeal that Jeffery had warned the Premier most lawyers thought would fail.

Except for Rowe's warnings during the campaign that a power shortage was imminent and the Premier's denials, the hydro issue remained dormant until just after the election. Then hydro matters began to light up behind the scenes. On October 16, the day on which Hydro announced that in September there had been a sharp increase in the demand for power (thirteen per cent over the previous year in the Niagara system), officials of the Beauharnois company learned that the Government might be interested in negotiating a new contract. One stumbling block to these negotiations would certainly be Lyon who had consistently opposed settling with Beauharnois, presumably with the Premier's backing. Hepburn moved swiftly to remove that obstacle. Two weeks after the election, he demanded and received Lyon's resignation. He then announced that Hydro's Chief Engineer, Thomas Hogg (who had warned of a power shortage in January, 1937), would replace Lyon as Hydro Chairman. Almost immediately negotiations began with Beauharnois for a new contract, and these proceeded so quickly that by early December the Government approved revised contracts not only with Beauharnois but with the other Quebec companies, Maclaren's and Gatineau, as well. (The fourth company, Ottawa Valley, had signed a revised contract in February, 1937.)

These new agreements called for taking all the power contracted for under the Conservative contracts except for about twenty thousand horsepower. The terms of the new contracts were somewhat better than the old ones: the price per horsepower was reduced from $15 to $12.50; if new taxation were levied during the course of the contracts by the Quebec Government, the companies, not Ontario Hydro, would absorb it, and the companies would be paid in Canadian not American funds.[13]

These were better terms (the Commission estimated net savings to the province of nearly eighty millions), but it was still humiliating for Mitch Hepburn to renew contracts that he had cancelled and had vowed he would never sign again. That bitter pill was not made any sweeter by accusations both in the press and by the Conservative Opposition that the Premier had deceived the electorate during the campaign by his assurance of ample power. "I charged at the time he was making those statements," said Leopold Macaulay, newly appointed Conservative House leader (Earl Rowe, while retaining the leadership, had decided to run again for the federal House), "that he knew Ontario was faced with a power shortage." These charges finally led to the appointment of a committee of the Legislature in 1938 to determine whether the Premier had deceived the electorate about the power situation, and whether the Government had secretly negotiated with the power companies prior to the 1937 election.

The Committee divided along Party lines. The majority Liberal report intimated that a power shortage threatened before the 1937 election, but that Hydro Chairman Lyon had deliberately kept this information from the Premier. No negotiations with Beauharnois had taken place prior to November 1, 1937. The minority report signed by Macaulay found that Hepburn knew for months it would be necessary to negotiate new contracts immediately after the election. "The only reasonable conclusion from the facts disclosed is that Mr. Hepburn deliberately misled the public and sought re-election upon an undertaking which he was well aware could not be fulfilled." What emerges from these conflicting conclusions is that Hepburn was aware prior to the election that a power shortage was a distinct possibility, that he told the voters there was ample power, and that, strictly speaking, no formal negotiations with the power companies took place until after the election. Just before the election campaign began, Provincial Secretary Harry Nixon told Lieutenant Governor Bruce that the Government "have enough power to last them for this year only." More damaging, in view of Hepburn's repeated denials, he informed Dr. Bruce that the Government "were going to have a deal with Beauharnois but Roebuck was going to come out against it so they called it off."[14]

The new contracts posed an immediate problem for the Hepburn administration, a problem that unfortunately involved Mackenzie King's Government. Instead of facing an imminent power shortage, Ontario now had contracted for more power than could be used in the immediate future. That, of course, was the reason for trying to cancel them in the first place.

It was the reason that almost from the time it took office the Hepburn Government tried to make provision for its power needs from provincial waters, independently of Quebec. This was the "back to Niagara" policy which Lyon advocated as Hydro Chairman and Hepburn had referred to in the 1937 campaign. It involved increasing the flow of water at Niagara in order to generate more power. From an engineering point of view, this could be done by constructing dams at Long Lac to divert water (which normally flowed to Hudson's Bay) into the Great Lakes, thereby increasing the flow at Niagara. The engineering problem was simple compared to the jurisdictional one. The rate of flow at Niagara was governed by an international agreement with the United States that established the division of waterpower flow between the province and New York State. For Ontario to obtain all the additional power from the Long Lac diversion, it would be necessary to renegotiate these treaties.

About a year after Hepburn took office, he requested the federal government to ask permission of the United States to increase the flow at Niagara by diverting water at Long Lac. The American Government would have acceded to this request on condition that the entire St. Lawrence Seaway development was proceeded with. Ever since this project had been defeated by the United States Senate in 1934, President Franklin Roosevelt had urged the Canadian Government to join the United States to build the Seaway. In any joint project, Ontario would play a large role. The Premier of Ontario was opposed to the Seaway for two reasons: it would provide competition to Canadian railways, already losing money; so far as the power aspects of the project were concerned, if the courts enforced the Quebec contracts, Ontario would have a surplus of power. From Ontario's point of view, the St. Lawrence Seaway was economical neither as a transportation avenue nor a power producer.

This was the position that Hepburn took when King visited him in his Queen's Park office in March, 1937, to ascertain how the Premier felt about Roosevelt's proposal to proceed with the Seaway. Hepburn did not close the door on Ontario's participation, but he would make no definite commitments until the Quebec power contracts were settled. After the Ontario election of October 6, 1937, the American Government again asked King to sound Hepburn out about the whole St. Lawrence development. King did so, and the Ontario Premier repeated his stock objection: Ontario had no need of power. When he made that reply on November 25, 1937, Mitch Hepburn knew he was in a box on the power situation. He had been boxed in from two directions: the American Government had rejected his plan to develop more power at Niagara unless he agreed to a full Seaway scheme; the Ontario courts had overturned his hydro legislation cancelling the Quebec contracts. Now, with the contracts renegotiated, Ontario Hydro had a surplus of power on its hands, a surplus that if it could not be disposed of economically would be a severe drain on Mitch Hepburn's treasury and might result in higher rates to consumers.

What could be done to get out of this box? Queen's Park had a plan: export the surplus to power-hungry New York State. There was a short in that circuit too. To export power required the consent of the federal Government, a prohibition based on the Electricity and Fluid Export Act of 1907. In 1929, an amendment to this Act (apparently not opposed by Hepburn, who was a federal Member at the time) specifically prohibited the granting of licences to export power except with the consent of Parliament. Although this amendment failed to pass in the Senate, Mackenzie King felt it was still the mind of the Commons. That was the jurisdictional situation when the Hepburn Government in the fall of 1937, faced with a power surplus, decided the best alternative was to export power to the United States. In the last week of November, Hepburn asked the federal Government for permission to export 120,000 horsepower to New York State. A meeting of the federal Cabinet, at which King was not present, decided that the request could not be granted without the consent of Parliament, an action that was, in effect, a refusal. This did not help Mitch Hepburn to extricate himself from his power box. On November 26, he phoned King and asked for a special Cabinet meeting to discuss Ontario's case, a request to which the federal Prime Minister reluctantly agreed.

King delayed a Florida vacation to be present when Hepburn personally presented Ontario's case for power export to a special Cabinet meeting at noon on November 29. King pointed out that the Cabinet had already refused two similar requests in 1937 from Quebec power companies for power export licenses, referred to the legislation of 1929, and reiterated that it was a matter for Parliament to decide. It was an angry disappointed Hepburn who returned to the Chateau Laurier while the Cabinet continued its deliberations. With some misgivings from the Ontario ministers about Hepburn's reaction, the Cabinet backed King's stand. In an unusual attempt to placate Hepburn, King visited the Ontario Premier's suite in the Chateau to give him the Cabinet's final decision. Mitchell Hepburn was not placated. He interpreted the federal Liberals' refusal to help him out of his power bind not only unjustified on principle (talk of Parliament's deciding was so much hair-splitting when all the Cabinet had to do was ram it through) but intolerable on personal grounds. It was nothing but another deliberate affront by King. Stormily Hepburn retaliated. Ottawa had refused Ontario permission to export power because the federal Government, annoyed by Ontario's refusal to co-operate in the St. Lawrence development, had buckled to pressure from Washington: "Now the cat's out of the bag," charged Hepburn on his return to Toronto. "Mr. King is taking a made-in-Washington policy and is trying to force it on Ontario."

Then he loaded his verbal blunderbuss with his own interpretation of some ancient history. "Mr. King was never friendly to Ontario. I happen to know because I was with him and watched him in Ottawa. His famous five-cent speech [which Hepburn had defended several times in the 1935 campaign] was directed at Ontario. I know that." Immediately, King, always reluctant to become embroiled in a slanging match with Hepburn, issued a mild statement saying that the allegation Washington had pressured Ottawa into denying Ontario an export license was "wholly without foundation." Now thoroughly angry, Hepburn retorted by attempting to provoke King into a verbal donnybrook. He charged that when the federal Prime Minister had called on him in March, 1937, King had tried to force him to back the St. Lawrence Seaway development. The correspondence between Ottawa and Ontario would prove this conclusively, and Hepburn telegraphed King demanding "that the official documents very improperly marked confidential by you should be made public."

Again, in a conciliatory reply, King denied he had tried to pressure Hepburn on the St. Lawrence plan. He had merely asked for Ontario's view so that he could inform President Roosevelt. He agreed to table the correspondence in the Commons. Hepburn did not wait for that. He released the correspondence between Queen's Park and Ottawa unilaterally with the comment, "Now we will see who is nearer the truth." The correspondence revealed that the American Government wanted Canada to proceed with the whole St. Lawrence development, that the Ontario Government wanted permission to develop more power at Niagara apart from the St. Lawrence plan, and that the King Government merely acted as the mailman. "The plain fact is," commented the *Globe and Mail*, "that the correspondence fails to substantiate Mr. Hepburn's wild charges." Ottawa had not succumbed to Washington pressure and had not pressured Ontario. That seemed to be the general view of the matter. King said he would have nothing more to say about power export until Parliament met in January, 1938. Mitch Hepburn was still in his power box.[15]

So the year 1937 ended with the feud between Ottawa and Queen's Park warming up again. After twelve months sizzling with politics and controversy, the combustible Oshawa strike, the hotly contested general election, and a short bitter December session of the Legislature to once again tighten up the Succession Duty Act, Mitch Hepburn welcomed the cool holiday weather. He spent a quiet Christmas at his Bannockburn farm with his family and guests, frequently enjoying the skating on Lake Laurier, the lovely artificial lake on his property. Dressed in his bright tam o'shanter and Hudson Bay sweater, the Premier looked relaxed and healthy as he joined the skating parties. But even at home he could not escape controversy. A record number of accidents in Toronto – three killed and sixty-seven injured – marred the Christmas holidays. The province's loose liquor laws were chiefly responsible for that, charged the Secretary of the Ontario Temperance Federation, Rev. A. J. Irwin. One man was answerable for those and the holiday carnage, "He is the Premier of this province."[16] Nineteen thirty-seven had been that kind of year for Mitch Hepburn.

chapter 10

King Must Go

At the beginning of 1938, as Mitch Hepburn left the skating parties at Lake Laurier for the affairs of Government at Queen's Park, one difficulty persisted like an abscessed tooth. The problem of power export had already infected relations between Hepburn and the federal Government. It could poison them further. Blocked for the moment in his attempt to sell surplus power to the United States, Hepburn enlisted the support of powerful friends to force the King Government to change its mind. One of those friends was the Union Nationale Premier of Quebec, Maurice Duplessis.

Almost from the time of his upset victory over the Liberal Taschereau regime in August, 1936, Maurice Duplessis had admired Ontario's dynamic Premier; the feeling was reciprocated. Temperamentally and politically, Maurice Duplessis and Mitch Hepburn had much in common: convivial, out-going, loyal to their friends, ruthless with enemies, decisive, impatient of protocol both constitutional and social, activists brooking neither opposition nor criticism, Mitch and Maurice became fast friends. As heads of the powerful central provinces, they faced problems that required consultation and joint action – power policy, timber rights, newsprint prices, and taxation. These gradually were subsumed into one growing knot of frustration and impatience with what both Premiers considered the vacillating policies of the Mackenzie King Government.

Mitch Hepburn, quick to respond to any gesture of friendship, even quicker to take umbrage at any supposed slight, could not help contrasting the treatment he received from King with the consideration that Duplessis displayed. Often the federal Government initiated programs affecting the provinces without prior consultation or warning. Yet during his first months as Premier, Maurice Duplessis sometimes phoned Mitch Hepburn to keep him informed about what the Quebec Government was doing. On November 21, 1936, Ontario Liberal Secretary, Harry Johnson, told Norman Lambert "that Duplessis had shown more co-operation towards Mitch than Ottawa & cited case of D. calling up at midnight to tell Mitch his Cabinet had just put through certain legislation." Throughout the Oshawa strike, when Hepburn felt that the Ottawa authorities had let him down, Duplessis publicly backed the Ontario Premier's strong anti-Communist stand. Quick to appreciate this support, Mitch Hepburn responded: "I'll give Premier Duplessis and his policies a blanket endorsement."

When Hepburn decided to make a formal application to the Cabinet on January 21, 1938, to export surplus horsepower to the United States (a matter that King still maintained was a question for Parliament to decide, a procedure that would require a private bill to gain the export licence), he turned for help to his good friend, the Premier of Quebec. Three days after the application, Hepburn wrote Duplessis: "I have just gone over the document in which we make formal application for the export of power. What do you think of the idea of introducing resolutions in the Legislatures of Quebec and Ontario in support of Ontario's application? We could project into the discussion the principle of the Provinces having sole control of their own natural resources."

A few days later, on January 27, Hepburn was again writing the Quebec Premier requesting that Duplessis should "indicate to the Prime Minister of Canada that the application for export of the Hydro Electric Power Commission of Ontario goes forward with the sympathetic and active support of the Province of Quebec." Duplessis (who shortly after Hepburn had a meeting with him in Montreal in December, 1937, said that if Mackenzie King wanted a "fight" on the power export issue, he could have one) replied that he would be happy to introduce a resolution in the Quebec Legislature declaring that the provinces had full control of their natural resources. He thought that the federal Prime Minister was clear about Quebec's attitude: "If you think, however, that Mr. King needs some more explanation, as far as I am concerned, we will be pleased to supply him with added informations."[1]

It is doubtful that "added informations" from the Premier of Quebec would have changed King's attitude concerning power export. If the Ontario Premier had approached the question more reasonably, not held the export request like a gun to the federal Government's head, King might have been more co-operative. Hepburn, in addition to enlisting Duplessis' help, did all he could to influence Parliament in favour of Ontario's application. He wrote to Cabinet ministers and private members urging their co-operation. This gave some of Hepburn's federal Liberal friends an opportunity to take him to task for his attacks on King. Hepburn told Dr. A. MacG. Young (Liberal, Saskatoon) that he "rather enjoyed your verbal spanking."

Insofar as your criticism of my attitude toward Mackenzie King is concerned, you must bear in mind at the time of the Coronation ceremonies, when he packed his trousseau and took his retinue and $300,000 of public funds to travel to England, we in the Province of Ontario were fighting single handed the invasion of Lewis and his Yankee racketeers, and from this perspective you will agree we did a mighty good job, not only for Ontario, but for the United States as well.

Then the Ontario Premier got his metaphors not so much mixed as reversed:

I was rather amused with your concluding paragraph when you quote Scripture, something unfamiliar to me. You say, "Let him who is without sin cast the first stone." In my opinion some of you statesmen at Ottawa could throw the whole Rock of Gibraltar.

With kindest personal regards and hoping that some time we can continue this argument with a nice quart of Haig and Haig between us. . . .

In his reply, Dr. Young (after noting that if Hepburn were going to cast stones he should throw them in the right direction), expressed the feelings of the majority of federal Liberals concerning the Ontario Premier's attacks on King: "You have done so many things of which I am proud and about which I have said so much, that honestly, I feel sorry that you did the thing referred to in my letter, which to me seems to be a way out of line with your genial personality and very fine sense of things."

Probably a majority of Parliament was prepared to support Ontario's request for a power export licence. King told the House that the Government had an "open-door" policy concerning the export of surplus power to the United States. He admitted that there "must be many cases where the granting of a licence would be wholly justified." Nevertheless, some of Hepburn's best friends at Ottawa, men like Arthur Slaght (Parry Sound), who would pilot Ontario's application bill through the House, were increasingly exasperated when Conservative members spiced their speeches with a fresh Hepburn attack on King. On March 11, Slaght wrote Hepburn with some asperity: "I trust that from now until the Private Bill is disposed of one way or another, you will not find it necessary to make any public utterance reflecting on the Federal Government in connection with this matter because there is a genuine desire here to help put this Bill through for you and it would be most unfair to me and your other good friends here for you to pursue such a course while we are so doing."

Ontario's application to export power to New York State soon became an academic question. The United States Government saved Mr.

King and the Ontario members (the Ontario Premier had dared them to vote against it) the embarrassment of standing up to be counted on Hepburn's request. On March 17, 1938, the American Government informed Ottawa that it objected to accepting Ontario power because it would make New York State too dependent on electricity that could be withdrawn by the Hydro Commission at any time. The American authorities also rejected Ontario's request to increase the power potential at Niagara. Mackenzie King explained to the Commons the Americans were prepared to negotiate both points if Ontario would agree to the entire St. Lawrence development. Annoyed by Roosevelt's rejection of his plan to sell surplus power, Mitchell Hepburn announced that Ontario was not interested. "The whole thing is off," he said at London. "We will not consent to the St. Lawrence scheme."

The power question remained there until the end of May, 1938, when American Secretary of State, Cordell Hull, acting for his Government, submitted a comprehensive new draft treaty to Ottawa for the development of the St. Lawrence Seaway and allied power projects. This treaty met two of Hepburn's long-time requests: it provided for both the export of power to the United States, and the diversion of waters at Long Lac to increase the flow at Niagara. King stated that the new proposals, which envisaged Canada's completing its share of the Seaway by the end of 1949, would be carefully studied. The Ontario Premier also promised that his Government would consider Hull's proposals "but I want to make it clear that I'm not going to be swept off my feet by any propaganda or ballyhoo."[2]

Apparently it was in the nature of "propaganda and ballyhoo" that Mitch Hepburn viewed a trip to Ontario by President Franklin Roosevelt in the late summer of 1938. On August 18, Roosevelt travelled to Kingston to accept an honorary degree at Queen's University and to open a new bridge at Ivy Lea. Besides his promise of military help at Queen's ("I give you the assurance that the people of the United States will not stand idly by if domination of Canadian soil is threatened by any other empire"), the American President used the occasion of the Ivy Lea Bridge opening to express some unvarnished views about the St. Lawrence Seaway. With Mackenzie King and Ontario's Lieutenant Governor Albert Matthews beside him, the American President rebuked the "prophets of trouble" (of whom the absent Premier Hepburn was one of the most vocal) who feared that the St. Lawrence Seaway would injure the railroads. "Such a waterway," said Roosevelt, "generates more railroad traffic than it takes away." He warned against selfish private power rings and, looking down at the St. Lawrence, foresaw "the day when a Canadian Prime Minister and an American President can meet to dedicate, not a bridge across the water, but the very water itself, to the lasting and productive use of their respective peoples."

What was Mitchell Hepburn's attitude toward Roosevelt's vision for the development of the St. Lawrence? He had consistently opposed the St. Lawrence project because it was needed neither for power nor for navigation. It would seem, however, that not only President Roosevelt but Mackenzie King too had begun to suspect that Premier Hepburn had other reasons for his opposition, that the man who had fought the power barons was somehow involved with the private power rings (and their natural allies, the mining interests). Whatever the connection, Hepburn's virulent campaign, supported by Duplessis, to export surplus power to the United States, played into the hands of the power barons on both sides of the border. In Canada, private power interests wanted to break into the rich New York industrial market; their American counterparts, especially in New York, hoped to import Canadian power so that the New York State Power authority and others (like President Roosevelt) pressing for the publicly owned development of the St. Lawrence would be unable to argue that more power was needed. In December, 1938, Prime Minister King intimated to his Defence Minister, Ian Mackenzie, that "he had power scandal on Duplessis & Hepburn & might have Royal Comm. to inquire." Shortly afterward, Senator Lambert received a memorandum "re Hepburn & the Power ring in Montreal and New York" which convinced him "that the power ring was behind Mitch."

Whatever truth there was in that, Premier Hepburn, both by his actions and his words, made his position toward President Roosevelt's exhortation at Ivy Lea to proceed publicly with the St. Lawrence development brutally clear. The Premier of Ontario refused even to welcome the American President to the province. He publicly boycotted the Ivy Lea ceremonies. If anyone had misinterpreted that outrageous display of bad manners from the King's First Minister in Ontario, Hepburn told the press what he thought of Roosevelt's proposal: "There can be no power development along the St. Lawrence river unless all the Governments concerned consent and there will be no consent from my Government." Then Mitch Hepburn wrote a corrosive letter to King asking what Ottawa's policy on the St. Lawrence was: "I would like to know what your policy is, if any, and should you have a policy, what proposal have you to submit to this Government for consideration"? Neither Roosevelt nor King were going to push Mitch Hepburn around: "Irrespective of any propaganda or squeeze play that might be concocted by you, you may rest assured that this Government will resist ["to the bitter end" is struck out in blue pencil] any effort to force us to expend public funds in such an unwarranted manner or to foist upon the people of Ontario an additional burden of debt and taxation."[3] Forthwith Hepburn made the letter public.

No action since he had become Premier was so unanimously condemned by the provincial press (and newspapers throughout the whole country) as Hepburn's snub to the American President by refusing to meet him at Ivy Lea. "His absence," deplored the *Globe and Mail*, "was an affront to the Ontario people, a violation of public amenities, and an incivility toward a very distinguished visitor." This constant sniping at King "is getting tiresome and nauseating. It will gain Mr. Hepburn nothing more than third-rate standing." King's first reference to the Ontario Premier's "squeeze-play" letter, made at a political picnic at Woodbridge, was moderate. He would be replying, he said, to Hepburn's letter in due course. Meanwhile, he added to resounding applause, he and his colleagues would "endeavour . . . to carry on the discussion of such questions [in accordance] with the wishes of the Canadian people as to how public business should be conducted."

To that end, on August 30, King wrote Hepburn a conciliatory letter (completely ignoring the latter's sarcastic jibes about a lack of policy), suggesting that experts from both Governments should begin a joint study of the technical problems of the St. Lawrence development. From these studies a policy could evolve. "We hope this will be acceptable and that you will find it convenient to designate representatives for this purpose at an early date." Nearly three weeks after receiving this request, the Ontario Premier asked his private secretary, Roy Elmhirst, to have Highways Minister McQuesten draft a reply. "In Mr. Hepburn's opinion," ran the memorandum from Elmhirst accompanying the request, "Mr. King has not declared his policy in this letter and he does not see any advantage in having any conference until such time as Mr. King declares himself."

Accordingly, on September 21, Hepburn informed King that Ontario was not interested in technical talks concerning the St. Lawrence. He added a new argument against the waterway. There would be too great an overhead for most ocean ships "meandering slowly up the inland course." He coldly asked King "where the pressure is coming from for the deep waterway?" Incredibly, and unknown to the Premier, some of the pressure was coming from his own Hydro Chairman, Thomas Hogg. During talks with American power officials in the fall of 1938, Hogg admitted that Ontario would need more power by the time the St. Lawrence project was completed years hence. He explained that Roosevelt's embarrassing frankness at Ivy Lea had hardened Hepburn against the plan. Despite this, Hepburn's own senior hydro official suggested that King should ignore Hepburn's opposition and proceed unilaterally with the St. Lawrence Seaway. King was not prepared to do this: it would take a world war to change Mitch Hepburn's mind about proceeding with the St. Lawrence project.[4]

Power export was merely one aspect of a larger problem emerging at this time – the complex of federal-provincial relations. Not unexpectedly, Mitch Hepburn and Maurice Duplessis were in broad agreement concerning the emphasis that their provinces should put on provincial rights. When the two Premiers met in Montreal in December, 1937, to review provincial problems – newsprint, tourism, mining – they also discussed the attitude their provinces should adopt toward the fundamental study of federalism that had been established by the King Government – the Rowell-Sirois Commission.

On August 14, 1937, the Commission had been set up "to investigate the economic and financial basis of Confederation and of the distribution of legislative powers in the light of the economic and social developments of the last seventy-five years." The growing responsibilities of all the provinces for unemployment relief and social services, shrivelled provincial revenues, and the increasing complexities caused by industrialization required that the financial arrangements made in 1867 be revised. There was a need to rationalize an antiquated system of government financing and determine a coherent plan of collecting and distributing the nation's tax resources that would be fair to all the provinces. The trouble was that what one province considered fair another might regard wholly unjust. It all depended on whose financial ox was being gored. Some of the western provinces were virtually bankrupt. Obviously they would need more help from the federal Government. Ottawa had only one major source for raising that money; the central Government would certainly have to turn to Ontario and Quebec for a larger share of succession duties and personal income taxes.

Duplessis and Hepburn made it clear what they thought of that. Two days after his sessions with the Ontario Premier at the Mount Royal and Ritz Carlton in Montreal, Maurice Duplessis, in a speech at Shawinigan Falls on December 15, 1937, warned that Ontario, Quebec, and the Maritimes had decided "we will not be run for the western provinces or Ottawa." The speech raised a storm of protest (Social Credit Premier William Aberhart of Alberta expostulated, "The East should take their hands out of our pockets"); the Maritime premiers denied any knowledge of an anti-western pact; Duplessis said he had been misquoted; and Mitch Hepburn rejected the theory that Ontario and Quebec were "ganging up" on the rest of the country, but warned that he would "fight to the last ditch any attempt by the Dominion Government to invade the provincial sphere of taxation."

At two further meetings, one in Toronto at the end of 1937 (which included a buffet supper at the suburban home of Senator Frank O'Connor), and one in Montreal at the beginning of 1938, the two Premiers co-ordinated their strategy. After their Montreal meeting, Duplessis declared that the two provinces had "got together" to "stop a raid against Confederation." Clearly Hepburn and Duplessis were laying the groundwork to oppose any changes in the federal taxing structure that would deleteriously affect their own provinces. A hard line on provincial rights coincided perfectly with Mitch Hepburn's anti-King feud, so much so that the Ontario Premier was now beginning to hedge on policies he had previously supported. During the 1937 provincial election campaign, Hepburn had advocated unemployment insurance. A bill providing for unemployment insurance passed by the R. B. Bennett Government had been declared unconstitutional because it infringed on the prerogatives of the provinces. When Mackenzie King wrote Hepburn in November, 1937, about further federal legislation for unemployment insurance, the Ontario Premier replied that his Government was willing to waive any provincial rights in the matter.

Early in 1938, after a further communication from King on the matter, and following his discussions with Duplessis, the Ontario Premier was more cautious. Before he gave King a final answer, Hepburn wrote to Duplessis on January 24, 1938: "It appears that he [King] is simply asking for a blank cheque insofar as amending the British North America Act is concerned and is using unemployment insurance as the thin edge of the wedge. You must appreciate the fact, however, that Ontario is solidly behind the principle of a national unemployment scheme but not at the expense of Confederation." Duplessis was certain that was the right line to take: "I am sure that the Federal authorities are using unemployment insurance as a smoke-screen to be able to temper [*sic*] with the constitution."

On February 14, Hepburn again wrote to Duplessis. He seemed sorry that he had ever publicly supported a national unemployment insurance plan at all:

> I rather regret that I was in a position of having to first endorse the proposed national scheme of unemployment insurance, for reasons explained to you by Heenan. However, if this means that we have to sacrifice Confederation I am quite prepared to withdraw any support whatsoever. It is clear to me that with the Western provinces hopelessly bankrupt, any national scheme of unemployment insurance will have to be borne by the two central provinces, and if unemployment insurance is necessary it probably will be better to run our own show.

In this same letter, Hepburn invited Duplessis to visit Bannockburn ("Don't forget the invitation you accepted to visit at our farm as soon as the session is over") and, more significantly, indicated how his thoughts were running on any changes in federal-provincial relations:

> This afternoon I intend to have a lengthy discussion with W. H. Moore, M.P., regarding our proposed submission to the Rowell Commission. The more I read of the representations made by the other provinces the more convinced I am of the necessity of Ontario and

Quebec resisting together, and in no uncertain way, the every increasing unreasonable and impossible demand. Our friend McQuesten is even more convinced on this subject than I am, if that is possible. I can readily understand the advantage it would be to the other provinces for them to raid the Federal Treasury, particularly when Ontario and Quebec contribute eighty per cent of the revenue.

Hepburn warned Duplessis to guard against encroachments by Ottawa on provincial revenues: "I have further information to the effect that the King Government is determined to take over the collection of succession duties. This would deprive us of our greatest source of revenue."

In addition to these views expressed privately to Duplessis, the Ontario Premier's public statements against Ottawa's financial policies became increasingly belligerent. When the King administration refused to raise relief grants to the provinces, Hepburn warned: "Ontario is going to cast off the role of milch cow for the rest of the Dominion," and introduced a resolution in the Legislature (which had convened on February 23) asserting Ontario's "prior right" to revenues from personal income tax. The Premier claimed that direct taxation should be left to the provinces. This had been understood in what he described as an unwritten agreement between the central Government and the provinces, an agreement honoured from the time of Confederation to the First World War. The resolution, which Hepburn wanted in his arsenal of arguments for the Rowell-Sirois Commission, was supported by the Conservatives and passed unanimously.[5]

Mitchell Hepburn's views on the taxing power and the whole area of Dominion-provincial relations were articulated more fully when the Commission sat in Toronto at the beginning of May, 1938. There was speculation about how hard a line the Ontario Government would take. When the federal Government had first announced the Commission, the Ontario Premier had said that he was "entirely satisfied with the personnel of the Commission, and I think the Dominion Government is fortunate to have such men available for such an important work." A number of conferences (with Maurice Duplessis) and a lot of verbiage (a good bit of it directed at Mackenzie King) had gone over the dam since Mitch Hepburn expressed that approval. Now he stood before the Commission in the green-carpeted Legislative Chamber at Queen's Park leading off for Ontario.

After a few words of welcome, the Premier began his submission on "a long deep note of discontent." The first he had ever heard of any Commission was at the breakfast table. "I was perplexed," continued the Premier, his voice dripping with sarcasm. "Perhaps I should have surmised something of the sort was around the corner from something the Prime Minister had said a year ago in the House of Commons. My attention is frequently drawn to the Right Honourable Gentleman's speeches, but somehow I missed that one, and upon inquiry, I learned that the Premier of another Province had also missed it." (This was an interesting introduction in view of the fact that Hepburn's own Government had suggested that one of the Commissioners should be Chester Walters, the Ontario Deputy Treasurer, a suggestion that the federal authorities had not seen fit to accept.) It was not only the formation of the Commission that Hepburn denigrated; he questioned its validity. If the nature of the constitution itself were to be dealt with, a Commission, no matter how distinguished its membership, was not the way to go about it: "There may be different views as to the approach to Confederation; personally, I have always regarded Confederation as the outcome of conference. . . . If there is to be change in Confederation (in my opinion) it can be brought about only by renewed conferences of the representatives of the people and with unanimity of approval." "It would have been better," explained the Ontario Premier, "to discuss Provincial relations in conference rather than by trying to make cases before a Commission."

Then Mitch Hepburn proceeded to make a case, not so much Ontario's case (except indirectly) as a case against the submissions previously made by the western provinces, particularly Manitoba, for a larger share of grants from the federal treasury. Hepburn's brief was, typically enough, at least two-thirds negative. What he proposed in a positive way was stated rather than developed. It rested on three assumptions: centralized power was dangerous; Canada was a heterogeneous country, and no attempt to "equalize" the various regions was practicable; "social services," when and if desirable, were best left to the provinces. This did not mean that Ontario was against changing the British North America Act. "We do not hold that the Constitution is inviolable just because it will be a year over three score and ten, next July." But the answer to the problem of "services that were not foreseen at the time of Confederation" was not to increase "the iron-hand of concentrated power." There had been enough of that in Ottawa already: "I do not, for a moment, suggest there is a formidably deliberate plan to destroy our parliamentary institutions; I do say: were the men of 1837 to take stock of our politics in 1938, they would find little left of the political ideals on which they placed such store."

There should be a rearrangement of the public services that would "bring government closer to the people all without changing the Constitution." This would involve a territorial dispersal of power not more centralization. "For we are a stupid people if we imagine ourselves immune from the consequences of concentrating power in a few hands. The accumulation of power leads to autocracy; its distribution is the safety-zone of democracy." Holding that principle, Hepburn also held that the provinces themselves should be responsible for both administering and paying for the new social services. The federal authority should be subordinate:

> The provinces charged with social services should make the initial levy on incomes arising within the provinces. The federal income-taxing officer should step in only when the provincial needs have been satisfied.
>
> Whatever our disagreements, I take it we agree that it is poor politics, and worse economy, that one government should tax for another to spend.

The effort to "equalize" the provinces by federal grants was at best unsound economically, at worst just a raid on Ontario's treasury. "Equality between the provinces is impossible," Hepburn stated. God had made them unequal and some of them had better face up to that fact. "The provinces are fiscal entities; and governments, like individuals, must learn to manage within their means." If some provinces were less equal than others, "the remedy that first suggests itself is amalgamation," an interesting suggestion that the Ontario Premier did not develop. He did, however, make some final observations which illustrated his traditional commitment to the primary industries and his suspicion of the welfare state. The way to a prosperous Canada was through increased production, not more government hand-outs:

> The need for . . . "social services" has come largely through lack of a national economy that insures a wide distribution of the proceeds of productive effort. The State is largely responsible. The State will pay the penalty with its life – unless it shapes its policy for the profitable employment of the great mass of its citizens. The government that arranges an economy under which one family out of ten lives on "social services" cannot survive; and does not deserve to survive.

If there were to be "social services," Hepburn insisted they should be on a contributory basis. In answer to a question from Commissioner Rowell, the Premier said he believed "in the contributory system, whether it applies to pensions or unemployment insurance. There are many abuses in the old-age pensions system. Certain old people's chief purpose seems to be doing away with their property and going on old-age pensions."[6]

Hepburn's brief annoyed many federal Liberals who considered it a mixture of "insolence and insularity." The *Globe and Mail* condemned it as "an instrument of destruction from the standpoint of national unity." Most prairie Liberals were outraged at what they considered a gratuitous attack on the West. If Mitch Hepburn had any national political aspirations at this time, his brief was not designed to advance them any. None of this appeared to worry Ontario's Premier. He was, in fact, just waiting for an opportunity to scuttle the Rowell-Sirois Commission completely so far as Ontario was concerned. The chance came with the Liberal budget of Charles A. Dunning in June, 1938. The budget included a minor change in the gift-tax. On June 29, Hepburn wrote to King of his "surprise and displeasure" at this change. "To introduce it at this time, with the Rowell Commission Report pending, constitutes little short of effrontery to the Provinces that entered protests, if not a snub to the Commission itself." In vain King replied that the purpose of the change was not to produce more federal revenue but to tighten up the administration of the tax act. This, in Hepburn's view, was more of King's hair-splitting. On July 13, he wrote to the Rowell-Sirois Commission's secretary, Alex Skelton, informing him that the Ontario Government had "decided to dissociate ourselves entirely from any participation insofar as these deliberations are concerned."

This precipitate action, another of the long series of slaps at the federal authority, was severely criticized. The *Globe and Mail* speculated that Hepburn had acted "under the increasing influence of his colleague and playmate, Maurice." Another colleague of sorts applauded Hepburn's withdrawal. Social Credit Premier William Aberhart of Alberta, who had already dissociated his Government from the Commission, explained in a letter to Hepburn that the differences between the provinces and the federal Government were greater than those between the provinces themselves. Therefore, suggested Aberhart, it was only logical that "the provinces should come together in conference without the intervention of the central Government." For Aberhart, like Hepburn and Duplessis, the face of provincial rights had an obverse side: a common dislike, for various reasons and in varying degrees, of Mackenzie King.[7]

Hepburn's squabble with King broke out in a rash of new headlines in the early winter of 1938 after the Ontario Premier himself caused scare bulletins across the province. Mitch Hepburn liked to fly. Near the end of June 1938, he flew to New York in J. P. Bickell's new amphibian plane for the Joe Louis – Max Schmeling championship boxing match. After an early afternoon party at Sell 'Em Ben Smith's New York apartment with Eddie Dowling, the Broadway producer, and other celebrities, the Premier arrived at Madison Square Gardens just in time to see Louis knock Schmeling out in the first round. Less than a month later, the Premier with Bickell and Smith again took off from Toronto, this time on a trip to Alaska. They planned to visit the Yukon and examine the Yellowknife mining area. On July 28, when the flight was near Whitehorse, the province was shocked by a report that Premier Hepburn's plane was overdue and perhaps lost. The Premier's wife, having her hair done when she heard the news, was not greatly perturbed, but Acting Premier Harry

Nixon took the precaution of arranging with Premier "Duff" Pattullo of British Columbia for an air search. Bad weather had interfered with radio communications near Juneau, but there had never been any danger to the Premier's party. "Held up by weather. Headed home. Back soon," was Mitch Hepburn's laconic reassurance to his wife.

The Hepburn flying party, enthusiastic about their ten-thousand-mile trip to the North, arrived home in time to celebrate the Premier's forty-second birthday at Bannockburn farms on August 12. It was quite a celebration. Sir James Dunn, just back from England, was there. J. P. Bickell flew in from Toronto with Maurice Duplessis. A few minutes later, a silver stream-lined plane with Harry McLean of Dominion Construction and Sell 'Em Ben Smith landed at Lambeth Airport, a few miles from Bannockburn. The Toronto distiller, Larry McGuinness, Harry Johnson, and Sir James met the New York party at Lambeth, then sped off for Bannockburn in two black cars escorted by Provincial Police officers. Seldom had the Hepburn farm hosted so many high-powered personalities, all of whom had become gentlemen farmers for the day. Mitch Hepburn was justly proud of his farms. Smiling and tanned, wearing white shoes, the sleeves of his shirt rolled up, he took the reins of his prize Percherons and Clydes to drive his friend Maurice around the property in a brightly painted wagon lettered "M. F. Hepburn, Bannockburn Farms." The first of a bumper onion crop (nearly thirty-thousand bushels) was graded. To work up an appetite, to say nothing of a thirst, the two Premiers took a shift at pitching sheaves into the threshing machine. For the *al fresco* buffet, graciously presided over by the Premier's wife, there were fried fillet of perch, freshly caught that morning in nearby Lake Erie. Maurice Duplessis stayed with the Hepburns for the night. The Premier assured newsmen that no sinister political implications should be read into the Quebec Premier's visit, his first to that part of Ontario. He came to enjoy himself and "to attend my birthday party."[8]

There were a number of Liberal strategists in Ottawa, who thought there was more to the relationship between Duplessis and Hepburn than riding around on a wagon behind prize horses. More than a year earlier, *l'Unité* of Montreal had speculated that Hepburn and Duplessis would eventually form a new federal union party. In a front-page news story in the *Globe and Mail,* in August, 1937, Blair Fraser reported a rumour that the two Premiers intended to construct an inter-provincial organization to dominate Eastern Canadian politics, an organization strong enough to challenge the central Government at Ottawa no matter who was in power there. At the time of these rumours (which first began to circulate shortly after Hepburn's union government attempt in Ontario and George Drew's reported comment, "Ontario and Quebec National and Canada is well-controlled"), Hepburn wrote to a Montreal friend: "There is quite a misconception with regard to any coalition with Premier Duplessis. I have a very high personal regard for him and might say he has been most courteous in all his dealings with the Ontario Government. As a matter of fact, I have received much more co-operation from him than I have from the administration at Ottawa. They seem to take great delight in treating me as some kind of burglar."

One of the federal Liberals most concerned with Hepburn's activities in concert with Duplessis and in Ontario itself was chief organizer, Senator Norman Lambert, who had been appointed to the Senate by Mackenzie King in January, 1938. Several federal by-elections were scheduled in Ontario for November. Hepburn's attempt to cut off campaign funds had continued; he had also refused to allow the Ottawa wing of the Party to use the Ontario Liberal offices. From time to time in 1938, Lambert had received disturbing reports about Hepburn's plans to cut into federal strength and his active hostility in several ridings. On March 12, 1938, George McIlraith, a federal Member from Ottawa informed Lambert that Frank Ahearn (Liberal, Ottawa West) "was quoting Mitch H.'s intention of taking twenty seats from Ontario out of the Federal House & that his efforts in West Ottawa at prov'l election time were anti-federal." Ahearn himself, once a good friend of the Ontario leader, explained to Lambert: "Soon after I came out for Albert Pinard against the Irish Catholic candidate – the late Bill Unger – in the Ottawa East by-election" he incurred "the enmity of Hepburn and Leduc, plus the local Irish Catholics." As a result of this hostility, according to Ahearn, the periodical *Jack Canuck* began to attack him in its columns, and the paper's Ottawa correspondent spread numerous pro-Hepburn pamphlets throughout the riding. Ahearn described *Jack Canuck* for Lambert's edification as "the well-known scandal journal published in Toronto, which recently folded up. This rag for some time, together with *Hush,* was, as you know, subsidized by the Hepburn regime."

As a result of this friction, particularly Hepburn's attempted freeze-out of campaign funds, Lambert favoured setting up an independent federal organization for Ontario. Ontario Liberal secretary, Harry Johnson, still loyal to Hepburn but hoping for a rapprochement with Ottawa, advised Lambert that a separate federal organization would be a mistake. By the early spring of 1938, King himself who had long thought that given enough rope the Ontario Premier would hang himself, seemed to be leaning toward a more positive attempt to bring Hepburn to heel. On May 4, 1938, he discussed the matter for two hours in his office with Senator Lambert: "He thought that a fight should be waged vs. Hepburn in Ontario & urged good representation for Ontario at the Federation meeting."

Senator Lambert immediately held a number of strategy meetings with key Ontario members: William P. Mulock, Hugh Plaxton, Sam Factor, Howe, Euler, and Rogers. An attempt was made to induce Senator Hardy (one of the three men to whom Hepburn gave most credit for the rebirth of the Liberal Party in Ontario in the early nineteen-thirties)* to enter the lists against the Ontario leader. Hardy's reaction, coming as it did from one of Hepburn's oldest political allies, was revealing. Lambert was informed "that Hardy wd. not take initiative in an Ont. fight because he was afraid of arousing Mitch's ire which wd. centre on his H.'s [Hardy's] estate." Hardy's response revealed to what an extent fear itself had tightened the lines of power running from Queen's Park.

Mitch Hepburn would not be satisfied with the removal of a few obnoxious federal Ministers like Howe and Rogers. He wanted to bring down Mackenzie King himself. When immigration authorities rejected Hepburn's application to have a European family emigrate to work at Bannockburn, he wrote to Mines and Resources Minister Thomas Crerar on May 30, 1938: "I am looking forward to the day when we, the electors of Ontario, will have the opportunity of electing at Ottawa a Government with some practical horse sense." Nor was it a big transposition from the removal of King to his replacement by Hepburn. Some of the Ontario leader's friends made that transposition easily. Larry McGuinness wrote from the Chateau in Quebec on June 22: "If you are drafted for Ottawa service, and that seems to be the general impression, you will have our gang with you."[9]

Mitch Hepburn battling Ottawa Liberals, freezing federal campaign funds, interfering with federal ridings, was one thing. Mitch Hepburn, with Maurice Duplessis as part of his "gang," was another. Immediately after the Hepburn birthday party, Senator Lambert, trying to prepare for the Ontario federal by-elections in November, phoned Harry Johnson to find out what Hepburn and Duplessis were up to. Johnson told the federal organizer somewhat cryptically that "he was 'on the spot' as result of developments over week-end. He said Mitch had Duplessis in his hippocket, & spoke about 'pressure from millionaires.' " C. D. Howe urged King to call the Ontario members together "to offset Hepburn in Ont., but P.M. did not want to do so just now. He felt Hepburn would do himself in." In Quebec City, Larry McGuinness did not think so. The Toronto distiller had been talking to Maurice Duplessis. On August 18, McGuinness wrote Hepburn that the Quebec Premier wanted him to lead the fight against King and Dr. Robert Manion (the newly elected Conservative leader who had replaced R. B. Bennett): "He suggests he would remain in Provincial politics but would stump the country and round up the French-Canadian vote." McGuinness, who despite his success as a brewery baron seems to have been a rosy-cheeked novice at politics, advised Hepburn to allow King and Manion to fight it out. In a short time he could pick up the pieces and go to Ottawa as Prime Minister.

---

* Senator Frank O'Connor and Arthur Slaght were the others.

There was no indication how this was to be accomplished, although during the fall Lambert heard intimations of an anti-King force led by Hepburn. On September 7, Harry Johnson called Lambert to inform him that "Gray of Alberta had been in Toronto in early August visiting at Queen's Park. He asked the question – what wd. happen if Ont., Que., Man. & Alta. were to start a farmer party." (Whatever would happen, nothing did which was true of all the schemes for overthrowing King.) Hepburn, himself, publicly disclaimed any federal ambitions. There is no question, however, that Hepburn, with Maurice Duplessis' backing, was working to change the federal leadership and to influence national policies. A letter from Sir James Dunn to Hepburn on November 5, 1938, indicates that the Ontario and Quebec Premiers were maintaining close liaison: "Maurice breakfasted with me and I told him of our last interview on policy with which I understand he is in agreement." One policy advocated by financial interests in Montreal and Toronto was the amalgamation of Canada's two railways, a step that apparently Hepburn and Duplessis had decided was in the national interest: "I gather he has some idea of an independent report before putting the railways together, but I do not think he holds any strong view on this subject that would be out of line with your policy."

In matters of defence and finance, too, Sir James assured Hepburn that Duplessis supported him:

> On defence I found him in entire agreement, stressing Canadian independent preparation ready to act with both Britain and the United States in defending this Continent but strongly preferring the British political association to the American. I understand him to see with you on the necessity of putting our financial house in order in Canada before calamity overtakes us. We discussed the ease with which Britain moved from a 5% to a 3% basis without any threat of repudiation – velvet glove method – I hope it will work with us. Maurice is 100% for your leadership. . . .

Sir James went on to explain that he intended "if it meets with your approval to have certain conversations in England, stressing the importance of Britain using Canada's facilities – geographical, raw material, and manufacturing – in carrying out the general Empire defence programme. Maurice approved of this idea." It was interesting that Hepburn and Duplessis seemed to be outlining policy in matters that were of almost exclusive federal concern. But as Sir James pointed out: "Since the days of Macdonald and Cartier, courageous leadership and effective co-operation have never been as necessary as now and it is fortunate that you and Maurice understand and believe in each other."[10]

The two Premiers had an opportunity to deepen this understanding in mid-November at the Royal Winter Fair (where Hepburn had entered his prize Clydesdale horses in several events). On that occasion, too, Hepburn chatted with one of his Ottawa political friends, James G. Gardiner, the Agricultural Minister. Hepburn told Gardiner that he would not support King in another election, but he indicated he would back a satisfactory federal leader, perhaps Gardiner himself, though the Agricultural Minister said he was entirely loyal to King. On November 25, Gardiner again visited Hepburn. The federal Minister (who had made the visits with King's knowledge) discussed the general results of these meetings with Senator Lambert:

> Lunch with J.G. who told me about his two visits to Mitch discussing leadership.
> (1) That King should get out as the price of unity.
> (2) That he not King wd. quit first, making the stake unity of the party. Three things wanted: (1) Power export (2) Long Lac diversion & (3) Niagara Bridge.*

More serious for Senator Lambert and the federal Liberals than these rather impractical and contradictatory conditions for Party unity was an action of Hepburn's a few days after Gardiner's last visit. On December 2, Lambert received a disconcerting phone call from one of the Liberals' leading financial men in Montreal, Gordon Scott. According to Scott, Ontario Liberal Secretary Harry Johnson had approached him and Senator Raymond a few days before:

> Gordon Scott phoned that Harry J. called on him last Monday morning, representing Mitch, and expressing concern over the unity of the Lib. party, & repeated what Gardiner had said to me about Mitch's proposition to him: he also said that Elliott's successor should be appointed at once in accord with Hepburn's wishes.† Gordon said also he had Johnson meet Raymond at his house in evening when he made same proposal to Raymond. Both of them, he said, laughed at the suggestion of J.G. taking King's place. J. also wanted both Raymond & Scott to see Mitch in Toronto.

Lambert placed a serious interpretation on this visit of a Hepburn representative to two prominent Liberals in Quebec: "I told P.M. all this &

---

* In the spring of 1938, Hepburn bitterly complained to King about the federal Government's delay in issuing a permit to replace the Niagara Falls View Bridge which had collapsed. (M.F.H. to W.L.M.K., telegram, April 6, 1938; W.L.M.K. to M.F.H., telegram, April 6, 1938. pao, Hepburn Papers.)

† King was having some difficulty naming a successor to Postmaster J. C. Elliott, partly because some of Hepburn's friends like Ross Gray and Arthur Slaght were in the running.

he agreed to see Scott on Mon. afternoon to hear the whole story. I told him I thought someone here had directed Johnson to Scott & underlying his visit was the idea of undermining federal financial sources."

If Hepburn were trying to put the financial squeeze on the federal Liberals in Quebec (King himself was later informed of Hepburn's claim that Duplessis would arrange the defeat of the Quebec wing of the Party), at the same time as he was tightening the money screws in Ontario, Lambert's whole federal organization could be in trouble. Lambert had already arranged that his Toronto collectors would ask for from one-and-a-half to two per cent contributions to campaign funds on federal contracts in Ontario. Hepburn was playing havoc with these collections. The Ontario Liberal treasurer, Bethune Smith, told Lambert through an intermediary "that any money spent in Ont. on roads or anything else by Ottawa must accrue to Ont." A Toronto construction company was warned that if it had any dealings with Ottawa it was out at Queen's Park. A prominent Hamilton contractor "had been cut out of 2 jobs by McQuesten as a penalty for helping us." The provincial Liberals had not lifted a finger to help the federal candidate in the losing by-election in Waterloo South in mid-November, a contest that Ottawa had expected to win.

Over lunch on December 5, Montreal organizer Gordon Scott told King and Lapointe about Hepburn's attempt to interfere with campaign funds in Quebec. Something had to be done. Mines and Resources Minister Crerar "favored calling of Ont. ministers & members in caucus & placing them all on record." Lambert decided that Ontario needed a separate federal organizer and a federal committee. He consulted some of Hepburn's old friends in Toronto. C. L. Burton of Simpson's promised that he would co-operate with a federal committee "if we set one up on basis of national unity with Hepburn as the issue." J. S. McLean of Canada Packers said "he would come to a luncheon to discuss federal matters if it were decided to make Mitch an issue. He said he had no use for him, but felt Mitch had a strong support still in Ontario."

Setting up an independent federal organization in Ontario would take time. Mackenzie King had already decided that something must be done immediately. By November of 1938, he was convinced, or had allowed himself to become convinced, that Hepburn and Duplessis were planning to intervene in federal politics, probably for the benefit of the financial and mining interests centred in Toronto and Montreal. He was also convinced (as he had perhaps not been a year earlier when Hepburn was fresh from a decisive electoral victory) that in any show-down with the Ontario leader he would have the support of the majority of the Ontario federal Members and of the people of the country. King was aware of the widely publicized fact that three members of his own cabinet – Ian Mackenzie, C. G. "Chubby" Power, and J. G. Gardiner – had long been on friendly terms with Hepburn. Lambert had received information from

Ontario sources that "we had traitors in the Dom. Cabinet." Ian Mackenzie was mentioned specifically.

But King was also convinced (quite rightly) that the entire Cabinet would support him in a fight with Hepburn. Possibly the news of Hepburn's attempt to interfere with campaign funds in Quebec was the determining factor. In any event, King decided that the time for a confrontation with Hepburn had come. One man's persistent treachery must not be permitted to destroy the national Liberal Party. For too long the Cabinet, especially the Ontario ministers, had worked with one eye on Queen's Park to ascertain Mitch Hepburn's reaction. There had been enough trimming sail to avoid Hepburn's tantrums. If one of his ministers would not speak out, King would do so himself. Better though for someone else to provoke Hepburn's wrath; then King, unsullied by petty partisan squabbling, would deliver the *coup de grâce*.

The strategy was meticulously worked out, the scene carefully chosen. This was to be no political sideshow in Madoc or Hastings with Mitch Hepburn gleefully firing balls at "Honest George" Henry or "Sparkplug" Earl Rowe; this was the big tent, and the top man himself was cracking the whip which had already stripped the hide from bigger politicians than Mitchell Hepburn. One of King's closest allies in the federal Cabinet, the precise, scholarly Labour Minister Norman McLeod Rogers (whom Hepburn after the Oshawa strike dubbed "a pink socialite") offered to take Hepburn on. The occasion was at hand. December 10 was nomination day in the federal riding of Port Arthur, represented by C. D. Howe. There had been rumours that a Hepburn candidate (the provincial Member, Charles Cox) would oppose Howe. In Ottawa, Norman Lambert had received reports that Howe's chances for renomination did not look favourable. A week before the convention, Howe told Lambert that he was very discouraged: "He proposed going up there, getting licked, & quitting. I told him he couldn't do that. He must go to Port A. a day earlier, & have the whole convention cancelled if any doubt about its outcome."

Howe went to Port Arthur and won the nomination unopposed. Cox did not stand and claimed subsequently in a letter to Hepburn that he had never intended running. He denied "there was an organized effort to take the Convention from Mr. Howe . . . but should there have been, I am quite sure he would not have secured it, as I consider him a most unpopular candidate here." What did make headlines all over the country was not Howe's uncontested nomination but the speech of Norman McLeod Rogers. The Labour Minister charged that "a conspiracy" headed by Hepburn and Duplessis had existed for some time. Its purpose was to force Mackenzie King's retirement and to gain control of the federal Government for the benefit of the two central provinces. This Ontario-Quebec alliance, according to Rogers, was based on "personal and political animosities and the desire of two men to gain power over national affairs without being subject to the responsibility of a national electorate." The conspiracy had already failed. Perhaps, warned Rogers, "Mr. Hepburn and Mr. Duplessis are ready to make overtures to Dr. Manion, the Conservative leader, with the same object of using provincial forces and political organizations to control the national Government." Howe reiterated Rogers' "conspiracy" charge.

Mitch Hepburn reacted promptly to the sensational charge of "conspiracy" (a word which seemed to have been carefully chosen, perhaps as much for its political leverage across the country as for its factual content). "Let me say here and now, there is no conspiracy whatever between Premier Duplessis of Quebec and me." (Duplessis termed the accusation "ridiculous," adding that he had "the very highest admiration for the very great qualities of heart, of spirit, and of mind of my friend, Hon. Mitchell Hepburn.") Hepburn denied categorically that he had any desire to go to Ottawa in any capacity. Mackenzie King's policies were "half-baked, impractical, and unworkable." Unless the King Government decided to give Ontario a fair deal, "I'm prepared to go out on the hustings and fight them and fight them to the limit. If that's the sort of thing that Howe and Rogers are looking for, let them say so. All they have to do is toss the gauntlet down to me . . . they'll get all they're looking for. More too." Hepburn would not lead a third party but he would support one. King was "living in another generation." The Ontario Premier was even prepared to "vote for Bob Manion – at least he's human." As for King, he should "lift the blinds of his summer retreat at Kingsmere, peek out, and then go back and hibernate again. It strikes me that's about all he has been doing for the last four years and he might as well continue."[11]

To this retort, King made his first formal reply in the long history of the feud with the Ontario Liberal leader. He supported the "conspiracy" charge that Hepburn and Duplessis were trying to force his retirement, a belief he claimed was shared by his entire Cabinet and most Canadian Liberals. Up to now he had kept silent to avoid saying or doing anything that would "widen the breach created by Mr. Hepburn's attitude toward myself and the Dominion Government." He had hoped that any legitimate differences might disappear or be removed. That had not happened, and the dispute had reached such proportions that King was prepared to fight:

> The issue as it has developed transcends the narrower considerations of personalities and parties. It has become one involving the standards which are to prevail in the public life of Canada, in the relations between the provinces and the Dominion, and the whole question of national unity.
>
> This issue must be and will be squarely faced. To that end, as a first step, I intend as soon as Parliament reassembles, to discuss the

situation in all its implications with members of the party in the House of Commons and the Senate.

There was no question that King would have the backing of the Ontario members though there was disagreeement, even in his own Cabinet, over how Hepburn should be handled. Ian Mackenzie told Lambert that he thought a mistake had been made at Port Arthur: "Saw Ian McK. who said he thought open break with Mitch was a mistake at this time. He thought somebody had poisoned P.M.'s mind." Whatever Mackenzie's misgivings, the Ontario members caucused on December 19 several weeks before Parliament met. King did not attend the meeting (which included Commons members, senators, and defeated candidates), but he wrote a letter to the caucus chairman expressing "the hope that today's meeting may serve to mark a place of new beginning in friendly and hopeful co-operation, on the part of the Party, in all parts of Canada." If it did not quite do that, the six-hour caucus did produce two results: a virtually unanimous resolution supporting King's leadership, and another plan to win Hepburn back to the fold. Two Members of a special subcommittee, Ross Gray and William Fraser (both friends of Hepburn), were despatched unofficially to sound out Hepburn about co-operation. Their chances of success did not seem promising. The Ontario Premier laughed off reports that the caucus would read him out of the National Liberal Federation by saying he had not been a member for two years. He accompanied that with another outburst against King: "I repeat that Mr. King is living in a past age and generation without hope of betterment so far as he is concerned. To anticipate any more would be comparable to the hope of getting results from putting a mustard plaster on a wooden leg."

That was the climate when Gray and Fraser saw Hepburn on December 20 at his Bannockburn farm. The talks were generally conciliatory, but the two federal Members returned to Ottawa carrying three conditions laid down by the Ontario chief: control of the appointing of two federal Ministers from Ontario; Norman McLeod Rogers' retirement; Harry Johnson (OLA Secretary) to be named to the Senate. Through another intermediary, Hepburn assured Norman Lambert that "he couldn't hope to interfere with local ridings and wouldn't." On December 22, Lambert discussed the whole matter with some of the Ontario Members: "Ross Gray & Fraser here. Met Euler, Howe & Rogers this A.M. Said that Hepburn was prepared to keep quiet; that united front from now on was to be the word." Hepburn denied that he had any knowledge of Harry Johnson's trip to Montreal in November to interfere with campaign funds.

There was some hope for peace in these negotiations, but it was significant that nothing was worked out about co-operation between the federal and provincial Liberals through the Toronto office. Significant, too, that despite the promise of keeping quiet, Hepburn was soon writing to

Rogers and Howe demanding that they prove their conspiracy charges.[12] Still at the end of 1938, Hepburn's feud with Ottawa seemed to be subsiding somewhat from the headline-hurling charges which had punctuated much of the year. What muted for a time the "King Must Go" movement was not so much any basic change of heart on Hepburn's part (his demand to interfere with federal Cabinet appointments was quite impossible) but an apparent breakdown of Mitch Hepburn's health. On December 15, the Premier addressed the Empire Club in Toronto. The speech, to a large but somewhat unenthusiastic audience dealt mainly with fiscal policy and constituted Hepburn's own blueprint for a solution to the national financial problems the Rowell-Sirois Commission had been examining.

The theme of Hepburn's speech was that Ontario's sound financial position (he had announced another surplus of three million in 1938), so carefully constructed, was being jeopardized by Ottawa's prodigality. All this talk of equalization payments to the underprivileged provinces would further endanger Ontario's treasury. Instead of more "hand-outs" to "have-not" provinces, Hepburn proposed to his blue-ribbon, Empire Club audience what he termed a genuine monetary reform that would reorganize the fiscal structure of the Canadian economy and render unnecessary any chimerical recommendations by the Rowell-Sirois Commission for equalization payments. Monetary reform fascinated Mitch Hepburn, as it has always fascinated most pseudo-reformers who think that tinkering with the money supply is an easy, magical way to cure all social ills. Monetary reform for Mitch Hepburn involved two steps: a refunding of public debts at lower interest rates (which he claimed would save the Canadian taxpayers nearly eight hundred million dollars annually); and a massive increase in the money supply. (He agreed with his Public Works Minister, Colin Campbell, that the federal Government should buy up Canadian gold and issue currency against it at the rate of four to one: "You may call that inflation if you like, but it would solve the problem.")

These views did not sit well with the business community, the very group that had backed Hepburn only a year earlier in his labour policy. The remedy sounded too much like the "funny money" policy of William Aberhart in Alberta. It was significant (and most upsetting to the Premier whose own budgets had been a model of fiscal orthodoxy) that immediately after the Empire Club speech on the iniquities of high-interest rates on government borrowing, trading in high-yield Province of Ontario bonds came almost to a stand-still in Toronto. It was not only the Government bond market that collapsed at the end of 1938. So did Mitchell Hepburn's health. After his Empire Club speech, a doctor was summoned to the Premier's Queen's Park office. Then it was announced that the Premier would join his Minister of Public Works, Colin Campbell, on a trip to Australia, ostensibly to study economic conditions in that country, which Hepburn often said he considered among the most advanced in the world. There was speculation that the Premier would resign because of ill health. Mackenzie King was informed that Hepburn was seriously ill and would be leaving public life within a matter of days.

Again numerous letters flowed into Queen's Park urging the Premier to continue. The St. Thomas *Times Journal,* which often disagreed with his policies, said the Premier's resignation would be a matter of regret. "Few public men have caught the imagination of the people as he has done." Hepburn himself, from his Bannockburn farms, where he spent Christmas with his family, said he was not "contemplating retirement at the moment at least." His carrying on would depend "on whether there is sufficient improvement by the time of the session."[13] The fact was that events and pressures – political, physical, and moral – were now beginning to close in on Mitch Hepburn, pressures that a sea voyage to Australia could only relieve, not resolve.

chapter 11

Point of No Return

When Mitch Hepburn, visibly tired, boarded the *Mariposa* at San Francisco in the first week of 1939 for his trip to Australia, he had been Premier of Ontario for four and a half years, leader of the Liberal Party for eight. These had been exciting and hectic years that would have taxed a man in the best of health. The fact that Mitch Hepburn's health was never robust had considerable relevance to the ups and downs of his public career.

As a boy of fifteen, he made a good recovery from typhoid fever. Two years later, he suffered the first of several attacks of pneumonia. While he was with the Flying Corps in the First World War, he recovered slowly from influenza. About that time too his hip and left kidney were injured in a car accident. Shortly after becoming Liberal leader, he was laid up for a month in the spring of 1931 with pneumonia, and in June underwent major surgery for the removal of his left kidney. The doctors were satisfied with his recovery, but he never seemed to regain fully his former strength and tired easily. Ten days after the kidney operation, pleurisy developed. In all, he was in bed for twelve weeks before resuming a strenuous speaking campaign. Later, when over-tired, he often suffered some pain at the site of the pleurisy infection.

Susceptible to colds which interfered with his speaking, Mitch Hepburn also experienced repeated bouts of bronchitis which not only weakened his resistance but interfered sometimes with his rest so that he could not fall asleep until two or three o'clock in the morning. By the time he became Premier, his doctors had diagnosed this condition as chronic asthmatic bronchitis. In March, 1935, the Premier's blood pressure was somewhat above normal, a symptom that recurred in subsequent years, and was thought by his doctors to be caused by the strain of his position and lack of rest. At this time too a doctor prescribed one and a half grains of Nembutal to help his sleep. After becoming Premier, he began to experience night sweats sufficient to warrant a change of pyjamas. All these symptoms indicate a man subject to severe tensions and susceptible to respiratory ailments.[1]

The fact that Mitch Hepburn's health was somewhat uncertain made him more conscious of the health problems of others. Health legislation, Premier Hepburn always maintained, was his administration's outstanding contribution to the betterment of the province. The legislation of which he was most proud was occasioned by a chat the Premier had with the well-known Toronto pediatrician, Dr. Alan Brown. The doctor told Mitch Hepburn of the incidence of disease and death among Ontario's children from impure milk. Although more than ninety per cent of the milk consumed in Ontario was pasteurized, the small percentage of raw milk produced in rural areas accounted for a disproportionate share of typhoid, undulent fever, and bovine tuberculosis. Because of the cost of installing purifying equipment (and, the mistaken belief that raw milk was the purest), a hard core of farmers was bitterly opposed to any compulsory pasteurization law. Dr. Brown frankly told the Premier that he did not believe the politicians had the "guts" to pass such a law because of the farm lobby.

Shaken by the information the doctor had given him on the rate of tuberculosis among children, Mitch Hepburn decided to see for himself. Together the Premier and the doctor visited one of the children's wards in the Toronto General Hospital. Down the ward they saw two long rows of cots. All were occupied by victims of bovine tuberculosis, the dread, milk-borne disease. There was no doubt about the horror of it or about the expression of compassion on Mitch Hepburn's face. Helplessly the Premier turned to the doctor. What could he do? The only solution, replied Dr. Brown, was compulsory pasteurization of milk: "Your Government has the power – if it wishes to use it – to empty hospital wards like these." Mitch Hepburn was silent for a moment. Then he said simply: "You have my word, doctor. It shall be done."

With that decision, the Premier unleashed a storm of protest that threatened to split his Cabinet and to alienate his rural support. Letters and telegrams bombarded Queen's Park when the Premier announced that a law providing for compulsory pasteurization (to be applied in rural areas gradually) would be introduced in the 1938 session. On February 15, 1938, a delegation of the Ontario Agricultural Council (including neighbours of Mitch Hepburn's from Elgin) met the Premier at Queen's Park to oppose the proposed law. As he looked at his friends, the Premier was well aware that if he lost the farm vote his Government was finished. Many were predicting that Mitch Hepburn would back down, that the political risk was too great.

The Premier said nothing as the farmers' spokesmen presented the case against compulsory pasteurization: the machinery was too expensive; there was no evidence that untreated milk was the cause of disease. Mitch Hepburn's expression changed as he listened to the arguments. He was obviously impatient and annoyed. A thin unpleasant smile crossed his lips and his eyes turned a cold blue steel as he suddenly looked at one of the men in the delegation. From the Premier's amazing memory a name and a face had emerged. He turned on the farmer, and as the delegation sat stunned, Mitch Hepburn's voice snapped like a whip: "I know you. How many children do you have?"

"I have five," replied the man, startled.

"Didn't you have seven?"

"Yes. Two died."

Tension crackled through the room. Mitch Hepburn, rigid and pale, his voice sharply pitched, barked: "They died of bovine tuberculosis, didn't they? They drank milk from your own cows and died?" There was a rasp of anger as the Premier continued: "You came here today to protest against the pasteurization of milk. You have already lost two children to bovine tuberculosis, but that doesn't prevent you from coming here to ask this Government to withdraw its bill and leave your children and other children open to the threat of death. What kind of man are you?" Then Mitch Hepburn turned to the other farmers and told them his decision on pasteurization was final: "I know it may be strenuously opposed . . . but we are determined to go through with it." Go through with it he did. In the session of 1938, a bill providing for the compulsory pasteurization of milk in progressive stages throughout all rural areas was passed by the Legislature.

Opposition did not cease with the bill's passage. Protests inundated Queen's Park, some of the most savage from the Premier's own constituents in Elgin: "I thought we had a real leader," wrote one farmer from the St. Thomas area, "but I find we have a damn stool pigeon." A petition from Yarmouth demanded that all townships be exempted from the Act, and a delegation of Elgin farmers travelled to Queen's Park to protest. Many of the letters addressed to the Premier were personally abusive: "What I would like to know is How is it that (judging by your actions) you think it is alright for People to drink Whisky but all wrong for them to drink raw milk? Why do you strain at a flea and swallow a Hippopotomus?"

Despite this fanatical opposition from many of the province's farmers and his voters in Elgin, despite the political dangers, Mitch Hepburn never wavered on his pasteurization program. He told his own people at a farmers' meeting at Aylmer that he was proud of his course and would not deviate from it: "I had to take the hard way, not the popular way, and I am going to live to see the day when the children of Ontario will be safe from the dangers of bovine tuberculosis." He lived to see that day. Within two years of the passage of Mitch Hepburn's pasteurization bill, the rate of death from tuberculosis in Ontario had dropped from 35.4 to twenty-six per 100,000 of population. Other factors were also involved, but Mitch Hepburn's bill had helped to empty the long wards. Whatever else he did or did not do, the bright laughter of healthy children would stand as a monument to Mitch Hepburn's courage, foresight, and compassion.[2]

The pasteurization program revealed Mitch Hepburn at his best, a man sensitive to the afflictions of others. The sick, the imprisoned, the jobless, the war veterans, all these at one time constituted Mitch Hepburn's constituency. He would remember an acquaintance in the hospital and send enough fruit for the entire ward. He would take a sick friend to a sanatorium and instruct the authorities to send the bills to him, "an act," wrote a man who knew of it, that "I shall always cherish in your favour as not political but humanitarian." Mitch Hepburn seemed to go out of his way to help his political opponents, especially those who were down on their luck. It might be finding a position for someone he had defeated in an election (something he did more than once), or it might be a helping hand for some die-hard Tory in Elgin who confessed that he had voted against Mitch Hepburn and now did not have enough cash to buy seed beans. To his plea for assistance Mitch Hepburn replied: "One can always appreciate frankness and honesty and although I have never had the pleasure of meeting you, I am going to loan you the money necessary to purchase your seed beans. Please believe me also that I have not made any inquiries in your community regarding your financial standing or anything else, this little transaction will be kept confidential between the two of us." He hoped that "these Grit beans will give you a good yield."

There were many transactions of that kind in Mitch Hepburn's career – a farmer helped with his crop, a young man given a stake to begin college, the time-consuming work of arranging parole for a prisoner. For some of them Mitch Hepburn was simply out of pocket; for most of them he gained no political credit. There was his concern for a prisoner at Guelph Reformatory whom he asked the warden's permission to visit: "I know the family very well and feel very keenly for the mother, especially as she is not in very good health, and worries continually over her son." There was the time at the beginning of a busy federal campaign when Mitch Hepburn wrote dozens of letters, made appointments with Cabinet ministers, and visited Kingston Penitentiary several times to secure parole for a man whose family lived in New York (where, needless to say, there were no votes for the federal Member for Elgin). After one of his visits to the Penitentiary, he wrote to encourage the prisoner's daughter:

I know you must realize that it is rather difficult for me to give you a detailed report of our interview, but one result I assure you is that I feel I am doing the proper thing in now pressing his case for clemency.

His chief concern seems to be that you and your mother should not worry too much about him. One with his culture and intellect can develop – even now – a certain peace of mind that would not be possible to others.

A letter from the man's daughter when her father's release was finally arranged largely through Mitch Hepburn's efforts was perhaps reward enough. She and her mother were "quite dazed with joy. We keep reading your letter over and over for the sheer pleasure of it. . . ."

Mitch Hepburn's compassion for the handicapped and the underdog was accompanied by a buoyant sense of fun. He once said that a politician would be lost without humour (though he would not necessarily have agreed with his friend Larry McGuinness that "to be a successful politician one must be young, vigorous, and heavily hung"). In answer to another friend, G. G. "Gerry" McGeer, the peppery Mayor of Vancouver, who telegraphed him on the eve of St. Patrick's day, "Wire me confidentially what part of you is Irish," Mitch Hepburn replied: "Sure me Mother's Father came from Ireland. Quite possibly our great grandfathers hoed potatoes together over there. The Irish in me is a fixed quantity and never varies, like the Scotch." When McGeer wired for permission to use the telegram in a speech, the Premier prudently replied: "Okay to use wire with the exception of the last sentence."

Mitch Hepburn laughed frequently and he made others laugh. His speeches (with the exception of the budget address) were never written out and were full of earthy humour. Preparing a speech, he first thought of a good joke and then built from that. Once at an impromptu meeting of farmers in the country, someone asked Mitch Hepburn to say a few words. He agreed and nimbly jumped on to the only rostrum available, a manure spreader. He looked down at the manure spreader and began with a wide grin: "This is the first time in my life that I have spoken from a Tory platform." As the farmers rocked with laughter, a voice from the back of the crowd roared: "Throw her into high gear, Mitch, she's never had a bigger load on." It was one of the few times on a platform that Mitch Hepburn did not have the last word.[3]

A man with a big heart and a ready smile, a man who instinctively liked people, a decisive man with the courage to take an unpopular position and see it through – that was one side of Mitch Hepburn. There was another side, a darker more unpleasant side, that eventually would alienate many of Mitch Hepburn's oldest friends, that would threaten his public career and would jeopardize his family life. Perhaps the drive that transformed Mitch Hepburn, "the boy from Yarmouth," into a dynamic, colourful, political leader, and Premier of his province also drove him to the excesses that blighted his career. Perhaps there was just too much drive and too little traction. Mitch Hepburn himself never stopped long enough to examine the pattern of his existence, to look back to ask what was happening and why. From its beginning, there had been disappointments and disturbances in Mitch Hepburn's life, serious enough to leave permanent scars. When he was just ten years old his popular, impulsive, somewhat unstable father fled his home, his promising political career ruined because of a widely publicized scandal reportedly involving liquor and women.

There is no exact way to measure the effect on a boy of a home life shattered by scandal. Nor is there any way to plumb the sadness of young parents when their only two children die in infancy, as did those of Mitch Hepburn and his wife in the first years of their married life. Their loneliness and sadness were not entirely assuaged when the couple adopted three children, Peter, Patricia, and Helen. Mitchell Hepburn took immense pride in his three adopted children (Peter's adoption in 1935 was a stimulus for the province-wide adoption drive launched by Minister of Welfare, David Croll). The Premier had a baseball field laid out at Bannockburn and outfitted Peter and his friends with uniforms. Early in 1937, he wrote his friend "Ned" Sparks, the Yarmouth-born movie comedian, in Hollywood: "Young Peter, age 4½ years, in my opinion is a real champion, while young Patsy, according to my wife at least, is going to develop into a Shirley Temple."

After he became Premier, however, Mitchell Hepburn had little home-life. During most of this period, the children and Mrs. Hepburn (upon whom devolved the responsibility of overseeing her husband's large farming interests) remained at Bannockburn while the Premier stayed at his King Edward Hotel suite in Toronto. Most weekends the Premier would return home in his black Cadillac with his faithful companion and jack of all trades, Eddie Wooliver (affectionately known as "The Bruiser") at the wheel. Frequently there were weekened guests – Jack Bickell, Sir James Dunn, Larry McGuinness, the Premier's close friend and personal physician, Dr. William Avery, his private secretary, Roy Elmhirst – and dozens of others from the sporting, political, and mining worlds to enjoy Bannockburn's hospitality presided over by Mrs. Hepburn.

It was convivial and hectic and informal, a good deal of fun for the Premier and a great deal of work for his wife. (Although she came from a politically oriented family, Mrs. Hepburn disliked politics: "If Mitch likes it, then I must give him all the help in my power." Through the ups and downs of the years already gone and the years to come, to the extent that she was able and was permitted, the Premier's wife did that faithfully.) Besides the conviviality of the weekends at Bannockburn, there was work for Mitch Hepburn too. A stranger driving past the Premier's farm on a Saturday, seeing the yard and the roads dotted with cars, might have thought there was a ploughing match or a fall-fair at Bannockburn. The place was swarming with friends, neighbours, job-seekers, political hacks, hangers-on – all trying to see Mitch Hepburn for a word, a favour, a deal of some kind. Usually there was too little time on these crowded weekends for Mitch Hepburn to talk to his wife and children, or to stroll over his twelve-hundred acres, to check the rich black soil where the well-publicized onions grew, or to examine his prize show-horses, the Percherons and Clydesdales.

By late Sunday it was time to drive out through Bannockburn's stone gates for the trip back to Toronto with Eddie Wooliver, back to the King Edward, to another week directing affairs from Queen's Park. It was a feverish life for a man in the best of health. For a man like Mitch Hepburn, it was a dangerous life and his recurring respiratory illness proved that. Shortly after he became Premier, he was warned by one of his examining physicians: "My own impression is that Mr. Hepburn is trying to carry too much for his own physical welfare. I quite appreciate it is almost impossible to get sufficient rest at present but every effort should be made towards this end when possible."[4] As Premier, it never seemed possible for Mitch Hepburn to obtain the rest he needed. There was the business of government, policies to be determined, legislation to be drafted and piloted through, politicians to be placated and hangers-on to be got rid of.

There was also that other life in Toronto that revolved around his new friends. Shortly after Mitch Hepburn's election, one observer wrote: "His greatest asset is his ability to make people like him, and his chief danger now consists of his friends." To some extent these friends – hard-driving and hard-drinking politicians, some of the wealthy mining crowd and the sporting fraternity, brewers, publishers, and contractors – reflected a need in Mitch Hepburn. He had started as a farm-boy in Yarmouth, but he was a hero worshipper who needed to prove a number of things to himself, one that he could move, if not with the best, at least with the fastest. It was a fast, driving, fun-loving crowd that Mitch Hepburn moved with in Toronto in the early years of his premiership. Some of that crowd, like Frank O'Connor, were genuine friends of Mitch Hepburn; others were just using him; almost all would be gone long before the end. For the moment it was an exciting, electric life, with its flying trips to the south, its parties at the hotel, at the sporting lodges, and on the suburban estates. It was the kind of life that Mitch Hepburn needed and craved. His was a restless, agitated spirit. He needed the wheel of excitement spinning dizzily, though he lacked and always had lacked a central axis to maintain balance. (An Indian tribe fittingly christened Mitch Hepburn the chief of "Turbulent Waters.")

An extrovert who vacillated between elation and depression, a vigorous leader who could not brook the slightest stricture on his policies (frequently criticism in one of the Toronto newspapers was followed by an emotional outburst from the Premier and a day or so of "illness"), a man who needed friends but was savage with his opponents (on one occasion, angered by criticism in the Toronto *Star,* the Premier, in one of his more despicable actions, revealed in the Legislature some minor misdemeanours of publisher Atkinson's grandsons), a beaming man often as tense as a coiled spring, Mitch Hepburn too often sought relief from his contradictions and frustrations in ways that might be overlooked in the ordinary citizens but were, for a public figure, both extreme and dangerous.

Mitch Hepburn did most things by extremes. Once at a dinner in his honour, when the speaker used several Latin quotations, the Premier remarked to a table companion that the only Latin he knew were the words he sometimes saw on a bottle – *Ne Plus Ultra.* Unfortunately, Mitch Hepburn rarely practised moderation. His political feuds, his towering tantrums, and his loyalty to friends who had long since become liabilities were examples of this. So at times was his consumption of alcohol and his relationships with certain women. Whatever the reason behind his need for friendship, conviviality, and excitement, Mitch Hepburn too frequently satisfied (or exacerbated) that need by liquor and female companionship. Sometimes these needs were so inordinate that they constituted a danger to Mitch Hepburn's health, his family life, and his political career. Even before he became Premier, some of Mitch Hepburn's closest advisors were concerned lest what one writer later termed his "fairly comprehensive extra-curricular capers" should damage his political hopes. Early in the 1934 campaign, the Secretary of the Ontario Liberal party, Harry Johnson, a friend of Hepburn's, twice warned Norman Lambert that there was a possibility of scandal: "If you hear anything break regarding Hepburn & women you'll know it's probably true."[5]

The record of most public men contains much that is good and some that is bad. Unfortunately, human nature being what it is, it is easier to remember sins than to recount virtues. Occasionally the Premier received a letter indicating this: "My advise [*sic*]," wrote one voter at the beginning of 1936, "is for you to cut out the liquor and the women and try and be a decent citizen while you are Premier, which I fear you won't be for long." Occasionally the Premier was castigated publicly for his habits, sometimes by a Protestant minister. Dr. George Little of the United Church Sunday School Publications once accused him of being a "playboy without either moral or commonsense." Dr. Little pointed out that during Premier Hepburn's term of office there had been an increase in admissions to mental hospitals, higher rates of divorce, illegitimacy, prostitution, and drunkenness, all of which seemed to prove nothing except that the Reverend gentleman had his causal sequence out of kilter. Criticism from a group that Mitch Hepburn once unjustly and intemperately called "Psalm-singing hypocrites" never seemed to worry the Premier much. Never a formally religious man (though nominally a member of the United Church), Mitch Hepburn nevertheless considered himself a Christian with little regard for ceremonial and pious cant. "It is hard," he once wrote to a friend, referring to certain ministers, "to understand the smug hypocrisy of these alleged pious Christians. For my part, I prefer to be one of the ordinary mill-run of humanity."

Whatever his disdain for ministerial anathemas, Mitch Hepburn was more than a little upset when a national magazine, the respected journal *Saturday Night,* published at the end of 1937 an article that suggested his private life was a little on the racy side. Written by the British author, Sir Anthony Jenkinson,* the article described an evening's visit in 1936 with the Premier in his suite at the King Edward. The suite was a spacious one, with a coloured picture of Mackenzie King on a centre table, a stack of government reports heaped in a corner, on the walls pictures of Dr. Allan Dafoe (a friend of the Premier and the doctor of the Dionne Quints), and another of the Premier's friends, actor "Ned" Sparks. Jenkinson described the Premier on that occasion:

> He had a round cheerful face and neatly brushed hair that grew far back on his forehead and a chin that was small but purposeful. He wore a well-tailored, double-breasted suit and had the appearance and manner of a popular young man-about-town. From the room behind him came the sounds of radio dance music and ice tinkling in glasses and girls' voices. . . .
>
> Mitchell Hepburn led me into the room where the radio was playing, and introduced me to his friends. They were his doctor and a member of his Government and two attractive girls who sprawled on a sofa and called the Prime Minister "Chief". . . . A big broad-shouldered fellow with the supple movements of a trained athlete mixed drinks and . . . periodically dashed out of the apartment after slipping on a camel-hair coat and a light felt hat with the brim turned up in front. . . . It was evident that he acted as a sort of bodyguard-cum-gentleman's servant to the Prime Minister. The latter called him "Eddie," but the girls just called him "Bruiser."

When the Premier protested to *Saturday Night,* the editor B. K. Sandwell expressed his regret "for any annoyance that the article may have caused you."[6]

One of Mitch Hepburn's former colleagues, Arthur Roebuck, reviewing the period of early 1937, noted: "Things were not going well with the Hepburn Government due to the Premier's drinking, loose living, and the company he was keeping." Still, from the welter of rumours that subsequently circulated about Mitch Hepburn's "loose living," two facts are easily forgotten: his family life did not break up (thanks in large measure to the loyalty and steadfastness of his wife), and the Hepburn administration was never tainted by scandal. No Hepburn minister ever resigned under the pressure of wrong-doing.† There were rumours of malfeasance as there are about most Governments. Two of the most persistent were that one Hepburn minister and some of his departmental associates had taken "kickbacks" on business contracts made for the Dionne Quintuplets (whose material welfare Premier Hepburn went to considerable lengths to safeguard); the other was that the Premier and others had made a good thing out of the timber contracts that were let by his Government in the Lakehead region, particularly those to his friend, the big lumberman, E. E. Johnson. If there was any truth to either of these allegations (and no conclusive evidence is available to substantiate them), nothing was ever proved. There were rumours, too, of graft and corruption in the awarding of road contracts especially to the Dufferin Paving Company, controlled by Hepburn's friends, James and Leonard Franceschini. Late in December, 1938, a federal Liberal official in Ontario showed Senator Lambert figures purporting to show padding of $248,000 on a stretch of highway construction in Northern Ontario. Specific charges were never substantiated, and the rumours remained just that.[7]

From time to time it was hinted that Mitch Hepburn had become a wealthy man as a result of stock-market tips from his mining friends. Undoubtedly the Premier speculated on the stock market under the guidance of men like George McCullagh, Jack Bickell, and Frederick Crawford. He invested in mining and other stocks. At the beginning of 1938, he wrote to "Ned" Sparks advising him to hang onto his Canadian gold stocks and added: "I was lucky in being quite a substantial holder of MacLeod-Cockshutt stock, much of which was purchased at the low level of ninety-seven cents. Today's quotations are around $3.00." If he made huge sums of money through speculation, Mitch Hepburn must have lost or spent his profits almost as fast as he made them. Eventually his total estate amounted to slightly more than $275,000 of which $138,000 was in real estate. (Life insurance, stocks, and cash totalled approximately $25,000). The only large personal donation that there is a record of

---

* This article was reprinted from Jenkinson's book *Where Seldom a Gun is Heard* (London: Arthur Barker Ltd., 1937)

† One of the ministers without portfolio, Charles Cox (Port Arthur), was scarred when a young woman acquaintance threw acid in his face. The woman was subsequently committed to a mental institution, and the minister resigned from the Cabinet shortly afterwards. (*Globe and Mail,* March 19, 24, 1937)

Mitch Hepburn's receiving during his lifetime amounted to $40,000 (spread over twenty years) from the estate of his friend, Senator Frank O'Connor.[8]

Whatever Mitch Hepburn's sins, venality and greed do not seem to have been among them. His "fairly comprehensive extra-curricular capers" are important in a political sense to the extent that they besmirched his administration's reputation or interfered with its effectiveness. A few days before the end of his public career, Mitch Hepburn confessed to his own electors in Elgin: "I have made mistakes in the past and I may make mistakes in the future but I didn't make any mistakes that impaired the efficiency of Government."

It is probably true to say that, on the whole, the Hepburn years at Queen's Park, so far as departmental administration was concerned, were years of efficient government. This was due in some measure to able civil servants like the Deputy Treasurer, Chester Walters, and Dr. Duncan McArthur who later became Minister of Education. The hydro contracts, of course, could have been renegotiated more quickly and with less fuss; still their final settlement represented an improvement over the original agreements. In a period of rising expenditures and revenues, Mitch Hepburn was proud of his string of budget surpluses. Although these surpluses restricted new welfare programs and services needed for economic recovery, they illustrated Hepburn's conservative fiscal approach and generally pleased the business community. It was only toward the latter part of its second term, when Mitch Hepburn, increasingly impatient and bored with the tedious details of day-to-day governing, spent more and more time away from Queen's Park, that Opposition Leader George Drew was justified in calling the Hepburn administration "a phantom government."[9]

Nevertheless Mitch Hepburn's "loose living," excessive drinking, philandering, and partying impaired his physical well-being, blurred his judgment, shortened his political career, and complicated his family life. The problem arises why a man with so many talents and opportunities should risk all for the ephemeral and diminishing pleasure of playing around. This was no young lad sowing his wild oats; this was a forty-two-year-old man whom his fellow citizens had twice elected Premier of the province by record majorities. The answer, in general terms, seems to be that for all his attainments, his shrewd intelligence, decisiveness, and dynamism, there was one side of Mitch Hepburn that never developed. In simple terms, he never grew up. When he was a child, Mitch Hepburn saw things with the eyes of a child; when he became a man he saw them, emotionally, the same way. He began his political career as "the boy from Yarmouth," and he always remained a boy – an exuberant, impulsive boy, generous to a fault, implacable with those who crossed him, jealous, hostile to authority, susceptible to flattery, somewhat naïve, over-sensitive to criticism, brash and cocky, yet all the while not quite sure of himself, constantly needing approbation, continually having to prove himself, throwing a temper tantrum if thwarted, demanding obedience from others, undisciplined himself, an extrovert who, like most children, had neither the time nor the ability for self-examination.

For the ordinary mortal, these are not necessarily fatal defects. For a political leader living in a pressure-cooker of steaming emotions and conflicting advice, they are tragic flaws. Unfortunately, some of Mitch Hepburn's closest associates seem to have been only too willing to cater to his whims and accommodate his juvenile excesses. Those who were his real friends, those who loved him most and who saw disaster written on the wall, could do nothing or were permitted to do nothing to save him from it. As he sailed for Australia at the beginning of 1939, Mitch Hepburn was fast approaching, if indeed he had not already passed, the point of no return.

chapter 12

Into the Breach

Before he travelled to Australia, Mitch Hepburn had referred several times to the worsening international situation. Shortly after the Munich Crisis in September of 1938, he told a gathering near Bala that Canada needed stronger defence forces: "I must confess that I held different views when I was a Member of the House of Commons . . . but now I realize Canada must arm herself in order to protect the peace she desires." His Australian trip reinforced his belief that international relations were deteriorating. On board the *Mariposa*, Hepburn became friendly with the Australian High Commissioner to London, S. M. Bruce, returning home to report to his Government. Bruce indicated to Hepburn that Germany would probably make another aggressive move by the fall of 1939.

When he reached Australia, the Premier saw the defence preparations in that country and was told about the fears of a Japanese attack. He noted in one of his speeches: "I am a good democrat but we have lessons to learn from the totalitarian countries. The democracies cannot hope to survive by simply patting each other on the back." Before leaving Sydney to sail for home, Hepburn told his hosts: "No one is more determined than I to force the issue of proper defence in Canada." When he landed in the United States in late February, 1939, the Ontario Premier did not mention, except in general terms, the economic panaceas he had supposedly gone to Australia to study. Instead, he stressed the apprehension in that part of the world of a Japanese invasion: "I will say that, as a result of my trip, I am even more fully convinced of the need of defence and a more adequate defence."

On his return, there was more interest in Mitch Hepburn's political future than in his military views. His blood pressure was down and his weight had dropped fifteen pounds to 175, but he seemed listless and discouraged about his political future. (Rumours current then and later suggested that just before leaving for Australia the Premier had been prepared to resign and offer the leadership to Harry Nixon. On January 10, Senator Lambert had been informed that Nixon "was ready to take over.") Hepburn refused to discuss these rumours. "You know," he told a newsman as he travelled to Toronto by train, "I don't like politics as much as some people think I do, and I suppose a person should not take chances with his health." Next day, February 24, 1939, he announced that he would lead the Government in the session and would be present as Premier to welcome King George VI and Queen Elizabeth to the province in May.[1]

On the first day of the session, which opened on March 8, attention centered on the new Conservative leader, George Alexander Drew. He had won the Conservative leadership in December, 1938, at a convention that revealed the virus still infecting the provincial Party from the coalition proposals of April, 1937. Earl Rowe, who had resigned the leadership, left no doubt that he felt George Drew had betrayed him at that time and in the 1937 election campaign. "Who is here among you," he cried to the Conservative delegates at the Royal York Hotel in his farewell speech, "who is so doubtful a Conservative that he would form a coalition with our common enemy? Him only have I offended." It was one of Earl Rowe's best speeches, as he told the Tories, his voice trembling with emotion. "I lost an election, but I saved you a Party." After he had won the convention easily on the first ballot, Drew admitted he had believed a coalition "was necessary at that time." Now all had changed. "Personally, I shall do everything I can to unite the Party for the purpose of defeating Mr. Hepburn."

Now the strapping, ruddy, good-looking lawyer from Guelph had his chance. The galleries were packed on Leaders' Day, March 14, to see the first clash between the new Opposition chief and Mitch Hepburn. Drew did not waste any time. He startled the Government benches by saying that to expedite the people's business he would be the sole Opposition speaker in the throne speech debate. When someone muttered "fascist," Drew's face reddened with anger. If there were any dictatorship in the house, he retorted sharply, it did not come from him. He would strengthen the central Government and confer "on provincial bodies only such powers as may be required for local purposes . . . I am for one strong Government dealing with national affairs." He then rebuked the Premier for his feud with Ottawa and moved an amendment condemning Hepburn's refusal to confer with Mackenzie King on problems affecting Ontario's welfare.

The Premier listened intently. There was just the trace of the old devilish twinkle in Mitch Hepburn's eyes as he rose to reply to the deadly serious, deep-voiced Drew. He looked over at the end of the Opposition front bench to the seat of former Tory House leader, Leopold Macaulay. Drew, remarked the Premier, like a man snapping a new whip, was about "as consistent as his predecessor who is now sitting there like the end man in a minstrel show." That flick brought Drew out of his seat explosively demanding a withdrawal. "I will withdraw," the smiling Premier replied, flicking the whip again, "and just say he is the end man." A roar of laughter swept the Liberals sitting behind the Premier. Obviously operating on the theory that the quickest way to deflate a balloon was to prick it, Mitch Hepburn went on to explain that it was he who had conceived the billboard picturing the sinking "Rowe Boat" in the election of 1937. He would now rechristen that "Show Boat," with George Drew as "Miss Canada Number One." At the next election, he would sink that boat too. If George Drew wanted to argue Ottawa's case, let him do so. It wouldn't get him far in Ontario.

By any tally, the Premier had won this first confrontation. The Liberals were delighted. So was Mitch Hepburn as he told Frank O'Connor vacationing in Florida: "The boys had a lot of fun over the battle between Drew and myself on Leaders' Day. There is one thing we all discovered and that is that he can't take it and loses his temper very easily. Our boys are in great humour and have caught the real old Liberal fighting spirit." The Premier and his boys again displayed the Liberal fighting spirit when the accusation that Drew had called the French Canadians a "defeated race" was revived in the House. Drew charged in a radio address that the Premier had deliberately resurrected that canard. The Premier dared him to repeat the charge in the House, and a claque of Liberal members shouted, "Say it!" An angry Drew protested: "We are certainly getting a fine lesson in dignity." The Premier shot back: "We are certainly getting a lesson in what a prima donna is like when he is cornered."[2]

As the session progressed, the two leaders co-operated more closely, a development that later was to have far-reaching consequences for Canadian politics. What seems to have occasioned this was their common impatience with the federal Government's reaction to the worsening international situation. In March, when Hitler seized part of Czechoslovakia, British Prime Minister Neville Chamberlain had asked the support of the Empire in resisting further aggression. "In my opinion," Hepburn told a group of Toronto business men at that time, "three nations have agreed on a conquest of the world and the rest of us must stand together and resist the inroads of dictators."

In Ottawa, Mackenzie King condemned the seizure of Czechoslovakia, and promised that if England were attacked Canada "would regard it as an act of aggression menacing freedom," a general policy statement supported by Conservative leader Robert Manion. At Queen's Park, neither Hepburn nor Drew considered this response adequate. Accordingly the Ontario Legislature unanimously passed a resolution petitioning the federal Government "that in the event of a war emergency, the wealth and manpower of Canada shall be mobilized . . . for the duration of the war."

Hepburn told the House he believed that a national emergency already existed. He realized that Canada was a difficult country to govern and that the contents of the resolution came under federal jurisdiction. Nevertheless, "I now believe that if the Government of Canada does not consider itself in a position to make a declaration as far as open sentiment is concerned, we, as the people of Ontario, can at least do that." The resolution, continued the Premier, who in his earlier career was never considered an anglophile, "will be a source of encouragement and a ray of hope to the people of the Motherland who, after all, have their backs to the wall, and a demonstration of loyalty to the Empire, and of our affection to the Crown."

The *Globe and Mail* was exultant: "Ontario struck for the Empire yesterday, and for all the Empire stands for in this hour of crisis." The Toronto *Star* thought that the resolution "voices the opinion of the great majority of this province's people." Reaction at the national level was considerably cooler to what seemed an unwarranted intrusion in a matter of federal concern. Mackenzie King told the Commons that he could not accept the view that in all circumstances Canada should be prepared to support any action decided by the Government at Westminster. Moreover, there would be no conscription for overseas service, a policy that Manion supported. The Conservative leader was having difficulty trying to hold the Quebec and imperialist wings of his Party together. "To cap it all off," he complained to his son, James, "this morning there is a report that in the Ontario Legislature yesterday Hepburn, another stay-at-home warrior in the last war . . . demanded that Canada have guts enough to say where she stands."

The resolution, besides embarrassing federal authorities of both parties (something that would now happen with increasing frequency) marked the first but not the last time that Drew and Hepburn would act in concert. Already Hepburn's view of the new Conservative chief had softened, as he explained to Senator O'Connor: "We are having lots of excitement in the House. Drew has calmed down considerably and is not the pompous individual who came in when the Session opened."[3] More frequently as the session progressed (highlighted by the war-mobilization resolution, another Hepburn budget surplus, and enabling legislation to permit Ontario to participate in a national unemployment insurance plan), Hepburn's attention and that of the Legislature was directed toward defence matters.

Hepburn's preoccupation with defence affairs took a dangerous turn when it seemed to threaten academic freedom. Near the end of the session, a storm broke out over statements which were allegedly detrimental to the defence effort made by two professors of the University of Toronto. G. M. A. Grube of the Classics Department of Trinity College and F. H. Underhill of the History Department of the University were the two well-known, socially minded academics in question. Grube had supported a resolution at a CCF meeting advocating less defence spending and a statement of Underhill's, "The poppies blowing in Flanders Fields have no further interest for us," made several years previously, upset Queen's Park members on both sides of the House. Tory Leader George Drew demanded an explanation of "such outrageous remarks." The Premier went further. If Trinity College did not discipline Professor Grube, the Legislature had the power to abrogate Trinity's affiliation with the University and might use that power: "Some have called me a precedent-buster. Well, I'm prepared to bust another precedent to get at a man of the character of this foreigner, Grube." (Unlike the Premier, "this foreigner" had served overseas in World War I).

The language of Hepburn's Minister of Education, Dr. Leonard Simpson, was more moderate. He announced that President H. J. Cody and other appropriate university authorities would deal with the two professors: "I would hesitate to support," said the Education Minister, speaking for the Government, "any measure that would take power away from those who are in control of our educational institutions." The Premier's outburst was another example of his intemperate and abusive language toward established institutions and individuals for whom he had little liking or respect. (His real targets, perhaps, were not the two professors so much as the University's President, H. J. Cody, and its Chancellor, Sir William Mulock.) The attack again reflected his narrow rural conservatism and, considering the threat of war, coincided with the pro-British sentiments of the majority of Ontario's people. It was a reminder too that his bark was often sharper than his bite. The Government took no action and the dispute subsided.* About the same time, when students of the University of Western Ontario in London publicly protested a lower legislative grant, the Premier (who never showed much sympathy for or awareness of the problems of higher education) remarked that universities were largely populated by the children of the rich, a state of affairs that would scarcely be ameliorated by cutting their grants.[4]

Of more interest to the Premier than the difficulties of higher education was the problem of national defence. One of the men who influenced Hepburn's thinking in defence matters was Sir James Dunn (still trying to lift Algoma Steel out of the red). Sir James made frequent trips overseas and informed the Premier concerning military developments there. In a letter written in November, 1938, Sir James emphasized the urgency of Canada's helping England to rearm:

> I believe our defense [*sic*] preparations should include a Canadian "Woolwich" where the nucleus of our armament can be created and maintaned [*sic*], situate [*sic*] well away from the seaboard and close to the American border since our defence operations must invisage [*sic*]

common action with the United States and at the start at any rate we will need the U.S. as well as the British technical aid. My mind naturally turns to the Soo with deep water frontage both above and below the canals and within reasonable distance of the nickel mines at Sudbury.

In the session of 1939, Hepburn urged the Legislature to pass a bill incorporating the Southern Algoma Railway as a subsidiary of the Algoma Steel Corporation. He told the members that he saw the day when continued industrial expansion would make the Sault "the arsenal of the British Empire" through expansion of its steel mills. About the same time the Premier was receiving urgent letters and memoranda from Sir James complaining that the King Government was not accepting orders from Britain for defence equipment. On April 24, Sir James wrote: "Are we going to take part in helping the Empire get ready in time and give our own people employment instead of relief and idleness, or are we going to lag and do nothing as has been the policy at Ottawa for so long on so many things?"[5]

The Ontario Premier's dissatisfaction with defence preparations and federal policies needed little fanning from Sir James Dunn or anyone else. This impatience was shared by a considerable number of citizens, particularly in Ontario, and was certain sooner or later to renew the conflict between Ottawa and Queen's Park. Since the explosion set off by the "conspiracy" charges at the end of 1938, Hepburn's feud with King seemed to have subsided. None of its underlying causes had disappeared, however, and the astute Norman Lambert had never fully accepted Hepburn's assurances at that time to keep quiet. More to the point, Lambert could discern no practical moves toward co-operation from the Hepburn machine. On the contrary, Lambert heard that if and when Postmaster-

---

* In the latter part of 1940, Professor Underhill was again criticized for his views on defence and foreign policy, and pressure was exerted to have him ousted from the University. Some believed that Premier Hepburn was behind this pressure, but the evidence available suggests that others, particularly certain members of the University's administration and the Board of Governors, wanted Underhill fired. A friend in Toronto sent Senator Lambert a "memo which showed that Cody not Mitch was responsible" for the attempt to oust Underhill. On behalf of the Government, Provincial Secretary Harry Nixon promised that no grant to a university would be cut because of the views of its staff members. About the same time, President Cody and Chancellor Mulock approached the Premier concerning his accepting an honourary degree from the University. Premier Hepburn, true to his anti-establishment bias, explained to a friend: "The matter of a University degree was thoroughly disapproved of by senior members of the Cabinet. Hence my own judgment was upheld – for better or for worse." (Lambert Diary, Jan. 17, 1941; Interview with C. W. Burns, May 25, 1967; PAO Hepburn Papers, C. Sifton to M. F. H., Jan. 10, 1941; M. F. H. to L. Dolan, Dec. 10, 1940.)

General J. C. Elliott resigned his London seat (a change contemplated for some time), Hepburn would see to it that the Liberals lost the riding.

When the time came to replace Elliott in the Cabinet, Mackenzie King, in view of Hepburn's reported hostility, took extraordinary pains with the appointment of a new minister from Ontario. He first offered the post to Arthur Slaght, whom Hepburn had recommended for a Cabinet position in 1935. When Slaght declined for personal reasons (apparently to King's relief), the Prime Minister adopted the astonishing course of asking the Ontario parliamentary representation to ballot on the appointment. One of the reasons King resorted to this unprecedented manner of choosing a Cabinet minister seems to have been to block party-whip Ross Gray, a Hepburn confidant, without antagonizing Hepburn's other Ottawa friends. Whatever the result of the balloting (most of the Ontario men did not vote, and some think that Gray did very well), King appointed Norman McLarty (Essex West) as Postmaster General.[6]

Meanwhile, Senator Lambert (whose request for the Ontario appointment for himself, because it would help straighten out the organizational mess in that province, was not accepted by King) proceeded with his plan to develop an independent federal organization in Ontario. When an attempt to have the President of the Ontario Liberal Association, Hepburn's Highway's Minister Tim McQuesten, call a meeting of that organization failed (none had been held since 1932), Lambert convened the Ontario federal ministers to see what could be done.

These efforts were stepped up early in 1939, when rumours began circulating in Ottawa among both Liberals and Conservatives that the Ontario Premier might start a new Party. In this venture, Hepburn's name was sometimes associated with that of George McCullagh. On January 31, 1939, Ontario Conservative strategist Donald M. Hogarth wrote to Dr. Manion:

> While I have no definite ideas, I believe it logical to assume that Duplessis and Hepburn would find it much easier to subscribe to a new political movement than to line up behind the Conservative Party. This line of thought is particularly applicable to Hepburn. I often ask myself why, outside of a desire to get away from things for awhile, he went to Australia, and sometimes wonder whether it did not form part of a plan which he had agreed with McCullagh and possibly Montreal, and to which he will contribute his part when he returns from his trip. I cannot conceive of him ever being brought into line behind King. His prime ambition is to defeat him.[7]

There is no doubt that Hepburn wanted to defeat King, but there was no conspiracy with McCullagh at this time. Following the election of 1937, relations between Hepburn and McCullagh cooled. When McCullagh differed with Hepburn over his plan to replace Lieutenant Governor Bruce with Duncan Marshall, Mrs. Bruce recalled: "G. McCullagh . . . told us . . . that he was going to break Hepburn during the next few months. If one could trust him to do this. On March 29 I reminded him of this and he says its [*sic*] taking him time but that he is laying careful plans, and will do it in the next 60 days."

In the spring of 1939, however, George McCullagh had other plans. He was a busy young man who had the politicians at Ottawa and else-were considerably perplexed. Shortly after Hepburn left for Australia, McCullagh began a series of radio broadcasts. In the main, these consisted of evangelical exhortations to reduce taxation, abolish provincial Legislatures, support Britain, form a National Government of the country's best brains at Ottawa, and place the children of the country firmly on the road to success. McCullagh seemed to think that his effervescent mixture of positive thinking, patriotic fervour, cold showers, spiritual calisthenics, and physical training could develop national greatness and a home-grown version of Jack Armstrong, the all-American boy. So potent was McCullagh's charismatic appeal, at least in the boondocks, that he established the Leadership League which developed into a kind of grass-roots lobby using the *Globe and Mail* as a clearing house for the little man to vent his spleen on governments in general and politicians in particular.

Conservative leader Robert Manion for one was not impressed with McCullagh's evangelism: "My own feeling is," he wrote one supporter, "that there is far too much acceptance without question of suggestions made by, for example, George McCullagh, who, after all, is only thirty-three and who has had no special experience except in making a bit of money." Although relations between Premier Hepburn and the publisher improved after the Premier's return from Australia ("He is becoming very friendly towards me again," Hepburn wrote O'Connor, "and invites me to his home frequently"), the Premier never appears to have been actively concerned with the Leadership League which, owing to lack of public interest and McCullagh's deteriorating health, disbanded in the early summer of 1939.[8]

More important than the fortunes of the Leadership League, so far as most Liberals were concerned, was the growing optimism that Mitch Hepburn's feud with Mackenzie King was subsiding. What occasioned this feeling was a meeting of the two men in Toronto in May at the time of the visit of King George VI and Queen Elizabeth. Just returned from a vacation in Georgia, Mitchell Hepburn was present at Union Station in Toronto on May 22 to greet the Royal Couple. It was a drizzly Monday and one of the few times that Mitch Hepburn was nervous. He explained later to George Challies, Conservative member for Grenville-Dundas, who had congratulated him on the ceremonies, "I must confess to you . . . that for the first time in my life I experienced a real attack of the jitters. If this was not obvious to those present, I am very much relieved." It was not obvious. The Premier moved smoothly through the complicated protocol (although he greeted the Queen ahead of His Majesty at Queen's Park). His wife looked charming and unflustered in a powder blue dress and a jacket of soft grey fox. In the Chamber at Queen's Park, His Majesty's First Minister in Ontario presented eight Victoria Cross winners, the members of the Cabinet, and George Drew ("Your Majesty, I have the honour of presenting a gallant soldier, an author, and the Leader of Your Majesty's loyal Opposition in Ontario") to the Royal Couple. The Premier seemed pleased as Mackenzie King presented the Hepburn children. "Peter almost doubled up when he made his bow, and Patsy made really a lovely curtsy," he proudly recalled later. During the banquet at the Great Hall in Hart House, Queen Elizabeth chatted animatedly to the Premier who sat on her right. At the far end of the table, Mackenzie King and Mrs. Hepburn appeared to get on famously.

For Mitch Hepburn, whose ancestors had fought the Crown's representatives a century before, the Royal Visit had been a tingling experience. The gracious couple made a deep impression on their first subject from Elgin County: "I am so enthusiastic I don't know what to say. . . . I know they are the right type to preside over British democracy." Mackenzie King also thought he had reason to be pleased with the ceremonies in the Queen City; surely Hepburn's personal animosity had been softened by the amenities of the occasion. King had gone out of his way to be friendly. The opportunity must not be lost. The Prime Minister spoke to C. D. Howe who spoke to Lambert who was asked to see Frank O'Connor again about a rapprochement with Hepburn. Two days after the Royal Visit, Lambert did so: "Called on Frank O'Connor & told him the suggestion of his friends in Ottawa about seeing Mitch & trying to consolidate the Ontario situation. He said he would do so, and . . . was emphatic about his stated efforts to restrain Mitch."

King was too sanguine. He had been criticized by the Conservative press for hogging the limelight on the Royal Tour and for including too many members of the Liberal establishment in the festivities. Hepburn shared this resentment. On the day after the Toronto visit, Robert Manion wrote to congratulate him on the magnanimous way he had treated Drew at the ceremonies, contrasting it "with Mackenzie King's caddish action so far as the Conservative Party, and indeed the other Parties down here, were concerned." In his reply, the Ontario Premier agreed that King had treated Manion shamefully. He thought, "King's idea to trail Their Majesties like a poodle dog was an effort to gain cheap publicity for his own political aggrandizement." So far as a personal reconciliation with King was concerned, Hepburn stated publicly, "My position is unchanged."[9]

The position was changed, however. It was weaker than a year earlier for three reasons. Hepburn's general health was deteriorating; because of the international situation, any alliance with Duplessis was becoming more of a liability; and it was now more uncertain to what extent Hepburn could hold his Ontario provincial members in line. One of them, Fergus Brownridge, Member for Stormont, told the Premier to his face in the Legislature that "in the event of a federal election I propose to assist the present federal member from Stormont in every possible way." Despite Hepburn's previous ukase that there was to be no co-operation with the federal Party, up to the middle of 1939 provincial members had attended every federal nominating convention in the province. The Premier seems to have realized that at the constituency level he could not control many of the members. On May 3, Lambert noted in his diary: "Euler told me about caucus of Ont. Leg. members who were told by Mitch that they were free agents in a federal election."

Rumours were now growing stronger that, barring international complications, a federal election would be held in the fall. Senator Lambert was operating on that schedule, and he was giving special attention to Ontario. He had finally succeeded in setting up a separate federal organization for the province to be called the National Liberal Committee for Ontario. An office had been leased in the Toronto *Star* building, and a federal man from Hamilton, Bartholomew "Bart" G. Sullivan, was hired as chief organizer aided by Toronto financial men like Peter Campbell, C. P. Fell, and D'Arcy Leonard. It was also decided there would be a major show of federal strength in the heart of Hepburn country – a monster testimonial dinner to Mackenzie King in early August to celebrate his twentieth anniversary as leader of the Party.

The Ontario Premier did not seem perturbed by this federal activity. At the beginning of July, he had another visit from his friend, Ian Mackenzie, who reported to Lambert: "Mitch's last & only grudge now was Howe and Rogers." Writing to Ottawa press gallery man, Tom Wayling, about the expected federal election, Hepburn noted: "I am not taking part in the election unless Rogers and Howe start something again." Early in June, the Ontario leader met Duplessis in Toronto amid rumours that both of them would support Manion to stop the drift toward state socialism in Ottawa. During part of July, the Premier enjoyed a relaxed holiday at Bannockburn where one of his guests was former heavy-weight champion, Gene Tunney. Both men swam in the cold waters of Lake Laurier and cantered about Bannockburn on two of the host's western saddle ponies. The same day an Orange parade was scheduled for St. Thomas. The Premier offered the Grand Marshall one of his white horses, but laughingly informed him that Gene Tunney's sister was a nun.[10]

Politics was never very far away, however, in the summer of 1939. There was much conjecture about the plans of Hepburn, Duplessis, Drew, and McCullagh in the expected federal contest. In the *Financial Post*, columnist Grant Dexter speculated that Drew wanted to replace Manion after the election. The Ontario Opposition leader wrote to Manion on August 3 to deny this and to say something of his strategy *vis-à-vis* Hepburn in Ontario, a strategy that he had discussed with the federal leader on previous occasions. Undoubtedly Drew believed that Dexter's suggestion of his replacing Manion originated with the Liberals. It was not the first time such a stratagem had been bruited about and probably would not be the last. What better way for Liberals to distract attention from the King-Hepburn vendetta than to stimulate or, at least, simulate a similar feud in Conservative ranks? If they were successful, the ground would be cut out from under Manion before he ever really gained control of the Party. He obviously could not go far as federal leader without the support of George Drew and his Ontario organization.

There had been rumours too that Drew and Hepburn were working closely with a view eventually to entering the federal field. It was not difficult to discover why these rumours should have started. There had been little or no criticism of the Hepburn administration from Drew and the provincial Tories. No doubt Drew felt that the best strategy in Ontario for the Conservative party was to sit on the side lines and permit King and Hepburn to slug it out. The Tories could scarcely hope to find an issue of their own that would cause more harm to the Liberals than the one handed them by the King-Hepburn feud. As long as Hepburn persisted in his running attacks on King, nothing would be gained by Drew's mounting any kind of campaign against the provincial Liberal leader. That would merely confuse the electorate and divert attention from the Liberals' internecine warfare. Let them fight each other to a standstill, then, so far as Ontario was concerned, Drew and his party could move in and pick up the pieces.

Manion told Drew the strategy of permitting Liberals to decimate each other was sound: "I am wholly in accord with your ideas about the Hepburn affair. It seems to me that it would be all to the bad if there were any row stirred up today over provincial matters. Under the circumstances, it is my feeling – as it is apparently yours – that until the Dominion election is out of the road, Hepburn, with his present attitude, should be left alone." Actually, Mitch Hepburn was fast becoming the ally, if not the unwitting captive of the Toronto Tory establishment. More and more frequently prominent Conservatives like Charles O. Knowles, Editor-in-Chief of the *Telegram*, and W. J. Stewart, Member for Parkdale, were guests at his King Edward suite. It was a measure of how far his political judgment had already been corroded by animosity for King that Mitch Hepburn did not seem to realize he was being used.

That animosity was bared again at the beginning of August. It was a sweltering night on August 8, when the cream of Liberalism gathered at the Royal York Hotel to honour Mackenzie King on his twenty years as

Party leader. There was no little irony in the orchestra's playing, "Hail, Hail, the Gang's All Here." The gang was not all there. The Prime Minister of Ontario was not there; no member of his Cabinet was there (though fourteen provincial Liberal members were). Still, most of the gang was present, including five provincial Premiers at the head table, thirty-five hundred roaring, perspiring Grits jammed into eleven dining rooms, and the federal leader standing under an immense portrait of himself flanked by bronze profiles of Laurier and William Lyon Mackenzie. It was the largest affair of its kind in the history of Canadian politics.

Hundreds of ecstatic Liberals crowded into the main ballroom when the chief himself, three hours and twenty-two speeches after the oratory began, rose to address his followers. King made only one reference to the Hepburn feud, and that indirect. One of the great lessons he had learned from Laurier was not "to cherish resentments." He expanded briefly on that: "I have always kept any differences I may have had in a personal sense from influencing, one way or another, my judgment on public affairs. It does not do to cherish resentment in public life." King had already proved more than once and would prove again that it certainly did not do to cherish them if Mackenzie King were on the receiving end.

Despite this dramatic display of federal strength in Hepburn land, King's speech was not one of his notable efforts. Manion, who had listened to it on the radio, told his son, that it "was the awfullest that I ever heard a prominent public man make – just terrible. . . . King must be indeed getting softening of the brain." Senator Lambert, trying to boost his new Ontario federal organization, noted that everything had been "wonderfully put on: but the speeches. The P.M.'s was disappointing." Even King seemed to recognize this. He was "full of excuses for his speech of last night, including Heeney, Mitch Hepburn, Pickering, and the weather."

The speeches aside, one of the amusing sidelights of the affair was the manner in which the two Toronto afternoon papers treated it. On the day of the banquet, the *Star* proclaimed: "Canada United for Premier King Provinces Declare." The *Telegram's* viewpoint was somewhat different: "All Hepburn Ministers Boycott King Banquet." Next day the *Star* trumpeted, "Enthusiastic Tribute to Mackenzie King Stirs Dominion." The *Telegram* did not seem overly enthused; its banner headline read, "Mad Heifer Terrorizes High Park District."[11]

Within days there was more to be concerned about than political banquets and amusing headlines. A deadly madness was loose in Europe. Adolf Hitler was massing his armies on the borders of Poland. As the war clouds darkened, Mitchell Hepburn, saddened by the death of Senator Frank O'Connor, one of his closest friends, declared: "We've got to stand or fall by the British Empire."

Saturday, September 2, was a hot day in Toronto. There were 146,000 spectators at the Canadian National Exhibition, the Leafs were at the bottom of the International baseball league, and at the Uptown Theatre Irene Dunn and Charles Boyer were playing in "When Tomorrow Comes." When tomorrow came, prayers were said for peace in the churches, the *Athenia* was torpedoed and at 7:00 A.M. Toronto time, Great Britain declared war on the German Reich. On Monday, September 4, the attendance at the CNE soared to 192,000, the Edmonton Eskimos came from behind to whip the Calgary Bronks, at the ball park the Maple Leafs split a double-header with Rochester, Hitler's panzer divisions rolled across Poland, and the Premier of Ontario and his Attorney General warned against enemy sabotage. At Ottawa, Parliament was summoned.

Tuesday, September 5, was a busy day for the Ontario ministers. Feuds were forgotten in the bigger crisis. After an all-morning Cabinet meeting, Premier Hepburn wired Mackenzie King "that each Minister places at disposal of Federal Government his services in any capacity. . . . The services of all departments of Government are available to you." The Premier then informed Defence Minister Ian Mackenzie that he would be glad to turn over the facilities of the new mental hospital at St. Thomas to the Defence Department. Attorney General Conant also wired Mackenzie urging that federal authorities help Ontario to guard the vital Niagara power installations which he and the Premier, after a quick flight from Toronto, inspected the same day.

While the federal ministers at Ottawa grappled with the complex problems of putting the nation on a war footing and formally declaring hostilities, there was no let-up in the flurry of activity at Queen's Park. Conant contacted Justice Minister Lapointe urging him to re-enact Section 98 of the Criminal Code dealing with subversive meetings and speeches. Then he wired Mackenzie again, insisting that Ottawa assume responsibility for guarding the power stations immediately: "Matter is most urgent and important. Would appreciate early attention and reply." (The Hepburn Government had already transferred four planes from the Ontario Government Flying Service based at Sault Ste. Marie to Toronto Island Airport for air patrol over the Niagara power stations.) Working his way through a maze of problems, the Defense Minister told Attorney General Conant that the matter of federal guards for the Niagara stations "will be taken up by Cabinet as soon as present session Pariament over." Other Ontario ministers were busy too. Harry Nixon wrote to Lapointe suggesting that more provincial Government buildings could be made available if prisoners serving short jail sentences were permitted to join the armed forces. It was also suggested to the federal authorities that the Ontario Government would supervise interned enemy aliens if Ottawa would permit them to work on Ontario sections of the Trans-Canada Highway.

Premier Hepburn took the lead in placing his administration on a war footing. He was pessimistic about the war and thought that drastic measures should be taken. "Make no mistake about it, Tommy," he wrote to Tom Wayling of the Ottawa Press Gallery on September 15, "this is going to be a long war, and a bad one, and I agree with you thoroughly that conscription should be put in force at once." Disturbed by reports that there was a shortage of military clothing in Ontario, the Premier wired King on September 18, warning him that this unsatisfactory situation might adversely affect recruiting:

> I am informed that there is a magnificent response from men rushing to enlist. Unfortunately so far recruits drilling must wear their own shoes, socks, and civilian clothing which are totally unsuitable and are causing severe physical hardships . . . will appreciate it very much if you will communicate with me advising when necessary supplies will be available in Ontario so that I may be able to give assurance to the large number of inquiries coming to me daily.

Mackenzie King, who presumably had more on his mind than socks for Ontario's recruits, asked his Defence Minister to inform the Ontario Premier that steps had been taken two weeks before to ensure sufficient clothing for all requirements.[12]

Besides prodding the federal Government on the defence situation in Ontario, Premier Hepburn was also busy in September with a special session of his own Legislature. It had been called to tighten up (for the third time) succession-duty legislation which had once again been challenged in the courts. Over the strenuous objection of George Drew, who deprecated its sweeping investigatory powers, the complicated Succession Duty law was passed by the big Liberal majority. The session, lasting only three days, also produced criticism of Canada's war effort. The Premier complained that he had "exhausted his persuasive powers" with federal defence officials trying to have them detail the militia for guard duty in Ontario. Conant said he could obtain no co-operation in the matter from the newly appointed defence minister, Norman McLeod Rogers. Several times the Opposition leader sat with the Ontario Cabinet to discuss the province's war measures. There was nothing unusual in that, explained the Premier: "My personal relations with Colonel Drew are of the very best. We have always co-operated and he has sat in conference with the Government a number of times. I hope to continue the present relationship." (One man who warned the Premier about "the present relationship" was his friend William Fraser, federal Liberal Member for Northumberland: "Watch Drew. He is the world's worst. Remember the story of the lady from 'Nigeria' & the tiger.")

One other federal politician was growing uneasy about the Drew-Hepburn relationship. Manion recorded on September 20 that he had heard "there was to be a blast put forward" the next day by a group of prominent Toronto politicians ("the names . . . were given to me as Mitch, George Drew, Nixon, Macaulay, and Conant") in favour of National Government. The blast did not materialize. The session at Queen's Park wound up not so much with a blast as a binge, which the Premier described to a friend. The session "prorogued in a burst of glory, following which some of the 'old gang' got together. Notwithstanding the increase in the excise tax on scotch whisky, we did our duty nobly – damn it."[13]

What resulted from the session was not pressure for National Government at Ottawa (to which Manion was opposed at that time) but an Ontario War Resources Committee composed of the Premier, Lieutenant Governor Albert Matthews, and George Drew. On September 27, Hepburn requested that this Committee might interview King or his officials "in order to discuss ways and means by which Ontario can best serve Canada in this great crisis." On October 3, the Ontario War Resources Committee ("this bizarre delegation," the secretary to the Prime Minister, J. W. Pickersgill, called it) met King and his aides for two and a half hours in the East Block. At the end of the conference, King warmly thanked the Ontario Premier for his province's co-operation, and the two men shook hands. King welcomed one major change of policy on Hepburn's part. As Pickersgill noted, "Hepburn used this occasion to reverse the attitude of the Government of Ontario to the St. Lawrence Seaway Development by favouring what he had previously opposed." Hepburn and Drew stressed the danger of sabotage to the Ontario hydro plants, and both intimated that the federal authorities were slow placing orders for munitions and supplies and raising troops.

At a Cabinet meeting later that day, Prime Minister King insisted that Ontario's representations should be taken at their face value and dealt with seriously. Perhaps, after all the derailments of the past five years, the federal and provincial Liberals were back on the rails. Norman Lambert immediately saw Bart Sullivan, the new Ontario federal organizer. Sullivan "proposed to McLarty, Howe, & Euler that steps be taken now by Ontario ministers to see *Mitch* so as to heal party breach in Ontario."[14]

Once again the federal men had misjudged Mitch Hepburn. The ups and downs that had marked his relationship with Mackenzie King for more than a dozen years could not be suddenly smoothed out, even by a national emergency. Mitch Hepburn was living on an emotional roller-coaster that was moving with increasing speed, fuelled by resentment, jealousy, a sense of inadequacy and frustration, a roller-coaster that could not be stopped, only slowed down. Those who could slow it down, like Frank O'Connor, were going or had already gone. More and more the bitterness was directed at Mackenzie King. He had been the one person who time and again had blocked the younger man. All of Mitch Hepburn's plans and emotions were, of course, not tainted. There is no reason to question his patriotism or his eagerness to lead his province in a vigorous war effort. If others were not producing a maximum effort, he himself wanted to move Ontario into the breach. At another level, Mitch Hepburn welcomed the war. It provided an opportunity to turn from the petty affairs of Ontario, which were a bore, and to flee the tortuous involvements of his personal life which were becoming a dead end. In a way that the trip to Australia could not, the war might provide an escape. From the moment hostilities were declared, Mitch Hepburn grasped this opportunity, galvanized his Government into action, fired off a barrage of suggestions to Ottawa, most of some value, but rating little priority with harassed federal ministers frantically coming to grips with the implications of a total national effort.

Mitch Hepburn could not understand why his spontaneous and friendly communications were not acted upon at once, why ministers did not drop everything else to prosecute what he almost considered his own war effort. No doubt the Ontario Premier had legitimate complaints concerning leadership at Ottawa; no doubt there was confusion there; no doubt Mackenzie King might have prepared the country for war with more foresight. These were, or would be, when time permitted, subjects for political debate. But Mitch Hepburn saw them as yet another personal rebuff. On his emotional scale, there was no modulation. There were only those keys ascending from impatience to resentment followed by the discordant crash of angry recrimination. It had all happened so many times before. When a national war effort seemed to bring Hepburn and King together, it happened again.

The Ottawa conference between King and Hepburn and their associates had taken place on October 3. The next evening Mitch Hepburn gave his version of what had occurred to newsman Jack Hambleton, a former associate of the Premier's at Queen's Park. This talk was off the record, but Hambleton wrote down Hepburn's conversation "as nearly as I could record it." According to Hambleton, the Ontario Premier had been completely disillusioned by the meeting with King:

> The situation at Ottawa would break your heart. We had intended to hold our tempers and we did, but it was very difficult. Mr. King apparently hasn't yet realized there was a war on, and we could not get a definite answer from him on anything.
>
> For instance, I offered to give in to Roosevelt on the St. Lawrence waterways if he wanted it. He agreed that would be an excellent gesture at this time – but I couldn't get any decision from him.

Hambleton's account noted that at the conference Hepburn had renewed most of the suggestions made previously by his Government – to use internees for road work, to release short-term prisoners who wanted to enlist so that the space could be used for other purposes, to have federal forces guard hydro plants – but no decisions were forthcoming. To convince King that he was sincere, Hepburn told him that he would pay for the federal militia "if he would order them to guard the plants. The result was the same – no answer." On the question of releasing short-term prisoners for enlistment, "Lapointe came in with a lot of bunk – and again we got no answer." Federal officials were not dealing adequately with war orders:

> I told Mr. King British manfacturers are waiting to place $60,000,000 worth of munitions orders in Canada but want to be assured of adequate supplies of power. He said: "I haven't heard anything of that and know nothing of it." I pointed out the recent British mission had interviewed hydro officials and asked about power supplies, and told him some of his ministers must know of it. At this point Ralston got up and said: "That is quite true, Mr. King." You can take that as an indication of the fact he doesn't know what is going on in the country.

Hambleton's record suggests that Ralston was the one man who had impressed Hepburn:

> The only man in the Cabinet who seems to know anything is Ralston, and he is about to quit in disgust. High defence officials are heartsick because they aren't getting anywhere. More than 100 soldiers in one section of Toronto are down with colds and flu from sleeping on the floors. We have ordered two lots of 1,000 blankets sent here and have another under way now.

The Ontario Premier was pleased with George Drew's contribution:

> I must pay tribute to Drew for the part he played in the conference. He told King quite frankly the wrong kind of carriage had been bought for Canadian artillery and said: "Do you know there isn't one Canadian gun which can be fired?" King said he could take pride in the fact that Canada was better prepared than it had been in 1914 and Drew leaned across the desk and asked: "Who told you that?" King said he had learned of it from his officials and Drew promptly told him to go back and check up for himself to find out.

Hambleton reported that Hepburn told him he hoped somebody would blow the lid off the situation:

> I went to Ottawa with the best intention. In wartime I realize any personal feelings must be submerged. But honestly, it would make you sick to see how confused and distraught everything and everyone is in Ottawa. I wanted to break the story and tell the country just what is

going on, but I realize my personal feelings towards King would neutralize any effort I made. Surely, some newspaper will sooner or later open up. It would be a great national service because we are unprepared for this war and we aren't anywhere towards getting prepared. . . .

Frankly, I don't want to issue any statement. I told Mr. King anything he cared to say would be quite satisfactory at this time. But I hope and pray someone will take the initiative and "blow the lid off" as did the British press in 1914. Until then, I honestly believe we are facing the most critical and dangerous period we've ever known.

Hambleton included this account in a letter dated October 5 and sent to Toronto *Star* editor, Jerry Brown, with the admonition: "I trust you will regard this information as confidential . . . as I assured Mr. Hepburn it would not be used in any way." The information was used immediately. Brown passed it on to the *Star's* Vice-President, Harry C. Hindmarsh, who mailed it to Coltrin Drive, Rockcliffe Park, Ottawa, the residence of Senator Norman P. Lambert. Hindmarsh noted, "It might perhaps be wise to destroy it after you have read it." Perhaps. After calling Hindmarsh, Senator Lambert considered it wiser to send the "P.M. copy of private memo about Hepburn." J. W. Pickersgill informed Lambert of the Prime Minister's reaction to the memorandum: "Heard from Pickersgill that P.M. had told Heeney Hepburn's statement ended everything: that Heeney was present at the conference & nothing comparable to Hepburn's statement transpired." Whatever happened at the Ottawa conference (and the supposition is that Hambleton's recollection was substantially correct but what the Premier said was highly selective, to say the least), the exchange of confidential correspondence further damaged the King-Hepburn relationship.[15]

The Premier, now more frustrated than ever by personal problems and federal apathy, was already planning a way out of the imbroglio. On October 4, he wrote his friend Collin Brooks of the London *Telegraph* in England: "I am really lonesome to see you and expect to get over with the first Canadian Contingent." He assured another friend that he had no aspirations for a federal position of any kind, "I have other ideas in mind and expect to go overseas with the first Expeditionary Force. I have, however, great confidence in Colonel Ralston and received his positive assurance that Canada will prosecute the war – not in the manner of the past or the present but with every possible effort put forward." Among the blizzard of suggestions from Queen's Park to Ottawa was one from Colin Campbell, the Premier's friend and Minister of Public Works who had enlisted in the Engineers. On October 11, Campbell wrote to the Commander of the Canadian Active Service Forces, Major-General A. G. L. McNaughton, urging the formation of a special unit of Engineers for immediate service with the Allies and another special unit of tunnelling troops. "I would like you to consider," Campbell asked McNaughton, "allowing Mr. Hepburn and myself to join the same unit with one of these services." Next day, October 12, the Premier wrote to a friend in Australia telling him of Campbell's enlistment and his own plans: "Collie is now in the army as a Lieutenant in the Engineers and I hope to join him shortly."

For the moment nothing came of the Premier's plans to enlist, and he and his ministers continued to jog Ottawa. Again they suggested the use of short-term jail prisoners for road work (rejected as impractical), offered such Ontario Government buildings as the Elgin Mental Hospital for military purposes (gratefully accepted), and proposed the use of the facilities of the Ontario Department of Health to control the spread of gonorrhoea. Defence Minister Norman Rogers thanked Hepburn for these suggestions, adding that he was certain "we can count on the co-operation of your Government in any reasonable request which we may make of it. . . ."[16] It was not much for a man hoping to be where the action was, but it was probably the best Rogers could do.

In any event, the perennial feud was again about to flare up. At the end of November, the Ontario Premier told a banquet at St. Thomas: "Just now there is a truce between the Dominion Government and myself. I don't know how long it will last, but I do know that I am going to support Wilson Mills [federal Liberal Member for Elgin] in the next general election." He was still dissatisfied with the federal war effort. "While I do not wish to appear in a critical attitude, I don't think the war is being prosecuted in this country the way Canadians like it." A modern mechanized force of two thousand men "could lick the whole Canadian army today." The shortage of clothing for the soldiers was scandalous. "Why, some of them haven't been issued a change of underwear since they signed up." The Americans were beginning to laugh at the Canadian war effort.

At a meeting in Aylmer, the Premier was more belligerent. The war effort was not being prosecuted because of Ottawa's policy "of putting the dollar in the driver's seat. The dollar appears to be the main and only consideration at Ottawa." At the Albany Club in Toronto, George Drew charged the King Government with "scandalous apathy" so far as the war effort was concerned. Mackenzie King in his diary termed these charges "direct lies." He added: "It is perfectly apparent that Hepburn and Drew . . . and their gang generally in Ontario intend to make matters as difficult for us as possible. Whatever impression they may be able to make in Toronto will not, I think, be shared in other parts of Ontario, and certainly not in other parts of Canada."

As usual, Mackenzie King had appraised the situation correctly, but there was no way to be certain of that in November, 1939. What was certain then was that Mitchell Hepburn was genuinely upset by Canada's lack of military preparedness, a feeling he shared with many Canadian citizens. What was just as certain was that this legitimate disagreement with the federal authorities, soaked by his bitterness for King, would sooner or later burst into another flaming quarrel. For the moment, however, Mitch Hepburn in his own way was trying to be helpful. In a gesture typical of his humanitarianism, he asked Defence Minister Rogers to supply lists of Ontario soldiers discharged from the services because of tuberculosis. If TB were definitely established, his Government would provide the patient with free hospitalization and place his wife on the mothers' allowance.[17]

As the Christmas season approached in 1939, and the armies in Europe settled down to the phony war on the Western Front, the lines of communication between Ottawa and Queen's Park, though buzzing with static, were open again. For his part, Mitch Hepburn had done his best to lead his province into the breach. He deserved a holiday. He was pleased when at the International Livestock Show in Chicago his three-year-old stallion, Torrs-Transformer, won first place in the Clydesdale class. At Bannockburn, the Premier relaxed and enjoyed skating on Lake Laurier. He seemed cheerful and relaxed.[18] But the membrane covering Mitch Hepburn's frustrations was as thin as the skin on a New Year's balloon. It could burst any minute, and in the first month of 1940 it did. The explosion rocked not only Ontario but the whole country.

chapter 13

The Gauntlet Hurled

On January 5, 1940, Mackenzie King phoned his chief political strategist, Senator Norman Lambert: "He said he hoped we would be ready for an early election; but also hedged on possibility of serious offensive on Western front. . . ." Despite his large parliamentary majority and his pledge to Opposition leader Manion that there would be another session before an appeal to the people, King wanted an early election to clear the air and give his administration a solid wartime mandate. Had the war not broken out, he might well have called one earlier on the issue of national unity, a political euphemism for neutralizing Hepburn and Duplessis. (Duplessis was already immobilized, soundly defeated in October, 1939, by Adélard Godbout with the help of Lapointe and Power and the federal Liberals in Quebec.) What King needed to justify a winter wartime election was a plausible excuse. That excuse was provided sooner than King or Lambert (who had departed on January 9 with Crerar for a holiday in Georgia) had expected or dared hope.

On January 10, 1940, the session opened at Queen's Park, its Chamber attractively recarpeted in rose plush. Much of the legislation outlined in the speech from the throne – to control fresh-air camps with respect to sanitation, water, and food supply – underscored once more to what an extent the province was on the periphery of real affairs. The Premier was not much concerned with fresh-air camps. Instead, as he told Senator Hardy, he was more and more pessimistic about the war: "I view the whole picture with great concern. I believe you will see Japan make a tremendous drive for complete supremacy in the Pacific. I think, under the circumstances, the closer United States and Canada are bound together the better it will be for all concerned."[1] This preoccupation with the war and with Canada's inadequate effort was evident from the session's first sitting. The Premier and Opposition leader George Drew regretted that the country was not doing more. Both men equated the nation's lack of effort with Mackenzie King's lack of leadership. "As for the leader of the Canadian Government," Premier Hepburn complained half-facetiously, "so profound is his addiction to peace that I myself have never been able to provoke him into the slightest demonstration of hostility, though I have tried my best to do so on frequent occasions."

Drew was determined to push the war preparedness issue for all it was worth – despite the express wishes of federal leader Robert Manion that the place to mount an attack on King's policies was in the federal House, scheduled to open on January 25. Manion was trying to find some formula that would at the same time retain the imperialist wing of the Conservative Party and command French-Canadian support, a neat trick if he could bring it off. The last thing that Manion wanted was to have George Drew making speeches in Toronto that would blunt his own attack and upset his delicate strategy. To forestall that, Manion held a two-and-one-half-hour conference with Drew about the time the Ontario Legislature opened at which Manion understood Drew had agreed the national leadership should direct the offensive against King.

Drew, however, was not nearly as convinced as Manion that criticism of the federal war effort and national affairs in general should be restricted largely to the national leadership or that Ontario provincial Conservatives should remain strictly in their own bailiwick. Even if Drew had wanted to co-operate fully with Manion in this matter, there were other Conservative members in Ontario who did not. That was not the only problem facing Drew in the matter of political strategy. Mitch Hepburn had indicated clearly on more than one occasion that he intended to deal with the federal war effort in the Ontario House. Drew would be placed in an ambiguous position if he were to remain silent. Presumably too he had concluded that vigorous criticism of Mackenzie King's war policies originating at Queen's Park would help put teeth into the national defence effort and at the same time would strengthen the Conservative Party right across the country. And George Drew was convinced that the national party needed plenty of strengthening.

Manion was more convinced than ever that the national point of view would be better served if George Drew stayed out of federal affairs. Nor did the fiery Tory chieftain who always called a spade by its name hesitate to tell Drew so:

I have no control, of course, over your actions but I should have thought that, since you have been speaking on the war fairly regularly for the last couple of months when I and my advisers thought it was wiser that we should refrain until the House opened, you would feel that now, with the Legislature in session, you should stick largely to your own field. I cannot stop you from coming into mine but I must tell you very frankly that I hardly consider it fair co-operation on your part if you carry out this proposal of yours.

So fearful was Manion that George Drew's militant speeches would damage the Party nationally that he asked the Conservative Member for Wellington South, Karl Homuth, to restrain the Ontario Opposition leader. Homuth informed Manion that he had already conferred with Drew: "He feels that he is widening the breach between Hepburn and King by encouraging Hepburn in the many things that he is saying. He is a very difficult man to handle, and I am afraid that if I approach him it might be too obvious that it came from you." By the time Manion received Homuth's letter, George Drew had urged the Ontario Legislature to "sound a clear trumpet call to action," Mitch Hepburn had blown the trumpet, Mackenzie King's chief enemies had been delivered into his hands, and the entire political situation in Canada had been changed.[2]

There was nothing to indicate that Thursday, January 18, would be an historic day at Queen's Park. George Drew was criticizing King's leadership but that was nothing new. Listening at his desk, the Premier seemed restless and preoccupied but he was often fidgety. A few of the members noticed a butter-yellow sheet of paper on the Premier's desk with a few lines scrawled on it. As Drew continued, Mitch Hepburn's agitation seemed to increase. He turned once to Harry Nixon beside him and when Nixon shook his head to Highways Minister Tim McQuesten for a few words. When George Drew finished his remarks, the Liberal member for North York, Morgan Baker, rose to defend the federal leader and began quoting from one of King's speeches. An impatient Mitch Hepburn was not going to stand for that. He jumped up, wheeled to face his own Member, and said to Baker coldly: "Why should we be subjected to that twaddle? . . . I ask to be associated with Colonel Drew in that atttack on the King Government to which you refer." Several others came to King's defence, including Arthur Roebuck (Toronto-Bellwoods) and one of the French-Canadians, J. A. Habel (Cochrane-North).

Then Mitch Hepburn rose again, the butter-yellow piece of paper, marked by his familiar blue-crayon pencil still lying on the desk in front of him. The time had come, he said in a voice a little higher, a little tighter than usual, the time had come to test the opinion of the House. The situation was deteriorating; now was the time for a showdown. The House quietened; the Liberal members looked puzzled; the Premier continued:

> I don't care if I am defeated – and you must construe the resolution I am about to put as a Government measure – I shall have done what I consider to be the right thing. Of course, if I am defeated, there is only one course left open to me – to resign. . . . I am ready to take

my political future in my hands. I'm not going to take it on the chin as Federal Cabinet ministers have done and go down without fighting.

By now most of the Liberals, who had been recently assured by the Premier in caucus that he intended to de-escalate his running war with Ottawa, looked not only puzzled but apprehensive as he continued: "Let me say again that I stand firm in my statements that Mr. King has not done his duty to his country – never has and never will. I sat with him in the Federal House for eight years and I know him."

The political bomb, which had ticked for so many months, was about to be detonated. Reaching down, Mitch Hepburn picked up the yellow piece of paper and began to read the text slowly. The resolution said that the Legislature joined the Premier and Drew "in regretting that the Federal Government at Ottawa has made so little effort to prosecute Canada's duty in the war in the vigorous manner the people of Canada desire to see." The bomb had gone off, but there was no immediate explosion, just the soft tread of Liberal members scurrying from the Chamber. The Premier, tense and grim-faced, summoned a page who took the sheet of paper to the acting Speaker, Roland Patterson: "All in favour, say . . ." began the Speaker, but the Premier cut him off. The Liberal members were not to get off that easily. There was to be no doubt, no doubt at all, that the gauntlet had been well flung. The Premier demanded a recorded vote. "Call in the members." It was reported later that twenty-two Liberals remained in the members' rooms and refused to answer the Speaker's summons. Of those who did, among them Arthur Roebuck, ten bolted the Party to vote against the resolution. All eighteen Conservatives present joined twenty-six Liberals (including Harry Nixon and the Cabinet) to vote affirmatively. So the final count, marking one of the most sensational moments in Mitchell Hepburn's political career, was forty-four to ten in favour of the Ontario War Resolution condemning the manner in which Mackenzie King was prosecuting the war effort.[3]

Now that the naked challenge from Queen's Park was on the record, the next move was up to Ottawa. It was not long coming. Mackenzie King heard of the Ontario Legislature's action as he was leaving his office after a Cabinet meeting on January 18. He recorded his reaction noting "how extraordinary it was that such a Resolution should be passed by a Legislature, but, even more, how extraordinary that any Liberals, worthy of the name, could have supported a resolution of the kind. It shows how completely Hepburn has become a dictator, and how fearful men have become of not bowing to his will and word." Mackenzie King did not spend much time speculating about the motives of those Ontario Liberals who had supported the resolution. Its implications were immediately clear to him as they apparently had not been to Mitchell Hepburn who had given King precisely what he had been seeking, an excuse to call an election: "I felt no concern about the Resolution, except for the unpleasant kind of campaign which it foreshadows – a campaign in which every effort will be made to make it as personal and contemptible as it is possible for men of Hepburn's and Drew's ilk to make it."

That same night, King discussed the Ontario Resolution with Ernest Lapointe and Norman Rogers. Both Ministers agreed with his view that it would mean an immediate election. The Prime Minister had no doubts about the outcome. He felt his Government was "in a very strong position from one end of the country to the other. That Hepburn's action is on all fours with Duplessis'. That he has been living in an atmosphere of groups around him in Toronto; is filled with his own prejudice and hate; and is entirely blind to the sentiments in other parts of Canada. I believe an appeal to the country will bring us back as strong, if not stronger, than we are at present." Mackenzie King had seen straight off that Hepburn's move had played into his hands: "Hepburn's action has given to me and my colleagues and to the party here just what is needed to place beyond question the wisdom of an immediate election and the assurance of a victory for the Government." An immediate election would "probably defeat wholly the intent that Drew and Hepburn have very likely had in mind, namely, dissolving the provincial house on an issue of more being done in the war by a Union Government." One other observer close to the provincial scene, former Lieutenant Governor Herbert Bruce, also thought that Hepburn's strategy was to force the National Government issue. Dr. Bruce noted that in his judgment, "Mr. Hepburn's purpose in submitting his resolution was not only to express his own personal dislike and distrust of King, but also to press for the formation of a National Government somewhat similar to that created in the closing years of World War I."[4]

Whatever his ultimate goal in forcing the War Resolution down the throats of many provincial Liberals (and the speculation that he somehow hoped to oust King in favour of a National Government was almost certainly correct), Mitch Hepburn's over-all plan (if indeed he had one) was frightfully faulty, another index of how much this political strategist, so sure of himself a few years before, had declined. Instead of challenging King on a clear-cut provincial issue in Ontario where his strength still lay, Hepburn would now be obliged to fight on the national scene where he was relatively unknown, disliked in the West for his Dominion-Provincial policies and where his strongest ally, Maurice Duplessis, had already been defeated. If King's war leadership could be criticized (as it could on a number of counts), Mitch Hepburn had chosen the worst possible forum in which to make the fight. Moreover, it was questionable to what extent he could command the support of his provincial Party in any anti-King campaign.

Conservative leader Manion (who had not yet realized that the

Ontario resolution had put him on a political limb that King was preparing to saw off cleanly and for good) had reservations about how Mitch Hepburn and George Drew could fit into a campaign against the federal Government. To an associate who wired him immediately after the Ontario resolution urging him to see Hepburn and Drew in order "to effect consolidation of the anti-King forces in this country," Manion replied on January 22: "Your suggestion about talking matters over with H. and D. I don't mind telling you in confidence has been carried out some time ago, but I can add that they are not easy men to deal with, and I think that is particularly true of D. I am saying this to you very confidentially but his idea apparently of co-operation is that you do as he says and he does as he likes."

While old-soldier Manion struggled to regroup the anti-King forces and to prepare his own strategy for the session that King had promised him before an election ("The session opens on the twenty-fifth," he had written his son. "I speak on the twenty-ninth and I may break loose and probably be accused of torpedoing Canada's war effort"), the Prime Minister had already decided on the strategy that would eliminate his chief opponents at one stroke. At noon on Tuesday, January 23, Senator Norman Lambert arrived back in Ottawa from his Georgia vacation. At one-thirty in the afternoon he was informed of King's plan: "P.M. called me to his office & said very privately that he intended to have an election at once & would announce it in the address from the throne on Thursday." While he was putting the finishing touches on the throne speech on Thursday morning, Mackenzie King thought that the best-laid plans of mice and politicians (even politicians as astute as King) could be improved on. He would not only announce an election; he would dissolve the House that very day, thus effectively choking off Opposition criticism of the war effort.

So it was done; no word to the members returning for a full session, no hint to the unsuspecting Manion who had counted on the session to establish his leadership potential, not even the customary courtesy of an advance copy of the speech from the throne. In his remarks to the Commons on the afternoon of January 25, King carefully developed the reason why it was necessary to strike down Parliament on the day it assembled – the challenge of the Ontario War Resolution: "That resolution was passed to start a political campaign, while this Parliament is sitting. . . . Already the leader of the Conservative Party in Ontario, speaking at a political meeting, has said the election should be held. And he gives the slogan for the election: 'King Must Go.' " King's voice was a cutting edge as he added, "I am quite prepared to accept that slogan and go to the people."

Across the aisle, Manion, stunned by the afternoon's breath-taking events, tore up the speech he had prepared. Eyes flashing and voice ringing with anger, he charged the Prime Minister with a cheap political trick: "What has happened?" he cried as the desperateness of his own political situation emerged. "The Prime Minister has been attacked by Mitch Hepburn. What is new in that?" What was new was that this time King had decided to cut Mitch Hepburn down to size and he would almost certainly take Manion down with him.

The Prime Minister moved swiftly to exploit the opportunity. Immediately after the House adjourned at six, the Cabinet met and adopted an order-in-council recommending dissolution. King took it to Government House where it was signed at seven minutes after seven. About four hours after it began, the sixth session of the Eighteenth Parliament abruptly ended. Manion himself, a doughty fighter and always the optimist at heart, was not totally displeased by this turn of events. He explained to his son:

> King scuttled the ship on January 25th – 3 hours after the House opened. . . . They say I did pretty well though King played a very dirty game in preparing his own speech and not hinting about anything that was going to be done. I was boiling mad and apparently that put some stuff behind my speech. I did very well and got a lot of praise and applause at caucus afterwards. Mr. King will know there is a merry fight on his hands whatever comes.[5]

Mackenzie King, for all the Tory leader's cheery optimism, seemed to be going into the campaign with all the high cards, and Manion, an untested leader who, despite his previous opposition, had now come out for National Government, might end up with nothing but a couple of political jokers at Queen's Park. As was his wont, King made sure his rear was covered. At a Party caucus on January 26, the Prime Minister asked the federal Liberals to stand up and be counted on the Hepburn issue. Senator Lambert noted: "P.M. read all disloyal people out of the Party: & asked any who wanted to leave the room to do so. None went." So much for Mitch Hepburn's influence with the federal Liberals. Later King discussed strategy with his two political experts, Senator Lambert and the Postmaster General C. G. "Chubby" Power. The Prime Minister would run a high-level campaign, staying close to his desk, projecting the image of a busy war leader with just a few sorties out of the capital. This would mean relying heavily on radio broadcasts. The Prime Minister told Lambert "he favored paying for national hook-ups especially in view of other parties having no money." When the Senator "objected on ground of principle, & costs," King "said he wanted to stay here & use radio rather than public speaking." Lambert and Power later decided on two other campaign tactics. In Liberal speeches and literature, there must be "no reference to 1914-18 war campaign, no reference to Mitch."[6]

Meanwhile, there was much speculation about what part Mitch Hepburn intended to play in the election scheduled for March 26. The man, who had said so often that Mackenzie King was unfit to govern, in the Legislature charged the Prime Minister with abject cowardice: "The commander of the *Graf Spee* sank his ship rather than face three little British ships. But Prime Minister Mackenzie King, with the greatest numerical strength ever accorded any Canadian Prime Minister, scuttled the ship of state rather than face the criticism of Dr. Manion and his 39 followers in the House of Commons." As if that were not enough, he compared King's obstructive presence on the Royal Tour of 1939 to that of "a mud turtle snapping its head up and down."

This was the kind of language ("gross personal abuse of Canada's Prime Minister," the *Globe and Mail* called it) which Mitch Hepburn was now using with increasing frequency. Sometimes it was good for a nervous laugh; in the end, it was self-defeating for a man in public life. Besides hurling insults, what did Mitch Hepburn plan to do in the campaign? It quickly became obvious that he could do very little about the campaigning of his provincial members or even his Cabinet ministers. They were in the invidious position of deciding whether or not to support the members of a Government they had just condemned in a recorded vote. Nearly all of them resolved their illogical position by ignoring it; most campaigned (some, like Gordon Conant, vigorously) for their federal Liberal counterparts. Not many were able to surpass the member for Toronto-St. David, Allan Lamport. He claimed that he supported both Hepburn and King. Reportedly angered by the open support his caucus was giving to King, the Premier did what he could to shore up the anti-King forces behind the scenes. A prominent Toronto Tory, H. Rupert Bain, told Hepburn that former Lieutenant Governor Herbert Bruce had been persuaded to stand in Parkdale not only because he considered King unfit to govern but also because of "my statement to him that you, personally, felt that his acceptance of the nomination would assist materially in the success of the election."

Without going on the stump himself (Hepburn did not accept Bain's offer of a half-hour national Conservative radio hook-up to attack King), the Premier easily managed to create a couple of diversions to embarrass the Government. The first revealed again his growing political ineptitude. During the early part of the campaign, the King administration was accused of censoring political speeches, particularly those of George Drew. Mitch Hepburn took it neatly off the hook on the censorship issue by banning in Ontario a "March of Time" film entitled "Canada at War" because it glorified King and was "nothing but political propaganda of the most blatant kind." Eight hundred people who had seen the film at a private showing in Ottawa, and considered it a balanced presentation of the country's war effort, were astounded. "Once more," the Toronto *Star* commented on the Premier's action, "he labels himself by subordinating all else to a private grudge."*

Mitch Hepburn's second intervention in the campaign had more serious implications. He charged that several hundred men at the St. Thomas Air Training School, fed up with inadequate courses, had walked out on February 10. Some were still absent three days later, despite the efforts of military police to round them up. The press, according to the Premier, had been warned not to publicize the walk-out. He challenged Defence Minister Norman Rogers to deny the charge: "I make the statement as Prime Minister of Ontario and let the censors say they can't publish that." American and European (including enemy) papers picked up the accusation and grossly inflated it. A headline in the New York *Post* referred to "Mutiny in Royal Canadian Air Force." In the strongest language yet used by a federal Cabinet Minister, Norman Rogers, campaigning in New Brunswick, termed Hepburn's charge a sheer fabrication: "It is high time for Premier Hepburn, for the good of all loyal Canadians everywhere, to desist from this intemperate abuse."† The Toronto *Star* asked in exasperation: "How much further can Mr. Hepburn go before his ministers resign?"⁷

Not much further. On March 11, there occurred the most dramatic event of the election campaign. The Premier's seat-mate and lieutenant in the Legislature, Provincial Secretary Harry Nixon, resigned from the Cabinet. Suddenly the quiet stable Nixon, the man with many friends and no enemies, the Premier's ally since 1932, the anchor man of the Hepburn Cabinet, was gone. He had been loyal to Mitch Hepburn up to voting for the war resolution; now things had apparently gone too far even for Harry Nixon who usually had no trouble straddling the fence on most issues. He explained to the press that the attacks on the King administration by the Drew-Hepburn alliance were too much. To the Premier he expressed "the sincere hope that this step, the serious consequences of which I fully appreciate, might not end the warm friendship which has existed between us personally and between our families for so many years."

For the Premier, Nixon's action was as upsetting as it was unexpected. Harry Corwin Nixon had played no little part in Mitch Hepburn's rise to power in 1934. He knew that this soft-spoken, colourless farmer from St. George (whom he sometimes humorously called "that tight-lipped Methodist") exuded an aura of respectability and righteousness that he could ill-afford to lose from his Government. From Bannockburn, the Premier termed Nixon's resignation a "terrible shock." If his long-time associate wanted to support King, that was no reason for him to resign: "I can't understand why Harry Nixon should do this. The principle of Cabinet solidarity does not apply outside provincial affairs." Then Mitch Hepburn prepared to leave for Queen's Park and a Cabinet meeting next day to discover where Harry Nixon's defection left his Government.

There were those, among them apparently Harry Nixon himself, who speculated that Mitch Hepburn would utilize this latest crisis to try a political power play in the last days of the federal campaign. There were two possibilities: reconstruct the ministry on an anti-King coalition government basis in Ontario; or dissolve the House immediately and go to the country on the union government issue. Senator Lambert noted in his diary on March 11: "Harry Nixon resigned today. Spoke with him over phone re possibilities of cabinet meeting to-morrow & consequent appeals to Lt.-Gov." Mackenzie King, gratified by Nixon's action, felt that genuine Ontario Liberals might now force Hepburn out of the leadership, though there was still the possibility that he would try to reconstruct his Cabinet through a coalition. Dissolution and an anti-King campaign were less likely: "I do not see how he could dissolve and hope to carry Ministers and Members with him through the campaign which will be directed at the federal Liberal Government. At this stage he could scarcely get Drew to join with him to try a union government experiment in Ontario as I have not the least doubt has been the intention of the two of them right along."

The expectation that Hepburn was again planning the unexpected increased on March 12, when Under Secretary of State, E. H. Coleman, and Arnold Heeney, Secretary of the federal Cabinet, who had been in contact with Ontario's Lieutenant Governor Albert Matthews, saw King. They told him that the Lieutenant Governor expected a call from Hepburn after the Ontario Cabinet meeting that afternoon. Matthews was anxious to ascertain King's views on the constitutional position if, as the Lieutenant Governor anticipated, the Premier advised him to form a coalition government with Hepburn and Drew its main members. King's advice was unequivocal: "Tell Matthews that my view was that he must accept the Premier all in all or not at all, and that I felt he should accept and act upon whatever advice he might tender."

---

* This was not the first time that Premier Hepburn had entered the censorship field. In June, 1936, he supported the provincial censorship board (under the Premier's jurisdiction in his capacity as Provincial Treasurer), when the board banned showing of the film "Green Pastures" on the grounds the Negro religious classic was sacrilegious: "I was shown the picture privately," explained the Premier, "and I can say I never saw a picture so silly, so ridiculous, so insulting to Church people. . . . Nobody can tell me that people wouldn't be shocked by such a picture." Undoubtedly that was the right line for the fundamentalists on the back concessions; fortunately, an appeal board quickly reversed the ban. (*Globe*, June 24, 1936)

† Subsequently an investigation revealed that there was a basis for the Premier's charge. Authorities admitted that owing to a misunderstanding in orders, 156 men had been absent without leave from the St. Thomas station on February 10. (PAO Hepburn Papers, Memorandum from Provincial Police Commissioner W. H. Stringer to G. D. Conant, March 11, 1940; *Globe and Mail*, March 13, 1940)

Before his visitors left, King elaborated on his interpretation of Hepburn's efforts, past and present, to form a coalition. King was not surprised by yet another attempt: "He and Drew have had it in mind right along. Hepburn had it in mind at the time of the last provincial election as was told me by McCullagh of the *Globe* himself in my library. While McCullagh was in England, Hepburn broke the understanding he had with the *Globe* and with Drew to form a National Government." The Prime Minister gave his view of the strategy behind the Ontario War Resolution, a view that probably credits the Ontario Premier with a bigger streak of Machiavellianism than he possessed. According to King, "Hepburn, in passing the Resolution he did in the Ontario Legislature, was at that time contemplating National Government. Had the Resolution been defeated, he would have there and then joined up with Drew for National Government and gone to the country before our Parliament met. That chance was spoiled by members of his own Government and following voting with him to the extent they did." King believed that a coalition could not yet be ruled out in Ontario: "Hepburn and Drew have been watching for a chance ever since to take the step which they were deprived of taking at that time. Their game, from the start, has been to get under way with it before the present federal Government appealed to the people. Hepburn will now make an effort to get under way with it before the present elections are over. I am pretty sure that the day will witness an effort on his part to effect this end."

What the day witnessed was not a Drew-Hepburn coalition at Queen's Park but an almost more surprising development, Harry Corwin Nixon's return to the Cabinet. After an hour's consultation with Nixon at the latter's Royal York suite, a smiling Mitch Hepburn called in newsmen and happily tore up his Provincial Secretary's resignation. The Premier was elated as he spoke of the sudden rapprochement: "We have now reached complete agreement and no one is more happy than I. Years ago we fought an uphill battle and it ended in the victory of 1934. Arriving at my office today, I realized how unwilling I would be to carry on the responsibility of government without my chief lieutenant at my side." Somewhat tense and pale, Harry Nixon endorsed the Premier's statement: "I am happy now to rejoin my colleagues . . . the Premier has made it clear to me that the views I hold on national affairs are my own affair." As he strode off toward the Royal York elevators with a bouncy step, Mitch Hepburn said he was feeling happier than he had for a long time. Even Mackenzie King, though surprised at Nixon's sudden reversal, was relieved: "I think it will mean a more decent kind of campaign in the next ten days. Hepburn's colleagues have come to a decision with him, that they are to be free to take their part in the campaign, he to keep quiet, if that is possible."[8]

Mitch Hepburn was not present at the monster Liberal rally for King held at Massey Hall in Toronto on March 14. It was the high point in the federal leader's campaign. To loud cheers, Justice Minister Ernest Lapointe introduced King as a man "who has serenity in his soul; who is free of hatred and jealousy." The real show-stopper and eye-mister of the evening was Harry Nixon's presence on the platform, and his few folksy words explaining that "my good wife and I just drove down from the farm to be here and to say to you that come what may we are behind Mr. King." At that a deep-throated ovation rose from the Ontario Liberals, an ovation that rocked the hall and obliterated all those previous statements of Nixon's that indicated he was a long way behind the federal leader.

It was a moving occasion, and no one was more moved than Mackenzie King himself. He was enchanted at the audience's response to Harry Corwin Nixon. The drama was the stuff of heroes and of history:

> His manner, speech and all was really heroic. His presence and what he said, all circumstances considered, reminded me of the types of men that my grandfather must have had around him in the Rebellion days who were prepared to endure all kinds of hardship for the sake of the cause and for personal loyalty. I felt a gratitude for Nixon no words could express. I confess in some measure an equal feeling of contempt for other members of Hepburn's Government who should have been present and were not. They will suffer for it all their lives. Their names in the history of the party and in the country's history will always have a question mark after them. Not a man of them had the courage of his own conviction at a time when it was up to them to show where they stood as Liberals and at a moment when the country itself was at war. One after the other made excuses to avoid embarrassment in their relations with a man who has betrayed his friends, his cause and his country.[9]

After that display, the remainder of the campaign was anti-climax. Mackenzie King was winning all the way. Money was no problem for the Liberals in Ontario. Senator Lambert checked over the financial situation with his Toronto bagmen two days after the Massey Hall meeting. He discovered that "after raising the candidates to a higher level all round," he would still have $50,000 left.* The campaign of old-soldier Manion,

---

* When the campaign ended in Ontario, Lambert had more than that left. The Ontario organization received official contributions totalling $458,989.53. Of this amount, approximately $250,000 was expended in the province. (Defence Minister Norman Rogers running in Kingston received the largest single amount, $7,000.) After disbursements of Ontario funds in other parts of the country, a balance remained of slightly more than $75,000. These figures include only those contributions recorded in the Liberal office. (Lambert Papers, C. P. Fell to N. Lambert, with enclosures, April 16, 1940)

built around the theme of a National Government to prosecute the war more vigorously, never got off the ground. One report suggested that Mitch Hepburn was the only Liberal Manion could induce to enter a National Government. References like those of George Drew to Defence Minister Norman Rogers – "that dyspeptic little son of Mars" who "has been a standing joke in every military camp since he blossomed forth as our new war lord last September" – did nothing to help Manion's cause. They merely but bite into King's final radio broadcasts.

A week before the election, Mitch Hepburn wrote to Colin Campbell overseas with the forces: "We are looking forward to the voting on Tuesday of next week, the outcome of which is very much in doubt." Shortly after the polls closed on that wintry Tuesday, March 26, there was no doubt. Mackenzie King's Liberals won overwhelmingly, taking 178 seats to thirty-nine for the National Government forces of Robert Manion who lost his seat in Fort William. At Bannockburn, where he listened to the returns with a group of friends, Mitch Hepburn accepted the results philosophically: "I am still taking the long range view of things." In Ottawa, Mackenzie King wanted to exploit the sweep. Manion had been taken care of. That left Hepburn and Drew. A few hours after the result, King called Senator Lambert "and wanted Mitch to be ousted in Ontario so that things could be consolidated vs. Drew."

Mitch Hepburn had had his showdown, and Mackenzie King had won easily. The Premier had done what he could to help the Conservative leader, but his help had been almost totally ineffectual, even in Ontario. Nevertheless, Manion wrote to thank him for his efforts:

> Just a word of appreciation for all you tried to do in our behalf – or at least against the fat little jelly fish out at Kingsmere, but somehow he seems to come out on top.
>
> I have rather reached the conclusion that it is because of an anti-war complex that exists across this country.

The Ontario Premier agreed with this analysis and added that the electorate would realize its error when the war worsened: "It is my opinion that when the real fury of this thing strikes us the people of Canada will realize they have made a tremendous mistake in endorsing King and his half-hearted war effort." To Colin Campbell, the Premier attributed part of the result to Manion's leadership: "Manion proved to be a very weak leader, particularly in connection with the radio broadcasts. He simply petered out at the finish."[10]

The election result clearly showed that Mitch Hepburn's political machine was no longer a threat to federal Liberal fortunes in Ontario. The question now was whether his grip on his provincial party had been severely loosened. After the election, demands increased that a meeting of the Ontario Liberal Association be held, even that Hepburn be replaced forthwith. The federal Member for Toronto Spadina, Sam Factor, said that it was "imperative that Ontario Liberals get together in some sort of convention to choose a new leader."

Amid charges that he had wrecked the Party, there were still those who remembered what Mitch Hepburn had done for the provincial Liberals in Ontario. Their case was put by Rupert Davies' Kingston *Whig-Standard*, a paper which had not always supported the Premier:

> The history of the Liberal Party in Ontario has not been so happy during the present century that a successful leader can lightly be asked to resign. Mr. Hepburn may have said things and done things of which many Liberals do not approve, but they must not forget that after thirty years in the cold shades of Opposition . . . it was Mitchell F. Hepburn and Mitchell F. Hepburn alone who brought them back into power. And furthermore, he repeated the triumph again in 1937.

Most of those yelling for Hepburn's head could not tie his political shoes:

> Now this one and that one . . . unimportant people who could not lead a party across the street – are demanding that "Hepburn Must Go." They forget what he has done for their party, they forget what he has done for the Province. They overlook, entirely, that he is successful because he wears no man's collar. Premier Hepburn occasionally says and does a lot of things with which The *Whig-Standard* does not agree. . . . We recognize, however, that he is the best leader the Ontario Liberal Party has had in forty years, and that his good works as Premier far outweigh those things which do not please us.

This agitation over Mitchell Hepburn's leadership was soon forgotten in the spring of 1940, relegated to the back pages by the searing war headlines: Norway Invaded; The Low Countries Over-run; France Collapses; Dunkirk; Italy Declares War; Defence Minister Norman Rogers Tragically Dies in the Flaming Crash of an RCAF Bomber Near Bowmanville. This timetable of disaster made partisan politics seem even pettier than usual. The Premier himself said: "They can call a provincial convention if they wish – they can call two provincial conventions – they can call a Dominion convention if they want to – I don't care. The issues are beyond that now."[11]

They were far beyond that for Mitch Hepburn personally. Once again his health had broken down. On June 10, Bannockburn was closed to visitors, and his personal physician ordered the Premier, suffering from bronchitis, to take a two-week rest. The next day, June 11, with Paris ringed by fire and the Western powers reeling, Mitchell Hepburn emerged from his illness to make the most fantastic statement of his career. Only the fact that his judgment seems to have been unbalanced by sickness – emotional as well as physical – can explain though not excuse its irresponsibility. According to the Premier, his Government had received "definite information that many Nazi and Fascist sympathizers in the United States are training; that they are well organized and in some instances well armed. They are only waiting for orders from across the Atlantic to act; to sweep in upon us and lay waste our land." This was incredible enough; what followed verged on sheer hysteria. In the face of this alleged danger (which American officials immediately branded "ridiculous"), Mitch Hepburn summoned the province to arms:

> I appeal to the able-bodied men of Ontario to act for the protection of their homes and their factories, of their wives and children.
>
> I am not an alarmist, but I am a realist. I want the people of Ontario to become realists with me and see the dangers. Geographically, Ontario is in a vulnerable position, for it virtually projects into one of the most thickly populated sections of the United States where undoubtedly there are hundreds of thousands of Nazi and Fascist sympathizers.
>
> I have no confidence in the Dominion Government, judged by its record. I have no confidence in the Dominion Government being of help to us in the event of such an invasion of our fair province. I fear that by the time the Dominion Government got ready to act, the damage would be done.
>
> We are prepared to give police instruction and the fullest cooperation in every way, and so far as it is within our power we are prepared to arm the civic guards and to provide ammunition. We are considering a plan at the present time of arming the guards.

There is no doubt that Premier Hepburn had become obsessed with the events of the war. Glued to the radio, he listened to war news by the hour. There is some reason to believe that this obsession was encouraged (though for what reason is not clear) by his friends, Sir James Dunn, and the American millionaire, Sell 'Em Ben Smith, the latter reported to have isolationist leanings. According to Air Minister, C. G. "Chubby" Power, the Premier "had built up in his own mind the fantastic belief that supporters of Wendell Willkie, a candidate for the Presidency of the United States, were all pro-Germans, and that Willkie himself would encourage them to sabotage Canadian installations." If Premier Hepburn had reliable information that the province was being threatened (an extremely unlikely supposition), it was his duty to inform privately the national authorities. Federal ministers ridiculed Hepburn's alarmist announcement as "just plain hysteria." His friend, Air Minister "Chubby" Power, remarked as much in sadness as in anger: "My own opinion is that Mitch Hepburn is crazy and I don't think I am alone in that opinion." The Premier's action can only be explained by a malaise that ran deeper than his neurotic hatred of Mackenzie King.

Two days after this indefensible proclamation, the Premier's physician announced that Mitch Hepburn was seriously ill with bronchial pneumonia. When he heard the news, Prime Minister King recorded his reaction:

> The afternoon paper made mention of the fact that Hepburn's bronchitis has developed into bronchial pneumonia. If this is so, it probably means the end of his earthly life. I don't often wish that a man should pass away but I believe it would be the most fortunate thing that could happen at this time. . . . The sympathy that will be expressed for him will be of a very different character than that expressed for Rogers whom he did all he could to destroy.[12]

There would be many, then and later, whose judgment of Mitch Hepburn with all his faults would be less harsh than that expressed by the federal leader.

On June 19, the sixth anniversary of his provincial victory in 1934, the Premier was still confined to Bannockburn. A week later, accompanied by his physician, Dr. W. H. Avery, Mitch Hepburn flew in Jack Bickell's private plane to Kellog Sanitarium, Battle Creek, Michigan, for a month's intensive treatment. For a time the emotional escalator would be slowed down, the excitable outbursts controlled. Perhaps rest and care could restore a man who had lived near the edge of personal dissolution for too long.

Within a month, the Premier was back at Queen's Park. August 12, his forty-fourth birthday, was spent at his desk. Cabinet colleagues said they had never seen the Chief looking better. Although there were several vacancies in the Legislature, the Premier announced that there would be no by-elections for the present and that wartime was no time to hold a general election. Rumours persisted that he was still considering some kind of coalition government for the duration of the war. A Conservative friend, C. O. Knowles, Editor of the Toronto *Telegram*, wrote Hepburn that he had "heard quiet repercussions regarding a possible reconstruction of your Cabinet and it is all favourable." Now, Knowles thought, was a good time to act: "You have an opportunity to get rid of three weak sisters and present an administration that will command universal respect. If you take in Drew, Macauley [sic] and Stewart you will immeasurably increase public confidence. There is no necessity for an election. In fact I feel very strongly that an election would be a great mistake." The fact that a Conservative could freely suggest the

Premier should take that arch-Tory William Stewart, a former Toronto Mayor, into his administration, revealed again how far Mitch Hepburn had been taken into camp by the Toronto Conservatives.

The Premier, however, had more on his mind than party politics which diminished further in importance as the war situation worsened. He still wanted to enlist or obtain a service appointment and had discussed his desire with Defence Minister J. L. Ralston. On August 14, the Premier wrote Ralston: "I have had a discussion with General Armstrong, following a complete medical check-up. The only obstacle in the way is the fact that I have a kidney removed, as a result of an accident suffered while in the Air Force in the last war. Apart from that, however, the doctors assure me that I could pass any medical test whatsoever. I hope you have not forgotten our conversation." For some reason this letter, mostly concerning the province's financial position, was neither signed nor sent. Informal efforts to obtain a war job for the Premier continued. On September 15, at the height of the Battle of Britain, Hepburn received a telegram from Colin Campbell in London. Campbell had lunched with Jack Bickell who had been overseas for some time attached to Lord Beaverbrook's Air Production Ministry: "You were discussed. Offer may be made soon. Advise acceptance. Miss you." Despite these efforts, nothing came of any overseas position for the Premier in 1940.[13]

Instead, Mitch Hepburn remained at Queen's Park dealing with routine matters. There was a friendly exchange of correspondence with King about negotiations for the St. Lawrence Seaway and the American Government's willingness to allow Ontario to increase the flow at Niagara, a decision that pleased Hepburn. For old time's sake, he invited Maurice Duplessis (who had requested that one of his Ontario friends be made a K.C.) to come to Toronto for some entertainment. "When I go to Toronto," replied Duplessis, certain he would soon make a political comeback, "I shall indeed be very glad to see you, not only for old time's sake but for yesterday, today, and tomorrow's sake." There was a friendly visit with Air Minister Power at St. Thomas to inspect the Air Training School. There were some Cabinet changes to attend to, the most important being the Premier's appointment of Robert Laurier (nephew of Sir Wilfrid and a friend of King's) to replace Mines Minister Paul Leduc who had accepted a federal position. The Premier was especially happy when Ernest Lapointe spoke for Laurier in the East Ottawa by-election and praised Hepburn for "the full measure of justice" he had shown Ontario's French-speaking Canadians. "It seemed like old times to be with you again," Hepburn wrote to Lapointe.[14]

After the bitter political struggles with which it began, 1940 seemed to be closing for Mitch Hepburn on a relatively quiet note. His health was improved, and relations with Ottawa were again returning to normal. There were pleasant diversions like the visit of movie-star Gene Autry and his wife. On December 3, the Premier wrote Autry: "When I took your autographed cowboy hat back to the farm it was promptly pounced upon by young Peter. While we did not object to him wearing it at the dinner table, we did with great effort manage to disassociate him from it when he went to bed, with the condition that it repose on one of the bedposts." But peaceful interludes with Mitch Hepburn did not last long; this one was no exception. He was again concerned about the lack of energy in the war effort. He expressed this in a letter to Lapointe:

> I trust you will pardon my apparent impatience at the lack of a whole hearted and full-out war effort. I do believe and most sincerely so that this situation is infinitely more serious than most of us realize and unless United States comes forward almost immediately with merchant ships and protective escorts it is very doubtful as to how much longer Britain can stand up under the concentrated U-boat and air attacks. I have endeavoured to make a careful study as to the conditions which obtain in the conquered areas of Europe. I am sure it would be much preferable for people to sacrifice their lives than their freedom to the German war lords.

These were sentiments that presumably most federal ministers shared. To make certain, Hepburn lashed out publicly at the King leadership again in Toronto on December 2: "It is three years since Prime Minister King said he knew war was inevitable. . . . One of the first duties of the leader of the Federal Government is to look after national security. Did we do anything? No we did not do a blasted thing."

King himself did not answer this speech, but it did provoke a reply from a curious quarter. A former Labour Minister in a King administration, Senator James Murdock, informed Hepburn by telegram that he was the father of two sons who had fought in France during the first war when Mitch Hepburn was safe in Elgin: "I am heartily sick of your repeated criticism of the war efforts of others." The Premier's reply revealed how sensitive he was on the point of his military service:

> Under ordinary circumstances I would not reply to an insulting telegram such as yours received today.
>
> I might advise you that at the time referred to I was a member of the Royal Canadian Air Force* and even in this war Ian Mackenzie and Colonel Ralston will both tell you that I have offered my services in the capacity of Second Lieutenant for overseas service, for which position I am fully qualified.

---

* Actually Mitch Hepburn was a member of the Royal Air Force. The RCAF was not formed until 1924, six years after he enlisted.

I can readily understand your position, however, as the poorest Minister of Labour Canada ever had and one who was thoroughly repudiated by the electors. Possibly the only thing you can trade upon is the worthwhile war record of your sons.

So far as I am concerned you need not bother cluttering up my desk in the future with any further communications, as I have for you, if it is possible, the same disdain apparently you have for me. So let's call it a draw.

To "call it a draw" suggested that Mitch Hepburn might be slowing up. On December 18, 1940, he had been leading the Liberal Party in Ontario for ten years. Late that afternoon, as he was sprinting from Queen's Park to make a radio appeal on behalf of the Greek War Fund, a newsman called after him: "What about another ten years?" The Premier stopped and smiled: "If I had another ten years like the last then I would need an elixir or something to pull me through."[15] There would not be another ten years for Mitch Hepburn. There would not be many more years at all.

chapter 14

Saints and Sinners

During the latter half of 1940, the federal Government had been sitting on several bulky volumes that were certain to cause a hassle, not only with Queen's Park, but with several other provinces as well. The Rowell-Sirois Commission,* appointed to examine the financial structure of Canadian federalism, had recommended sweeping changes in the taxing relation of Ottawa and the provincial administrations. In return for assuming provincial debts and responsibility for unemployment relief, the federal Government would acquire sole taxing authority in the personal income, corporation, and inheritance fields.

The principle of provincial equalization was to be made both more important and more flexible by replacing fixed provincial subsidies with a system of National Adjustment Grants payable annually according to provincial need. If these radical recommendations were adopted, at least two objectives would be achieved: Canada's complicated taxing structure would be rationalized by centering it in the federal authority, and several of the Western provinces, on the verge of bankruptcy would be bailed out of their financial difficulties.

On November 2, 1940, King wrote to the nine provincial Premiers inviting them to a Dominion-Provincial conference to discuss the Rowell-Sirois recommendations. "The Report commends itself strongly to our judgment. We believe that no time should be lost in arranging for a conference with the provinces in order to secure, if possible, the adoption of the Commission's recommendations." More than a year before, in a fit of pique with King's financial policies, Mitch Hepburn had publicly dis-

---

* In November, 1938, Chief Justice Newton Rowell, Chairman of the Commission, resigned because of ill health. He was succeeded by Dr. Joseph Sirois, Professor of Law at Laval University, who had been Acting Chairman during Rowell's absence.

sociated his Government from further dealings with the Rowell-Sirois Commission. Since then the war had intervened, and the Premier recognized that the federal authority would require the widest possible taxing powers. Nevertheless, Hepburn regretted, as he told King, that a conference on the problems of federalism could not have been postponed: "I was hopeful that a discussion of this problem could be delayed until after the war so that there could be no possibility of any controversial issue arising which might impair the national unity and the effective prosecution of the war." Despite these reservations, he informed King that Ontario would be represented at any conference "after the middle of January, as suggested by you."[1]

As the date of the conference, set for January 14, 1941, approached, there was speculation that Mitchell Hepburn and at least two other Premiers – Aberhart of Alberta and Pattullo of British Columbia – would oppose permanent changes in the federal structure. It was well-known that Hepburn, as head of one of the "have" provinces, thought that the best financial contribution Ontario could make toward a total war effort was to maintain its own viable economic position. The Premier gave no hint in public about what his attitude would be at the conference.

The federal Government, however, was well aware of Premier Hepburn's view. In October, Finance Minister James Ilsley conferred with the Premier at Queen's Park concerning the Rowell-Sirois recommendations. It was a friendly meeting, but the Premier emphasized that he did not favour the Report's major recommendations of transferring most of the taxing authority to Ottawa and assuming provincial debts. Ilsley referred to these conversations in a letter to Hepburn on November 1, in which he said if the Report were brought up in the House of Commons either he or King might "have to state that the views of the Government of Ontario have been ascertained and that they are unfavourable to the adoption of the Report."

The federal Government itself was not optimistic about the outcome of the conference. At a cabinet meeting on December 13, most of the ministers were of the opinion that nothing would be achieved. King himself, who seemed to view the whole exercise as a kind of political charade, shared their pessimism if he did not encourage it. He thought that "in the preliminary speech, we would have to construct a mattress that would make it easy for the trapeze performers as they dropped to the ground one by one. I have never believed that the Conference could succeed at this time of war." For the sake of the record, and to protect its rear, the Government should make the attempt. If it did not, according to King, "it would be blamed for whatever financial disaster will follow, as it certainly will, in the course of the next year or two."

Even in peacetime it would have been difficult to achieve substantial agreement on the radical changes in the federal structure recommended by the Rowell-Sirois Report. Disagreement concerning what attitude Hepburn should adopt was reflected in the provincial press. Consistent with his own predilection for a strong centralized administration, George McCullagh supported the Commission's proposals. Preceding the conference, the *Globe and Mail* ran a series of editorials reiterating the national as opposed to the narrow provincial point of view. At the same time, the Toronto *Star* considered that Ontario would be paying too high a price if the Report were adopted. The Premier preparing to lead a strong delegation to the capital, kept his own counsel and the province guessing. Before the conference, he wrote to Air Minister Power: "I am looking forward to meeting you in Ottawa next week. I am going down with blood in my eye and dandruff in my moustache – but of course that's the way you expect me."

That was the way they expected him, and Mackenzie King for one was taking no chances. At a Cabinet meeting on January 9, he urged a conciliatory approach to the provinces, noting his Government "must consider the use that could be made particularly by Hepburn and others, of any opening we might give them for stage play at this time."[2] The others that King expected to try some kind of political high-wire act were Aberhart and Pattullo. Strongest support for the new financial arrangements would come from Premier John Bracken of Manitoba. As the provincial delegations began to arrive in Ottawa on January 13, attention centered on Mitchell F. Hepburn. It is doubtful that he knew himself what he would do, unlike Mackenzie King who knew every minute the consequences his actions might have. It was the difference between a man who played his cards close to the vest and one who played them with a reckless abandon which had little or no relationship to the chips he held. Mitch Hepburn did not like card games much. If he had, he would have been a poor poker player.

On Tuesday, January 14, a crisp sub-zero morning in the capital, the Dominion-Provincial Conference convened in the Commons Chamber. About 150 delegates and members of Parliament almost filled the 244 seats. Before the proceedings opened, Mackenzie King and Mitchell Hepburn chatted briefly. The federal Premier, who six months previously had wished for Mitch Hepburn's demise, "was as pleasant and natural with Hepburn as if we had always been on most cordial and friendly terms. His attitude was, for the most part, quite the same." Then amid the pop of flashbulbs and the expectation of verbal fireworks, the conference began. King's opening statement, which recommended that the new financial arrangements be adopted, was balanced, moderate, cautious, uninspiring, and uninspired.

Then the delegates' attention rivetted on the man sitting two feet to Mackenzie King's right. Mitch Hepburn stood up quickly, looked around the Chamber, and began to speak. The Ontario Premier did not even take time to warm up. He contemptuously dismissed the Rowell-Sirois Report out of hand as "the product of the minds of three professors and a Winnipeg newspaper man."* They had concocted a blueprint for the destruction of Confederation: "To lay hands on the lifetime work of Sir Wilfrid Laurier and Sir John A. Macdonald is nothing short of national vandalism." The centralizing philosophy underlying the Rowell-Sirois Report would damage all the provinces, continued the Premier, and none more so than the province of Quebec: "By this deal, according to the best constitutional advice I can get, Quebec and the rest of us will have to agree to a surrender to the central authority of rights and privileges granted by the North America Act." Ontario, promised the Premier, would "stand solidly beside Quebec if at any time her minority rights are threatened."

No one now had any doubt where Mitch Hepburn stood. He was not yet finished. In a peroration which sounded more like a page from a nineteenth-century textbook on elocution than the product of a stump-speaker who had begun his oratorical career in a one-room country school in Elgin County, Mitch Hepburn proceeded to ridicule the whole idea of a conference at a time when Britain and the Empire were concerned with national survival:

> Is this the time to send a courier to bomb-torn London with a document in his hand and have him step into the Hall of Westminster and ask the British Parliament to pause in its consideration of questions determining the very life of the British Empire in order to debate the question of a new Constitution for Canada? To me it is unthinkable that we should be fiddling while London is burning. In the heart of the Empire the citizenry – men, women, boys and girls – with their bare hands are beating out the flames spread by the ruthless vandals upon the housetops and the roofs of their homes. . . .
>
> Today, while these brave people are shielding their homes with their bodies and braving the bursting bombs and the hail of machine-gun bullets, do we read that the Lord Mayor of London has paused in his efforts to save the nation and has called a meeting of the aldermen to consider a readjustment or a revision of the borough system of the great metropolis which is now a beleaguered fortress?

Down to the alliteration and rhetorical questions, it was quite a performance, and like most performances it received mixed reviews. Mackenzie King's special assistant, Leonard Brockington, was disgusted. He remarked to Senator Lambert at the luncheon break after Hepburn's speech: "The Fathers of Confederation at least are responsible for leaving one bastard in the family." Lambert told the editor of the Ottawa *Journal*, Grattan O'Leary, that "he should write an editorial representing

Mitch as the Duplessis of Ontario, but unfortunately Ont. has no Lapointe, Cardin, or Power to oppose him." Not surprisingly, Mackenzie King thought that his own statement "made a good impression." Not so Hepburn's: "Many spoke of the contrast between Hepburn's attitude and my own, particularly in the manner of speaking." George McCullagh was fed up with both leaders. Hepburn, complained the *Globe and Mail*, had opted "to match Mr. King's languid but well-calculated innocuity with all the fiery effervescence of a parochial demagogue." The Toronto *Star*, while deprecating Hepburn's reviling and rancour, supported his substantive position that adoption of the Rowell-Sirois Report would provoke "discord rather than unity. . . . It is unfortunate," added the *Star*, "that when he goes to Ottawa with a strong case he should weaken it by hostility and exaggeration."

This time Mitch Hepburn not only stole the show; he stopped it. Over the protests of Premier John Bracken, both Aberhart and Pattullo followed Hepburn in opposing the Report. The Alberta Premier provided one of the few touches of humour in the discussion when he compared the original pact of Confederation to an historic marriage of states: "I think," Aberhart remarked, turning to King who joined in the laughter, "that the chairman will agree with me in opposing second marriages." (Later King noted: "Aberhart, while amusing and plausible, was pretty much all humbug.") Hepburn and the two opposing Premiers were willing to discuss with the federal Government how the war might be more effectively financed and prosecuted, but they refused to be tied down to the Report itself.

This was not acceptable to the federal authorities. After an impassioned speech by Finance Minister Ilsley in favour of the Report, Highways Minister T. B. McQuesten announced on behalf of Ontario "that our association with this so-called convention is over." Premier Hepburn had the last word. Ontario was still prepared to co-operate with the Dominion to prosecute the war but not if the Prime Minister continued to insist that the discussions must be predicated on a Report to which Ontario objected. In that event, "there is no alternative open to my colleagues and myself but to withdraw and leave these wreckers of Confederation, under the guise of patriotism, to continue to carry on their nefarious work." After a hurriedly called Cabinet at the supper hour on the meeting's second day, Mackenzie King returned to the Chamber to say quietly that, with three Premiers opposed, it would be useless to continue. The delegates then sang "God Save the King" (not Mr. King either, Mitch Hepburn later remarked), and the Dominion-Provincial Conference on the Rowell-Sirois Report was over.[3]

---

* J. W. Dafoe, Winnipeg *Free Press*; Dr. Joseph Sirois, Laval University; H. F. Angus, University of British Columbia; R. A. Mackay, Dalhousie University.

Mackenzie King was not displeased by the failure of the conference, or by Mitch Hepburn's absence from a dinner given by the federal Government for all the provincial Premiers. King had gained from the provinces a firm acknowledgement that for the duration of the war federal financial needs would receive priority. By deliberately missing the dinner, King thought that Hepburn had once again put himself in a bad light. Some other federal ministers were not so sanguine about the conference's failure. T. H. Crerar told Senator Lambert how disappointed he was at the results: "He said that if it hadn't been for Ilsley and himself the Conference would not have been held." Mitch Hepburn received the lion's share of the blame for the break-up. Premier A. S. MacMillan of Nova Scotia complained that Hepburn's "personal animosities and political ambitions" were responsible for wrecking the conference. To his old antagonist, the Toronto *Telegram*, however, Hepburn's action was the height of patriotism. The conference was a waste of time. Energy that should have been devoted to the war effort would have been indefinitely diverted but for "the courageous refusal of three provincial Prime Ministers, Messrs. Hepburn, Aberhart, and Pattullo." The *Globe and Mail* sensed partisan politics in the Premier's action. Hepburn, wrote the newspaper "has no doubt ensured for himself another term of office as Prime Minister of Ontario. His portrait will not, however, be included in that group of patriots whom later generations will revere as the founders of a rejuvenated Canada. He has chosen to sacrifice an opportunity for national service in order to ensure continuance in office."

In the on-again, off-again McCullagh-Hepburn relationship, it is difficult to decide whether George McCullagh was chagrined because he could not control Mitch Hepburn or because he could not rely on him. Perhaps the publisher equated the two. In this instance, McCullagh apparently believed that Premier Hepburn had committed himself to supporting the Rowell-Sirois Report. That is what McCullagh told King when the latter visited Toronto some time after the conference to consult his dentist. Following his dental appointment, the Prime Minister visited McCullagh, then ill in the Toronto General Hospital. Mackenzie King had a certain liking for the bluff, brash young publisher but no confidence whatever in his political judgment. During the hospital visit, McCullagh "talked very strongly against Hepburn. Told of how Hepburn had promised, in the presence of his colleagues, to support the Sirois Report. I gathered that he, McCullagh, had promised the Globe's support to him if he supported the Sirois Report." King had little use for political dilettantism: "The truth is there are a lot of amateurs alike at Queen's Park and in the Globe office. The latter really want to govern. Think they know as much about the country's needs as the people's representatives."[4]

Shortly after his return from the abortive conference, the political amateur at Queen's Park announced that he had alternative proposals to strengthen the country's financial position. These were based on Mitch Hepburn's theories of monetary reform. In a carefully worded statement, he condemned high-interest rates, criticized the federal Government's "three per cent war," and urged Ottawa to "make available sufficient new currency in order to take care of expanding requirements of wartime." Finance Minister Ilsley termed Hepburn's scheme "a defeatist inflationary policy," claimed it would cause a drastic wage reduction for every worker, and paired the Ontario Premier with Aberhart as an advocate of "rubber money." Hepburn countered this by saying that the Bank of Canada could issue approximately 480 millions of new currency without any danger of inflation. He pointed out that the level of currency in Canada amounted to thirty dollars per capita, whereas England's stood at sixty-five dollars per capita and that of the United States at seventy dollars: "Currency expansion for the utilization of labour and materials is not inflation, but common horse sense." He did not object to being bracketed with William Aberhart: "We have to get away from the orthodox system of money and we might as well come to it now."

These were not new ideas with Mitch Hepburn. For many years he had advocated getting away from the orthodox system of money. Several of Hepburn's friends encouraged his predilection for monetary change. Among these were the colourful mayor of Vancouver, G. G. "Gerry" McGeer, who once threatened to repudiate municipal debts, and the mildly socialistic publisher of the Vancouver *Sun*, Robert Cromie. Two other men sent Hepburn voluminous letters concerning monetary reform: the first, Huntley Sinclair, a one-time professor in the Department of Economics, Washington University, St. Louis, ran as a Liberal candidate in the provincial election of 1934 and was soundly defeated; the other was Neil McLean, president of a fishing firm in Saint John, New Brunswick, a man whom Senator Lambert considered a thorough-going economic planner.[5]

If there was one thing that disturbed the predominantly conservative business group which helped Mitch Hepburn to win the Liberal leadership, it was his monetary theories. Senator Hardy protested in 1933 that some of Hepburn's speeches sounded wildly inflationary. Hepburn replied he was convinced some measure of monetary reform was necessary:

I have settled in my mind at least the question of whether we will have to have currency expansion or not. During the Chsitmas [*sic*] holidays I had as a guest in my home Huntley Sinclair, Professor of Economics in the Washington University at St. Louis. He has written several books recently and informs me that it is the consensus of opinion of the economists of the United States that there will have to be measures of monitory [*sic*] reform even in the United States. . . .

If we try to maintain our high money value in this country it means in time complete isolation from world trade.

"Truly," Hepburn once said in a sentence that might have been spoken by William Aberhart himself, "our problem is an economic one in a land of plenty." When Social Credit under Aberhart swept to power in Alberta in the summer of 1935, Mitch Hepburn confessed to a friend in that province that he could make neither head nor tail of its theories: "I have read over carefully literature just received on Social Credit, and the more I look into it, the more confusing and impossible the whole proposition seems to me."[6]

About the time of the conference on the Rowell-Sirois Report, Mitch Hepburn apparently looked into Social Credit again. The Premier of Ontario was now saying about monetary reform: "Let us tackle this thing in a big way as suggested by my honourable friend from Alberta." It is difficult to judge whether Mitch Hepburn had made any more sense of Social Credit's theories or whether he saw in Aberhart another vocal ally to fight Mackenzie King. Perhaps both. If, in fact, Mitch Hepburn's vague proposals for currency expansion were distilled with Social Credit's basic theory of keeping consumption and production in balance, there would remain in each instance an inflationary residue.

"Bible-Bill" Aberhart was quick to encourage a potential convert to Social Credit's hot fiscal gospel. He stated publicly that he had "nothing but the highest words of praise" for Hepburn's "masterly statement" advocating currency expansion. That was just the beginning of Aberhart's proselytizing. On February 11, 1941, Aberhart wrote Hepburn: "I believe we should go further in this matter and I have in the course of preparation a little memorandum that I shall send to you in the next few days for your consideration and revision." Three days later, Aberhart wrote urging Hepburn to join with him "to submit to the people of the Dominion, in definite form, the proposals that we would make as a substitute for the recommendations of the Sirois Report." He enclosed a seven-page compendium "for a Sound Reform of the Monetary System to Serve the Nation's War Effort and to Provide a Strong Foundation for Post-War Reconstruction," a resume of Social Credit theories. It was as if a prospective convert had received a catechism from the pope.

Mitch Hepburn promised the Alberta Premier that he would study his doctrine carefully:

I am thoroughly convinced that only by the recasting of our monetary system can this democracy survive. The alternative will mean an upheaval the like of which this nation has never witnessed. We cannot continue forever increasing debts and taxation without a financial

crisis being created. My one regret is that I did not have an opportunity of discussing this problem with you while we were in Ottawa.
. . . After the smoke of battle in the Legislature clears away, I shall
communicate with you with a view to arriving at some common
ground on which to present some definite proposals to the people of
Ontario.

Mitch Hepburn added that Ontario, far from the monetary bible-belt,
would take some saving: "My position here is more difficult in view of
the fact that Toronto is the centre for entrenched finance for the Dominion, and the Press, generally speaking, are very hostile."

Mitch Hepburn's seed of faith was not strong and seems from the
outset to have fallen on the rocky ground of eastern financial orthodoxy.
Aberhart did not give up. On March 12, he pressed Hepburn again,
stressing that a national program of monetary reform would require preparation, pamphlets, and probably radio addresses to educate the people,
who, insisted Aberhart, were ready for the message if only Mitch Hepburn heard the call: "We have been waiting very patiently for a final
word from you regarding some plan of Monetary Reform which you
would propose as an outcome of our Dominion-Provincial Conference
and as a counter proposal to the Sirois recommendations." As in most
conversion attempts, there was no time to lose: "I am dropping you these
few lines urging you give us your considered opinion on the whole matter
of Monetary Reform at as early a date as possible."[7]

For the moment, Mitch Hepburn had slipped out of Aberhart's grasp.
Perhaps the Ontario Premier realized that it would have been impossible
to carry even his provincial Party on a nebulous platform of monetary
reform. Perhaps as Ontario Treasurer, always rigidly orthodox in his own
financing, Mitch Hepburn preferred to keep monetary reform in the attic
of theory, where it could be dusted off periodically as an interesting piece
of bric-a-brac. Perhaps it was just that Mitch Hepburn, his attention span
for any problem now steadily diminishing, again fed up with provincial
affairs, was once more making an attempt to escape monetary theory and
everything else. On February 17, 1941, the eve of the opening of the
Legislature, as the war situation worsened, the Premier cabled Jack
Bickell, still in England with Lord Beaverbrook: "As crisis approaches
can you persuade our great Canadian Lord Beaverbrook to arrange for
me to assist you in your work. Will resign and leave here soon as advised.
Affectionately, Mitch Hepburn." The reply from Lord Beaverbrook arrived a week later: "Jack Bickell has told me of your message to him
and I am deeply grateful for your support which means much to me.
Stop. Shortly I may have to ask you for help which I will not hesitate
to do."

It was not a very satisfactory answer for a man impatient to get into a theater of action, to slough off his personal problems, and to serve his country in some more exciting way than overseeing routine affairs at Queen's Park. But the summons to higher service did not come and Mitch Hepburn was obliged to sit out the sixth session of the Twentieth Legislature answering such questions as the cost of the lighting equipment on the Queen Elizabeth Way and the price of installing a comfort station at Port Burwell. The 1941 session was an uneventful one in which the Premier rehashed many of his arguments against the Rowell-Sirois Report, and George Drew, echoing the *Globe and Mail*'s line, blamed him for walking out on the conference. The highlight of the brief session was the Premier's budget address which occasioned the loudest and longest ovation Mitch Hepburn ever received in the Legislature. It was his seventh budget, and he announced, to deafening Liberal desk-thumping, a surplus of more than twelve million dollars, the largest in the province's history. Much of the increased revenue came from the higher yield on corporation taxes whose rates had been more than doubled. When the Premier sat down, tired and happy, the Liberals stood and cheered. Mitch Hepburn enjoyed the ovation; there would not be many more.[8]

After the session ended in early April, the worsening war news overshadowed political events in Ontario. After the break-up of the Dominion-Provincial Conference, there had been rumours that the Premier planned to call an election on the issue of provincial rights. Senator Lambert discussed this possibility with some of the federal ministers: "McLarty thought Hepburn shd. be opposed but didn't have any ideas how it shd. be done. No leadership. . . . Gardiner said Hepburn would win Ontario." Occasionally Lambert received reports that the Ontario Premier was experiencing problems with his Cabinet and that George McCullagh's hostility was increasing. Ian Mackenzie told Lambert that he had written to King "about McCullagh whom he had seen in Toronto . . . & who was bitterly opposed to Mitch. He wanted P.M. to see George with idea of promoting opposition to Hepburn. Nixon, McArthur, & Conant ready to leave he said." There was no doubt about McCullagh's hostility or the fact that George Drew had now replaced Hepburn in the publisher's affections. On February 8, the *Globe and Mail* was acidulous: "The more we see of Mr. Hepburn's political antics the more we are convinced that the people were right in the last Federal election in choosing Mr. King, with all his faults, rather than listening to the Ontario Provincial Leader." McCullagh warned Drew and the Conservatives to be on guard: Hepburn was planning a snap election on a platform of "rubber money." "There can be no doubt that the erratic young ruler at Queen's Park has been impressed with the election technique of Mr. Aberhart."

Probably, in the spring of 1941, Hepburn considered an appeal to the people on the issue of provincial rights. The year 1941 would have been the normal time to call an election, and men like Harry Nixon and

Farquhar Oliver (appointed to the Cabinet in January 1941) urged Hepburn to go to the country. He told them that he would not subject the province to the turmoil of an election in wartime, a position he had been urged to take by his friend, Thomas L. Kennedy, Member for Peel and later a Conservative Premier. Whether this was the real reason or whether Mitch Hepburn, increasingly unsure of himself and his supporters, simply could not make up his mind, there was no election. Instead, the Premier announced extensive Cabinet changes at the end of May. These included Norman Hipel to Lands and Forests, Peter Heenan to Labour, and Farquhar Oliver's assuming Welfare in addition to the Public Works post he had acquired the previous year.[9]

The citizens of Ontario were not much interested in affairs at Queen's Park in the early summer of 1941. Too many other things were going on at home and abroad: Germany invaded Russia; Joe DiMaggio broke the major-league hitting mark; Bob Hope and Dorothy Lamour were playing "Caught in the Draft"; and Mackenzie King was touring the West, reiterating that his Government would not renege on its pledge of no conscription for overseas service. If all this was too complicated, the man on the street could get away from it all to a place like Ronville Lodge, Lake of Bays, where there was swimming, tennis, and golf for seventeen dollars a week and up. The Premier took a cruise on the Great Lakes with some of his wealthy business friends. On his return, looking bronzed, rested, and considerably overweight, rumours began again that he was going to England for a war job.

Instead, the Premier flew to New York in late September (thereby missing an appointment in Toronto to have his portrait done by the writer and artist Wyndham Lewis) for a trip combining business and pleasure. After his flight, the Premier lunched with the executives of the Chase National Bank, then put the finishing touches on a radio broadcast to be delivered that evening, September 23, over the Columbia Broadcasting System. The speech warned that if the United States and Canada did not shake off their apathy the continent would fall prey to Hitler's legions just as Europe had. At this time both countries were plagued by numerous strikes. Hepburn lashed out at "those who cause strikes in war industries." After referring to his fight against the CIO in 1937, he explained how he would deal with professional labour agitators in wartime: "In Canada, there should be no room for such trouble-makers. They should be listed, classified, condemned, and divorced from society." To cope with these strikes and fifth-columnists, Hepburn suggested that use could be made of veterans' organizations.

The speech, heard in Canada over the CBC, brought a large number of congratulatory letters and telegrams from Canadians (and Americans) who were fed up with strikes and liked Mitch Hepburn's tough solution for them. (The Premier had made short-shrift of a strike at the New

Toronto plant of Campbell's Soup by trucking in farmers to help unload tomatoes before they spoiled, and he was keeping a tight lid on CIO agitation in the Kirkland Lake mining areas.)* "It's too damn bad that you are not the Minister of Labour at Ottawa," wrote one admirer from New Brunswick, "instead of the useless tool we have there." A friend in Elgin also was delighted: "I can't express, Mitch, how proud I am that I have had the privilege of knowing you from the time you started out in politics, and to my mind you never have risen to greater heights in your whole career, than you did when you gave the speech I have just listened to with so much interest."[10]

The trip to New York was not all business. The Premier was inducted into the Saints and Sinners Club, an American fraternal and charitable organization associated with the Shriners. His membership in this group was sponsored by his friends Gene Tunney and newscaster Lowell Thomas. Before leaving for New York, the Premier remarked to a group of his constituents at Aylmer that he was a bit concerned about becoming a Saint and Sinner: "My only hope is that I can hold my own in company with the big names of the United States. At least I hope I can get a spoonful every time one of them digs in for a shovelful." Mitch Hepburn need not have worried. He was right at home with high-jinks: "Don't pull any punches on my account," he smilingly told nine hundred Saints and Sinners packed into the Astor hotel ballroom to see the Premier of Ontario as "the fall guy." They didn't. Dressed as John Bull, with a garland of onions around his neck, a topper, and an empty monocle, Mitch Hepburn laughed as uproariously as anyone when five men with CIO placards exploded a bomb beneath his chair.

Before boarding his plane for home, the Premier led a couple of dozen well-wishers at the airport lustily singing:

Ontario, Ontario
There's no place like Ontario,
All Sons of Mitch-ell Hepburn know
There's no place like Ontario.

"These Canadians impressed us greatly," noted the Saints and Sinners bulletin (under an item headed "The Case of the Well-Primed Minister or Pleased to Mitchell, Hepburn"), "and acted as if each drink were their last." One of the Saints and Sinners, the former Governor of New Jersey, Harold G. Hoffman, told Mitch Hepburn: "You were certainly a swell 'Fall Guy' and I must reiterate that you are the best salesman Canada has ever sent to the United States."[11]

High-jinks of a different kind were being prepared in Ontario in the autumn of 1941. Mitchell Hepburn was again the "fall guy" in one of his last political burlesques with Mackenzie King. The stage for this was set when Arthur Meighen was again chosen to lead the Conservative Party, replacing Robert Manion who had resigned after his personal defeat in 1940. Meighen supported compulsory military service for overseas, a policy King was pledged against. So that Meighen might enter the House of Commons as quickly as possible, the Member for South York, Allan Cockeram, resigned the seat he had won in 1940 by nearly 2,500 votes, a seat that had never elected a Liberal. Despite King's notorious dislike for Arthur Meighen, the Liberals, in keeping with the tradition of facilitating a Party leader's election to Parliament, did not put up a candidate. Any hope that Meighen may have had for an acclamation ended, however, when the CCF nominated a Toronto high school teacher, Joseph W. Noseworthy. In the general election of 1940, Noseworthy had polled less than one-sixth of the votes. Besides South York, King called three other by-elections for February 9, 1942: Welland, where the newly appointed Labour Minister, Humphrey Mitchell was opposed by Douglas Watt, a pro-conscriptionist independent candidate; and two in Quebec (where the new Minister of Justice Louis St. Laurent was running).

This little general election was critical so far as King's controversial manpower policy was concerned. The Prime Minister told his Cabinet on more than one occasion that he might resign if the newly appointed Ministers were defeated. The all-out conscription issue, which Meighen was stressing in York South, became blurred when, in the speech from the throne on January 22, 1942, King announced that a plebiscite would be held to ask the people to relieve the Government of its no-conscription pledge for overseas service. Announcement of the plebiscite catapulted Mitch Hepburn into the Ontario by-election campaigns. It also occasioned his bitterest attack on Ottawa since the war began: "The calling of a plebiscite on the question of conscription is the most dastardly, contemptible, and cowardly thing ever perpetrated on a respected and dignified country by any Government." The historians of the future, he told a sales convention in St. Thomas, would consider the plebiscite a "dastardly act." The memoirs of King, which the federal leader prized so highly, would not grace many Canadian libraries in the future. So that King's memoirs would recount one less victory, Hepburn wrote to his old foe,

---

* Late in November, 1941, a strike, potentially disruptive of the war effort, broke out in the mines of the Kirkland Lake area. After eleven weeks, the important issue of CIO recognition still unresolved, the strike leaders ordered their men back to work. Both the President of Macassa Gold Mines (in whose stocks Premier Hepburn had previously invested) and the Managing Director of Lake Shore Mines thanked Mitchell Hepburn for his assistance (provincial police strength at Kirkland Lake had been substantially increased) "in staving off, for the present, the taking over of control of operations by the CIO." (PAO Hepburn Papers, Robert A. Bryce to M. F. H., February 14, 1942; A. L. Blomfield to M. F. H., February 24, 1942)

Arthur Meighen, on January 27, 1942: "As a Liberal I am quite prepared to, and shall, deliver an address to the electors on your behalf.
Wishing you every success, to which I add a sincere hope that you may
long be spared to do your part to take our central legislative authority
out of the valley of humiliation and incoherence." "Your offer to speak
as a Liberal on my behalf," replied Meighen who had the backing of
Drew and McCullagh, "is accepted with gratitude."

Hepburn's plan to intervene in the Ontario by-elections against King
further unsettled a complicated political situation. The federal Ministers
were edgy. Air Minister Power told Senator Lambert that "things were
disintegrating. Bad atmosphere in Cabinet. King spoke in caucus rather
roughly, he said; and threatened to resign if Mitchell and St. Laurent
beaten." Mackenzie King was pessimistic about the chances of beating
Meighen in South York. On February 2, he noted: "Reports keep coming in from CCF and Liberals that Meighen will have a hard fight. That
they may beat Meighen. This I do not believe at all . . . Hepburn's
machine will be combined with the Tory machine and will spare . . .
nothing to ensure Meighen's return."

The Prime Minister did not note that his own machine had been
thrown into low gear to ensure Meighen's defeat. Two weeks before
voting day, the Liberal Member for Montreal St. Lawrence-St George,
Brooke Claxton, informed Senator Lambert that he wanted $1,000 for
the CCF in South York. Lambert sent the money to be picked up by one
of Noseworthy's aides, Andrew Brewin. Another CCF strategist, David
Lewis, was also informed of the matter. These transactions were handled
gingerly. When one of Toronto's leading Liberals, Peter Campbell, called
to inform Lambert that C. D. Howe had suggested some financial help
be given to Arthur Roebuck (who was speaking against Meighen in
South York), Lambert advised Campbell to see Brewin personally about
it.[12] Mackenzie King's machine was not making much noise, but it was
geared to run down Hepburn and in the process was giving Arthur
Meighen's opponent in South York a bit of a lift.

Mitch Hepburn was making a good deal of noise. In Welland, campaigning against Humphrey Mitchell, he charged that King had followed
a policy of "appeasement in every critical issue" since the war began. "I
don't care whether I stick my chin out the length of this hall just so long
as I help defeat the Mackenzie King candidate." Referring to his appearance in Niagara Falls with George Drew in support of Mitchell's opponent, the Premier commented, "I don't know how long this strange
relationship will last. I do hope we will live together long enough to end
the sham Government at Ottawa." Four days before the voting, he delivered a radio address for Arthur Meighen, the man he had all but called
a criminal because of the hydro-bond transactions a few years before.
The Conservative party needed Meighen's brilliant qualities: "With Mr.
Meighen its leader in the Commons, it will be an inspired force to see

that the Government gives Churchill and our allies a total effort and our enemies a total war."

Hepburn's support of the anti-King candidates again split the Liberals, including members of his own Cabinet, wide open. The federal Member for Leeds, George Fulford, once a friend of the Premier, now hung his head in shame when he thought "that I was chairman of the meeting that chose Mitchell Hepburn to lead the Liberal Party in Ontario." He hung it lower when he thought "that I sat complacently in the Ontario Legislature three years and four months suffering the indignities imposed upon private members of that body by the dictator of Ontario." More serious than federal Liberals hanging their heads was the threat of defections from Hepburn's Cabinet. Mines Minister Robert Laurier had informed King privately that he intended to resign. (The federal leader was delighted: "I told him that his uncle would be very proud of his actions today.") Laurier now formally submitted his resignation to Hepburn because "with all due respect for your judgment," he could not agree with the Premier's support for Meighen. Mitch Hepburn ignored the resignation and several weeks later Laurier resumed his portfolio, a performance that moved Mackenzie King to write in disgust that the "whole business of Ontario politics . . . is so amateurish and school-boyish that it makes me rather nauseated."

No Cabinet could long survive the fissures opened by Hepburn's support of Meighen. Attorney General Gordon Conant said that Meighen's defeat would be "a tragedy." Harry Nixon avowed that his election would be a "national calamity." Nixon accompanied his statement with another resignation attempt, this one more half-hearted than usual. On February 6, he wrote the Premier:

> If the public statement which I released this morning following your address last night for Arthur Meighen embarrasses you or interferes with your plans and policies for the future, do not hesitate to accept this as my resignation.
>
> I am extremely sorry that this Ottawa business has come between us again but there has never been any secret of my convictions in the matter.

Nixon would be proud to continue in the Government "if it is your wish, but I can never be a party to an alliance with Drew and Meighen." Nixon's public repudiation of Meighen was ignored by Hepburn (as was his letter of resignation) but pleased Mackenzie King: "The best thing of the day is Harry Nixon having come out strongly against Meighen, saying it would be a disaster for him to be re-elected. This will help getting out the vote against Meighen in Toronto, and should help in bringing the farmers out in Welland."

Still, when C. D. Howe told King that the betting was three-to-two against Meighen's winning, the Prime Minister thought it "sheer non-sense." Continuing his efforts to ensure the defeat of the King candidates, Hepburn spoke at Port Colborne. He was prepared to sacrifice his own premiership if that would bring about a stronger war effort. He had jeopardized his position at the time the Ontario Legislature voted to condemn King's conduct of the war: "It caused a breach that has not healed and that will never heal. I have lost friends and supporters. . . . I nearly lost my position as Prime Minister – I may lose it yet if you endorse the King candidate in this by-election by an overwhelming majority, but I don't care about that." "The true authentic voice of Liberalism in this province," Highways Minister T. B. McQuesten told the meeting, "is the voice of Mitchell Hepburn."[13]

"The true authentic voice of Liberalism" in Ontario was somewhat muted after the election returns on the night of February 9. All four King candidates won handily. In a stunning upset, the new leader of the Conservative Party, Arthur Meighen, the man chosen to make King toe the mark, lost York South by nearly 4,500 votes, a loss probably caused more by Meighen's inept campaign and the vigorous door-to-door bell-ringing of the CCF than by federal Liberal intervention which seemed to have been directed as much at Hepburn as at Meighen. With a wry grin, Mitch Hepburn told a banquet at Chatham: "After those returns, I feel somewhat like a darn small minority." He admitted he had been spanked by the voters but promised to keep his chin up and keep smiling.

There was a smile also on the usually bland, inscrutable face of Mackenzie King. Of the two men he hated most in public life, one had been eliminated, the other's influence again proved inadequate when put to the test. According to King's analysis, Meighen's defeat "was in large part due to the treacherous action on Hepburn's part going on to his platform, and also trying to organize the defeat of the federal Minister in Welland. There never was such treachery on the part of a Leader of a Government towards another Government supposed to be of the same political stripe." Mackenzie King attributed his enemies' come-uppance to Providence: "I felt tonight that public life in Canada had been cleansed, as though we had gone through a storm and got rid of something that was truly vile and bad. . . . I felt most grateful to Providence for what Canada had been spared of division and strife."[14]

Put that way, Mitch Hepburn should not have felt too badly about the political set-backs of early 1942. If he had been on the side of the saints (like many mortals, Mitch Hepburn spent his share of time on the other side) and had been feeling at the top of his form (he was not), it was too much to expect that Mitch Hepburn could take on God and Mackenzie King too. Before the year ended, neither King's hostility nor the attitude of the deity would be very relevant so far as Mitch Hepburn's political future was concerned.

chapter 15

Reaping the Whirlwind

On February 11, 1942, two days after Arthur Meighen's defeat in York South, the Ontario Legislature opened, an event noted by the Toronto *Star* on page 29. The main business of the session was an agreement transferring corporation and income taxes to Ottawa for the duration of the war in return for federal grants to the province. Premier Hepburn was generally pleased with the new arrangement because he believed it gave the province better financial terms than those recommended by the Rowell-Sirois Commission. He agreed with Leopold Macaulay, however, that this reduced the Legislature to the status of a "glorified county council."

Liberals hailed the Premier's budget address when he announced a surplus of $1.3 million. Nothing very exciting happened during the short session. On April Fool's Day, a bird got into the Chamber and flew wildly around the chandeliers and ornately moulded ceiling until Public Works Minister Farquhar Oliver and his efficient staff managed to chase it out. Some considered it a bad omen. After unanimously extending its life for a year because of the war, and passing legislation to change the name "undertaker" to "funeral director and embalmer," one of the dullest and the first divisionless session in the history of the Legislature ended.

The funereal debates obscured the program mounted by the Hepburn administration to aid the war effort. For a man who felt so frustrated because he was not on active service, Premier Hepburn did what he could at the provincial level with vigour and imagination. The main thrust was in agriculture: to increase the production of foodstuffs for shipment to Britain and provide a mobile working force for the short-handed farmers. Subsidies, which substantially increased production, were paid for hogs and cheese. With the financial assistance of the federal Government, a Farm Labour Force was organized utilizing the services of students and retired people to help on the farms. A retraining program provided many workers for hard-pressed war industries. The province also made available to the federal authorities eleven institutions comprising 141 buildings.[1] Premier Hepburn and his Government were justifiably proud of these efforts, though they did not command headlines in the spring of 1942. These were reserved for the war itself, dominated by the German drive into Russia's heartland.

There seemed little political activity in Ontario in the spring and summer of 1942 (the Premier himself was hospitalized for a tonsil operation), and what there was emanated from the rejuvenated CCF, under its new young leader, Toronto lawyer Edward B. Jolliffe. The CCF took legal action to force Hepburn to call by-elections for six vacant seats. Because both George Drew and the Premier had supported the motion extending the Legislature's term for a year, there seemed little likelihood of a general election. There was some difference of opinion among the Conservatives themselves concerning how much longer the political truce with Hepburn should continue, especially since the CCF was showing signs of strength. One of Drew's advisors, Harold Robbins, warned his chief: "There is nothing I can do personally to overcome the business of sabotage which is being pursued by the neutralized portion of your followers." Robbins warned, "I still think Hepburn would pull an election if he thought it would help him." Liberal strategists at Ottawa were also concerned. Senator Norman Lambert met C. D. Howe and other Ontario Members in Postmaster General W. P. Mulock's office on May 5: "After showing situation in Ont. now in hands of CCF and a prospective Union of Hepburn & Drew followers, it was decided to have an Ont. caucus to decide upon a convention for Ont. by July 1st."

While continuing his spasmodic indictment of King's policies (and strongly defending Colonel Drew when he was charged but not prosecuted for alleged subversive statements), the Premier was engaged in a number of murky manoeuvres which defy analysis but seem to have had as their objective the structuring of some kind of coalition to combat King. He invited William Aberhart to come East, and the two men discussed strategy early in the summer. The Alberta Premier wrote to Hepburn on July 30 that he was "more convinced than ever, that, in the disastrous crisis which is developing, immediate and strong action is the urgent need." Aberhart enclosed a blueprint for action entitled "Draft National Platform" which included general plans for a total war effort, post-war reconstruction and rehabilitation, and financial readjustments. There was a suggestion that traditional party alignments were breaking down and the time had arrived to place before the country a coherent national program. Aberhart urged his friend at Queen's Park to get on with it:

I would suggest that as a preliminary you and Drew (if you both concur in the views I have expressed) should get together and draft a popular platform, brief and progressive, to give the people a chance to choose their proper course. You people must give leadership to Canada! You will pardon that statement – I say it as a challenge.[2]

For the moment, Premier Hepburn was too busy to accept that challenge, worded in generalities and based largely on Social Credit theory. Inexplicably, he had veered off in another direction. At the end of July, he telephoned former Lieutenant Governor Herbert Bruce, now the Conservative federal Member for Toronto Parkdale, to inquire if he were returning to Toronto from Ottawa for the first weekend in August. When Bruce replied affirmatively, the Premier asked that he meet him Saturday morning in his King Edward Hotel suite. Bruce recalled the meeting in his autobiography, *Varied Operations*:

I was amazed when he asked me if I would head a Provincial Coalition Government. He said that he had consulted his Cabinet members and they had all agreed to this suggestion except Nixon. But, he added, Nixon's refusal would make no difference and he could be left out. He even went so far as to suggest those who might fill the various positions and to say that if I had any difficulty in forming a Cabinet that included him, he would drop out!

To this, I replied that although I was not inclined to consider doing what he was asking, I would think the matter over in the next few days, and then give him my answer.

After thinking this astonishing proposal over, Bruce replied:

When you approached me with the suggestion that I head a coalition Government in Ontario, I felt that, coming from you, it merited serious consideration. After giving it some thought, I am not able to see how such a proposal would contribute to the important object we are both most concerned about, namely, the more vigorous prosecution of the war and, therefore I would not be willing to act in the role you suggest. I believe that whatever ability I may have can be used to best advantage in representing my constituency in the Parliament at Ottawa.[3]

Mitch Hepburn's attempt in the summer of 1942 to form a union government in Ontario with a strong anti-King Tory at its head did not make much political sense. A union government at the provincial level is difficult to justify at any time. Why the Premier, leading a large majority in a Legislature whose tenure had been extended and whose importance in wartime was steadily decreasing, should again suggest something that had been decisively rejected by the electorate at the federal level is difficult to comprehend. The manoeuvre was of a piece with many of the Premier's actions at this time – confused, incoherent, almost irrational.

By the summer of 1942, whatever pattern there had been to Mitch Hepburn's personality was beginning to unravel in a snarl of inconsistencies. The house had been built on sand and the sand was shifting. As Richard M. Alway has remarked in his study, "Mitchell F. Hepburn and the Liberal Party in Ontario, 1937-1943," what one sees are the footsteps, not the man.[4] The footsteps were those of a man staggering under the weight of instincts he could no longer control; of nerves jangling from the vicious circle of too little sleep and too much medication; of a physical and emotional malaise that a few of his so-called "friends," whose influence over the Premier was anything but healthy, did nothing to alleviate. Not many of the old friends remained. Some, like Percy Parker and Senator Frank O'Connor, had died. Others had gradually extricated themselves from a way of life that was deteriorating. Still others had tried to remain in contact with their old friend, the Mitch Hepburn they once knew, only to discover that he had changed if they could arrange to see him at all. Private Liberal members of the Legislature now found it increasingly difficult to contact the Premier. Cabinet ministers, never his confidants, were scarcely consulted. More and more the routine business of Government, so boring and uninteresting, was carried on in the Premier's absence by civil servants and Deputy Ministers like Chester Walters, an able man with a towering ego whose influence with the Premier over the years had nettled not a few Liberals. The Hepburn Government, in the phrase of Opposition Leader Drew, was becoming "a phantom administration."

The Premier's aloofness and inaccessibility were noticed now even in Elgin where his supporters saw less and less of Mitch Hepburn. Even when they did, they remarked that his once hearty greeting was perfunctory, his geniality restrained. One of these, A. W. "Bertie" Ward, who had been a chum of Mitch Hepburn's in the early days in St. Thomas, who had helped Mitch Hepburn with his homework, shared his escapades in the banking days, enjoyed his hospitality in Ottawa, and had tried to maintain the friendship through the years of power and aloofness at Queen's Park, now in 1942 tried again:

I have long ago given up hope of ever receiving an answer to any personal letter or telegram I send you – or even of being able to get in touch with you or see you. In fact, the last time I was in St. Thomas, a year ago, I started out to see you but changed my mind as I did not want to call you and be told you would not see me. I sometimes wonder if I, inadvertently, offended you somehow. But all that is as it may be – because I cannot forget the old days &, as far as I am concerned, the close affection I had for you as a boy still remains.

After congratulating his friend for pressing a vigorous war effort, Ward added: "Well, old partner, keep up the good work – &, although it may not mean much to you now, – I am proud of you. My very best to Eva – & I hope that some day I shall be allowed to come & see you both." A month passed, then Mitch Hepburn wrote, "My dear Bertie: Your letter was most welcome. It does seem that we have travelled a long ways apart although I often think of you and our many escapades. . . . I hope to be in Ottawa in a short time . . . and maybe we can get together then."[5] In the last years, Mitch Hepburn had indeed "travelled a long ways apart" from the friends of earlier days. Some of this is inevitable in the life of any man, certainly in the life of a busy Premier. For Mitch Hepburn, who had alienated or forgotten many of his supporters, the price involved was too high. There was nothing to replace the stabilizing influence of the solid friends he had lost. He was now surrounded for the most part by people using him for their own purposes or just along for the ride. The ride was now moving on a careening course at a sickening pace.

Nevertheless, in the summer of 1942, Mitch Hepburn summoned his resiliency and energy to make another effort to find some way out of the political and emotional maze. After a wedding celebration for his old friend, Sir James Dunn, and Dunn's long-time secretary, Christoforides, at Bannockburn (a celebration that took a more hilarious and convivial turn than usual when Maurice Duplessis challenged the groom, in his late sixties, along with Hepburn and Jack Bickell, to a milking contest, somewhat surprisingly won on points by Sir James), Premier Hepburn embarked on a heavy speaking tour that took him to all parts of Ontario. If the tour had any objective, it would seem to have been an attempt to test the political temper of the province and to retaliate against Mackenzie King for the many defeats that Mitch Hepburn had suffered at the hands of the federal leader.

To an audience in Elgin, Hepburn charged that Canada was "governed by a group of men whose autocracy and stupidity are doing irreparable damage to this country." At the opening of the Shand Dam near Fergus, the Premier was scornful. "Don't listen to these men at Ottawa, these men with the Vichy minds, who tell you we are winning the war comfortably. We are not." A police banquet at Niagara Falls heard the Premier appeal to federal Ministers like Ralston, Macdonald, Ilsley, and Howe. "For God's sake, I ask them, in this hour of trial, to forget politics and put your country before living men; never mind whether you save King, let's save the country." In some of his speeches, Mitch Hepburn sounded vaguely as though he were summoning his audience to organize a new national party. "I say to you," he urged a crowd at the Oshawa fair, "whether you be CCF, Conservative, King Liberals, or Hepburn Liberals, let us raise a political umbrella under which those who believe in fighting shoulder to shoulder may rally in this struggle for existence. Let us line up together." He had no politics himself any longer, he explained at the Maxville fair, "only a desire to waken this country to what it is up against, and to stress its responsibilities to our men overseas."[6]

In view of this strenuous speaking tour, it seemed that Mitch Hepburn, despite disclaimers, was preaching for a call. Just what his new charge would involve never clearly appeared. It is doubtful that Mitch Hepburn knew himself. If he had a definite plan either to retain power in Ontario or to dislodge King, it is probable that his blurred vision could not focus on it for long, certain that his resources were too far spent to sustain it. Nevertheless, Premier Aberhart kept pressing Mitch Hepburn to take the lead in an "All-Canada" organization that would get the country moving again and, presumably, oust King. When Aberhart received no answer to his letter of July 30 urging action, he wrote Hepburn again on August 26:

> I am wondering whether you are contemplating disposing of your provincial election before tackling the larger issue.
>
> I sincerely hope that this is not the case, for I am convinced that you will not only strengthen your position in the Province by coming out on the national issue *first*, but I think that you run a grave risk of weakening your position in the national field, should the Socialists make a good showing in the provincial election.
>
> At the present time the majority of people are desperately concerned about the national situation. Because they have no alternative, many of them are giving their support to socialism – it is a protest support, born of despair. I believe that there is a real danger of this being reflected in your provincial election if it precedes action in the national field. Whereas if your provincial election followed, the effect would be the reverse. . . .
>
> Every moment counts if we are to be organized for an All Canada organization.
>
> Have you talked with Col. Drew and what was the result?

Whether Hepburn spoke to Colonel Drew, he does not seem to have answered Aberhart's letter. But the Alberta Premier was persistent. On September 28, he wrote Hepburn again, and this time he was more specific. In order to save the national situation "from the disaster toward which we are drifting," he intended to convene a provincial conference of the people of Alberta early in December: "I suggest that a Provincial

Conference, such as we propose to hold in Edmonton, would provide an excellent springboard for the whole country. I am satisfied that the people will respond enthusiastically to a definite policy of postwar reconstruction and a courageous lead on the war effort."

If, as Premier Aberhart apparently hoped, the Edmonton conference was to be the kick-off for a new national grouping with an All-Canada label, Social Credit theories and his own tailor-made slogan ("No party politics in war and a Canada worthy of maximum sacrifices"), he also had the men in mind to boot this shiny new ball into the political arena. He pleaded with Hepburn not to miss the opportunity:

> Would you come West to speak at this Conference? It would strengthen the position immeasurably if Drew would join you and you both appeared on the same platform. I can promise you a tumultuous welcome, and if you both put over the right stuff, as I am sure you will, you could electrify the whole country. I think you will readily appreciate the potentialities of such a move.

According to Aberhart, both the Liberals and the Conservatives were through as Parties: "The only alternative is non-party action by men who place their country's welfare above all else. You and Drew can give this leadership. I urge you to do so."

After explaining he had failed to answer earlier because he had been on a speaking tour, Mitch Hepburn replied to Aberhart's summons on October 6. His answer was couched in general terms which may indicate either that he found Aberhart's proposals nebulous or that he was wrestling with problems far more pressing than a conference in Edmonton:

> Everywhere in Ontario I found that which you described as an utter sense of frustration among the people and whole-hearted condemnation of the vacillating record of the Ottawa Administration.
>
> I do believe we are arriving near the point where the resentment of the people will crystallize in some form or other and seek expression.
>
> I am interested in your suggestion that I attend a Provincial Conference in Alberta. Please let me have another week to take stock and inventory of my own problems here before making a definite reply. Needless to say, I am whole-heartedly in support of the general idea.[7]

Even as he indicated vague interest in Aberhart's "All Canada" scheme, Mitch Hepburn had shot off on another tangent in his own province. The man who had fought to keep out the Communist agitators in 1937 was now agitating on behalf of well-known Communist leaders

like Tim Buck and advocating the lifting of the ban on the Communist
Party in Canada. Reasons for Hepburn's puzzling change of attitude toward the Communists can only be conjectured. Because of the war, of
course, the public's attitude toward Russia had changed. Perhaps, too, by
championing the civil liberties he had played fast and loose with previously, he hoped to shore up his waning labour support and steal a
march on the political up-and-coming CCF. Perhaps he wanted another
stick with which to belabour King: "A total war effort is not possible,"
said the Premier, "so long as an autocratic political party in office abuses
its extreme power and persecutes those who criticize its policies and
record, and differ in economic theory." One probable reason for the
Premier's *volte-face* concerning the Communists was his acquaintance
and growing admiration for A. A. MacLeod, the articulate, witty, and
clear-minded publisher of the Communist *Tribune*. MacLeod became not
only a close friend of the Premier but also a political adviser whose
judgment Mitch Hepburn came to respect.

On September 21, the Premier of Ontario was seated on the platform
in Maple Leaf Gardens at a rally for total war. Beside him were some of
the men with whom he had clashed over labour matters in the past:
George Burt of the United Auto Workers, J. A. "Pat" Sullivan, President
of the Seamen's Union, and such well-known Communists as Joseph
Salsberg and Norman Freed. (The author, Theodore Dreiser, had been
scheduled to speak but fled the city amid an uproar over his reported
remark: "I would rather see Germans in England than the damn snobs
we have there now.") The Premier told the crowd of sixteen thousand in
the Gardens: "I believe in total war and so do you, so in that regard I
find myself tonight among many friends, although there are many here
with whom I have differed politically in the past." To applause, the
Premier summoned a Red Army girl sniper to the platform and presented
her with a 30-30 sporting rifle on behalf of the province: "We hope that
your present record of slaying 309 Nazis is a mere rehearsal."

Mitch Hepburn's concern for the Communists occasioned his last
dispute as Premier of Ontario with Mackenzie King. When Tim Buck
and other Communists voluntarily surrendered to police and were lodged
in Toronto's Don Jail (where Hepburn had his secretary, Bert Lyman,
take them candy and cigarettes), the Premier and Attorney General
Gordon Conant telegraphed Justice Minister St. Laurent requesting that
they be released "to co-operate and assist in every way in the prosecution
of the war." The Justice Minister freed the men within a few days, but
Hepburn's further recommendation that the King Government lift the
ban on the Communist Party was rejected. "This move," Hepburn had
explained to King, "will be in the interest of national unity and will
enhance the prestige of your Government, both of which stand in need
of additional strength at the present time." It was ironic that one of the

last public appearances Mitch Hepburn made as Premier was on October 13 at another rally in Maple Leaf Gardens in support of lifting the Communist ban. He looked overweight, his face somewhat puffy, as he chatted with Tim Buck.[8]

A number of the things that Mitch Hepburn did in the fall of 1942 seem ironic. The man whose administration had so much trouble with strikes told the convention of the AFL in Toronto that his Government would bring in special legislation to guarantee the rights of labour to collective bargaining: "I believe that the future peace of this world is only secure in the hands of labour and the great masses of society." The man who had been accused of a "conspiracy" to topple Mackenzie King was now upbraided by his partner in crime, Maurice Duplessis, for not obtaining a K.C. for an Ontario friend of the former Quebec Premier. Duplessis wrote jocularly:

> I understand that, since the war, no K.C. were appointed by your Government. I cannot but help telling you that I don't know why. Billy King, of Ottawa, needs counsels and our Gracious King, of England, is always pleased to have counsels. . . .
>
> I may say frankly to you that I would be very much disappointed if the first favour I ask you, which is not of so much consequence, were not amicably received.

The Premier promised his friend that he would discuss the matter with the Attorney General. Then the man who had so often threatened to retire from public life wrote to the Liberal Member for Northumberland, Harold Carr, on October 15, to express his shock that Carr had decided not to stand again "although I can well understand anyone today desiring to retire from the controversial atmosphere of public life." The Premier then turned to the future: "At the moment we are not contemplating an election but there may be an early Session this fall in order to consider two important bills. I do hope you will drop in to see me the first time you are in Toronto as there are other matters I would like to discuss with you."

On Friday evening, October 16, Premier Hepburn addressed the third annual meeting of the Queen's Park War Service Guild held in the Legislative Chambers. He congratulated the women on their devoted labours for the war effort and told them the greatest contribution to the province his administration had made was in the field of health, particularly the prevention of tuberculosis. His final words to the ladies in the Chamber, where he had been Premier for more than eight years, seemed to carry no special significance: "I do not know what the events in the future will bring forth, whether I will be Premier or whether George Drew will be Premier and I the leader of the Opposition, but whatever happens I hope you will carry on your work and I can assure you you will always have my very best wishes." When the meeting of the War Service Guild ended at 10:25 P.M. on Friday, October 16, with the singing of "O God, Our Help in Ages Past," no one present thought he or she had listened to a valedictory; perhaps Mitch Hepburn did not realize he had delivered one.[9]

The Premier spent the weekend of October 17 at his Bannockburn farm where he was visited by a number of his political associates in Elgin. He returned to Queen's Park on Tuesday. There were conferences, apparently routine, with several members of the Cabinet including Provincial Secretary Harry Nixon. Wednesday, October 21, was a warm, showery October day in Toronto. Headlines from the war fronts dominated the news. In savage hand-to-hand fighting, the Russians slashed through German holdings in Stalingrad to recapture several buildings. Royal Air Force planes prepared to bomb Genoa. General Montgomery, his Eighth Army backed by strong air support, had completed plans to assault Rommel's El Alamein line. Premier Hepburn reportedly lunched with his friends, Sell 'Em Ben Smith and Jack Bickell. Afterwards he was again in his office at Queen's Park. In mid-afternoon, he received two deputations, one of them headed by Mayor F. J. Conboy of Toronto. By this time excitement had begun to crackle through the corridors of the Parliament Buildings as a rumour spread that a major announcement was imminent. About 4:30 P.M., the Premier again conferred in his office with Harry Nixon for fifteen minutes.

After Nixon left, the clerk of the Crown in Chancery, C. F. Bulmer, who had assisted at the swearing in of several Premiers, was summoned to Premier Hepburn's office. Moments later, Attorney General Gordon Conant arrived. About 5:30 P.M., the Premier, looking unusually serious and preoccupied, put on his hat and coat, left his second-floor office and drove north with the Attorney General to the Warren Road home of Lieutenant Governor Albert Matthews. Flashbulbs popped yellowishly in the light drizzle as the two men walked up the front steps of the Lieutenant Governor's residence. The Premier turned up his coat collar and ignored the cameras, something that photographers could never remember his having done before. A few minutes after six in the Matthews' spacious drawing room, Mitchell F. Hepburn resigned as Prime Minister of Ontario. Attorney General Gordon Conant was immediately sworn in as his successor. The new Premier returned to Queen's Park, the former one to his King Edward suite.

"Hepburn Resigns; Conant Succeeds Him as Ontario Premier," blared the banner headline of the *Globe and Mail*. The province and the former Premier's closest friends were stunned. Even the handful of associates in Elgin, to whom he had confided over the weekend that he had offered the Premiership to Conant, did not really expect that he would go through with it. This time there was no bluff. Mitchell Hepburn not only resigned as Premier but also submitted his resignation as Provincial Treasurer and said it was his intention to retire completely from public life. In his formal resignation statement, he explained: "It has not been my desire to seek a third term of office. One year ago I called a meeting of my colleagues of the Cabinet and urged then that my successor be selected. I was, however, prevailed upon to lead the Government through the last session of the Legislature." He felt it was his duty to continue until the attempt of the CCF to force by-elections in Ontario was settled. When the CCF case was rejected on October 16, "I at once asked the Attorney General to accept the position as head of the Government. Yesterday he consented. I have now handed to him my resignation as provincial treasurer, but at his request have agreed to retain the portfolio for a short time, after which I shall retire from public life."[10]

A few days later, when he had second thoughts about retiring from public life, Mitch Hepburn told the press there were two reasons for his resignation from the Premiership: his unwillingness to kow-tow to Ottawa and his refusal to call a provincial election:

As was to be expected my adamant and consistent stand on the war effort, my lack of blind adhesion to Party welfare as against national interests in this unprecedented crisis in world history, annoyed the purely partisan section of the Liberal Party, and as a consequence my position as leader became untenable. A serious division gradually developed within the Government and the Party which became intensified even as the war came closer to our shores.

Two issues stood out above all others; complete subservience to the Ottawa political machine and the calling of a snap election whenever the time appeared opportune.

Hepburn claimed that he resisted this pressure to call an election:

In this respect I was in an anomalous and yet vulnerable position. I was elected leader of a political party at a properly constituted convention. True the Liberal Party was the vehicle by which the Government was elected to office, but on all great issues and particularly in terms of war it is not the political party but the welfare of all the people which must be of paramount consideration. It is regrettable and a national disaster that such a fact has been entirely overlooked by the Federal Government. . . . I was forced to choose between the party and the well-being of the nation. I have put my country first.

Whatever else the Premier's statement revealed, it obviously did not give the complete reasons for his sudden resignation. He elaborated on these in a letter to Premier Aberhart on November 7: "In announcing my resignation . . . I did not make public one of the main reasons which I am now giving you in a confidential way." He would use this later "when the King crowd becomes a little bolder and insistent in their demands for a convention and a general election." The ex-Premier then gave Aberhart this version of the steps that led to his resignation.

> Some while ago I was warned that King had decided to use his prestige and many Senate vacancies with a view of forcing an Ontario General Election in order that a racial issue could be raised in Ontario and which would, if he succeeded in his effort, result in a repetition in Ontario of the bitter 1917 fight where the slogan was "Take them out of Quebec at the point of the bayonet."
>
> The French-Canadian Federal Members are outraged over King's political manoeuvre on the plebiscite as the result of which the French minority in Ontario and the people of Quebec are smarting under the increasing criticism, particularly of that emanating from publications in the United States. He has put the Province of Quebec in the position of occupying a sour spot on the North American Continent. He, at the same time, has witnessed the aftermath of the plebiscite in the growing resentment and the falling away of his Quebec support.
>
> This move on the part of King is becoming very obvious now to the French-Canadians and the citizens of Ontario. All we have to do . . . is let him become a little bolder.

Hepburn also wrote to two leading Conservatives, Robert Manion, and the man who would soon become the Conservative federal leader, Premier John Bracken of Manitoba. He told Manion:

> I am proud of the fact that I did not succumb to the demand for a General Election and have this Province in a turmoil when the actual blood-bath in Europe is about to take place. There would be created, among other things, a sharp division between labour and industry at a time when we are trying to attain maximum production. Even worse, there would have been raised, in all probability, a bitter racial issue which would have destroyed the last vestige we have of national unity.

Hepburn also explained to John Bracken that King had tried to force a general election in the province in order to hold his French-Canadian support by championing Quebec against the imperial issue in Ontario. He added that George McCullagh had warned him of this federal strategy in July.

The best that can be said of these reasons for his resignation is that they were the product of an imagination diseased and warped by hatred for King. No doubt there was pressure from both provincial and federal Liberals for the Hepburn Government to call an election rather than extend its term of office, usually a fatal political recourse. But to charge that Mackenzie King, whose over-riding aim was to maintain national unity at almost any price, would deliberately foment racial strife in Ontario in order to consolidate his French-Canadian support is so incredible that it must be dismissed out of hand. Mackenzie King himself, the man Mitch Hepburn was trying to make the villain of the piece, had his own theory about why the Ontario Premier resigned so suddenly. King's feeling was "that something personal has occasioned his resignation . . . I cannot imagine his real reason for resigning being other than something personal to himself." King was sure that Hepburn "had been planning to get out for some months past, and has finally acted in an impetuous, impulsive way, as he has done in everything else." In postulating "something personal to himself" as the occasion of Mitch Hepburn's resignation, King was almost certainly correct.

Two weeks before his resignation, Mitch Hepburn had asked Premier Aberhart to give him a little more time to decide about going West for a conference. "Please let me . . . take stock and inventory of my own problems here."[11] When, to the extent that he was able, Mitch Hepburn took stock of his own problems, he found that they were too complicated, the burden was too heavy, the web had become too entangled, the candle, burnt so long at both ends, had now begun to consume itself. Tired and frustrated, he was no longer capable of coping with either the responsibilities of the Premiership or even the exigencies of daily living. Most of those who might have helped him, had he wanted help, those who had been his genuine friends, had long since departed or had been replaced and their replacements, for the most part, were no help at all. It was a sad commentary on his own dissolution as a man that Mitch Hepburn now appeared almost mesmerized by a few companions who seemed, at least indirectly, to be inviting him to destruction. But, like many other things about him, Mitch Hepburn's ability to choose friends had also deteriorated.

When Ontario's eleventh Prime Minister took a cab to the Lieutenant Governor's residence on the drizzly evening of October 21 to resign the office he had laboured so long and so hard to attain, he had been leader of the Liberal Party for almost twelve years (longer than any other man in the twentieth century), and Premier a little more than eight years and three months, the third longest term (after Sir Oliver Mowat and Sir James Whitney) in the province's history. It was paradoxical that a man so heedless of his own well-being should have considered the greatest achievement of his premiership the pasteurization law which gave his province better health*; paradoxical too that the Government of a man who would be remembered as anti-labour should have been among the first in Canada to pass enlightened laws raising the wages and bettering the conditions of the working man.

Despite these achievements, the time of Mitchell Hepburn's premiership was not noted for legislative enactments in Ontario or, for that matter, in any other province. The years of the Hepburn administration coincided with the depression and the war. The first hampered significant legislation at the provincial level; the second reduced the legislature's importance as more and more power devolved on the central authority. Even if these conditions had not obtained, it is doubtful that an administration led by Mitchell Hepburn would have left behind a constructive, progressive record. Despite all his qualities – a quick, shrewd intelligence able to grasp a problem almost intuitively, break it down into its component parts, and act on it decisively; his considerable executive ability; and his astonishing gift for communicating with people at almost any level – the fact remains Mitch Hepburn had serious inadequacies, both intellectual and emotional, which weakened his effectiveness as a Government leader.

Intellectually, Mitch Hepburn lacked any kind of philosophical base, any firm commitment, any real sense of direction. At a time when the running of a provincial Government was a much less complex operation than it would later become, requiring less long-range planning and expert advice, this was not necessarily a fatal defect. It does indicate, though, that one will look in vain through the Hepburn era in Ontario for any positive, progressive theme. Beyond his two broad inherent tendencies – a liberal humanitarianism (epitomized in his health legislation) and his rural conservatism (exemplified in his economies and balanced budgets) – Mitch Hepburn had no thought-out or sustained political program. Politically, he lived pretty much from hand-to-mouth, showing contempt today for his opinions of yesterday. He did not lack political courage, but this too often meant that he was merely a political opportunist able to base a policy on a headline. Seldom if ever has a Canadian political leader executed so many reversals of policy during his term of office.

Whatever consistency there had been in his earlier years was replaced by an impatient drive for personal power, a drive that, on occasion, threatened civil rights and other prerogatives (especially those of labour unions, the medical profession and the academic community), interfered with legitimate property rights (the Hepburn administration's Succession Duty legislation undoubtedly gave too much discretion to government officials), and even personal freedom (when a deputation of the unemployed visited Queen's Park in 1938 to protest reduction in relief allowances, the Premier had the Council Chamber ringed with police and ordered several of the men, who had earlier been involved in relief disturbances, arrested on the spot). It was with some justification that for several years Toronto's *Saturday Night* had considered Mitch Hepburn "a danger to democracy in this province and in this Dominion."[12] His conniving with Maurice Duplessis, his contemptuous attitude toward the Rowell-Sirois Commission, and his irresponsible attacks on the federal Government's war effort were also a danger to national unity.

If Mitch Hepburn's want of a sound intellectual base heightened his authoritarian tendencies, his lack of emotional discipline was equally destructive. To be successful most political leaders must relegate their personal feelings about associates and opponents to a secondary role in governing their behaviour. This Mitch Hepburn was rarely able to do. Despite some of his other characteristics – boundless energy, immense personal charm, audacity and a kind of earthy wit – Mitch Hepburn's decisions and policies often were motivated not by the objective reality of the situation but by his own animosities and antipathies. Nowhere was this more evident than in his long feud with Mackenzie King. Too frequently Premier Hepburn dismissed proposals by Ottawa for better housing and social services, not because they lacked merit, but because they emanated from King's administration. Even when he had legitimate grievances – the absence of a consistent federal economic policy through the later years of the depression; the lack of a vigorous defence effort during the early part of the war – he usually corroded his arguments with irrelevant emotional acid. This was true of the one theme that perhaps more than any other characterized the Hepburn era – the Premier's consistent championing of provincial rights. In the spring of 1937, Premier Hepburn and his Ministers made some valid points before the Rowell-Sirois Commission. Mitch Hepburn had the opportunity to provide constructive leadership in the delicate area of co-operative federalism. But the opportunity was missed; his case was compromised when, as so often, he confused policies with personalities.

Eventually personal animosity toward Mackenzie King would prove an inadequate base from which to govern the Province of Ontario. As Richard Alway has noted:

In an era when the politics of consensus, under the direction if not the leadership of Mackenzie King, reigned supreme in Canadian national life, Hepburn presented it with a strong and persistent chal-

---

* The officials of the medical profession did not always agree that Premier Hepburn's actions furthered the health of the province. His most celebrated dispute with the College of Physicians and Surgeons concerned a Kitchener doctor, J. E. Hett, who claimed considerable success (attested to by some of his patients) for his own cancer cure. Stricken from the rolls of the profession because he refused to have the cure examined on the terms required by medical authorities, Hett's right to practise was restored through the intervention of Queen's Park. Mitch Hepburn considered this another example of his championing the underdog against a closed bureaucracy and the establishment. So did most of Hett's patients and a good many voters. (CAR, 1937-38, p. 187; Personal Interviews).

lenge. But unlike Duplessis and Aberhart who also mounted their own challenges, Hepburn's policies and attitudes presented a clear threat to the unity and integrity of the chief political vehicle of national consensus in the 1930's and early 1940's – the Liberal Party of Canada. If during this period Mackenzie King was the leader who divided Canadians the least, Mitchell Hepburn was chief among those leaders who divided Canadians the most.[13]

One of the major reasons for this divisiveness was that Mitch Hepburn, like some of his rebellious Elgin forbears, had always known more clearly what he was against – the establishment, the big interests, the hydro barons, labour racketeers, George Henry and the Tories, the federal Liberals and Mackenzie King – than what he was for. Despite his native intelligence and executive ability, the expeditious way he presided over Cabinets in the earlier years, his domination of the House, Mitch Hepburn was more effective opposing than governing, more at home on the hustings than in the Legislature. He was the prince of campaigners, a master of the surprise attack with a deadly instinct for the jugular, the ambush, the false trail, the *tour de force*. But he never matured very much politically after the campaign of 1934 when he rejuvenated the Party and led it to its greatest victory.

Now eight years later, in the fall of 1942, the electoral triumphs had been forgotten and Mitch Hepburn – his Party weakened, his friends alienated, his record of bluster and bombast obscuring his achievements – now Mitch Hepburn was reaping the whirlwind. As the St. Thomas *Times-Journal* noted on another occasion, he had started out well. But he had become "reckless and erratic, crude and rude in statement. . . . Slowly but surely he lost favor with his own people as well as with the Liberals of the province, and . . . he reaped what he sowed." Like his father thirty-five years earlier, Mitch Hepburn decided it was time to get out.

For all that, there were many in the province who were sorry to see Mitch Hepburn go, many who thought that Ontario's political life would be the poorer for his going: "It will be a dull Ontario if he makes no more speeches and devotes himself to onion-growing in Elgin County," remarked the London *Free Press*, a strong Conservative paper. "Mr. Hepburn has added to the gaiety of politics in Ontario. He has been the only colorful figure in an arena which has been noted in recent years for its drabness." Political opponents were generous in their praise. The Member for Victoria, Leslie M. Frost, wrote to the ex-Premier: "As one who has been on the opposite side and has differed with you on many occasions, I want to say that I think your retirement from the political field is a great loss to Canada. . . . From the first you were one of the few who had the war situation properly sized up. . . . I believe that you deserve the thanks of the country." Even the Toronto *Star*, so often at odds with Mitch Hepburn, now had kind words for the retired Premier:

He might well have claimed – and we think it is for this that his premiership will be chiefly remembered – that he has not been disregardful of the humanitarian needs of the province. His insistence upon the pasteurization of milk – a move which required some courage, and Mr. Hepburn does not lack it – his measures looking to the better control of tuberculosis, and his provisions of better accommodation for the mentally afflicted are instances of a trend of mind entirely admirable.[14]

When he had first been elected to the premiership, Mitchell Hepburn said that he hoped when his term was over he would leave Ontario a little better place in which to live. For the children of the province, who had benefited by his health legislation, Mitch Hepburn had accomplished that, an accomplishment that all the mistakes could not erase. That would stand no matter what had gone before or what was to come. And despite his resignation, there was much to come. For Mitch Hepburn personally, for his family, and for the Liberal Party of Ontario, it would have been better had the story ended when he left the Premier's chair.

chapter 16

Tears at the End

For several years the Liberal Party in Ontario, weakened by its split from the federal wing and by its lack of democratic organization, had been disintegrating as a coherent political force. Now, with Mitchell Hepburn's resignation as Premier (though not as Party leader), the Ontario Liberals began to fly apart into disparate factions. This was inevitable. By his autocratic domination over the Party machinery (despite numerous requests, no annual meeting had been held since 1932), his dictatorial control of the Cabinet, his tight-fisted handling of patronage, Mitch Hepburn had virtually been the Liberal Party.

He had been able to maintain this domination unquestioned for so long for two reasons: gratitude from the rank-and-file Liberal because he had resurrected the Party and maintained it in power through two record election victories; the fear of provincial members and potential leaders that they would be dealt with ruthlessly. Since 1934 no one in the provincial arena commanded the strength to challenge Mitch Hepburn's supremacy. The one man who might have mounted such a challenge, Harry Nixon, had neither the power base nor the inclination to do so. As the Toronto *Telegram* noted at the time of the Premier's resignation: "It is not necessary to have agreed with all Mr. Hepburn's performance in office to feel that with his departure the cabinet is deprived of what ability and driving force it had. . . . The Liberal Party in Ontario has dropped its pilot."

What complicated this situation for the Party and caused an immediate crisis in its affairs was Hepburn's choice of a successor. Second only to the surprise occasioned by the Premier's resignation was his naming fifty-two-year-old Attorney General Gordon Conant to succeed him. "I am convinced," said Conant on one of his early morning walks near his Oshawa home, "the situation does not call for anything more than a

plain man with a thorough sense of duty. That I hope I have." Almost
certainly he did, but as Premier of Ontario and leader of the Liberal
Party, he lacked many other qualities. The dull, plodding, cautious,
small "c" conservative lawyer from the Motor City was not popular with
the Cabinet and commanded little support in caucus. One observer noted
this when commenting on the fragmented state of the Party after Hepburn's resignation: "The Government following includes Hepburn Liberals, Nixon Liberals, McQuesten Liberals, and King Liberals, plus
Farquhar Oliver in a stage of political metamorphosis, and nary a
Conant Liberal in sight unless as an unidentified sub-species."

Not only the naming of Conant was surprising but the manner of his
choice was questioned. Hepburn had not consulted the caucus about his
successor, nor had he discussed the matter with most of his ministers.
Harry Nixon expressed the general resentment at this high-handed procedure by remarking caustically that the office should not be handed
around "like an old dirty shirt when somebody else is tired of it." Nixon
and Public Works Minister Oliver showed their displeasure by immediately resigning from Conant's Cabinet. Nixon also let it be known that he
was interested in the premiership himself, and agitation began to hold a
leadership convention either to confirm Hepburn's choice or to make a
new selection.

Mackenzie King took a hand in the move to upset Hepburn's nominee. He would have preferred Nixon to Conant: "He could have carried
the Province as the leader of the Liberal party. I rather doubt if Conant
can do that. He is too much of the Hepburn type in his belief in force and
in his irreconcilable attitude toward those who do not share his views." On
October 26, King phoned four of the Ontario federal ministers suggesting
that they urge the constituency organizations to pass resolutions requesting a provincial convention. He contemptuously rejected a request from
Conant, made through Mines Minister Robert Laurier, that Harry Nixon
be neutralized by appointing him to the Senate. King thought it "infernal
cheek . . . [that] Conant who has opposed us bitterly, to ask, as a first
request, that we should help him out of his difficulty by side-tracking the
one man who is really entitled to the leadership and who has adopted the
sound course."[1]

All these manoeuvres – Nixon's desire for the leadership, the agitation for a Party convention, Conant's Cabinet reorganization, and his
efforts to strengthen his position – ignored one factor: Mitch Hepburn
himself. One week to the day after he resigned the premiership, Mitch
Hepburn was back at Queen's Park using Harry Nixon's old office. Now
there was no more talk of leaving the Cabinet. Instead, he would continue to serve Conant (who had not accepted his resignation as Treasurer) "and the people of Ontario with loyalty and devotion." He
maintained that he had followed the ordinary procedure in the change of

leadership, revealing also that he had offered the premiership to Nixon during the summer when the Provincial Secretary had turned it down: "As a matter of fact, when I discussed the Premiership with Mr. Nixon some months ago he suggested Mr. Farquhar Oliver as my successor. Had I appointed Mr. Nixon's nominee I am sure he would not have challenged the constitutional aspect of the matter. . . . I did discuss the leadership with Mr. Oliver, not, however, in the way of a formal offer."

Formal offer or not, it would seem plausible that both Nixon and Oliver refused the premiership because they felt it must be the decision of caucus and not the personal gift of Mitch Hepburn.* That was all somewhat academic now. With Mitch Hepburn back at Queen's Park, back as Provincial Treasurer at Conant's right hand, opposed to an immediate leadership convention, all bets were off. "It is not beyond the bounds of possibility," acidly commented the Toronto *Star*, "that he has it in mind to play Bergen to Mr. Conant's Charlie McCarthy." Not beyond the bounds of possibility at all. And much easier to regain a premiership which had been given as a personal gift to a weak man politically than one whose transferal had been ratified by the party caucus. In any event, the man who had just dealt himself out of the game was back picking up part of his old hand and apparently asking for a new pile of chips. Once more he would take up the fight against King as he explained to Premier Aberhart on November 7: "I had to go back and retain my position as treasurer for the Province in order to help Conant over this critical period, and now intend to stay and we shall fight this King conspiracy to the finish."

Accordingly, Hepburn wrote a letter (which he requested be destroyed) to the provincial Liberal members a few days prior to the first caucus under Conant. Again he gave his version of the reasons for his resignation – to frustrate King's plot to foment racial strife by forcing an election in Ontario in order to consolidate Liberal strength in Quebec. "This and this alone in the opinion of the Ottawa Board of Strategy would hold the wavering Quebec support against a common enemy to be created in Ontario." An election would have been a disaster because the Party lacked the support of the three Toronto newspapers.

> I knew the *Star* intended to support the CCF and George McCullagh told me definitely that he would oppose the Government for bringing on an election in this critical period. I am convinced that under the circumstances as they existed then we would have been annihilated even with probably the best record any government has ever had so far as administration is concerned in Ontario.

The ex-Premier went on to explain why he had chosen Gordon Conant to succeed him:

My decision to name Gordon Conant as my successor was one which I considered carefully. . . . You can readily understand what would have happened had we called a caucus to name a successor to myself. Again we would have been torn to shreds. You know and I know that during the last two sessions, I have suffered from continuous headaches as a result of tonsil infection which the doctors had not then properly diagnosed. Gordon Conant was the real truck-horse for the Party on the front benches. . . . If there is one thing I can commend Gordon Conant for, it is his absolute honesty and keen devotion to duty. No Attorney-General has ever been popular or can be popular, but in his new sphere he can do and will do an excellent job. A convention after this important session can deal with his leadership.

At the caucus held on November 25, Hepburn gave this explanation in person. The Liberal members then voted by a large margin to support Conant for the coming session, expressed "appreciation of the services of former Premier Hepburn and regret in his resignation as Premier of Ontario," and directed that a leadership convention be held within two months of the session's close.[2]

When the session began on February 9, 1943, with Gordon Conant in the Premier's chair, there was wide-spread speculation about where Mitch Hepburn, still on the front bench as Provincial Treasurer, fitted into the political picture. He remained the centre of attention, Ontario's number-one political mystery man. Since his resignation, he had continued his attacks on the King administration. The House of Commons, he told a meeting in Hamilton, had become "the only lunatic asylum operated by the inmates themselves." Before a hotel convention at the Royal York in Toronto, he ridiculed King's new policy of restricting liquor consumption: "He put on his red underwear and flannel socks and decided he would track down demon rum to his lair." These attacks renewed rumours that Hepburn was planning to run as a Progressive Conservative in the next general election under John Bracken who in December had defeated several candidates, including John Diefenbaker, for the leadership. A few weeks before Bracken's victory, Hepburn had written to him: "The people of Ontario are thoroughly disgusted with the incompetence and waste of the political machine at Ottawa at a time when we should be considering all our problems from the point of view of getting Canada geared for total war. . . . We are following your speeches with great interest. Keep up the good work."

There does seem to have been a haphazard attempt to line up

---

* Oliver's recollection of this meeting is that Hepburn offered him the premiership, that he was prepared to consider the offer if it were ratified by the caucus, and the Premier replied, "To hell with the caucus. I can get someone to take it without going to caucus." (Interview with Farquhar Oliver, November 23, 1966)

Bracken, Aberhart, and others in an anti-King movement. A friend of Hepburn's, Kenneth McLaren, conferred with the Alberta Premier and his Cabinet in mid-November. He reported the results to Hepburn:

> When I return I expect to be authorized to convene a meeting between yourself, Cardin, Aberhart and Bracken. In this connection it might be well for you to wire or phone Bracken that I shall call on him in Winnipeg . . . your friend Bill is right behind my organized and constructive movement along the lines we have been discussing and he says Bracken will be also. Hence my desire to now get an expression of opinion from Bracken. With you four men on common ground we can push forward from there and nothing can stop you.

Nothing came of this anti-King cabal, if indeed there had been much to it in the first place. Not that John Bracken did not want or would not need all the help he could muster against King. But it was becoming more questionable how much support Mitch Hepburn could deliver.[3]

The ex-Premier's vitriolic attacks on Mackenzie King, eroding the hard core of support which remained to him among provincial Liberals, reached a new pitch of violence in the 1943 session of the Legislature. On February 19, as Provincial Treasurer, Hepburn announced in the Chamber that Ontario was facing a twelve-million-dollar loss because of Ottawa's "raid on revenues." He coupled this with a vicious attack on federal ministers. "They are men without honour and I propose to prove that statement. They are something like Hitler's Nazi tactics, making an agreement and then breaking it." His face flushed, Hepburn turned to face the Liberals: "I want some of the members of the House who have a blind partisan adhesion to Ottawa to listen to what I am going to say." The Treasurer then ticked off a list of agreements that he alleged Ottawa had broken. He was especially incensed at Finance Minister Ilsley for his policy of controlling liquor sales: "Something like Hitler, that's the way he did it. Made an agreement and then broke it. Nazi tactics." Members on both sides sat embarrassed as they listened to the language of a man who seemed emotionally demented. When his former Minister, Eric Cross, electrified the house by rising to protest Hepburn's indefensible language, even some Liberals applauded.

It was perhaps inevitable that Mitch Hepburn's last words in the Legislature as a Minister of the Crown should have been an attack on Mackenzie King. Ironic too that this final onslaught on the federal leader, who had thwarted him on so many occasions, now brought about the downfall of Mitch Hepburn himself. Gordon Conant, whom Mitch Hepburn had made king, now decided that the king-maker was too much of a liability. In the political context he reached that conclusion simply. If Conant were to have any chance of being confirmed in the leadership, he would need federal support. To gain that he could no longer afford to retain as the best-known Minister in his Cabinet a man whose only policy was violent opposition to the federal leader. It was even rumoured Hepburn had urged that the entire Cabinet resign to protest Ottawa's policies. On March 3, 1943, Premier Conant regretfully informed Hepburn that his resignation as Provincial Treasurer (originally submitted when he resigned as Premier) would now be accepted immediately. No matter what legitimate differences of opinion existed with Ottawa, Conant wrote to Hepburn, the war effort required co-operation with the federal authorities. He added: "It grieves me more than I can tell you to write this letter. The performance of what I consider my duty in this regard is made indescribably painful to me because of my very high regard and great affection for you."

Two hours after his successor, A. St. Clair Gordon, was sworn in as Provincial Treasurer, Mitch Hepburn gave the press a venomous letter to Conant in which he charged that Mackenzie King's "political machine has long endeavoured to set up a Quisling Government in Ontario and has now succeeded temporarily by employing the Hitler policy of breaking an agreement and by autocratic use of power." Quisling was a strange term for Mitch Hepburn to use about the man he had made Premier and about Cabinet colleagues he had chosen. Strange was also the word to describe most of Mitch Hepburn's speeches and actions during this period. Mackenzie King's prediction at the time of Hepburn's resignation from the premiership was being fulfilled: "Ambition, combined with venom, has helped to bring about his destruction. . . . Hepburn will find, once he is no longer Premier and ceases to be a Minister of the Crown, that few will be left to do him honour or to honour his name."[4]

Others, remembering Mitch Hepburn's comebacks in the past, were not so certain that this was the end of the Hepburn story. "We won't believe he's gone from politics," remarked the Toronto *Telegram*, "until the asbestos curtain comes down." George McCullagh was not sure either. In a generous editorial, the *Globe and Mail* commented on the resignation:

Mr. Hepburn . . . leaves the Government, but not the Legislature, with a record as a careful administrator of the affairs of his Province and as a contributor to the gaiety of the nation by the constantly enlivening influence of his exuberant vigor and salty wit in the almost unrelieved dullness of our political world. Those Liberals who are now so triumphantly rejoicing over his elimination from official power cannot forget that he was the chief revivalist of their party's fortunes in this Province, and that the qualities of energy, courage, and humour and imagination which made him so formidable in this role still survive as his personal assets, which he may employ in further unpredictable measures.

Most unpredictable of all was how much remained of the reservoir of affection and personal obligation that Mitch Hepburn had accumulated during the years he had reconstructed the Party and led it to power. Could that reservoir, much shallower now, be channelled for yet another political victory? There were some who still remembered the happy warrior of the early thirties and hoped that his political career had not ended at the age of forty-six. One of the friends who had fought shoulder-to-shoulder with Mitch Hepburn in those years now wrote to the ex-Premier:

> No one who looks back to 1930 can forget what you did for the Liberal Party in Ontario in those days. Almost alone, you brought it from practical oblivion to the highest point in its history. And too, one cannot forget the splendid Government you gave this Province during your years as Premier. . . . I hope nothing will ever change the marvellous personality that God gave you. . . . I sincerely trust that you will soon again be giving of your ability in the public life of Canada for, if not, the loss will be Canada's. In looking back over these thirteen years, I think I can best express my feelings by quoting some words from Bob Hope's theme song, "You sometimes were a headache but you never were a bore."

A civil servant whom Hepburn had appointed in 1936 also remembered with gratitude:

> For my part I wish to say "Thank you" for your kindness in the past. You treated me with more honesty and humanity than any other politician and I shan't forget.
>
> In the public scene your retirement except from ill health is inconceivable. To those of us who followed you in the bleak days before June, 1934, you were and are a peerless leader. Others climbed on the chariot of victory and in many cases fared better than the original troops but to "the Old Gang" you will remain "the Happy Warrior of 1934."

"If this is to be the end of what promised to be a notable career," commented the St. Thomas *Times-Journal*, "it is tragic. But few will believe that it is the end."[5]

It was not the end; it would have been better had it been. Two days after his ousting from the Cabinet, the irrepressible Mitch Hepburn was back where he had always been most effective – on the stump. His smile as broad as ever, he told the Brotherhood of Threshermen meeting at

Waterloo: "You are threshermen. Well, I've threshed in my day and I have been threshed by experts." With a fine sense of irony, he asked to be seated in "bad boys' row," the front section of the northwest corner of the Legislative Chamber which he had set apart for Liberal mavericks like Roebuck and Croll. In another unpredictable reversal, he seemed to be throwing his support to Harry Nixon for the Liberal leadership. Over tea at the Nixon farmhouse at St. George, Hepburn predicted: "My friend, Mr. Nixon, may be the next Premier of Ontario, the next leader of the Liberal Party. If I were a betting man, I'd bet on Harry Nixon to carry the next Liberal convention."

There were other betting men who thought that Mitch Hepburn himself would make a spectacular attempt to regain his lost leadership at the convention at the end of April. "Please attend the convention," wrote one Hepburn supporter, "and I am sure after one of those addresses you are so famous for you could carry it . . . and come out the absolute leader of the Liberal Party." Neither of the leading leadership candidates, Nixon or Conant, could discount the possibility that Mitch Hepburn would decide to stand. Both of them tried to strengthen their positions by making a pilgrimage to seek the blessing of Mackenzie King who told them he must remain neutral. King noted Nixon's "tremendous relief to be rid of the incessant wrangles they have had in the Cabinet. He said on no account would he let Hepburn participate in his campaign or give him any support. I think he is the man who deserves to be chosen." As for Conant, "It was really pathetic his appeal for understanding and sympathy, having regard specially for the way he joined in with Hepburn against myself."

On April 28, as the delegates to the leadership convention gathered at the King Edward Hotel, there were those who remembered the midnight "Yellow Room" conference which had helped nominate Mitch Hepburn in the same hotel twelve years before, those who wondered if it might happen again. Cards bearing the words "We Want Mitch" appeared. Harry Nixon, the front-runner, denied that he had made any deal in return for Hepburn's support. A late entry, Highways Minister T. B. McQuesten, avowed, "In my opinion, Mr. Hepburn matches any leader in my lifetime." Rumours circulated through the King Edward that Mitch Hepburn would make a dramatic appearance at the convention. That possibility may have been one of the reasons why no less than eight federal Ministers, headed by C. D. Howe and Mitch Hepburn's old friend, Ian Mackenzie, descended on the convention. There were to be no slip-ups. The Ontario Liberal Party, for so many years a maverick under Mitchell Hepburn, was now to be roped, branded and returned to the federal corral.

There was really no need for so large a federal delegation to ride herd on the convention. If Mitch Hepburn had ever contemplated a strike to regain power, he abandoned it. The day of the balloting, April 30, the delegates were informed that the former Premier had left for New York on the advice of his doctors. Moments before the leader was named, the chairman read a terse, one-sentence letter from the old chief: "I wish to tender my resignation as leader of the Ontario Liberal Party." There was a hush, a memory, then a crash of applause as the new leader was announced. Harry Nixon had easily defeated three other contenders to become, perhaps unluckily, the thirteenth Prime Minister of Ontario.*6

Thus Harry Nixon, a good serviceable grey ("grey-haired, grey-suited, grey-personalitied Harry Corwin Nixon," one writer described him) replaced the colourful, dynamic, erratic Mitch Hepburn as Party leader. For the time being, the Liberals had had enough colour, corn-popping, balloon busting, side-shows, and merry-go-rounds. They wanted to get off the political midway and back on the main track. So they had swapped horses, swapped a highly geared, excitable runner with a tendency to bolt for a good reliable pacer who presumably would wear well in the stretch.

Whatever else the change portended, it signified that the forces of Mackenzie King had won the day. To King himself, Nixon's victory was further evidence, if he needed any, that benign spirits hovered in smoke-filled rooms to guard King's fortunes:

> The whole affair is a remarkable evidence of the moral forces that work in the unseen realm, of the vindication of right in the end. It has taken a long time to get Hepburn and his gang out of the control of the party's affairs, but they have each in turn killed themselves, beginning with Hepburn himself. Nixon, the man who has been most outspoken in his support of myself . . . is now the leader by an overwhelming majority.

King interpreted the result as a final victory in the war that Hepburn had started and had now lost for good:

> It was a King-Hepburn battle so far as the province generally was concerned, with a complete routing of all the Hepburn forces, and he and his right and left bowers left wounded and bleeding on the field – no one prepared to lend them succour of any kind. . . . It is a great triumph – a wonderful expression of loyalty. It reveals the extent to which, despite "everything," I have been able to keep the party together, in provincial as well as federal politics and this by "non-resistance," by refusing to enter a quarrel and through allowing my enemies to confound and destroy themselves. Again I say it is the evidence of a moral order that controls in the end.

The good spirits may, on occasion, intervene in the choice of a Party leader; their success in electing Premiers is more difficult to discern. Considering the public image of the Liberal Party in Ontario in the spring of 1943, with three leadership changes in six months, Harry Nixon would need all the help he could get, spiritual and otherwise. The new Premier hesitated a month before appointing his predecessor, Gordon Conant, to be Master of the Ontario Supreme Court, almost twice that long before announcing a general election for August 4. Attempting to project the image of a solid rural squire (which he was), Nixon confessed that he preferred farming to politics ("A herd of Holsteins is a lot more dependable for a living than a fickle electorate") and promised to eschew political pyrotechnics ("If they want common sense I'll give it to them. But they'll have to look elsewhere for dinner orations that will bring them up from their chairs").[7]

The voters of Elgin did not have to look elsewhere. On July 12, in the Masonic Temple at St. Thomas, where he had been first nominated seventeen years before, Mitch Hepburn was chosen to run as an Independent Liberal. He told the meeting that Nixon had asked him to stand, that he would not criticize Conservative leader George Drew (campaigning vigorously on a twenty-two point platform headed by his promise that the provincial government would assume fifty per cent of education costs) and would not speak outside his own riding. Mitch Hepburn's organization in Elgin responded once more for "the boy from Yarmouth," his opposition was weak, and the Hepburn platform magic was still there. Mitch Hepburn could convulse an audience in his home township of Yarmouth as he ridiculed the financing policies of CCF leader Edward Jolliffe. They reminded him of a school board deciding to build a new school. First they resolved to build the school; then they resolved to use the materials from the old school; finally they planned to use the old school while the new one was being built.

Mitch Hepburn had not lost his touch with the boys on the back concessions in Elgin. Others in the province also welcomed his candidacy. "Sitting in the Legislature as an Independent Liberal," noted the *Globe and Mail*, "Mr. Hepburn can continue to be a very healthy force in our public life." The newspaper thought it must be galling for Hepburn to see the men who had ousted him using his own administrative record as their main election plank: "For, no matter what anyone has said or thought of Mr. Hepburn, it has never been questioned that he was the driving force of his Government from 1934 to the time of his resignation."[8]

What Elgin thought of Mitch Hepburn was clear as the returns started coming in on the night of August 4. "Can Elgin County Afford

---

* Results of the ballotting were: Harry Nixon, 418; Arthur Roebuck, 85; T. B. McQuesten, 49; Walter Thompson, 22. On the morning of the voting, Premier Gordon Conant, with very little evident convention support, had been rushed to Toronto General Hospital suffering from what his doctor termed nervous exhaustion. (*Globe and Mail*, May 1, 1943)

to Lose Mitch Hepburn?" was the question his numerous political advertisements had posed. Elgin obviously thought it could not. Mitch Hepburn was re-elected by more than 2,500 votes, winning a majority in the
city of St. Thomas and in every township. Meanwhile, across the province, the Party, which he had led to power, was overwhelmingly turned
out of office. The Conservatives under George Drew won thirty-eight
seats followed by Edward Jolliffe and the CCF with thirty-four. The
Liberals, who had held sixty-three seats at dissolution, were now reduced
to fourteen, the same number they held when Mitch Hepburn took over
the leadership from William Sinclair in 1930. The voting blocks so
laboriously constructed by Mitch Hepburn had now collapsed. Much of
the North was gone, as were most of the cities and the French-Canadian
vote.

Amid the crumbling of the Party he had built, Elgin county remained
with Mitch Hepburn. The St. Thomas *Times-Journal* remarked:

> The result of the election in Elgin was almost a foregone conclusion,
> proving that Mitchell F. Hepburn is still "the white-haired boy" of
> the people of his native county. With all his faults they have shown
> that they love him in December as they did in May. . . .
> The man is probably not yet born who can defeat M. F. Hepburn
> in this constituency. . . . He has done things that were bad, and
> almost broken the hearts of his friends, but he has done many things
> which were good which have won the approval of friends and foes
> alike. . . .

Mitch Hepburn, excited as a school boy while he watched the returns,
and delighted with the response of "those grand old friends and neighbours" in Elgin, interpreted the results across the province as a rebuke
for Mackenzie King. It was significant, he told his cheering supporters,
that none of the ridings near Elgin had elected Liberals: "Ontario has
said to Ottawa today in no uncertain terms, 'Hands off.' "9

It was an incredible rationalization from a man who in his career had
made some real ones and whose antics in recent years were primarily
responsible for the crushing rejection of the Liberals. Mackenzie King
was closer to the real reasons for the outcome. Before the votes were
counted, he noted:

> I do not see how the Liberals could win a majority for the following
> reasons: first, a house divided against itself is sure to fall. Hepburn
> began to divide the house immediately after taking office. This division
> has been kept up throughout. Cleavages in the party extending con-
> tinuously over four or five years. In the second place, the Liberals
> perpetuated themselves in office – two terms. This contrary to views

of electorate and also always a sign of weakness. Should have had an election without any extension of term. Third, Hepburn's action transferring leadership to Conant – Conant hanging on, and later ousted by convention, and later appointed to office by Liberals. Delay on Nixon's part in bringing on election. Should have prepared for election the day after the Liberal convention. . . . No preparation for campaign in constituencies. No literature. Next, no platform for campaign. Greatest weakness of all running on the record of the Liberals which is really a thoroughly bad record. Nothing positive presented. Hepburn's nomination as Independent and supporter of Nixon. People bewildered as to the relationship.

When he heard the results, Mackenzie King was more convinced than ever that they signified a total rejection of Hepburnism. Most of Hepburn's former ministers had been defeated:

This showing pretty conclusively that men who had any association with Hepburn were doomed. The three men that stood by me against Hepburn were: Nixon, Oliver, and Laurier. Those three were returned. All others were defeated. . . . Results would seem to indicate that large bodies of Liberals had lost confidence in the Government. The Conservative-minded had thrown their support to the Conservatives and the radical-minded, their support to the CCF. I must confess that while I deeply deplore the breakup, the collapse of the Liberal party in Ontario, which may be the beginning of the end of the power of the Liberal party federally, it has seemed to me all along that the results which have now come to pass were inevitable, with Hepburn retained as a Liberal leader and allowed to play the fast-and-loose part he did. In my inner nature I feel a sense of relief that a Cabinet that has been so unprincipled and devoid of character has been cleaned out of Queen's Park. . . .[10]

If Mackenzie King thought that at last Mitch Hepburn's political career was ended, he miscalculated. For some months after the election of 1943, little was heard from the provincial Member for Elgin. He did not attend Liberal meetings at Queen's Park. He took little part in the debates of the session of 1944, when George Drew carefully led his minority Government through a business-like session. It was not until October, 1944, that Mitch Hepburn broke his political silence. The occasion was an invitation by a group of Elgin friends that he stand for the House of Commons in the next federal election. It was not so much the occasion as the content of the ex-Premier's statement that left many observers, including the St. Thomas *Times-Journal*, "pop-eyed, wondering that it all means, and where the former Premier is headed politically."

What it all meant was that Mitch Hepburn, longing for the lost seats of power, was about to make a final attempt to regain them. To this purpose he executed one of the sharpest zigs in his zagging career. No longer did he have any quarrel with the federal Liberals at Ottawa. "My argument is not with Mr. King." It was with his former political crony, Premier George Drew. As Mitch Hepburn now saw it, his duty was to fight "against reactionary Toryism as it rears its ugly head in Ontario." Specifically, he attacked Drew's opposition to the plan for family allowances proposed by the federal Government. In a speech several weeks earlier, Drew was reported to have said that his administration would go the limit "to make sure this iniquitous bill does not go into effect." According to Mitch Hepburn, Drew's words constituted the "most irresponsible utterance ever made by a Canadian public man within memory." It was nothing less than an attempt to inflame passions against the French-Canadians who presumably would benefit most by the "baby-bonus" legislation. Hepburn also challenged Drew's policy of encouraging large-scale immigration from the British Isles: "It begins to look as though Colonel Drew aspires to become the president of a separate republic of Canada." He insisted again that the hatchet he had brandished so often on the federal Liberals was buried: "I hold no issue with the Liberal Government in Ottawa. My grievance is with the Drew Government in Toronto, which I believe is attempting to breed racial disunity in Canada."

It was pretty thin stuff, scarcely the stuff that would enable the Liberals to dislodge even a minority Government at Queen's Park. But the provincial Liberal Party, still in a state of shock after the defeat of 1943, its leader Harry Nixon incapable of finding any remedy for its revival, was willing to try the Hepburn magic once more. On December 6, 1944, at a Party caucus, on the motion of Harry Nixon himself, Mitchell Hepburn was unanimously chosen Liberal House leader. It was almost fourteen years to the day since he had first become the Party's chieftain. Hepburn looked cheerful as he left the Queen's Park caucus for his Bannockburn farm: "I know," he remarked with a grin, "this isn't going to make my wife happy."

There were others who were not happy either. Some of Mitch Hepburn's closest Elgin friends, the men from Yarmouth who had been with him from the beginning, thought that Mitch Hepburn would have been better to leave it alone. The smile, a little more forced, the gaiety, a little less spontaneous, would not be enough now. This was not the world of the early thirties; this was a new world requiring positive programs. It was doubtful that Mitch Hepburn could provide them. His agile mind had been dulled, his emotions allowed to run riot, too many of the assets had been spent, prodigally wasted in the pursuit of ephemeral amusements, dissipated in innumerable animosities. Still, there was always the chance that the happy warrior of 1934 could pull it off again, that the old magic would work one final time. Despite the fears of his Yarmouth friends, perhaps it was worth that chance. The Toronto *Star* remarked: "Mr. Hepburn has ability, energy, and courage. If he can throttle down his engine and have his brakes tightened up, there are real services which he can perform for Ontario."[11]

On February 15, 1945, Mitchell Hepburn, leading fifteen Liberals, was again in his place at Queen's Park for the opening of the session. Most of the headlines in the spring of 1945 concerned the allied armies racing to victory in Europe. But the situation of Drew's minority Government, the Liberals holding the balance of power, and Mitch Hepburn's return to the leadership ensured full galleries and growing excitement at Queen's Park. It sounded like the old slashing Mitch Hepburn who tore into Premier Drew, especially for his attitude on family allowances. Even the phrases were the same. Obtaining information from Drew was like "trying to nail jelly to the wall." The Liberal leader warned that he would lead a fighting group: "We are small in numbers but we represent a lot of people. Neither the Party nor Old Man Ontario is going to be crucified on the twisted cross of reactionary Toryism."

It sounded like the Mitch Hepburn of the thirties, and it sounded a little sad. In the challenging post-war world of 1945, Mitch Hepburn, not yet fifty, was already an anachronism. The scatter-gun fusillades, which a decade before had mowed down a Government, now left the Tories smiling indulgently. George Drew could now afford to be patronizing, an attitude he was extremely good at: "Members of the House," he explained with an olympian smile, "should realize that these gestures of the Member for Elgin should not be taken seriously." The Member for Elgin who had enjoyed baiting George Henry and had always claimed he could take it now found Drew's barbs intolerable. What Drew did have to take seriously was the position of his own minority Government and the possibility of Mitch Hepburn's combining with the CCF to upset it. Basic to Hepburn's strategy for a return to power was his plan to construct some kind of combination to defeat Drew, thereby forcing either an election or a Coalition Government of which he would be a Member, perhaps eventually the First Minister.

His first attempt to strengthen the Liberal position was through a working alliance with the two able Labour-Progressive (Communist) Members of the legislature, A. A. MacLeod (Bellwoods) and Joseph Salsberg (St. Andrews). Hepburn did not disguise his admiration for MacLeod. "I've said privately and I'll say publicly . . . I consider him to possess the most brilliant mind in the Legislature." Before he announced his political comeback, Hepburn had convened a meeting of Liberal Members at the Royal Connaught Hotel in Hamilton to discuss ways and means of co-operating with the Labour-Progressives to bring down Drew.

The CCF would have to be convinced of the wisdom of this course, and Mitch Hepburn apparently thought he could swing Jolliffe into line. He approached the CCF leader who was sceptical of the proposal's political wisdom and its constitutional feasibility. To defeat the Drew administration in the House, in the hope that Lieutenant Governor Matthews would deny the Conservative leader a dissolution and call on an alternative combination to form a Government, as Mitch Hepburn apparently hoped, was a piece of strategy that even Ontario's provincial Liberals could scarcely swallow.

With a national election near, Senator Lambert and the federal Liberals were concerned about reports that Mitch Hepburn was attempting to force the issue at Queen's Park. A provincial election in Ontario might adversely affect federal fortunes there. On February 18, Senator Lambert travelled to Toronto to discuss these developments with Senator Peter Campbell, C. D. Howe, and Mitch Hepburn himself:

> Saw Peter at lunch & heard about Mitch being approached by Agnes Macphail, and thinking he could ally with the CCF crowd & form a Gov't.
>
> C.D.H. came along to Peter's office at 4; and Mitch came down; and we discussed the whole situation federally and provincially and it was finally agreed (or agreement was implied) that no election or change of gov't shd be forced in Ont. just now. Give more time for Drew to kill himself, and the CCF to split. Mitch's contacts are with MacLeod and his Prog. Labor group, not CCF's.[12]

Agreement or not, as the session progressed at Queen's Park the threat of an election increased. If there were one, George Drew said "the Liberal-Communist alliance for disunity" would be to blame. Unless the CCF were to support Government measures down the line, Mitch Hepburn held the key to dissolution. He was in good form in the throne speech debate. Tory efforts to block a distinctive Canadian flag (which he favoured) were "like putting a mustard plaster on a wooden leg." He was opposed to Drew's program of religious education in the public schools. He was "sorry indeed that I indulged in personal attacks on Mr. King." He wished that sometimes George Drew would make a mistake and admit it: "I have made a lot of mistakes. I am just an ordinary human individual, and will probably make a lot more. I will probably be apologizing for my mistakes as long as I live."

On the night of March 22, the galleries at Queen's Park were filled. It was expected that a CCF motion amounting to non-confidence in the Government would come to a vote. The fate of the administration would then depend on Mitch Hepburn and the Liberals, most of whom did not favour forcing an election immediately. Tension had been building for several days. So large were the crowds that tickets were distributed for standing room in the galleries. Drew told the house that he would view an adverse vote as want of confidence in the Government. The Tory front bench (which would welcome a forced election) seemed confident. Moments before midnight, the CCF motion was put. A hush swept over the House and the packed galleries as the assistant clerk polled the last CCF name, then turned toward the Liberals: "Mr. Hepburn, Elgin," he intoned. The hands of the clock stood just after midnight as, amid a din of desk-thumping, Mitch Hepburn slowly rose in his place to support the motion. The Government was defeated. With a smile and a wide gesture, Mitch Hepburn indicated the "Door Out" exit to the Tories. He had gambled; he looked confident; but the sweeping hands of the clock, which had signalled the defeat of a Government, were also marking the end of Mitch Hepburn's parliamentary career.

Within a few days, George Drew announced a provincial election would be held on June 11 (later changed to June 4, when King chose the same date for a federal contest). A meeting of about 250 Liberals at the King Edward Hotel named Mitch Hepburn Party leader, pending a convention after the election, which would be asked to confirm him in the post. Provincial politics, even with the prospect of a general election, seemed a little irrelevant in the spring of 1945. The real news was elsewhere: Roosevelt Dead; Russians Strike for Berlin. Newspaper advertisements reflected an air of excitement and anticipation as the arduous years of the war ended:

Be Prepared.
Official announcement of Victory in Europe may result in the closing of Retail Food Stores for 24 to 48 hours.
We suggest that it might be advisable for housewives to be prepared for such a situation.
Your Dominion Store.[13]

With unconditional victory for the United Nations only days distant in Europe, Liberal leader Mitchell Hepburn set off for Windsor on April 23 to begin his campaign to regain power at Queen's Park. His group of personal aides, much smaller now, hoped against hope that it would be 1934 over again, a sharp, clear sustained thrust through the province climaxed at the end by the ringing bells and tooting whistles of victory. Surprisingly, Hepburn's opening speech was one of the most positive he had ever made. In the labour stronghold of Windsor, he pitched his remarks to recapture the urban support lost in 1943. The Liberal platform promised a minimum wage of twenty-five dollars a week for men; shorter working hours; a modern labour code guaranteeing the worker full rights of free association and collective bargaining; universal health insurance;

higher old-age pensions; lowering of the voting age from twenty-one to eighteen; a new Cabinet post of Youth Welfare; more money for teacher training; later a new university for Northern Ontario was promised.

To read this blueprint for a better post-war Ontario was one thing; to see and hear Mitch Hepburn deliver it was another. He was no longer the smiling troubadour of the early thirties, no longer the happy warrior of the 1934 campaign. He looked heavy, his blue eyes slightly red and bleary, his touch sluggish and unsure. The Hepburn snap, crackle, and pop were gone. The puffiness of too many nights of revelry, too much unbridled turmoil, too little self-discipline were now painfully visible. There was much heckling from the heavily pro-labour audience, and Mitch Hepburn, the man who had once revelled in repartee, could no longer handle it. One of the hecklers strode onto the platform, interrupted the speech, and demanded the microphone. Confused and unsteady, Mitch Hepburn stepped back and sat down, a prematurely aged man. One of his aides was aghast: "What's the trouble with the chief?" he whispered. The trouble was that at the beginning of a province-wide campaign, Mitch Hepburn, enervated physically, drained emotionally, and relying as he had for a long time on alcohol to take up the slack, was at the end of his tether, a spent force.

Somehow he went on with the help of a few friends who managed to get him to meetings and onto platforms, into trains and cars, hurtling over empty roads that had been the scene of past victory parades, looking down at audiences that sometimes were just a blur. The Hepburn campaign party in 1945 was pathetically small. Most of the friends of the old victorious days were gone, dead like Frank O'Connor, or busy about other things, men who had once toasted Mitch Hepburn and used him, and now for their own reasons no longer wished to be associated with him. Some of those who remained, men like Vincent Barrie of St. Thomas, were more concerned now about saving the man than saving a Party. If his campaign staff was small, Hepburn campaign funds were hard to come by, and significant newspaper support almost non-existent. But the Hepburn party plodded on to meeting after meeting; now and then there were flashes of the old Hepburn wit. The fact that none of the major newspapers was supporting him (neither was the St. Thomas *Times-Journal*) reminded him, he said at St. Thomas, of the old woman who, when she was asked if she wanted her husband embalmed, buried, or cremated, answered: "Take no chances, give him all three."

The Hepburn party was a dispirited group as it moved across the North of the province and back into the smaller cities and rural areas of the South where the Liberal victories of the thirties had been fashioned. In his speeches (which, despite pleas from Liberal secretary Bert Lyman and his staff, he did not seem to have either the energy or the enthusiasm to vary much), Mitch Hepburn returned to the familiar role of negative criticism. He pounded at Drew for his attitude on family allowances and for his plan to increase immigration from Britain. "Colonel Drew," he warned one audience in the North, "is the most arrogant and reactionary Tory I have ever known." No one seemed to pay much attention to this, including Colonel Drew. Still, the crowds which turned out to hear and see Mitch Hepburn in 1945 were generally good and often astonishingly large. Five hundred sloshed through a heavy rainstorm at New Liskeard; nearly a thousand waited in the Galt Armouries until ten-forty-five at night to hear a few words from the Liberal leader two hours late; twelve hundred at the Collegiate in London; almost two thousand in the Capital Theater in Sudbury.

They came, the hard core of supporters who would stick with Mitch Hepburn no matter what had happened, others for old time's sake, some for amusement, others curious to see the man who had for so long almost single-handedly dominated the political life of his province. Except for occasional flashes, they never saw the real Mitch Hepburn. It was left to George McCullagh, who had so often tried to manipulate Mitch Hepburn, and now took to the radio to support George Drew, to put in plain, almost brutal language a judgment of the Mitch Hepburn of 1945 that was near the truth: "I have known him many years and he was endowed with one of the shrewdest, most agile minds that any man could possess. Mr. Hepburn has deteriorated as a public man. He is now a lamentable and sorry figure."[14]

A lamentable and sorry figure he was, his face growing more florid and strained, his eyes more tired and bloodshot, his speeches unfocussed and rambling. As the campaign progressed, he reverted to the slogans and cliches so effective in 1934, trying with all the energy he could muster to recapture the magic he had then commanded so easily: "If the Liberals are returned on June 4, I promise we will put an end to these Tory boards and commissions, the same way we did in 1934." He would look into the excessive use of Government cars which was creeping in again. For his one-time friend and advisor, George McCullagh, the ex-Premier had an answer that was ironic in the extreme: "I have known Mr. McCullagh for forty years and I want to tell you if you want to see the Government transferred from Queen's Park to the W. H. Wright Building, vote for Mr. Drew."

Premier Drew and CCF leader Edward Jolliffe practically ignored Hepburn's speeches. In its final days, the campaign was dominated by Jolliffe's sensational charge that Drew had organized a secret political police force, a paid Government Gestapo to report on all opposition to the Tory administration and keep it in power. It was a charge that Mitch Hepburn himself might have made, analogous to some of those he did make effectively in the 1934 campaign, a last-minute roorback designed to smear the Government with scandal. But it was negative, the kind of thing that might have worked in a depression but was irrelevant for the voter looking to the bright promise of an affluent post-war world. George Drew categorically denied it, and subsequently a Royal Commission found there was nothing in it to implicate the Conservative leader. The Gestapo issue raised by the CCF, and blown into horrendous headlines by the Toronto *Star*, added bitterness to the final days of the campaign and virtually eliminated Hepburn's spotty addresses from the press.

So at the campaign's end, after giving more than sixty speeches and travelling eighteen thousand miles, sometimes lurching over roads where the water came up to the car's floor-boards, Mitch Hepburn returned to Elgin. He had done practically no campaigning there, had been forced to cancel his one major meeting because of his efforts in the rest of the province. Some of Mitch Hepburn's oldest supporters, like A. V. "Archie" Coulter, had turned out again to work for "the boy from Yarmouth." They knew this time that it would be an uphill fight, even in Elgin. The rumours of Mitch Hepburn's excesses had now reached the back concessions, and these stolid family men did not like what they heard. Years before Mitch Hepburn had said, "I hope that I shall never get too far out of touch with the people." He had been out of touch with the people, including his "ain folk" of Elgin for a long time. Furthermore, Mitch Hepburn was facing strong opposition in his own riding. Fletcher S. "Tommy" Thomas, a personable young farmer and family man who had been Elgin's agricultural representative for nearly twenty years, was the Conservative candidate. A personal friend of Mitch Hepburn's, a man the former Premier had helped to become one of the best agricultural representatives in the province, "Tommy" Thomas had reluctantly agreed to stand against his former benefactor. He had run a strong race and he was well-known and well-liked in Elgin.

Now, in the dying hours of the campaign, Elgin turned out once more in driving rain to welcome Mitch Hepburn home. There was the mile-long parade, the brass band, and the soggy streamers proclaiming "Elgin Needs Mitch." Beneath a picture of a smiling, much younger-looking Mitch Hepburn, his newspaper advertising – "The Man who has done more for Elgin than any man since Confederation" – stressed the theme that Mitch Hepburn had earned another chance: "By all the rules he deserves what Elgin has in store for him – the grateful thanks of his own people." As he stood in the drafty Granite Rink, his wife beside him, to acknowledge the cheers of his own people, Mitch Hepburn predicted that the Liberals would win fifty-six seats, easily enough to form a Government.[15]

As the cheers rang out, it sounded for a moment like the old confident Mitch Hepburn. It had to be said just as "For He's a Jolly Good Fellow" had to be sung. But long before he returned to Elgin, Mitch Hepburn knew that he would not win fifty-six seats, knew that he had no chance to form a Government. It is doubtful that he really cared any more. Just surviving the campaign had been a sufficient ordeal without worrying about much else. There was one thing, though, that Mitch Hepburn still cared about; he wanted desperately to hold Elgin. To lose Elgin – which had supported him faithfully for nearly twenty years, through five general elections, where his real friends had always been; to lose Elgin, which had turned down his father forty years before; to lose Elgin to a personal friend like "Tommy" Thomas, who owed much to Mitch Hepburn – that was not to be thought of, that was not to be borne.

The unthinkable and the unbearable happened. On Monday, June 4, while George Drew's Conservatives were easily sweeping the province to win sixty-six seats (the Liberals won eleven and the CCF eight), Mitch Hepburn lost Elgin. He lost it by an astounding 2,500 votes, lost even his home polling station, Number Four Yarmouth, where Bannockburn was and where he had been born and gone to school and lived all his life. It was unbearable but somehow it had to be borne. So as the dimensions of his personal defeat among his "ain folk" of Elgin mounted, Mitch Hepburn, helped by his loyal supporters from Yarmouth, faced for the last time an election night crowd in St. Thomas.

He looked tired and upset, a little unsteady on his feet, a bewildered man, perspiration beading his face, his smile forced. He summoned all the resources he could to control his shakiness and disappointment: "For the first time in my long political career," he told the throngs in front of the *Times-Journal* building, "I have tasted defeat, but I can take it on the chin and come up smiling." From a small section of the crowd came the sound of booing. Mitch Hepburn looked puzzled and embarrassed. He lurched slightly to one side, then tried to focus his eyes, glazed with tears, out over the crowd from where the booing had come. In a voice that was slurred and scarcely audible, he said simply he did not think he deserved that kind of reception from the place he had tried to serve so well. He didn't. Not publicly in Elgin.[16]

Epilogue

On the night of his first and last political defeat in Elgin, Mitch Hepburn said he was going home with his wife and family, going back to Bannockburn where it had all begun, "going back to my farm to listen to the grass grow." He listened for a little more than seven years. On the whole they were quiet and uneventful years. The gaiety and glitter of the days at Queen's Park, gone forever, were never altogether forgotten, but the bitterness of Elgin's final rejection gradually lost its sting. To the extent that his health, never completely recovered, permitted, Mitch Hepburn personally supervised the work on his twelve-hundred-acre farms, started to raise western cattle, and showed keen interest in the rich gravel deposits uncovered on Bannockburn.

Not many friends from the old days came to visit, but there were the good people and neighbours of Yarmouth. Sometimes one of them would ask Mitch Hepburn for a favour; invariably he would do what he could. Sometimes, not often, he attended a political meeting. In the provincial election campaign of 1951, against the advice of his doctors, he spoke for the Elgin Liberal candidate. To the four hundred who jammed the Legion Hall in St. Thomas to hear him, Mitch Hepburn seemed as witty, fiery, and persuasive as ever. When he sat down to waves of laughter and applause, the crowd demanding more, Mitch Hepburn looked pleased and happy.[1]

Then it was over. Early on the morning of January 5, 1953, in the upstairs room at Bannockburn, where he had been born nearly fifty-seven years before, Mitch Hepburn died in his sleep. Down the road, Union School, which he had attended as a boy, was the first to lower its flag to half-mast for the man who had been Elgin's only Premier. Across the province, people who had known Mitch Hepburn paused briefly to remember the campaigner, the leader, and the friend, to remember what he had done and to speculate on what might have been. One tried to describe the real Mitch Hepburn:

He was youthful in spirit and his extravagances were of the youthful kind. Yet what a refreshing spirit it was, in the fusty, cautious-ridden realm of Ontario politics! . . . Let there be no mistake about it. Mitch Hepburn was a man of intelligence and executive power, but he chose to express his intelligence and show his power like a school boy. The charm, which was so potent on the platform, was a boy's charm.[2]

So on January 7, a bright cold day in Elgin, they buried "the boy from Yarmouth." Among the hundreds from all over the province who crowded into Knox Presbyterian Church for the funeral (including Premier Leslie Frost and four former Ontario Premiers, Harry Nixon, George Drew, T. L. Kennedy, and George Henry), was a blind man for whom Mitch Hepburn had once done a favour. He was led to his seat and he could stand for all those whom Mitch Hepburn, without fanfare or publicity, had helped through the years. It was a simple eulogy that Mitch Hepburn's friend, the Reverend Harry S. Rodney, delivered:

> You met him, you shook hands with him, you were warmed by his famous smile, and you heard him say, "I'm Mitch Hepburn"; and in a few minutes you were calling him Mitch, and you liked it, and you felt you had always known him.

It was the short, simple service that Mitchell Hepburn, always eschewing ceremony, had requested. In just over half an hour, the funeral cortège was moving through the hushed streets of St. Thomas, through the streets where the great political triumphs had been celebrated. It was a time to forget the bright promise cut short, the opportunities missed, the disappointments, and the sadness; a time to remember the friendships made, the service given, the victories fashioned, to remember that this man, often so heedless of his own well-being, considered his efforts to better the mental and physical health of Ontario's citizens, his greatest achievement.

The cortège stopped on the knoll high in the cold snow-covered St. Thomas Protestant Cemetery. Below were the rolling white fields of Yarmouth, and just beyond was the hospital that would always stand as a memorial to Mitch Hepburn in Elgin. A shaft of weak wintry light glinted momentarily on the walnut casket of the eleventh Premier of Ontario as it rested by his native soil of Yarmouth. Leslie M. Frost, the Province's sixteenth Prime Minister, stood bare-headed and silent, then turned to a friend and said: "No one could dislike Mitch, not if you really knew him."[3]

Notes

A NOTE ON SOURCES

The principal manuscript sources used in this work are the Hepburn Papers in the Provincial Archives of Ontario. They are primarily valuable for the period from 1932 until 1942. Unfortunately, a considerable amount of this material concerns routine administrative matters of no interest to the general reader. It is obvious that some of the Hepburn Papers have been destroyed or removed and this, added to the fact that Mitch Hepburn was not ordinarily given to writing lengthy letters, makes the researcher's task a more difficult and less rewarding one. Among other provincial collections that proved helpful were the Howard Ferguson Papers and the George S. Henry Papers.

Of the collections consulted in the Public Archives of Canada, the most illuminating were the Mackenzie King Papers, which are now open to the end of 1932, the Robert Manion Papers, and the Arthur Meighen Papers. Excerpts from Mackenzie King's diary are quoted from *The Mackenzie King Record* by permission of Mr. King's Literary Executors and the University of Toronto Press. I am especially grateful to John Lambert, son of Senator Norman Lambert, for making available to me his late father's diaries. These were invaluable in supplementing the King Papers. My thanks also to Mrs. Herbert Bruce who graciously permitted me to consult her Diary and Journal, both of which helped clarify the political situation in Ontario in 1937.

Nothing of any length has been published on Hepburn. Of those works that refer to him, the most helpful were *The Mackenzie King Record*, Volume 1, edited by J. W. Pickersgill, the autobiography of Dr. Herbert Bruce, *Varied Operations*, and an article in the *Canadian Historical Review* for September, 1966, entitled "C. George McCullagh and the Leadership League" by Brian J. Young. Among unpublished sources, I relied heavily on Richard M. Alway's splendid thesis, "Mitchell F. Hepburn and the Liberal Party in Ontario, 1937-1943." For certain aspects of the Hepburn era, a manuscript written by Larry Zolf, "Rowell or Dewart?" was also valuable.

Relatives and friends of Mitch Hepburn were helpful with their recollections. Close political associates of the former Premier, especially Colin Campbell, Farquhar Oliver, Paul Leduc, Senator Arthur Roebuck, and Senator David Croll, offered valuable insights. Of the many interviews that provided material for the book, none were more enjoyable than those in Elgin County with Mitch Hepburn's old friends "on the back concessions." The Toronto daily newspapers and the St. Thomas *Times-Journal* were the main newspaper sources used, supplemented, when necessary, by other Ontario publications. In order to avoid extensive numbering in the text itself, the footnotes, where this seemed practicable, have been consolidated. It is hoped that this method will be useful to the student without being a distraction to the general reader.

Abbreviations

C.A.R.   *Canadian Annual Review of Public Affairs*

C.H.R.   *Canadian Historical Review*

C.P.G.   *Canadian Parliamentary Guide*

M.F.H.   Mitchell F. Hepburn

M.H.P.   Mitchell Hepburn Papers

P.A.C.   Public Archives of Canada

P.A.O.   Provincial Archives of Ontario

W.L.M.K.   William Lyon Mackenzie King

M.K.P.   Mackenzie King Papers

Notes

CHAPTER 1   UNDER THE SHADOW

1. St. Thomas *Daily Times*, June 29, 1906; St. Thomas *Evening Journal*, June 29, 1906; *Evening Journal*, Jan. 8, 1901; Jan. 5, 1904; March 29, 1904; C.P.G. 1908, p. 168; Aylmer *Express*, Nov. 10, 1904.
2. *Elgin County Atlas* (Toronto: H.R. Page & Co., 1877), pp. III, V, ix, x, xiii.
3. St. Thomas *Times-Journal*, Oct. 16, 1922; Records of the Elgin County Registery Office; *Times-Journal*, Souvenir Issue, July 19, 1934; Records of St. Thomas Protestant Cemetery; Personal Interviews. *Times-Journal*, Oct. 16, 1922.
4. James Fulton Family Tree, compiled by Kenneth A. Fulton, 1963; Interviews with Mrs. Sam Fulton, Feb. 28-9, 1966, and Mrs. J.F. Light, Feb. 25, 1966; *Times-Journal*, Oct. 22, 1922; Interview with George Millman, March 1, 1966.
5. Registery of St. Thomas Wellington.

Street Public School, 1900-1905. *Evening Journal*, March 29, 1904; Interview with Roy Johnson, Feb. 27, 1966; *Times-Journal*, Souvenir Issue, July 19, 1934.
6. *Daily Times*, Sept. 18, 1906; *Evening Journal*, Sept. 18, 1906. July 5, 6, 14, 31; Aug. 2, 1906; *London Advertiser*, Sept. 19, 1906; London *Free Press*, Sept. 19, 1906; *Evening Journal*, Sept. 19, 1906, Sept. 22, 1906.
7. *Evening Journal*, Sept. 24, 1906; London *Free Press*, Sept. 24, 1906.
8. *Daily Times,* Sept. 26, 1906; *Evening Journal*, Sept. 29, 1906, Oct. 1, 1906, Oct. 2, 1906; *Daily Times*, Oct. 3, 1906; C.A.R., 1906, p. 548; *Evening Journal*, Oct. 5, 1906; *Daily Times*, Oct. 8, 1906.
9. *Evening Journal*, Nov. 8, 1906; *Daily Times*, Nov. 8, 1906. Personal Interviews.

CHAPTER 2   THE BOY FROM YARMOUTH

1. Personal Interviews; M.F.H. to Sam Fulton, Feb. 28, 1909; Margaret Hepburn to Sam Fulton, March 9, 1909 (both in possession of Mrs. Sam Fulton).

2. *Daily Times*, March 10, 1909; *Report of the Commissioner into Conduct of W.R. Andrews*, April 6, 1909 (Ontario Legislative Library).
3. Margaret Hepburn to Sam Fulton,

March 30, April 5, 7, 19, 29, 1909.
(In possession of Mrs. Sam Fulton).
4. James Beeson to M.F.H., Dec. 15,
1926 (P.A.O., M.H.P.); St. Thomas,
Collegiate Register, 1910-11-12; Interview with George Gray, May 18,
1966; *Times-Journal*, Souvenir Issue, July 19, 1934; Letter to author
from Rev. James M. Finlay, April
10, 1967.
5. *Evening Journal*, Oct. 8, 1912;
Times-Journal, Souvenir Issue, July
19, 1934; Interview with George
Gray, May 18, 1966; Personnel
Records of Canadian Bank of Commerce.
6. Interviews with W.G. Whiteside,
May 13, 1966; Mrs. George Ponsford and Mrs. Alice Glover, Feb.
27, 1966; *Times-Journal*, Souvenir
Issue, July 19, 1934; Records of
Elgin County Registry Office; Personal Interviews.
7. *Daily Times*, March 15, 1916;
Times-Journal, Souvenir Issue, July

19, 1934; *Daily Times*, March 15,
1916; Interview with Matt Loney,
Feb. 26, 1966.
8. Personal Interviews.
9. Records of Elgin County Registry
Office; Personal Interview; *Times-
Journal*, Oct. 17, 1922; Will of
Mitchell Hepburn Sr., May 18, 1920
(Elgin County Court House).
10. Interviews with A.V. Coulter, Feb.
18, 1966, and with Percy R. Locke,
Feb. 21, 1966; Minutes of East Elgin
U.F.O., May 10, 1923 (M.H.P.);
Times-Journal, May 11, 1923; Oct.
19, 21, 28, 1925.
11. *Times-Journal*, July 29, 1926; Per-
sonal Interviews.
12. *Times-Journal*, Aug. 13, 1926;
Times-Journal, Aug. 13 to Sept. 15,
1926; Interviews with Percy Locke
and A.V. Coulter; *Times-Journal*,
Sept. 8, 1926; W.L.M.K. to Percy
Parker (Telegram), Aug. 20, 1926
(P.A.C., M.K.P.); *Times-Journal*,
Sept. 15, 1926.

CHAPTER 3 MEMBER FOR ELGIN WEST

1. M.F.H. to Albert P. Conley, Dec.
10, 1926 (M.H.P.); A. Darrach to
W.L.M.K., Jan. 6, 1927 (M.K.P.);
W.L.M.K. to A. Darrach, Jan. 21,
1927 (*Ibid.*); M.F.H. to J.A. Mc-
Pherson, Feb. 9, 1927 (M.H.P.);
M.F.H. to A. MacIntyre Bruce,
March 25, 1927 (*Ibid.*); M.F.H. to
E. Lee, April 26, 1928 (*Ibid.*)
2. M.F.H. to J.R. Galbraith, Jan. 17,
1927 (M.H.P.); M.F.H. to H.H.
Roberts, Feb. 8, 1927 (*Ibid.*);
M.F.H. to A. Aveling, April 9, 1930
(*Ibid.*); M.F.H. to A. Darrach,
March 9, 1928 (*Ibid.*); *Can. H. of
C. Debates*, Feb. 10, 1927, p. 206;
April 9, 1929, p. 1426; M.F.H. to
W.A. Galbraith, Feb. 25, 1927
(M.H.P.); Interview with Senator
C.G. Power, March 23, 1966.
3. *Can. H. of C. Debates*, March 2,
1928, p. 961; April 5, 1927, p. 1924;
April 17, 1928, p. 2112; March 15,
1929, p. 1001.
4. M.F.H. to A.W. Roebuck, March 7,
1928 (M.H.P.); M.F.H. to J.C.
Elliott, June 7, 1928 (*Ibid.*); M.F.H.
to E. Lee, April 26, 1928 (*Ibid.*).

5. Toronto *Star*, Sept. 13, 1927;
Farmers' Sun, Oct. 27, 1927; C.A.R.,
1927-8, p. 41; *Times-Journal*, Oct.
20, 1927; M.F.H. to C. Jones, Nov.
8, 1927 (M.H.P.); Toronto *Star*,
Nov. 30, 1927; *Globe*, Dec. 9, 1927.
6. M.F.H. to Imperial Tobacco Co.,
April 12, 1929 (M.H.P.); *Times-
Journal*, April 29, 1929; R.J. Deach-
man to A. Haydon, April 29, 1929
(M.K.P.); A. Haydon to R.J.
Deachman, April 30, 1929, (*Ibid.*);
Times-Journal, April 8, 1930.
7. Blair Neatby, *The Lonely Heights*
(Toronto: University of Toronto
Press, 1963), pp. 287-9; Senator J.
Spence to W.L.M.K., Jan. 6, 1930
(M.K.P.); M.F.H. to F.W. Hay,
Jan. 21, 1930 (M.H.P.); M.F.H. to
H. Johnson, Jan. 28, 1930 (*Ibid.*);
A. Darrach to W.L.M.K., March
10, 1930, (M.K.P.); Neatby, *op.
cit.*, pp. 314-15; W.L.M.K. to A.
Darrach, March 15, 1930 (M.K.P.).
8. M.F.H. to R.J. Deachman, June 23,
1930 (M.H.P.); Toronto *Star*, April
5, 1930; Statement with London
Advertiser, July 30, 1930 (M.H.P.);

M.F.H. to R.J. Deachman, June 16, 1930 (M.H.P.); *Times-Journal,* July 26, July 29, 1930; C.A.R., 1929-30, p. 100, 635.

CHAPTER 4 THE HEATHER AFIRE

1. This resume of the provincial Liberal Party in Ontario relies primarily on two sources: Larry Zolf, "Rowell or Dewart?" an unpublished manuscript, and Neil McKenty, "Rum, Romanism, and Power," an unpublished M.A. thesis (University of Toronto Library, 1963).
2. J.E. Atkinson to W.L.M.K., May 1, 1926 (M.K.P.); W. Sinclair to W.L.M.K., Dec. 26, 1929 (*Ibid.*); W. Sinclair to W.L.M.K., Dec. 4, 1928, Feb. 5, 1930; Aug. 15, 1930 (*Ibid.*); W.L.M.K. to W. Sinclair, Aug. 19, 1930 (*Ibid.*); A.C. Hardy to W.L.M.K., Sept. 25, 1930 (*Ibid.*).
3. Toronto *Star,* Oct. 21, 1930; *Globe,* Oct. 29, 1930; Oct. 31, 1930; *Mail and Empire,* Oct. 31, 1930.
4. P. Parker to W.L.M.K., Nov. 21, 1930 (M.K.P.); W.L.M.K. to P. Parker, Nov. 6, 1930 (*Ibid.*); W.L.M.K. to Senator J. Spence, Nov. 27, 1930 (*Ibid.*); W.L.M.K. to H. Johnson, Nov. 27, 1930 (*Ibid.*); W.L.M.K. to A. Darrach, Nov. 27, 1930 (*Ibid.*); A. Darrach

9. *Can. H. of C. Debates,* Sept. 18, 1930, p. 411; C. Campbell to M.F.H., Sept. 23, 1930 (M.H.P.).

to W.L.M.K., Nov. 20, 1930 (*Ibid.*).
5. M.F.H. to A.W. Roebuck, Nov. 26, 1930 (quoted in Zolf MS); A.W. Roebuck to M.F.H., Dec. 2, 1930 (*Ibid.*); P. Parker to W.L.M.K., Dec. 1, 1930 (M.K.P.); A. Roberts to W.L.M.K., Dec. 11, 1930 (*Ibid.*)
6. A. Roberts to W.L.M.K., Dec. 11, 1930 (M.K.P.); Interview with P. Locke, Feb. 21, 1966; P. Parker to W.L.M.K., Dec. 15, 1930 (M.K.P.); W.L.M.K. to A. Roberts, Dec. 15, 1930 (*Ibid.*).
7. Information on the Ontario Liberal convention of 1930 was obtained from the following newspapers covering the period Dec. 16 to 18: Toronto *Star; Globe; Mail and Empire; Telegram; Times-Journal;* Interviews with Colin Campbell Nov. 16, 1966 and Percy Locke, Feb. 21, 1966; P. Donnelly to P. Parker, Oct. 26, 1931 (M.H.P.); P. Donnelly to M.F.H., April 12, 1934 (*Ibid.*); H. Johnson to W.L.M.K., Dec. 20, 1930 (M.K.P.).

CHAPTER 5 RUM, ROMANISM, AND POWER

1. *Telegram,* Dec. 18, 1930; Toronto *Star,* Dec. 18 and 22, 1930; Ross Harkness, *J.E. Atkinson of the Star* (Toronto: University of Toronto Press, 1963), p. 231; Alex Darrach to W.L.M.K., Dec. 19, 1930, and Jan. 2, 1931 (M.K.P.); W.L.M.K. to M.F.H., Dec. 18, 1930 (*Ibid.*); W.L.M.K. to W. Sinclair, Dec. 18, 1930 (*Ibid.*); W. Sinclair to W.L.M.K., Dec. 30, 1930 (*Ibid.*).
2. Merrill Denison, *The People's Power* (Toronto: McClelland & Stewart Ltd., 1960), 178-9.
3. Franklin A. Walker, *Catholic Education and Politics in Ontario* (Toronto: Thomas A. Nelson & Sons, 1964), p. 355, *ff.*
4. Neil McKenty, *op. cit.,* p. 152, vii.

5. Biographical sketch of George S. Henry, n.d. (P.A.O., George S. Henry Papers); *Globe,* March 15, 1933; *Saturday Night,* May 12, 1934.
6. W.L.M.K. to Alex Darrach, June 12, 1931 (M.K.P.); W.L.M.K. to James Malcolm, June 12, 1931 (*Ibid.*); *Globe,* May 22, 1931; Beauharnois Inquiry (Toronto Hydro Library); *Globe,* July 18 and 29, 1931; Roderick Lewis, *A Statistical History of All the Electoral Districts of the Province of Ontario since 1867* (Toronto: Queen's Printer, n.d.), p. 315; Paul Munro to W.L.M.K., Nov. 26, 1931 (M.K.P.).
7. H. Nixon to W.L.M.K., Oct. 18, 1932 (M.K.P.); G. Henry to H.

Ferguson, Dec. 24, 1931 (Henry Papers); *Report of the Royal Commission Appointed to Inquire into Certain Matters Concerning the Hydro-Electric Power Commission of Ontario* (Toronto: King's Printer, Oct. 31, 1932); Kingston *Whig-Standard*, Nov. 5, 1932; *Globe*, March 4, 1933; London *Free Press*, March 23, 1933; *Whig-Standard*, March 25, 1933; *Globe*, April 6, 1933; *Mail and Empire*, April 6, 1933; G. Henry to H. Ferguson, April 28, 1933 (Henry Papers).

8. Walker, *op. cit.*, p. 356, *ff.*, p. 378; *Globe*, March 14, 1933; Martin Quinn to M.F.H., Jan. 21, 1933 (M.H.P.); M.F.H. to M. Quinn, Feb. 2, 1933 (*Ibid.*); M. Quinn to M.F.H., April 10, 1935 (*Ibid.*); M.F.H. to R.R. Cromarty, April 10, 1933 (*Ibid.*); H. Ferguson to G. Henry, Oct. 24, 1933 (Henry Papers); Daily *Star*, March 31, 1934.

9. H. Ferguson to G. Henry, Oct. 24, 1933 (Henry Papers); Brockville *Recorder and Times*, March 10, 1932; H. Nixon to M.F.H., March 11, 1932 (M.H.P.); M.F.H. to M.W. Rossie, Oct. 9, 1933 (*Ibid.*); Windsor *Border-Cities Star*, March 22, 1934; M.F.H. to Dr. G. McQuibban, March 24, 1934 (M.H.P.); M.F.H. to T.B. McQuesten, March 24, 1934 (*Ibid.*); Globe, March 28, 1934; London *Free Press*, April 3, 1934.

10. Windsor *Star*, April 13, 1934; Leo McLaughlin to M.F.H., April 3, 1934 (M.H.P.); *Mail and Empire*, May 16, 1932; *Globe*, May 30, 1932; Toronto *Star*, Sept. 30, 1933; *Telegram*, Feb. 17, 1934; Margaret Stewart and Doris French, *Ask No Quarter* (Toronto: Longmans and Green, 1959), p. 173; W.L.M.K. to Albert Roberts, April 16, 1932 (M.K.P.).

11. M.F.H. to R.J. Deachman, Oct. 23, 1931 (M.H.P.); M.F.H. to Allan Kneale, Oct. 12, 1932 (*Ibid.*);

M.F.H. to P. Parker, Oct. 14, 1932 (*Ibid.*); A.C. Hardy to M.F.H., Dec. 22, 1932 (*Ibid.*); M.F.H. to T.B. McQuesten, Oct. 12, 1932 (*Ibid.*); M.F.H. to W.P. Mulock, Oct. 21, 1932 (*Ibid.*); Ottawa *Citizen*, Nov. 19, 1932; M.F.H. to M.W. Rossie, Feb. 28, 1933 (M.H.P.).

12. *Globe*, Jan. 8, 1934; Toronto *Star*, Jan. 12, 1934; *Mail and Empire*, Jan. 1, 1934; *Globe*, March 17 and 23, 1934; M.F.H. to Dr. L.J. Simpson, Oct. 11, 1933 (M.H.P.); St. Catharines *Standard*, May 27, 1932; Diary of Senator Norman Lambert, April 8, 1934; Ottawa *Citizen*, May 18, 1934; *Globe and Mail*, Jan. 6, 1953.

13. Memorandum from A. Ellis for G. Henry, Jan. 25, 1934 (Henry Papers); *Globe*, Jan. 1, 1934; *Mail and Empire*, April 6, 1934; London *Free Press*, April 27, 1934; G. Henry to R.B. Bennett, March 22, 1934 (Henry Papers); *Globe*, April 23, May 1, 1934; G. Henry to H. Ferguson, April 28, 1933 (Henry Papers).

14. *Mail and Empire*, May 7, 1934; *Globe*, May 10 and June 14, 1934; *Whig-Standard*, May 14, 1934; *Globe*, May 17, June 5, May 28, 1934; Windsor *Star*, June 15, 1934; *Globe*, June 1, 1934; North Bay *Nugget*, May 30, 1934.

15. *Mail and Empire*, June 11, 1934; Toronto *Star*, June 14, 1934; Ottawa *Citizen*, June 15, 1934; Toronto *Star*, June 16, 1934; *Telegram*, June 13, 1934; *Globe*, June 19, 1934; Interviews with Douglas Oliver and Ralph Hyman; Brockville *Recorder and Times*, June 20, 1934.

16. Toronto *Star*, June 20, 1934; *Mail and Empire*, June 20, 1934; *Globe*, June 20, 1934; *Times Journal*, June 20, 1934; G. Henry to H. Ferguson, June 21, 1934 (Henry Papers).

CHAPTER 6 POWER POLITICS

1. *Globe and Mail*, Jan. 6, 1953; *Mail and Empire*, June 25, 1934; Toronto *Star*, June 22, 1934; *Times-*

Journal, June 20, 1934.

2. Interview with Leopold Macaulay, Dec. 1, 1965; *Telegram*, June 20,

1934; D.M. Hogarth to Robert Manion, July 4, 1934 (P.A.C., Robert Manion Papers); Neil McKenty, "Mitchell Hepburn and the Election of 1934," *C.H.R.*, Dec. 1965, pp. 309-10; *op. cit.*, pp. 375-80.
3. Toronto *Star*, July 11, 1934; Mrs. H. Bruce Diary, July 10, 1934; Toronto *Star*, July 11, 1934; Harkness, *op. cit.*, p. 231; W.L.M.K. to M.F.H., May 24, 1934 (M.H.P.); *Telegram*, June 21, 1934; W.L.M.K. to M.F.H., Sept. 1, 1934 (M.H.P.).
4. W.L.M.K. to M.F.H., July 12, 1934 (*Ibid.*); *Financial Post,* Aug. 18, 1934; Toronto *Star*, June 23, 1934; Thelma Le Cocq, "Mitch Hepburn," *Maclean's Magazine*, March 15, 1943; *Whig-Standard*, Sept. 13, 1934; *Globe*, July 31, Oct. 24, 25, 1934; C.A.R., 1934, p. 182; M.F.H. to A.C. Hardy, Aug. 22, 1934 (M.H.P.); *Mail and Empire*, Sept. 7, 14, 1934; *Globe*, Oct. 1, 1934; Arthur Meighen to Colonel Hugh Clark, July 21, 1934 (P.A.C., Arthur Meighen Papers); C.A.R., 1934, p. 183.
5. *Globe*, July 20, 1934; *Times-Journal*, July 20, 1934; Toronto *Star*, July 20, 1934.
6. W.L.M.K. to M.F.H., July 12, 1934, (M.H.P.); Lambert Diary, July 14, 1934; W.L.M.K. to M.F.H. July 16, 1934 (M.H.P.); *Globe*, Sept. 20, 1934.
7. Lambert Diary, July 23, 26, 30, June 28, 1934; G. Fulford to M.F.H., July 3, 1934 (M.H.P.); Lambert Diary, Aug. 20, Oct. 24, 1934.
8. *Globe*, Feb. 21, 1935; *Mail and Empire*, Feb. 21, 1935; Herbert A. Bruce, *Varied Operations* (Toronto: Longmans, Green and Company, 1958), p. 225; Cobourg *World*, quoted in *Mail and Empire*, Feb. 20, 1935; *Mail and Empire*, Feb. 20, 1935.
9. *Globe*, April 9, March 14, 15, 1935; *Mail and Empire*, March 16, 1935;

Globe, March 29, 1935.
10. *Globe*, March 1, March 2, April 2, 1935; Lambert Diary, March 2, 1935; Mrs. Bruce Diary, April 10, 1935.
11. *Globe*, April 2, 3, 5, 1935; *Mail and Empire*, April 2, 1935; Lambert Diary, April 4, 1935; *Globe*, April 2, 9, 10, 1935; *Mail and Empire*, April 10, 1935; *Globe*, April 12, 1935; *Mail and Empire*, April 19, 1935.
12. *Mail and Empire*, June 3, 1935; *Globe*, June 5, 6, 12, 13, 1935; London *Financial News*, June 14, 1935 (M.H.P.); *Globe*, June 14, 15, 20, 1935.
13. *Times-Journal*, Jan. 28, 1935; Lambert Diary, April 23, May 10, Sept. 11, 1935; W.L.M.K. to M.F.H., Aug. 6, 1935 (M.H.P.); *Times-Journal*, Aug. 14, 1935; *Globe*, Aug. 14, 1935.
14. M.F.H. to W.L.M.K. (2), Aug. 31, 1935 (M.H.P.); W.L.M.K. to M.F.H., Sept. 2, 1935 (*Ibid.*); *Globe*, Sept. 10, 1935; M.F.H. to A. Roebuck, Sept. 24, 1935 (M.H.P.); D.M. Hogarth to R. Manion, Oct. 10, 1935 (Manion Papers); C.A.R., 1935-36, p. 68; *Times-Journal*, Oct. 15, 1935.
15. W.L.M.K. to Fred J. Regan, Nov. 28, 1932 (M.H.P.); Paul Martin to M.F.H., Aug. 17, 1932 (*Ibid.*); Lambert Diary, July 14, Dec. 6, 1934; March 1, 6, 8, April 29, May 4, 6, June 9, July 8, 1935; March 30, April 3, Sept. 20, 1935.
16. Lambert Diary, Oct. 15, 1935; May 10, 1939; W.L.M.K. to M.F.H., Oct. 22, 1935 (M.H.P.); J.W. Pickersgill, *The Mackenzie King Record*, Volume 1, (Toronto: University of Toronto Press, 1960), p. 34.
17. *Globe*, Oct. 24, Nov. 6, 1935; *Mail and Empire*, Nov. 5, 1935; New York *Daily News*, Dec. 4, 1935 (M.H.P.); *Globe*, Dec. 4, 7, 12, 14, 1935.

CHAPTER 7 TOOLS OF ROME

1. *Globe*, March 19, 1936.
2. *Mail and Empire*, Jan. 23, Feb. 15,

1935; M.J. Quinn to M.F.H., April 10, 1935 (M.H.P.); R. Elmhirst to

M.J. Quinn, April 11, 1935 (*Ibid.*); M.J. Quinn to M.F.H. April 13, 1935 (*Ibid.*); *Globe*, May 4, 1935.
3. M.J. Quinn to Robert Kerr, Feb. 7, 1936 (M.H.P.); Toronto *Star*, Feb. 10, 1936; M.J. Quinn to M.F.H., (telegram), Feb. 10, 1936 (M.H.P.); Ivers Kelly to Mr. Knowles, Feb. 11, 1936 (*Ibid.*); M.F.H. to M.J. Quinn, Feb. 21, 1936 (*Ibid.*); Toronto *Star*, Feb. 11, 1936; J.E. Atkinson to M.F.H. (enclosure), Feb. 24, 1936 (M.H.P.); M.F.H. to E.M. Macdonald, March 5, 1936 (*Ibid.*); *Telegram*, March 25, 1936; M.H.P., *passim*, Jan. 1, 1936, to March 24, 1936; *Globe*, April 1, 1936.
4. *Mail and Empire*, April 4, 1936; *Globe*, April 4, 1936; P. Parker to M.F.H., April 3, 1936 (M.H.P.); M.F.H. to C.G. Power, April 4, 1936 (*Ibid.*); *Telegram*, April 4, 1936; *Globe*, April 6, 1936; *Mail and Empire*, April 7, 1936; *Globe*, April 7, 1936; W.O. Weaver to M.F.H., April 8, 1936 (M.H.P.); C.G. Power to M.F.H., April 9, 1936 (*Ibid.*); *Mail and Empire*, April 8, 1936; W.R.P.P. (Percy Parker) to M.F.H., April 8, 1936 (M.H.P.); *Globe*, April 9, 1936; *Mail and Empire*, April 9, 1936; *Globe*, April 10, 1936.
5. C. Mell to M.F.H., April 18, 1936 (M.H.P.); Toronto *Star*, May 22, 1936; *Mail and Empire*, May 29, 1936; *Globe*, May 29, 1936; *Telegram*, May 29, 1936; *Globe*, May 22, June 25, 1936; *Times-Journal*, June 26, 1936.
6. *Telegram*, Nov. 6, 1936; *Globe and Mail*, Nov. 25, 1936; *Globe and Mail*, Nov. 27, 1936; *Telegram*, Nov. 28, 1936; *Globe and Mail*, Dec. 1, 1936; *Globe*, Nov. 10, 1936; *Globe and Mail*, Nov. 30, 1936; Nov. 23, 1936; *Globe*, Nov. 20, 13, 1936; *Globe and Mail*, Dec. 8, 1936; Dec. 2, 3, 9, 10, 1936; Lewis, *op. cit.*, p. 95; Mrs Bruce Diary, Nov. 27, 1936; M.F.H. to Neil McLean, Jan. 4, 1937 (M.H.P.); *Globe and Mail*, Dec. 10, 1936; Lambert Diary, Dec. 21, 1936.
7. Lambert Diary, March 19, 1936; M.F.H. to C.G. Power, April 4, 1936 (M.H.P.); Lambert Diary, April 18, 19, 1936; June 20, 1936.
8. Lambert Diary, April 29, May 28, Aug. 12, Sept. 9, 1936; N. Lambert to M.F.H., Nov. 5, 1936 (Lambert Papers); M.F.H. to N. Lambert, Nov. 12, 1936 (M.H.P.); Lambert Diary, Nov. 16, 20, Dec. 7, 10, 16, 1936.
9. *Globe and Mail*, Nov. 23, 1936.
10. Pierre Berton, "The Amazing Career of George McCullagh," *Maclean's Magazine*, Jan. 15, 1949; J.C. Furnas, "Canada's Boy Wonder," *Saturday Evening Post*, Jan. 22, 1938; *Globe*, Oct. 15, Sept. 29, 1936; *Globe and Mail*, Nov. 30, 1936; G. McCullagh to W.L.M.K., Dec. 5, 1936, quoted in Bryan Young, "C. George McCullagh and the Leadership League," C.H.R., Sept., 1966, p. 204.
11. *Globe and Mail*, December 17, 1936; *Telegram*, Dec. 17, 1936; *Globe and Mail*, Dec. 18, 19, 29, 1936.

CHAPTER 8 RIDING WITH GENERAL MOTORS

1. M.F.H. to R.S. McLaughlin, Jan. 4, 1937 (M.H.P.).
2. *Globe and Mail*, Jan. 14, 16, 21, 1937; M.F.H. to Friend, Jan. 20, 1937 (M.H.P.); Harold Kirby to M.F.H., Jan. 21, 1937 (*Ibid.*); T.H. Hogg to M.F.H., Jan. 21, 1937 (*Ibid.*); H. Nixon to M.F.H., Jan. 21, 1937 (*Ibid.*); D. Croll to M.F.H., Jan. 23, 1937 (*Ibid.*); Interview with Senator Croll, March 24, 1966; *Globe and Mail*, Jan. 23, 30, 1937.
3. G. McCullagh to M.F.H., Jan. 29, 1937 (M.H.P.); Interview with Senator A. Roebuck, Dec. 1, 1965; Mrs. Bruce Diary, Nov. 29, 1936.
4. Interview with Senator D. Croll, March 24, 1966; H. Nixon to M.F.H., Feb. 5, 1937 (M.H.P.); M.F.H. to F. O'Connor, Feb. 10, 1937 (*Ibid.*); *Globe and Mail*, Feb.

13, 1937; *Telegram*, Feb. 13, 1937.
5. M.F.H. to F. O'Connor, Feb. 10, 1937 (M.H.P.); Lord Beaverbrook, *Courage* (Fredericton: Brunswick Press, 1961), pp. 115-119; M.F.H. to J. Curran, Feb. 10, 1937 (M.H.P.); J. Curran to M.F.H., Feb. 13, 1937, (*Ibid.*); *Telegram*, Feb. 16, 18, 1937; March 5, 6, 9, 10, 1937.
6. C.A.R. 1935-1936, p. 206.
7. M. Quinn to M.F.H., Feb. 22, 1937 (M.H.P.); M.F.H. to F. O'Connor, Feb. 26, 1937 (*Ibid.*); *Globe and Mail*, March 3, 24, 25, 1937.
8. Rev. E.A. Doyle to M.F.H., March 25, 1937 (M.H.P.); A.C. Hardy to M.F.H., March 25, 1937 (*Ibid.*); *Telegram*, March 25, 1937; M. Quinn to Edward F. Murphy, April 7, 1936 (M.H.P.); M. Quinn to Albert H. Murphy, Sept. 7, 1937 (*Ibid.*); *Telegram*, March 27, 1937; *Globe and Mail*, March 26, 1937; *Times-Journal*, May 16, 1937.
9. Robert Caygeon, "Hepburn, Liberal St. George," *Saturday Night*, Nov. 11, 1933; The point of Mitchell Hepburn's fundamental conservatism is also made by M.G. Decarie in his unpublished essay "The Depression of the 1930's: Three Movements of Political Revivalism" (Queen's University, 1966); *Canadian Forum*, July, 1934; *Toronto Star*, Sept. 17, 1934; *Canadian Forum*, February, 1935.
10. *Can. H. of C. Debates*, 1932, p. 330; Sir J. Dunn to M.F.H. Aug. 4, 1937 (M.H.P.); *Toronto Star*, July 16, 1934; H.A. Logan, *Trade Unions in Canada* (Toronto: Macmillan, 1948), pp. 220, 458; Lambert Diary, March 1, 1935; Feb. 16, 1935; *Telegram*, Nov. 2, 1934; W. Fraser to M.F.H., Sept. 28, 1936 (M.H.P.); M.F.H. to W. Fraser, Oct. 2, 1936 (*Ibid.*).
11. *Globe*, April 5, 26, 1935; *Mail and Empire*, April 25, 26, 1935; *Globe*, April 29, 30, May 10, 13, 1935.
12. *Telegram*, March 3, 5, 1937; *Globe and Mail*, March 5, 6, 8, 1937.
13. M.F.H. to Ian Mackenzie (telegram), Feb. 25, 1937 (M.H.P.); Ian Mackenzie to M.F.H. (telegram), Feb. 25, 1937 (*Ibid.*); T.H. Crerar to M.F.H., March 4, 5, 1937 (*Ibid.*); M.F.H. to A.C. Hardy, April 9, 1937 (*Ibid.*).
14. *Globe and Mail*, April 1, 1937; Logan, *op. cit.*, pp. 233-34; *Globe and Mail*, April 1, 1937; Memorandum of meeting with David Croll, April 2, 1937 (M.H.P.); Interview with Senator Croll, March 24, 1966; *Globe and Mail*, April 5, 1937; M.F.H. to G. Fulford, April 9, 1937 (M.H.P.); *Toronto Star*, April 8, 1937.
15. *Globe and Mail*, April 9, March 10, 1937; M.F.H. to Ernest Lapointe (telegram), April 8, 1937 (M.H.P.); Memorandum from R.H. Elmhirst to M.F.H., April 8, 1937 (*Ibid.*); Ernest Lapointe to M.F.H. (telegram), April 8, 1937 (*Ibid.*); *Globe and Mail*, April 9, 1937.
16. *Toronto Star*, April 10, 1937; *Globe and Mail*, April 12, 1937; *Toronto Star*, April 12, 1937; M.F.H. to Ernest Lapointe (telegram), April 13, 1937 (M.H.P.); *Globe and Mail,* April 13, 1937; M.F.H. to W.L.M.K. (telegram), April 13, 1937 (M.H.P.); *Globe and Mail*, April 14, 1937; W.L.M.K. to M.F.H. (telegram), April 13, 1937 (M.H.P.); *Globe and Mail*, April 14, 1937; W.L.M.K. to M.F.H. (telegram), April 13, 1937 (M.H.P.); Ernest Lapointe to M.F.H. (telegram), April 14, 1937 (*Ibid.*); M.F.H. to Ernest Lapointe (telegram), April 15, 1937 (*Ibid.*).
17. *Toronto Star*, April 16, 1937; *Globe and Mail*, April 16, 1937; H. Foote to M.F.H., April 17, 1937 (M.H.P.); *Toronto Star*, April 16, 1937; Officers 133rd Battalion C.E.F. to M.F.H. (telegram), April 13, 1937 (M.H.P.); A. Hall to M.F.H. (telegram), April 13, 1937 (*Ibid.*); *Globe and Mail*, April 9, 1937; April 14, 15, 1937; M.F.H. to D. Croll, April 14, 1937 (M.H.P.); M.F.H. to A. Roebuck, April 14, 1937 (*Ibid.*); Interviews with D. Croll and A. Roebuck; D. Croll to M.F.H., April 14, 1937 (M.H.P.); *Toronto Star*, April 15, 1937.

18. M.F.H. to C.E. Finley, July 8, 1937 (M.H.P.); M.F.H. to T.E. Wilson, April 15, 1937 (*Ibid.*); Memorandum from R.H. Elmhirst to M.F.H., April 17, 1937 (*Ibid.*); *Globe and Mail*, April 19, 1937; General Manager Hollinger Mines to M.F.H. April 16, 1937 (M.H.P.); *Globe and Mail*, April 19, 20, 1937; C.A.R., 1937-38, p. 165; *Globe and Mail*, April 21, 1937.

19. M.F.H. to R.S. McLaughlin (telegram), April 20, 1937 (M.H.P.); *Globe and Mail*, April 22, 1937; Memoranda to D. Oliver, April 21, 22, 1937 (M.H.P.); *Globe and Mail*, April 23, 1937; Ian Mackenzie to M.F.H. (telegram), April 22, 1937 (M.H.P.); Toronto *Star*, April 23, 1937; *Globe and Mail*, April 24, 1937.

20. Harkness, *op. cit.*, p. 235; Copy of Agreement with G.M. (M.H.P. April 1937); M.F.H. to T.H. Crerar (telegram), April 23, 1937 (*Ibid.*); T.H. Crerar to M.F.H. (telegram), April 23, 1937 (*Ibid.*); *Globe and Mail*, April 24, 26, 1937; G. McCullagh to R.H. McMaster, Jan. 18, 1943, quoted in Bryan Young, *loc. cit.*, p. 206; D. Croll to M.F.H., April 14, 1937 (M.H.P.).

21. Windsor *Star*, April 9, 1937; *Globe and Mail*, April 15, 19, 1937; M.H.P. during April and May, 1937; J.J. Gibbons to M.F.H., April 9, 1937 (M.H.P.); T.J. Taylor to M.F.H., April 15, 1937 (*Ibid.*); J.O. Nix to M.F.H., April 17, 1937 (*Ibid.*); A.R. Mosher to M.F.H., April 24, 1937 (*Ibid.*); D.P. Campbell to M.F.H., June 14, 1937 (*Ibid.*).

22. *Globe and Mail*, June 18, 1938; Harkness, *op. cit.*, p. 232-33; Toronto *Star*, April 12, 16, 17, 20, 22, May 1, 1937; G. McCullagh to R.H. McMaster, Jan. 18, 1943, quoted in B. Young *loc. cit.*, p. 206; G. McCullagh to R.S. McLaughlin, Jan. 26, 1945 (*Idem.*); Sir Anthony Jenkinson, "Premier At Home," *Saturday Night*, Dec. 4, 1937; M.F.H. to L.H. Dingman, May 5, 1937 (M.H.P.).

CHAPTER 9 BACK TO POWER

1. Toronto *Star*, May 1, 4, 1937; *Globe and Mail*, May 3, 1937; Mrs. Bruce Journal, p. 94 *ff.*; L.B. Birdsall to M.F.H., April 25, 1937 (M.H.P.); Mrs. Bruce Diary, April 25, 26; March 14, 1937; Personal Interviews; Mrs. Bruce Journal, p. 94 *ff.*; Lambert Diary, April 30, April 29, 1937; H. Johnson to M.F.H., May 3, 1937 (M.H.P.); *Globe and Mail*, May 5, 1937.

2. Pierre Berton, "The Amazing Career of George McCullagh," *Maclean's Magazine*, Jan. 15, 1949; R.E. Knowles, Jr., "President and Publisher," *Saturday Night*, Nov. 4, 1936; *Telegram*, Dec. 3, 1938; Anthony Jenkinson, "Premier at Home," *Saturday Night*, December 4, 1937; *Telegram*, May 6, 1937; *Globe and Mail*, May 3, 1937; Toronto *Star*, May 5, 1937.

3. Rowe's speech was printed in pamphlet form entitled "The Path to Industrial Peace" (M.H.P. 1937); *Globe and Mail*, May 6, Dec. 5, 1938; Toronto *Star*, May 7, 1937; Mrs. Bruce Diary, April 25, 1937; Mrs. Bruce Journal, p. 94 *ff.*; *Telegram*, Dec. 5, 1938; *Globe and Mail*, Dec. 5, 6, 1938; *Telegram*, Dec. 6, 1938, May 8, 1938; M.F.H. to R.S. Colter, June 1, 1937 (M.H.P.); D. Hogarth to R. Manion, May 17, 1937 (Manion Papers).

4. *Globe and Mail*, June 4, 1937; M.F.H. to T.D. Pattullo, July 27, 1937 (M.H.P.); Lambert Diary, Feb. 3, 5, 9, 10, 11, 12, 17, 18, 22, 23, 1937; "Rt. Honorable C.D. Howe – A Memoir" (Lambert Papers); G. Fulford to M.F.H., Aug. 3, 1937 (M.H.P.).

5. M.F.H. to W.G. Nixon, May 3, 1937 (*Ibid.*); M.F.H. to T.D. Pattullo, July 27, 1937 (*Ibid.*); *Globe and Mail*, May 11, Aug. 13, 1937; *Times-Journal*, Aug. 13, 1937; *Globe and Mail*, Aug. 16, 19, 21, 23, 27, 1937; Oct. 4, Sept. 13, 1937.

6. *Globe and Mail*, May 31, 1937; D. Hogarth to E. Rowe, July 5, 1937

(Manion Papers); R. Manion to D. Hogarth, April 18, 1937 (*Ibid.*); *Globe and Mail*, Sept. 10, 16, 27, 1937; *Times-Journal*, Sept. 23, Oct. 2, 1937; *Globe and Mail*, Aug. 28, Sept. 17, 1937; R. Manion to Earl Rowe, Sept. 17, 1937 (Manion Papers); *Globe and Mail*, Sept. 28, 21, 1937, Aug. 26, Oct. 1, 1937.

7. M. Quinn to A. Murphy, Sept. 7, 1937 (M.H.P.); A. Murphy to M.F.H., Sept. 8, 1937 (*Ibid.*); A. Murphy to P. Leduc, Sept. 4, 1937 (*Ibid.*); M. Quinn, "The Frustration of Lay Catholic Effort in Ontario," p. 27, quoted by Walker, *op. cit.*, p. 460; *Globe and Mail*, Sept. 6, 15, 1937; A. Murphy to M.F.H. Sept. 27, 1937 (M.H.P.).

8. *Globe and Mail*, Sept. 8, 9, 18, Oct. 2, 4, 1937; *Telegram*, Oct. 4, 1937; *Globe and Mail*, Oct. 1, 4, 5, 1937; Ottawa *Citizen*, Oct. 6, 1937; *Globe and Mail*, Sept. 29, Oct. 1, 6, 1937.

9. *Times-Journal*, Oct. 7, 1937; *Globe and Mail*, Oct. 7, 1937; D.M. Hogarth to R. Manion, Jan. 20, 1939 (Manion Papers); C.A.R., 1937-8, p. 178; Lewis, *op. cit.*, p. 47; *Times-Journal*, Oct. 7, 1937; *Globe and Mail*, Oct. 7, 27, 1937; C.A.R., 1937-8, p. 169; Toronto *Star*, Sept. 22, 1937; *Globe and Mail*, Oct. 8, 1937; G. McCullagh to E. Wooliver, Aug. 28, 1937 (quoted in Young thesis, p. 53); G. McCullagh to M.F.H., Oct. 7, 1937 (M.H.P.).

10. *Globe and Mail*, Oct. 13, 1937; *Telegram*, Oct. 13, 1937.

11. *Saturday Night*, April 22, 1939; Bruce, *Varied Operations*, p. 226; W.L.M.K. to E.G. Long, Oct. 8, 1937 (Lambert Papers); W.L.M.K. to M.F.H., Oct. 8, 1937 (M.H.P.); Bruce, *Varied Operations*, p. 225, 226; Mrs. Bruce Journal, p. 110; M.F.H. to W.L.M.K., Oct. 12, 1937

(M.H.P.); Bruce, *Varied Operations*, p. 226; Mrs. Bruce Journal, p. 110 *ff.*; Mrs. Bruce Diary, Oct. 19, 24, 1937.

12. R.E. Knowles Jr., "Genial and Hard-Boiled," *Saturday Night*, Aug. 4, 1937; *Globe and Mail*, April 7, 1938; *Telegram*, Nov. 20, 1937; *Globe and Mail*, Oct. 23, Nov. 22, 1937; Mrs. Bruce Journal, p. 110 *ff.*; G. Fulford to M.F.H., Nov. 19, 1937 (M.H.P.); Dr. Joseph Sullivan to Roy Elmhirst, Nov. 24, 1937 (*Ibid.*); Bruce, *Varied Operations*, p. 227; Mrs. Bruce Diary, Nov. 15, 17, 1937; *Globe and Mail*, Nov. 22, 24, 1937; Lambert Diary, Feb. 19, 1937; *Globe and Mail*, Nov. 24, 1937; *Telegram*, Nov. 24, 1937; D. Marshall to M.F.H., Nov. 25, 1937 (M.H.P.).

13. *Globe and Mail*, Sept. 27, 1937; *Statement of R. T. Jeffery before Hydro Inquiry*, May 25, 1938 (M.H.P.); *Telegram*, June 22, 1937; M.F.H. to T.S. Lyon, Oct. 21, 1937 (M.H.P.); T.S. Lyon to M.F.H., Oct. 28, 1937 (*Ibid.*); *Globe and Mail*, Nov. 1, 1937; Dec. 11, 1937; C.A.R., 1937-8, p. 153.

14. *Telegram*, Dec. 11, 1937; *Globe and Mail*, April 6, 1939; Mrs. Bruce Diary, July 22, 1937.

15. H. Nixon to F. Rinfret, July 21, 1937 (M.H.P.); W.L.M.K. to H. Nixon, Sept. 7, 1937 (*Ibid.*); W.L.M.K. to M.F.H. Nov. 12, 1937 (*Ibid.*); M.F.H. to W.L.M.K. Nov. 25, 1937 (*Ibid.*); C.A.R., 1937-8, p. 81; *Globe and Mail*, Dec. 17, 18, 1937; C.A.R., 1937-8, pp. 156-7; *Globe and Mail*, Nov. 30, Dec. 14, 17, 1937; Dec. 18, 20, 1937; *Telegram*, Dec. 20, 1937; *Globe and Mail*, Dec. 22, 1937.

16. *Telegram*, Dec. 27, 1937.

CHAPTER 10 KING MUST GO

1. Lambert Diary, Nov. 21, 1936; *Globe and Mail*, May 15, 8, 1937; M.F.H. to W.D. Euler, Jan. 21, 1938 (M.H.P.); M.F.H. to Maurice Duplessis, Jan. 24, 1938 (*Ibid.*); M.F.H. to M. Duplessis, Jan. 27, 1938

(*Ibid.*); C.A.R. 1937-8, p. 157; M. Duplessis to M.F.H., Feb. 14, 1938 (M.H.P.).

2. M.F.H. to Dr. A. MacG. Young, Feb. 9, 1938 (M.H.P.); Dr. A. MacG. Young to M.F.H., Feb. 10,

1938 (*Ibid.*); *Can. H. of C. Debates*, 1938, pp. 1207-8; *Globe and Mail*, March 11, 1938; A. Slaght to M.F.H., March 11, 1938 (M.H.P.); C.A.R., 1937-8, p. 82; *Globe and Mail*, March 22, 1938. W.L.M.K. to M.F.H. (enclosure), May 31, 1938 (M.H.P.); *Globe and Mail*, June 1, 1938.

3. *Globe and Mail*, Aug. 19, 1938; Lambert Diary, Dec. 12, 1938, Jan. 2, 3, 1939; *Globe and Mail*, Aug. 19, 1938; M.F.H. to W.L.M.K., Aug. 19, 1938 (M.H.P.).

4. *Globe and Mail*, Aug. 20, 22, 1938; W.L.M.K. to M.F.H., Aug. 30, 1938 (M.H.P.); R. Elmhirst to T.B. McQuesten, Sept. 19, 1938 (*Ibid.*); T.B. McQuesten to M.F.H., n.d. (*Ibid.*, 1938); M.F.H. to W.L.M.K., Sept. 21, 1938 (*Ibid.*); Frank Walsh Memorandum, Sept. 1, 1938, p. 156 (Franklin Roosevelt Papers).

5. E.H. Coleman to H. Bruce (copy enclosed Order-in-Council P.C. 1908), Aug. 24, 1937 (M.H.P.); *Globe and Mail*, Dec. 17, 1937; *Telegram*, Dec. 16, 1937; *Globe and Mail*, Jan. 11, 1938; W.L.M.K. to M.F.H. Nov. 5, 1937 (M.H.P.); M.F.H. to W.L.M.K. Nov. 25, 1937 (*Ibid.*); M.F.H. to M. Duplessis, Jan. 24, 1938 (*Ibid.*); M. Duplessis to M.F.H., Jan. 31, 1938 (*Ibid.*); M.F.H. to M. Duplessis, Feb. 14, 1938 (*Ibid.*); *Globe and Mail*, Feb. 17, March 12, 15, 1938.

6. Toronto *Star*, March 17, 1937; *Statement by the Government of Ontario to the Royal Commission on Dominion-Provincial Relations, Book I, The Prime Minister's Statement, passim* (Legislative Library of Ontario); Lambert Diary, May 4, 1938; *Globe and Mail*, May 5, 1938.

7. *Telegram*, May 3, 1938; *Globe and Mail*, May 4, 1938; M.F.H. to W.L.M.K., June 28, 1938 (M.H.P.); W.L.M.K. to M.F.H., June 30, 1938 (*Ibid.*); M.F.H. to A. Skelton, July 13, 1938 (*Ibid.*); *Globe and Mail*,

Aug. 16, 1938; W. Aberhart to M.F.H., Sept. 9, 1938 (M.H.P.).

8. *Globe and Mail*, June 22, 1938; E. Dowling to M.F.H., Oct. 3, 1938, (M.H.P.); *Telegram*, July 28, 1938; Personal Interview; *Globe and Mail*, July 29, 1938; *Times-Journal*, Aug. 12, 13, 1938; *Telegram*, Aug. 12, 13, 1938; *Globe and Mail*, Aug. 13, 1938.

9. D.P. Gillmor to M.F.H., July 10, 1937 (M.H.P.); *Globe and Mail*, Aug. 6, 1937; Mrs. Bruce Journal, p. 94; M.F.H. to D.P. Gillmor, July 26, 1937 (M.H.P.); Lambert Diary, Feb. 5, March 13, 1938; F. Ahearn to N. Lambert, April 10, 1938 (Lambert Papers); Lambert Diary, April 30, May 4, 5, 1938; M.F.H. to T. Crerar, May 30, 1938 (M.H.P.); L. McGuinness to M.F.H. June 22, 1938 (*Ibid.*).

10. Lambert Diary, Aug. 15, 16, 1938; L. McGuinness to M.F.H., Aug. 18, 1938 (M.H.P.); Lambert Diary, Sept. 7, 1938; *Globe and Mail*, Oct. 10, 1938; Interview with C.G. Power, March 23, 1966; Sir J. Dunn to M.F.H., Nov. 5, 1938 (M.H.P.).

11. *Telegram*, Dec. 14, 1938; Lambert Diary, Nov. 29, Dec. 2, 1938, Oct. 18, 1938, Dec. 3, 10, 7, 5, 8, 9, 1938; C. Cox to M.F.H., Dec. 24, 1938 (M.H.P.); *Globe and Mail*, Dec. 12, 13, 15, 1938; Toronto *Star*, Dec. 13, 17, 1938; *Telegram*, Dec. 13, 1938.

12. *Telegram*, Dec. 13, 1938; Lambert Diary, Dec. 12, 13, 1938; Toronto *Star*, Dec. 20, 1938; Lambert Diary, Dec. 19, 20, 1938; *Globe and Mail*, Dec. 20, 1938; Lambert Diary, Dec. 20, 22, 1938; M.F.H. to Norman Rogers, Dec. 29, 1938 (M.H.P.); Lambert Diary, Dec. 29, 1938.

13. Text of Empire Club Speech, Dec. 15, 1938 (M.H.P.); Toronto *Star*, Dec. 16, 17, 1938; *Globe and Mail*, Dec. 16, 20, 1938; Personal Interview; *Times-Journal*, Dec. 21, 1938; *Telegram*, Dec. 21, 1938.

CHAPTER 11 POINT OF NO RETURN

1. Medical Reports of M.F.H., Nov. 28, 1932, March 11, 1935 (M.H.P.);

Dr. C.G. Brink to M.F.H., Nov. 28, 1932, March 19, 1935 (*Ibid.*).

2. Ralph Hyman, "Mitch's Fighting Spirit Assured Pasteurization," *Globe and Mail*, Nov. 28, 1953; *Globe and Mail*, Feb. 16, March 8, 1938; L.H. Harries to M.F.H., Aug. 3, 1938 (M.H.P.); Petitions against Pasteurization, February, 1939, March 14, 1939 (*Ibid.*); C.L. Biggar to M.F.H., April 22, 1939 (*Ibid.*); *Times-Journal*, Nov. 24, 1939; Toronto *Star*, Feb. 20, 1941; Records of Ont. Dept. of Health.

3. H.A. Horton to M.F.H., Dec. 9, 1926 (M.H.P.); M.F.H. to G.B. Backstock, April 16, 21, 1938 (*Ibid.*); M.F.H. to Warden, Guelph Reformatory, June 11, 1929 (*Ibid.*); M.F.H. to Miss E.G., April 30, 1930 (*Ibid.*); Miss E.G. to M.F.H., May 28, 1930 (*Ibid.*); M.F.H. to G. Moir, Jan. 27, 1928 (*Ibid.*); L. McGuinness to M.F.H., April 6, 1932 (*Ibid.*); G.G. McGeer to M.F.H. (telegram), March 16, 1937 (*Ibid.*); M.F.H. to G.G. McGeer (telegram), March 16, 1937 (*Ibid.*); G.G. McGeer to M.F.H. (telegram), March 16, 1937 (*Ibid.*); M.F.H. to G.G. McGeer (telegram), March 17, 1937 (*Ibid.*); Thelma LeCocq, "Mitch Hepburn," *Maclean's Magazine*, March 15, 1943; Interview with Percy Locke, Feb. 21, 1966.

4. *Times-Journal*, Souvenir Issue, July 19, 1934; M.F.H. to Ned Sparks, Feb. 10, 1937 (M.H.P.); *Telegram*, June 20, 1934; Interview with A.V. Coulter, Feb. 18, 1966; Medical Report of M.F.H., prepared by Dr. C.G. Brink, March 11, 1935 (M.H.P.).

5. R.T.L., "Mr. Hepburn," *Maclean's Magazine*, Aug. 15, 1934; T. LeCocq, *loc. cit.*; *Globe and Mail*, Jan. 25, 1940; Mrs. Bruce Journal, Feb. 14, 1935; S. Levington, "What Kind of Man is Ontario's New Premier?" *Saturday Night*, Oct. 31, 1942; Lambert Diary, Jan. 19, 1934; Feb. 5, 1934.

6. J.W. McKay to M.F.H., Feb. 12, 1936 (M.H.P.); *Saturday Night*, October 18, 1941; M.F.H. to George Smith, Dec. 13, 1939 (M.H.P.); A. Jenkinson, "The Premier At Home," *Saturday Night*, Dec. 4, 1937; B.K. Sandwell to M.F.H., Dec. 17, 1937 (M.H.P.).

7. A.W. Roebuck, *The Roebuck Story* (Don Mills: T.H. Best Printing Company Ltd., 1963), p. 156; Lambert Diary, Feb. 11, 1937; Mrs. Bruce Diary, Oct. 23, 1936; Mrs. Bruce Journal, Sept. 29, 1937; C.D. Howe to M.F.H. (telegram), Sept. 16, 1940 (M.H.P.); G. Wardrope to M.F.H. (telegram), Sept. 16, 1940 (*Ibid.*); Mrs. Bruce Diary, Jan. 20, 1937; *Journal of the Legislative Assembly of Ontario*, vol. LXXI, 1937, pp. 19-43; Lambert Diary, Dec. 8, 1938.

8. Statement from Mara and McCarthy for M.F.H., Feb. 24, 1936 (M.H.P.); Frederick Crawford to M.F.H., Oct. 20, 1937 (*Ibid*); M.F.H. to Ned Sparks, Feb. 19, 1938 (*Ibid.*); Will of M.F.H., June 10, 1952 (Elgin County Court House, St. Thomas); Copy of Portion of Will of Frank O'Connor, n.d. (M.H.P.).

9. *Times-Journal*, June 2, 1945; *Globe and Mail*, April 13, 1943.

CHAPTER 12 INTO THE BREACH

1. *Globe and Mail*, Oct. 27, 1938; Interview with Colin Campbell (Nov. 16, 1966) and Roy Elmhirst (Nov. 30, 1966); *Globe and Mail*, Jan. 24, Feb. 4, 21, 1939; Toronto *Star*, Feb. 24, 1939; Lambert Diary, Jan. 10, 1939; *Globe and Mail*, Feb. 24, 1939.

2. *Globe and Mail*, March 9, 1939, Dec. 9, 10, 1938, March 15, 1939; M.F.H. to F. O'Connor, March 16, 1939 (M.H.P.); Toronto *Star*, March 17, 1939; *Globe and Mail*, March 22, 1939.

3. *Globe and Mail*, March 18, 21, 24, 1939; Toronto *Star*, March 25, 1939; *Globe and Mail*, March 31, 1939; R. Manion to James Manion, March 24, 1939 (Manion Papers); M.F.H. to F. O'Connor, March 25, 1939 (M.H.P.).

4. *Globe and Mail*, April 13, 14, 15,

1939; *Saturday Night,* April 22, 1939.

5. Sir J. Dunn to M.F.H., Nov. 5, 1938 (M.H.P.); *Globe and Mail,* April 22, 1939; Sir J. Dunn to M.F.H., April 24, 1939 (M.H.P.).

6. Lambert Diary, Jan. 8, 11, 17, 18, 19, 20, 22, 1939; Interview with C.G. Power, March 23, 1966.

7. Lambert Diary, Jan. 20, 16, 17, 1939; D. Hogarth to R. Manion, Jan. 31, 1939 (Manion Papers).

8. Mrs. Bruce Journal, March 1938; Brian J. Young, *loc. cit.,* p. 210; R. Manion to J. McIntosh Tutt, Feb. 7, 1939 (Manion Papers); M.F.H. to F. O'Connor, March 16, 1939 (M.H.P.).

9. M.F.H. to G. Challies, May 29, 1939 (M.H.P.); *Toronto Star,* May 22, 1939; *Globe and Mail,* May 23, 1939; Lambert Diary, May 25, 26, 1939; R. Manion to M.F.H., May 23, 1939 (M.H.P.); M.F.H. to R. Manion, May 29 (*Ibid.*); *Globe and Mail,* May 30, 1939.

10. *Saturday Night,* April 29, July 22, 1939; Lambert Diary, May 3, June 20, 22, July 4, 10, 11, 1939; M.F.H. to T. Wayling, July 4, 1939 (M.H.P.); *Globe and Mail,* June 6, July 12, 1939; *Times-Journal,* July 13, 1939; Interview with J. Pethick, Feb. 16, 1966.

11. G. Drew to R. Manion, Aug. 3, 1939 (Manion Papers); R. Manion to G. Drew, Aug. 8, 1939 (*Ibid.*); Interview with J. Pethick, Feb. 16, 1966; *Saturday Night,* Aug. 19, 1939; *Globe and Mail,* Aug. 9, 1939; *Telegram,* Aug. 9, 1939; *Toronto Star,* Aug. 9, 1939; R. Manion to P. Manion, Aug. 11, 1939 (Manion Papers); Lambert Diary, Aug. 8, 9, 1939; *Saturday Night,* Aug. 19, 1939.

12. *Globe and Mail,* Sept. 1, 1939; M.F.H. to W.L.M.K. (telegram), Sept. 5, 1939 (M.H.P.); M.F.H. to Ian Mackenzie (telegram), Sept. 5, 1939 (*Ibid.*); G.D. Conant to Ian Mackenzie (telegram), Sept. 5,

1939 (*Ibid.*); *Globe and Mail,* Sept. 9, 1939; G.D. Conant to Ian Mackenzie (telegram), Sept. 11, 1939 (M.H.P.); *Globe and Mail,* Sept. 6, 1939; Ian Makenzie to G.D. Conant (telegram), Sept. 12, 1939 (M.H.P.); N. Rogers to H. Nixon, Oct. 11, 1939 (*Ibid.*); M.F.H. to T. Wayling, Sept. 15, 1939 (*Ibid.*); M.F.H. to W.L.M.K. (telegram), Sept. 18, 1939 (*Ibid.*); Ian Mackenzie to M.F.H. (telegram), Sept. 18, 1939 (*Ibid.*).

13. *Globe and Mail,* Sept. 20, 1939; *Toronto Star,* Sept. 23, 20, 1939; *Globe and Mail,* Sept. 15, 1939; W. Fraser to M.F.H., Sept. 26, 1939 (M.H.P.); R. Manion Confidential Memorandum, Sept. 20, 1938 (Manion Papers); M.F.H. to E.J. Krause, Sept. 23, 1939 (M.H.P.).

14. R. Manion to Paul Manion, Sept. 11, 1939 (Manion Papers); M.F.H. to W.L.M.K. (telegram), Sept. 27, 1939 (M.H.P.); Pickersgill, *op. cit.,* p. 36; *Globe and Mail,* Oct. 4, 1939; Lambert Diary, Oct. 5, 1939.

15. Jack Hambleton to Jerry Brown (enclosure), Oct. 5, 1939 (Lambert Papers); Lambert Diary, Oct. 7, 11, 1939. *Globe and Mail,* Oct. 12, 1939.

16. M.F.H. to C. Brooks, Oct. 4, 1939 (M.H.P.); M.F.H. to A. Jarvis, Oct. 10, 1939 (*Ibid.*); C. Campbell to Gen. A.G.L. McNaughton, Oct. 11, 1939 (*Ibid.*); M.F.H. to Miles Cox, Oct. 12, 1939 (*Ibid.*); E. Lapointe to T.B. McQuesten, Oct. 17, 1939 (*Ibid.*); N. Rogers to M.F.H. (telegram), Oct. 14, 1939 (*Ibid.*); M.F.H. to K.S. Maclachlan, Oct. 11, 1939 (*Ibid.*); M.F.H. to N. Rogers, Oct. 16, 1939 (*Ibid.*); N. Rogers to M.F.H., Oct. 18, 1939 (*Ibid.*).

17. *Times-Journal,* Nov. 23, 1939; *Globe and Mail,* Nov. 23, 24, 1939; Pickersgill, *op. cit.,* p. 36-7; M.F.H. to N. Rogers, Dec. 5, 1939 (M.H.P.); N. Rogers to M.F.H., Dec. 7, 1939 (*Ibid.*).

18. *Globe and Mail,* Dec. 8, 27, 1939; *Times-Journal,* Dec. 27, 1939.

CHAPTER 13 THE GAUNTLET HURLED

1. Lambert Diary, Jan. 5, 1940; *Globe and Mail*, Jan. 11, 1940; M.F.H. to A.C. Hardy, Jan. 9, 1940 (M.H.P.).
2. *Globe and Mail*, Jan. 11, 1940; *Saturday Night*, Jan. 20, 1940; G. Drew to R. Manion, Jan. 15, 1940 (Manion Papers); R. Manion to G. Drew, Jan. 16, 1940 (*Ibid.*); R. Manion to K. Homuth, Jan. 16, 1940 (*Ibid.*); K. Homuth to R. Manion, Jan. 20, 1940 (*Ibid.*); *Globe and Mail*, Jan. 17, 1940.
3. *Globe and Mail*, Jan. 19, 1940; Interview with Farquhar Oliver, Nov. 23, 1966; Toronto *Star*, Jan. 19, 20, 1940; *Saturday Night*, Jan. 27, 1940.
4. Pickersgill, *op. cit.*, p. 62; Bruce, *Varied Operations*, p. 285.
5. Brigadier J.A. Clark to R. Manion, Jan. 19, 1940 (Manion Papers); R. Manion to Brigadier J.A. Clark, Jan. 22, 1940 (*Ibid.*); R. Manion to James Manion, Jan. 16, 1940 (*Ibid.*); Lambert Diary, Jan. 23, 1940; Pickersgill, *op. cit.*, 63-5; *Globe and Mail*, Jan. 26, 1940; Lambert Diary, Jan. 25, 1940; R. Manion to James Manion, Feb. 8, 1940 (Manion Papers).
6. Lambert Diary, Jan. 26, 30, Feb. 14, 1940.
7. *Globe and Mail*, Jan. 30, Feb. 1, 1940; *Saturday Night*, Feb. 10, 1940; H.R. Bain to M.F.H., Feb. 26, 1940 (M.H.P.); *Globe and Mail*, March 5, 1940; Toronto *Star*, March 5, 1940; *Globe and Mail*, March 7, 1940; Toronto *Star*, March 8, 1940.
8. Toronto *Star*, March 11, 1940; *Globe and Mail*, March 12, 1940; Lambert Diary, March 11, 1940; Pickersgill, *op. cit.* pp. 69-70; *Globe and Mail*, March 13, 14, 1940; Pickersgill, *op. cit.*, p. 71.
9. *Globe and Mail*, March 15, 1940; Toronto *Star*, March 15, 1940; Pickersgill, *op. cit,*, p. 71-2.
10. Lambert Diary, March 16, 1940; Toronto *Star*, March 19, 1940;

Pickersgill, *op. cit.*, p. 72; M.F.H. to C. Campbell, March 20, 1940 (M.H.P.); Toronto *Star*, March 27, 1940; *Times-Journal*, March 27, 1940; Lambert Diary, March 27, 1940; R. Manion to M.F.H., March 27, 1940 (M.H.P.); M.F.H. to R. Manion, April 1, 1940 (*Ibid.*); M.F.H. to C. Campbell, April 1, 1940 (*Ibid.*).

11. Toronto *Star*, March 28, 1940; *Whig-Standard*, April 1, 1940; *Globe and Mail*, May 22, 1940.
12. *Globe and Mail*, June 11, 1940; Toronto *Star*, June 12, 1940; Interview with Douglas Oliver, Nov. 23, 1966; C.G. Power, *A Party Politician* (Toronto: Macmillan, 1966), p. 193; Toronto *Star*, June 13, 1940; *Globe and Mail*, June 15, 1940; Pickersgill, *op. cit.*, p. 93.
13. *Times-Journal*, June 27, 1940; *Globe and Mail*, Oct. 22, 1942, Aug. 13, July 27, 1940; C.O. Knowles to M.F.H., June 21, 1940 (M.H.P.); M.F.H. to J.L. Ralston, Aug. 14, 1940 (*Ibid.*); C. Campbell to M.F.H. (telegram), Sept. 15, 1940 (*Ibid.*).
14. W.L.M.K. to M.F.H. (enclosure), Oct. 10, 1940 (*Ibid.*); *Globe and Mail*, Oct. 15, 1940; M.F.H. to W.L.M.K., Oct. 16 (telegram) and Oct. 18, 1940 (M.H.P.); M. Duplessis to M.F.H., Oct. 1, 1940 (*Ibid.*); M.F.H. to M. Duplessis, Oct. 8, 1940 (*Ibid.*); M. Duplessis to M.F.H., Oct. 11, 1940 (*Ibid.*); *Globe and Mail*, Oct. 8, 15, Nov. 21, 1940; M.F.H. to Ernest Lapointe, Dec. 4, 1940 (M.H.P.).
15. M.F.H. to Gene Autry, Dec. 3, 1940 (M.H.P.); M.F.H. to Ernest Lapointe, Dec. 4, 1940 (*Ibid.*); *Globe and Mail*, Dec. 3, 1940; James Murdock to M.F.H. (telegram), Dec. 3, 1940 (M.H.P.); M.F.H. to J. Murdock, Dec. 3, 1940 (*Ibid.*); *Globe and Mail*, Dec. 19, 1940.

CHAPTER 14 SAINTS AND SINNERS

1. Royal Commission on Dominion-Provincial Affairs, Report (1940), "Confidential Preliminary Memorandum of the Main Findings of the

Sirois Commission," prepared for the Ontario Government (M.H.P., 1940); W.L.M.K. to all Provincial Premiers, Nov. 2, 1940, *Report of the Proceedings of the Dominion-Provincial Conference*, 1941, V; M.F.H. to W.L.M.K., Nov. 8, 1940 (*Ibid.*), p. ix.

2. *Globe and Mail*, Oct. 22, 1940; J.L. Ilsley to M.F.H. Nov. 1, 1940 (M.H.P.); Pickersgill, *op. cit.*, p. 159; *Globe and Mail*, Dec. 25, 1940; Toronto *Star*, Jan. 3, 4, 1941; M.F.H. to C.G. Power, Jan. 7, 1941 (M.H.P.); Pickersgill, *op. cit.*, p. 160.

3. Pickersgill, *op. cit.*, p. 161; *Globe and Mail*, Jan. 15, 1941; *Report of the Proceedings*, etc., pp. 11, 15, 16; Lambert Diary, Jan. 14, 15, 1941; Pickersgill, *op. cit.*, p. 161; *Globe and Mail*, Jan. 15, 1941; Toronto *Star*, Jan. 15, 1941; *Globe and Mail*, Jan. 15, 1941; Pickersgill, *op. cit.*, p. 161; Toronto *Star*, Jan 16, 1941; *Globe and Mail*, Jan. 16, 1941; *Statement of M.F.H. at Dominion-Provincial Conference*, 1941 (M.H.P.); *Globe and Mail*, Jan. 29, 1941.

4. Pickersgill, *op. cit.*, p. 161; Lambert Diary, Jan. 16, 1941; Hamilton *Spectator*, Jan. 21, 1941; *Telegram*, Jan. 18, 1941; *Globe and Mail*, Jan. 15, 1941; Pickersgill, *op. cit.*, p. 175.

5. *Globe and Mail*, Jan. 20, 1941; Toronto *Star*, Jan. 20, 1941; *Globe and Mail*, Jan. 22, 1941; *Telegram*, Jan. 22, 1941; R. Cromie to M.F.H., Aug. 24, 1933 (M.H.P.); G.G. McGeer to M.F.H., (enclosure "The Conquest of Poverty"), Feb. 16, 1934 (*Ibid.*); H. Sinclair to M.F.H., Feb. 19, 1933 (*Ibid.*); N. McLean to M.F.H., (*Ibid.*, 1938); Lambert Diary, Oct. 30, 1941.

6. A.C. Hardy to M.F.H., Jan. 23, 1933 (M.H.P.); M.F.H. to A.C. Hardy, Jan. 30, 1933 (*Ibid.*); Toronto *Star*, Aug. 7, 11, 1934; *Times-Journal*, Aug. 13, 1934; M.F.H. to J.A. MacKinnon, Aug. 27, 1935 (M.H.P.).

7. *Globe and Mail*, Jan. 22, 1941; W. Aberhart to M.F.H., Feb. 11, 1941 (M.H.P.); W. Aberhart to M.F.H. (enclosure), Feb. 14, 1941 (*Ibid.*); M.F.H. to W. Aberhart, Feb. 18, 1941 (*Ibid.*); W. Aberhart to M.F.H., March 12, 1941 (*Ibid.*).

8. M.F.H. to J. Bickell (telegram), Feb. 17, 1941 (M.H.P.); Lord Beaverbrook to M.F.H. (telegram), Feb. 23, 1941 (*Ibid.*); *Globe and Mail*, Feb. 28, 26, March 15, 1941.

9. Lambert Diary, Jan. 17, Feb. 3, 1941; *Globe and Mail*, Feb. 8, 27, 1941; Interview with Farquhar Oliver, Nov. 23, 1966; Thomas L. Kennedy, "Mitchell Hepburn — He Trusted Too Many People," *Globe and Mail*, May 28, 1959.

10. *Globe and Mail*, Aug. 13, 1941; R. Elmhirst to Wyndham Lewis (with enclosure from W. Lewis to M.F.H.), Sept. 24, 1941 (M.H.P.); Copy of speech of M.F.H. delivered over C.B.S., Sept. 23, 1941 (*Ibid.*); *Globe and Mail*, Sept. 11, 1941; P.M. Tamlyn to M.F.H., Sept. 23, 1941 (M.H.P.); V. Buchanan to M.F.H., Sept. 25, 1941 (*Ibid.*).

11. *Times-Journal*, Sept. 23, 1941; *Globe and Mail*, Sept. 25, 1941; "Short Hauls" (monthly publication of Saints and Sinners Club), Oct., 1941 (M.H.P.); H.G. Hoffman to M.F.H., Oct. 8, 1941 (*Ibid.*).

12. Lambert Diary, Jan. 29, 1942; *Globe and Mail*, Jan. 23, 1942; *Times-Journal*, Jan. 23, 1942; M.F.H. to Arthur Meighen, Jan. 27, 1942 (M.H.P.); A. Meighen to M.F.H., Jan. 28, 1942 (*Ibid.*); Lambert Diary, Jan. 29, 1942; Pickersgill, *op. cit.*, p. 347; Lambert Diary, Jan. 27, 30, 31, 1942.

13. *Globe and Mail*, Feb. 3, 5, 1942; text of radio address delivered by M.F.H., Feb. 5, 1942 (M.H.P.); *Globe and Mail*, Feb. 4, 1942; Pickersgill, *op. cit.*, p. 344; R. Laurier to M.F.H., Feb. 5, 1942 (M.H.P.); Pickersgill, *op. cit.*, p. 345; *Globe and Mail*, Feb. 7, 1942; H. Nixon to M.F.H., Feb. 6, 1942 (M.H.P.); Pickersgill, *op. cit.*, p. 347; *Globe and Mail*, Feb. 7, 1942.

14. *Globe and Mail*, Feb. 10, 1942; Toronto *Star*, Feb. 10, 1942; Pickersgill, *op. cit.*, p. 348-9.

CHAPTER 15 REAPING THE WHIRLWIND

1. Toronto *Star*, Feb. 12, 1942; *Globe and Mail*, March 25, 1942; Toronto *Star*, March 25, 1942; *Globe and Mail*, April 2, 3, 11, 1942; *Telegram*, April 11, 1942; *Globe and Mail*, April 15, 1942; *Report on War Activities of Departments in the Hepburn Government*, Oct. 27, 1942 (M.H.P.); *Globe and Mail*, Dec. 19, 1942.

2. *Globe and Mail*, May 11, 1942; H. Robbins to George Drew, Private and Confidential Memorandum, March 29, 1942 (Drew Papers); Lambert Diary, May 5, 1942; Memorandum from G.D. Conant to M.F.H., July 13, 1942 (M.H.P.); *Globe and Mail*, July 18, 1942; W. Aberhart to M.F.H., July 30, 1942 (M.H.P.).

3. Bruce, *Varied Operations*, p. 285; H. Bruce to M.F.H., Aug. 5 or 6, 1942, (M.H.P.).

4. Richard M. Alway, "Mitchell F. Hepburn and the Liberal Party in the Province of Ontario, 1937-1943," (University of Toronto Library: unpublished M.A. Thesis, 1965), p. 375.

5. Interviews with A.V. Coulter, Feb. 18, 1966, and F. Oliver, Nov. 23, 1966; A. Ward to M.F.H., Jan. 24, 1942 (M.H.P.); M.F.H. to A. Ward, Feb. 23, 1942, (*Ibid.*).

6. Lord Beaverbrook, *op. cit.*, p. 159; *Globe and Mail*, July 30, Aug. 8, 14, Sept. 17, 19, 1942.

7. W. Aberhart to M.F.H., Aug. 26, 1942 (M.H.P.); W. Aberhart to M.F.H., Sept. 28, 1942 (*Ibid.*); M.F.H. to W. Aberhart, Oct. 6, 1942 (*Ibid.*).

8. *Globe and Mail*, July 17, Sept. 22, 1942; Interview with E.B. Jolliffe,

March 14, 1967; *Globe and Mail*, Sept. 22, 1942; M.F.H. to Capt. W. Rayfield, Oct. 5, 1942 (M.H.P.); M.F.H. to Louis St. Laurent (telegram), Oct. 3, 1942, (*Ibid.*); *Globe and Mail*, Sept. 26, 1942; M.F.H. to W.L.M.K. (telegram), Oct. 5, 1942 (M.H.P.); L. St. Laurent to M.F.H. (telegram), Oct. 7, 1942 (*Ibid.*); *Globe and Mail*, Oct. 14, 1942.

9. Globe and Mail, Oct. 6, 1942; M. Duplessis to M.F.H., Oct. 1, 1942 (M.H.P.); M.F.H. to M. Duplessis, Oct. 15, 1942 (*Ibid.*); M.F.H. to H. Carr, Oct. 15, 1942 (*Ibid.*); Text of address of M.F.H. to Queen's Park War Service Guild, Oct. 15, 1942 (*Ibid.*).

10. *Times-Journal*, Oct. 22, 1942; *Globe and Mail*, Oct. 22, 1942; *Telegram*, Oct. 22, 1942; F.A. Brewin, "The Ontario Political Pot Boils," *The Canadian Forum*, Dec., 1942; M.F.H. to Hon. A. Matthews, Oct. 21, 1942 (M.H.P.); M.F.H. Resignation Statement, Oct. 21, 1942 (*Ibid.*).

11. Statement of M.F.H. to press, Oct. 28, 1942 (M.H.P.); M.F.H. to W. Aberhart, Nov. 7, 1942 (*Ibid.*); M.F.H. to R. Manion, Nov. 13, 1942 (*Ibid.*); M.F.H. to J. Bracken, Nov. 13, 1942 (*Ibid.*); Pickersgill, *op. cit.*, pp. 454-5; M.F.H. to W. Aberhart, Oct. 6, 1942 (M.H.P.).

12. *Globe and Mail*, April 30, 1938; *Saturday Night*, Oct. 31, 1942.

13. Alway, *op. cit.*, p. 387.

14. *Times-Journal*, June 5, 1942; London *Free Press*, Oct. 22, 1942; L. Frost to M.F.H., Oct. 22, 1942 (M.H.P.); Toronto *Star*, Oct. 22, 1942.

CHAPTER 16 TEARS AT THE END

1. *Telegram*, Oct. 22, 1942; Toronto *Star*, Oct. 22, 1942; S. Levington, "What Kind of Man is Ontario's New Premier?" *Saturday Night*, Oct. 31, 1942; Toronto *Star*, Oct. 22, 1942; *Globe and Mail*, Oct. 23, 1942; F. Oliver to G.D. Conant, Oct.

27, 1942 (M.H.P.); Pickersgill, *op. cit.*, p. 454-6.

2. *Globe and Mail*, Nov. 4, 1942; Statement of M.F.H., Oct. 28, 1942 (M.H.P.); *Globe and Mail*, Oct. 29, 1942; Toronto *Star*, Oct. 29, 1942; M.F.H. to W. Aberhart, Nov. 7,

1942 (M.H.P.); M.F.H. to Frank Kelly (and all Ontario provincial Liberal members). Nov. 18, 1942 (*Ibid.*); *Globe and Mail*, Nov. 26, 1942.
3. *Globe and Mail*, Dec. 1, 1942, Jan. 20, 1943; M.F.H. to John Bracken, Nov. 17, 1942 (M.H.P.); M.F.H. to W. Aberhart, Nov. 16, 1942 (*Ibid.*); K. McLaren to M.F.H., Nov. 19, 1942 (*Ibid.*); Interview with John Bracken, March 19, 1966.
4. *Globe and Mail*, Feb. 10, 1943; Toronto *Star*, March 2, 1943; G.D. Conant to M.F.H., March 3, 1943 (M.H.P.); M.F.H. to G.D. Conant, March 3, 1943 (P.A.O., Conant Papers); Pickersgill, *op. cit.*, p. 454.
5. *Telegram*, March 3, 1943; *Globe and Mail*, March 5, 1943; Leo McLaughlin to M.F.H., March 4, 1943 (M.H.P.); E. Carroll to M.F.H., March 9, 1943 (*Ibid.*); *Times-Journal*, March 5, 1943.
6. *Globe and Mail*, March 6, 1943; Toronto *Star*, March 6, 1943; *Globe and Mail*, March 8, 1943; Dr. F. Belden to M.F.H., March 24, 1943 (M.H.P.); Pickersgill, *op. cit.*, pp. 491, 492; *Globe and Mail*, April 29, 1943; *Telegram*, April 29, 1943; *Globe and Mail*, April 30, 1943; *Times-Journal*, May 1, 1943; *Telegram*, May 1, 1943.
7. Thelma LeCocq, "Farmer in the Saddle," *Maclean's Magazine*, June 15, 1943; Pickersgill, *op. cit.*, p. 492; *Globe and Mail*, May 18, July 1, 1943.
8. *Times-Journal*, July 13, 1943; *Globe and Mail*, July 9, 1943; *Saturday Night*, July 24, 1943; *Times-Journal*,

July 23, 1943; *Globe and Mail*, July 14, Aug. 3, 1943.
9. *Times-Journal*, July 30, 1943; Lewis, *op. cit.*, p. 47; *Globe and Mail*, Aug. 5, 1943; *Times-Journal*, Aug. 5, 1943.
10. Pickersgill, *op. cit.*, pp. 568-70.
11. *Times-Journal*, Oct. 3, 4, 1944; Toronto *Star*, Oct. 4, 1944; *Globe and Mail*, Aug. 10, 1944; Oct. 7, Dec. 7, 1944; Toronto *Star*, Dec. 7, 1944.
12. Toronto *Star*, Feb. 21, 1945; *Globe and Mail*, Feb. 20, 23, 1945; Oct. 4, 5, 1944; Interview with E.B. Jolliffe, March 14, 1967; Lambert Diary, Feb. 19, 1945.
13. *Globe and Mail*, Feb. 28, March 7, 1945; Interview with F. Oliver, Nov. 23, 1966; *Globe and Mail*, March 23, 1945; *Telegram*, March 23, 1945; Toronto *Star*, March 23, 1945; Globe and Mail, April 3, 14, 1945.
14. *Times-Journal*, April 24, 1945; *Globe and Mail*, April 24, 1945; Interviews with Bert Lyman, Dec. 30, 1965 and Jack Pethick, Feb. 16, 1966; *Times-Journal*, May 7, 1945; Toronto *Star*, May 22, 1945; *Globe and Mail*, May 22, 25, 1945; *Times-Journal*, May 28, 1945; *Globe and Mail*, June 1, 1945.
15. Toronto *Star*, May 30, 1945; *Globe and Mail*, June 1, 1945, May 25, 1945; Interview with A.V. Coulter, Feb. 18, 1966; *Times-Journal*, April 28, 1945; Toronto *Star*, June 2, 1945; *Globe and Mail*, June 2, 1945.
16. *Globe and Mail*, June 5, 1945; Lewis, *op. cit.*, p. 47; Toronto *Star*, June 5, 1945; *Times-Journal*, June 5, 1945; Interview with V. Barrie, Feb. 20, 1966.

EPILOGUE

1. *Globe and Mail*, June 5, 1945; Oct. 21, 1949; London *Free Press*, Oct. 25, 1949; *Globe and Mail*, Nov. 1, 1951; Toronto *Star*, Nov. 9, 1951.
2. London *Free Press*, Jan. 5, 1953;

Times-Journal, Jan. 5, 1953, Jan. 8, 1953, quoting editorial from the Peterborough *Examiner*.
3. *Times-Journal*, Jan. 7, 1953; *Globe and Mail*, Jan. 8, 1953.

Index

A

Aberhart, William: on Dominion-Provincial relations and the Rowell-Sirois Commission, 162, 226-7, 229, 230; monetary policy and Social Credit theory, 172, 231-3; new political grouping, 242, 246-7, 262; also 70, 157, 234, 252, 260

Ahearn, F., 164

Aird, Sir John, 43

Aird, John Jr., 43-4

Alway, R.M., 244, 255

Andrews, William, 7-9, 12

Angus, H.F., 229n

Atkinson, Joseph E.: and Liberal leadership (1930), 37, 39; attitude to labour, 114, 117, 139; also 32, 34, 60, 78, 121, 181

Autry, Gene, 222-3

Avery, Dr. W.H., 179, 221

Aylesworth, A.B., 6

B

Bain, H. Rupert, 213

Baird, W.E., 97

Baker, Morgan, 208

Barrie, Vincent, 274

Beaverbrook, Lord, 222, 233

Beck, Sir Adam, 14

Bennett, R.B.: election and special session (1930), 28-9; election of 1935, 71; also 26, 36, 49n, 52, 62, 121, 124, 126, 158, 165

Bickell, J.P.: trips with M.F. Hepburn, 68, 75, 162; contribution to election of 1935, 70, 73n, 86; also 87, 90, 101, 112, 163, 179, 183, 221-2, 233, 245, 250

Birdsall, L.B., 120

Bolan, Rev. M., 116

Borden, Sir Robert, 4

Boughner, Mahlon, 8, 9, 12

Boyce, Harold A., 81, 84

Bracken, John, 227, 229, 252, 261, 262

Brewin, Andrew, 238

Brockington, Leonard, 228

Brooks, C., 203

Brower, Andrew, 9, 12

Brown, Dr. Alan, 175

Brown, Jerry, 203

Brownridge, F., 195

Bruce, Herbert: and union government proposal (1937), 119-20, 124; elec-

E

F

G

L

Lambert, Norman: campaign finances, 69, 73n, 217, 238; friction with Ontario organization, 72, 85-7, 127, 164, 166-7, 169, 191, 195, 234, 242; and Ontario federal organization, 164-5, 168, 192, 195; federal election of 1940, 206, 211-2; attempts to conciliate Hepburn, 194, 200, 272; also 51, 63-4, 75n, 121, 152, 171, 181, 183, 187, 191n, 197, 203, 215, 218, 228, 230

Lambie, J., 100

Lamport, Allan, 213

Lang, M., 24

Lapointe, Ernest: and Oshawa strike, 107, 109; federal election of 1940, 210, 217; also 168, 198, 202, 206, 222-3, 229

Laurier, Robert, 222, 239, 259, 269

Laurier, Sir Wilfrid, 4-5, 7n, 73, 98, 197, 228

Leduc, Paul: and separate school legislation, 99, 133; also 50, 60, 138, 145, 164, 222

Legault, Theodore, 50

Leonard, D'Arcy, 195

Lewis, David, 238

Lewis, John L., 104-118 *passim*, 130-31

Lewis, Wyndham, 235

Little, Rev. George, 181

Long, E.G., 140

Louis, Joe, 162

Lyman, Bert, 248, 274

Lyon, T.S., 93, 145-7

M

Macaulay, Leopold: and separate school legislation, 80, 98; hydro report, 146; also 55, 187, 200-221, 241

MacBride, M.M., 49, 139

Macdonald, Angus L., 245

Macdonald, Sir John A., 228

Mackay, R.A., 229n

Mackenzie, William Lyon, 2, 197

Mackenzie, Ian: relations with Hepburn, 168, 171, 195; also 105, 131, 155, 169, 198, 265

MacLeod, A.A., 248, 271

MacMillan, A.S., 230

Macphail, Agnes, 24, 272

Malcolm, James, 32-3, 35, 42

Manion, J., 189, 212

Manion, Robert: relations with George Drew, 196, 199-200, 207-8, 210; election of 1940, 211-2, 218, 237; also 59, 120-21, 125, 130, 132, 133n, 136, 165, 170, 188-9, 192-5, 206, 252

Marshall, David, 6, 8-9, 12

Marshall, Duncan: as possible Lieutenant Governor, 141-4; also 49, 55, 60, 66, 137, 193

Martin, Homer, 108, 111, 113-4

Martin, Paul, 32-3, 36, 63-4, 72

Massey, Vincent, 73, 75n

Matthews, Albert, 143, 154, 200, 215, 250, 272

McArthur, Duncan, 184, 234

McCrea, Charles, 53, 55-6, 63n, 67n

McCullagh, George: on power bills, 89, 91-2, 94; on Hepburn's investments, 92-3; on separate school legislation, 97, 99; labour policy and the Oshawa strike, 105, 107-10, 114-5, 117-8; on union government proposal (1937), 120-22, 124-5, 216; and Hepburn Cabinets, 92, 111, 120, 138-9; and provincial election of 1937, 134-5; Leadership League, 193; and Rowell-Sirois Commission, 227, 229-30; also 88-9, 143, 183, 192-3, 195, 234, 238, 252, 260, 263, 275

McGeer, G.G., 178, 231

McGuigan, Archbishop J.C., 99, 133

McGuinness, Larry, 73n, 163, 165, 178-9

McGuire, William, 32-3, 35-6, 46-7, 97

McIlraith, G., 164

McKillop, Hugh, 20

McLaren, K., 262